# POWER AND INTIMACY IN THE CHRISTIAN PHILIPPINES

What kind of reciprocity exists between unequal partners? How can a 'culture' which makes no attempt to defend unchanging traditions be understood as such? In the Christian Philippines, inequalities – global and local – are negotiated through idioms of persuasion, reluctance and pity. Fenella Cannell's study suggests that these are the idioms of a culture which does not need to represent itself as immutable. Her account of Philippine spirit-mediumship, Catholicism, transvestite beauty contests, and marriage in Bicol calls for a reassessment of our understanding of Southeast Asian modernity. Combining a strong theoretical interest in the anthropology of religion with a broader comparative attention to recent developments in Southeast Asian studies, she offers a powerful alternative to existing interpretations of the relationship between culture and tradition in the region and beyond. This book addresses not only Southeast Asianists, but all those with an interest in the anthropology of religion and post-colonial cultures.

FENELLA CANNELL is lecturer in Social Anthropology at the London School of Economics and Political Science

*Cambridge Studies in Social and Cultural Anthropology*  109

The monograph series Cambridge Studies in Social and Cultural Anthropology publishes analytical ethnographies, comparative works and contributions to theory. All combine an expert and critical command of ethnography and a sophisticated engagement with current theoretical debates.

*A list of books in the series will be found at the end of the volume.*

Founding Editors:
Meyer Fortes, Edmund Leach, Jack Goody, Stanley Tambiah

# POWER AND INTIMACY IN THE CHRISTIAN PHILIPPINES

FENELLA CANNELL

CAMBRIDGE
UNIVERSITY PRESS

CAMBRIDGE UNIVERSITY PRESS
Cambridge, New York, Melbourne, Madrid, Cape Town, Singapore, São Paulo

Cambridge University Press
The Edinburgh Building, Cambridge CB2 8RU, UK

Published in the United States of America by Cambridge University Press, New York

www.cambridge.org
Information on this title: www.cambridge.org/9780521641470

First published 1999
Reprinted 2001

*A catalogue record for this publication is available from the British Library*

*Library of Congress Cataloguing in Publication data*

Cannell, Fenella
Power and intimacy in the Christian Philippines / Fenella Cannell.
    p.   cm. – (Cambridge studies in social and cultural
anthropology)
Includes bibliographical references and index.
ISBN 0 521 64147 0 (hardcover). – ISBN 0 521 64622 7 (pbk.)
1. Philippines – Social life and customs.   2. Philippines –
Religious life and customs.   I. Title.   II. Series.
DS663.C35   1998
306′.09599–dc21   98–24883   CIP

ISBN 978-0-521-64147-0 hardback
ISBN 978-0-521-64622-2 paperback

Transferred to digital printing 2007

*For Jeanne Frances I. Illo, and all the other Bicolanos who helped me, especially the people of Calabanga, Camarines Sur. Dios mabalos po sa saindo gabos.*

# Contents

# Illustrations

**Figures**

**Map**

**Diagrams**

# Acknowledgements

Like any book which has taken longer to write than its author intended, this one has accumulated more debts than can ever be properly acknowledged. Those who are mentioned here, therefore, also stand for the many other colleagues and friends whose conversation and support have been important over the years.

Fieldwork was undertaken in Bicol from March 1988 to December 1989, and this fieldwork and the rest of my doctoral work was supported by an Economic and Social Research Council state studentship. I was attached to the Institute of Philippine Studies, Ateneo de Manila University, throughout my fieldwork period. Assistance in the final stages of writing up the thesis came from my parents, and from a Malinowski Grant from the Department of Social Anthropology, London School of Economics. During 1991–2, I was a Junior Research Fellow of Sidney Sussex College, Cambridge, while the Evans Fund of the Cambridge Department of Social Anthropology and the British Academy provided funds for a return visit to Bicol and attendance at the International Conference of Philippine Studies at the Australian National University in Canberra during the summer of 1992. The British Academy again funded my attendance at the Association of Asian Studies and the International Philippine Studies Conferences in Honolulu, Hawaii, in April 1995, where various arguments were further developed. The conversion of thesis into book was crucially enabled by a research and sabbatical period spent in Cornell University in 1995, at the invitation of the Cornell Department of Anthropology under David Holmberg and the Southeast Asia Program under John Wolff, which was partially funded by STICERD at the London School of Economics. A Poste Rouge appointment at the Institute de la Recherche sur le Sud-Est Asiatique, Aix-en-Provence, under

Charles MacDonald, in the summer of 1996 allowed me to complete the writing of the manuscript. I am most grateful to all these persons and institutions for their support, and to the members of my department at the London School of Economics, especially Jonathan Parry, who was Convenor between 1994 and 1997.

For providing the opportunity to become an anthropologist in the first place, and for invaluable teaching and inspiration during the writing of my doctoral thesis, I would like to thank Maurice Bloch, who was my supervisor. Maurice Bloch also visited me in Bicol, as did Michael Stewart, and my parents Hugh and Judy Cannell, and in different ways I have learned a great deal from and with each of these people. Others whose support and comments on parts of the thesis were especially important include William Christian, Rineke Coumans, Alice Magos, Doreen Fernandez, Malcolm Mintz, Fernando Zialcita and David Lewis. Sections of the thesis were presented to the London School of Economics post-graduate writing-up seminar of 1989–90, the 1989 London School of Economics workshop on Christianity organised by Peter Loizos, who also provided helpful comments, the 1991 European Conference on Philippine Studies at CASA in Amsterdam and the 1990 London School of Economics Departmental Seminar. I was extremely fortunate to have as my examiners Benedict Anderson and the late Alfred Gell, to the quality and originality of whose thinking in each case most of us can only aspire. I thank them for their comments and criticisms.

In the Philippines, Jeanne Illo provided my first introduction to Bicol via her own family, friends and colleagues, as well as lending me a place to feel at home in Manila during breaks from fieldwork. Her friendship, in-depth knowledge and intellectual relish for the crazy notions of anthropologists, as well as her generous feedback on whether my interpretations made sense to a Bicolana, have contributed centrally to both thesis and book. Marilyn Flores's friendship also made the Philippines a good place to be, and punctuated my fieldwork with both keen insights and gales of laughter, especially and most appropriately at myself. Her brother, Tata Flores, was my host at the Miss Gay Naga City contest and to him and the **bakla** community in Naga and Bicol go my thanks and admiration. The family of Attorney S. Adan first made me welcome in Naga City. At Ateneo de Naga University, Jesus 'Jess' Volante began teaching me Bicol with great patience, and he and his colleagues in the Social Science Research Center provided continual support and suggestions. Danny Gerona made me aware of issues in Bicol history which he was then pioneering, and was generous with his insights. Josephine Asug is another friend who has helped in many different ways, practical and intellectual, and thanks are also due to her family including Mr and Mrs Salvacion Rivera in Calabanga.

So many people in Calabanga deserve my thanks, that it is difficult to select anyone for special mention, and I would like to express my gratitude to everyone who offered help, hospitality and guidance, especially in San Lucas, Santo Domingo and at Hinulid, and including the Azanes, Alto, Encilla, Sepre, Capal, Marescal, Isaac, Esmarin, Remella, Tuazon, Hemady, Garinga, Guerrero, Medroso, Esperida and Dulce families. I particularly thank Mr Antonio and Mrs Ellen Alto, Mr Manuel and Mrs Maria Azanes and Merly Azanes Villareal, Mr Russell and Mrs Norma Hemady, Mr Ernesto and Mrs Sideria Azanes, Mr Apolinar and Mrs Recilda Caraan, Mr Manuel and Mrs Alejandra Azanes, Mr Alfredo and Mrs Lolita Azanes, Mr Pio and Mrs Lillia Borok, Mr Herzon and Mrs Concing Sepre, Mrs Leonida Gisic, Mr Vicente and Mrs Corazon Capal, Mr Pasqual and Mrs Gloria Remella, Mr Elpedio and Mrs Elizabeth Capal, Mr and Mrs Dulce, Mrs Felicitas Marescal, and Mrs Dolores Llanete, as well as all my co-godparents (*mga padi sagkod mga madi ko*), my godchildren, and the *paratarok* (rice-planting) groups of the barangay. In Libmanan, particular thanks are due to Mrs Felicitas del Carmen and to Mrs Erna Guiruela.

The writing of the book in its present form has particularly involved a number of other people. Vince Rafael's continuing intellectual influence, first through his work, and latterly through conversations and his comments on my own writings, will be evident to everyone who reads on the Philippines. Tom Gibson and Michael Lambek have also each been important to my thinking, and I was lucky enough to have them both as readers of the manuscript for Cambridge University Press; both have provided many useful suggestions, and Michael Lambek has given his time to reading the manuscript at both the beginning and the end of its conversion into a book. Benedict Anderson's influence has also bridged the first and second stages of the writing of this book, and his comments while I was in Cornell in 1995 are gratefully acknowledged, as are those of Jim Siegel, John Wolff and many other members of the Southeast Asia Program and the Anthropology Department seminars at Cornell, as well as Marc Perlman. The members of the seminar series on the Comparative Ethnography of the Lowland Philippines at Cornell, including Steve Graw, Smita Lahiri, Carole Hau and Andrew Abulahim, all taught me a great deal, and Rineke Coumans and Nancy Stage are also owed a special thank-you. At the Association of Asian Studies Conference in Hawaii in

April 1995, Mark Johnson, Neil Garcia and I were able to discuss Filipino gay identity in a way I found most valuable. In England, Lotta Hedman and John Sidel have constantly reminded me what it is to be really knowledgeable about Southeast Asia, while Sue Benson, Harvey Whitehouse, Paola Filippucci, Simon Coleman, Chris Fuller, Charles Stafford and Simon Jarvis have read or listened to the argument in whole or in part. Peter Loizos most helpfully read the final draft, while Danilyn Rutherford read the whole thing twice, discussed several sections in detail with me over many months, and added her own exceptionally interesting remarks. Miranda Snow kindly produced the illustrations. Finally, Carol Sobritchea and Jeanne Illo read the book for Ateneo de Manila University Press, and Esther Pacheco agreed to publish it in the Philippines.

# Glossary

| | |
|---|---|
| abaca | Manila hemp |
| abay | bystander (spirit) |
| agaw-buhay | death-struggle |
| agom | spouse |
| agta | ethnic minority 'pygmy' population in Bicol |
| alok | invite |
| ama | father |
| Amang Hinulid (Ama) | the 'dead Christ' |
| amateuran | amateur contest |
| ambag | contribution to wedding costs by groom's side |
| amerikana | men's formal Western suit |
| Amerikano/a | American/white person |
| an mga pobre (pl.) | the poor |
| anayo | soul-loss |
| anitos | spirits/ancestors |
| ano | what |
| anting (Bicol/Tag.) | amulet |
| aray! | exclamation of pain |
| areglado | sorted out (of disputes) |
| arindo | mortgaging of land |
| artista | a star |
| aso | smoke |
| asog (archaic) | effeminate priest |
| aswang | viscera-eating 'witch' |
| atado | heap (of goods measured for sale) |
| ataman | person or animal cared for by humans/adoptee |
| atang | offering cast on the sea or river |

| | |
|---|---|
| Ate (Tag.) | Older Sister |
| babaylanes (Visayan) | traditional healers |
| baduy | vulgar |
| bahon | orator of courtship rituals |
| bakla | transvestite man |
| bakya (Bicol/Tag.) | wooden clog |
| balak | intermediary/go-between |
| balao | small salt shrimp |
| balayi | in-laws (parents of newlyweds) |
| balos | pay back |
| baloslos | mythical creature with reversible face |
| bansag | nickname |
| barangay | 'village'; smallest administrative unit |
| bawi | to swap, or to give something back |
| bayaw | brother-in-law (spouse's brother/sibling's husband) |
| bilas | spouse's siblings' spouses (either sex) |
| binucot (Visayan, archaic) | enclosed elite woman |
| birthdayhan | Filipino birthday party |
| bisa | kiss the hand of senior kin |
| boot | inner feelings |
| buhay | life |
| bukid | mountains, rural areas |
| contravida | villainess |
| daghan | breast/heart |
| dai | no/not |
| daog | defeated |
| dapit | to accompany a funeral procession |
| datu (historical, except Mindanao) | local Filipino leader/aristocrat |
| disponir | borrow money |
| diwata | high supernaturals |
| drama | film melodrama |
| duende | dwarves |
| dulok | approach |
| emsee | master of ceremonies |
| endono | wedding gifts from parents of newlyweds |
| engkanto | magic being/spirit |
| entregar | trousseau |
| espiritu | soul |
| gadan | dead/a dead person |
| gi'til | vain |

| | |
|---|---|
| guapo | handsome |
| gusi | form of sharecropping |
| gusto | like/wish |
| habay | belt |
| hadi | king |
| halo-halo | sweet snack with crushed ice |
| hanapbuhay | a living |
| harana | serenade |
| harong | house |
| harong-harong | sort-of-house/hut |
| hawak | body |
| herak | pity/compassion |
| higda | lying down |
| hilot | traditional massage |
| hipag | sister-in-law (spouse's sister/sibling's wife) |
| hito | catfish |
| hulit | little sermon |
| ibos | type of sticky-rice cake |
| igwa | there is/there are |
| ilustrado | elite of Spanish period |
| Inay | Mother |
| incenso | type of incense |
| Itay | Father |
| Jueteng | lottery |
| kadikloman | darkness/domain of the dead |
| kagawad | councillor |
| kalag | dead soul |
| kamangyan | type of incense |
| kami | we (exclusive) |
| kampusanto | cemetery |
| kapwa | fellow-humans |
| katabang | (domestic) helper |
| kaya | able to cope/match |
| keme (bakla slang) | nonsense |
| komedya | folk drama |
| kulam (Bicol/Tag.) | sorcery |
| kulkul | carrying a child over one's shoulder |
| kumpliaño | birthday |
| kuripot | stingy |
| kursinada | 'fancy' (romantically) |
| Kuya (Tag.) | Older Brother |
| laban | struggle/martial arts movie |

| | |
|---|---|
| laki | mythical being, half-horse |
| lang | only |
| laog | inside |
| laway | saliva; heal with saliva |
| librito | 'little book' (of spells) |
| lote | form of sharecropping |
| lugod | might as well/ faute de mieux |
| lumay | love-potion |
| luwas | outside |
| ma-arte | artful |
| maboot | good, accommodating |
| madaldal | talkative |
| madi | co-godmother |
| mag-adal | study |
| mag-agi | pass (a house or person) |
| mag-arog | imitate/make something like something else |
| mag-atubang | be (sit) opposite/facing |
| magbantay | keep guard/perform brideservice |
| mag-blowout | host an extravagant meal |
| magbulong | heal |
| maghagad | beg |
| maghale | leave/remove |
| maghugot | commit suicide |
| mag-iba | accompany |
| mag-intindi | understand |
| magkakan | eat |
| magpangisi | comedy |
| magpoon | begin |
| magpresentar | propose marriage formally |
| magribay tasa | 'exchange of cups' |
| magtugang | group of siblings/be siblings |
| magtungod | deal in rice wholesale |
| magurang | parents/old people |
| maimon | selfish |
| maisog | fierce |
| makahibi | likely to make one weep |
| makiulay | discuss, negotiate |
| makulog | painful |
| maligno | evil spirit |
| malungsi | deathly pale |
| Mamay | Uncle |
| mamundo | sad |

| | |
|---|---|
| manambitan | ritual wailing |
| Manay | Older Sister |
| Mang (Tag.) | Old Man |
| Manoy | Older Brother |
| manugang | parents-in-law/children-in-law |
| marhay | good, very |
| masakit | difficult |
| masiram | delicious |
| masuba | jokey |
| matibay/on | (very) clever |
| may | there is/are |
| mayaman | wealthy |
| maybahay (Tag.) | householder/housewife |
| mayo | there is/are not |
| misteriohan | prayers, e.g. for death anniversaries |
| naibanan | 'accompanied' (by spirits) |
| naigo | reprimanded/served right (by spirits) |
| Nana | Aunty |
| napikon | hurt/tricked |
| nawili | fascinated |
| negocio | business |
| nguog | coconut |
| Ninang | Godmother |
| Nini/Ni | Little Girl |
| Ninong | Godfather |
| nipa | type of palm |
| Nono/Nonoy/Noy | Little Boy |
| om'om | nightmare |
| orasion | spell/prayer |
| oripon | oppressive |
| pabasa | reading |
| padangat | darling/favourite |
| padi | co-godfather |
| pagkamoot | love |
| pagkatawo | consciousness |
| paglaog | entry |
| pagtapat | riddling contest |
| palad | palm/fate |
| palagayon | black spirit-rice |
| palihion | death observances |
| pamaghat | herbal infusion |
| pangontra | protective spell |
| pantomina | wedding dance |

| | |
|---|---|
| paraanitos | healer with anitos |
| parabulong | healer |
| paradaog | 'defeater' |
| paralibot | circulating |
| parigos | bathe |
| parong | smell |
| pasalubong (Bicol/Tag.) | greeting gifts |
| pasayan | shrimp |
| Pasion | Bicol Passion text |
| pasma | humoral illness |
| Pasyon (Tag.) | Tagalog Passion text |
| patianak | abortion-causing spirit |
| pilosopo | sceptic |
| pilya | feisty |
| pinsan | cousin |
| Pistang Kalag | All Souls' Day |
| po | respect particle used in address |
| poblacion | town centre |
| pogi (slang) | handsome |
| promesa | religious vow |
| pula | dumb |
| puyo | mudfish |
| remontados | outlaws |
| restos | secondary tomb |
| ribay | exchange, swap |
| rigaton | deal in fish |
| sabi | say |
| sadiri | self |
| sakop | dominion |
| salabat | ginger tea |
| salapi | 50 centavo coin |
| sampot | spirit-companion |
| sana | just/only |
| sanib (Tag.) | spirit-companion |
| santiguar | form of divination |
| santo/a | M/F saint |
| saro | spirit-companion |
| sentencia | judge |
| sentimiento | sentimental |
| sikat | famous |
| silahis (Tag.) | double-blade/ man with dual sexuality |
| sinda | they |

| | |
|---|---|
| sundang | farmer's knife |
| sungkohan | final meal in courtship ritual |
| supog | shame/embarrassment |
| suwerte | luck |
| swardspeak | bakla slang |
| talusog | mudfish |
| tandan | wage |
| tanggal | passion-play |
| tawad | discount/forgiveness |
| tawo na dai ta nahihiling/tawo | people we don't see/people |
| tentasion | temptation |
| togot | allowed |
| tontonan | Easter ceremony blessing children |
| tood | used to/accustomed to |
| tribo | clan |
| tugang | sibling |
| tulod | spirit meal |
| tunay | true/real |
| turog | sleeping |
| turubigan | hopscotch |
| tuytoy | canopy extending a house |
| ugali | customs/ways |
| ugat | body vessels |
| urulay | discussion/talk |
| usog | illness caused through 'influence'; a form of mystical 'contagion' |
| utang | debt |
| utang na loob (Tag.) | 'debt of the inside' |
| vetsin | monosodium glutamate |

# Note on language and names

The Philippines is rich in languages, and the Bicol language is itself rich in dialects, including mutually incomprehensible dialects. The people with whom I lived speak standard Camarines Sur Bicol, and it is their dialect which is quoted here, and which for the sake of brevity is referred to as 'Bicol' throughout. Some words in Tagalog (the language of the national capital region of Metro Manila) are also quoted, and are marked by the abbreviation 'Tag.' Other Philippine languages are referred to by their full name in the text.

The Bicol language, like other Filipino languages, makes plurals by inserting a plural marker (in this case, **mga**) before the noun; hence **harong** (a house) becomes **mga harong** (houses). For the sake of ease of reading in English, the plurals used here (except of course in passages of Bicol quotation) are 'false plurals'; I have either added a final -s to Bicol words (as in **saros** from **saro**, a spirit-companion), or omitted pluralisation altogether (as in **amateuran** for singing contests) if the Bicol ending already suggests a possible plural to the English ear (on the model of sheep/sheep). I hope these bits of DIY 'Biclish' will not offend Bicolano and Filipino readers too greatly.

Spelling in Bicol and other Filipino languages was not fully standardised during the Spanish period, and writers in local languages may still adopt a number of variant spellings. Contemporary Philippine spellings in many local languages, however, now tend to be modernised according to the pattern of the constructed official national language, Pilipino. The reader may therefore notice a number of different spellings of cognate words, according to the period and source. My Bicol spellings generally follow M.W. Mintz and J. del Rosario Britanico's *Bikol–English dictionary (diksionariong bikol–ingles)*, except in quotations from, for example, the

Bicol **Pasion**, in which more old-fashioned spelling is used, especially -c for -k. However, I prefer 'Bicol' to the modernised 'Bikol', and have used this spelling throughout.

## Names

Some pseudonyms have been used to protect the identity of my informants.

# Introduction: mountains and plains

This is a book about people who for a long period have been described in academic literature – and even at times describe themselves – as having no culture worth the name, and as being in many senses a vexing puzzle for social and political theory. Disturbingly devoid, as it was thought, of social backbone, lowland Filipinos have frequently been said to be 'merely imitative' of their two sets of Western colonisers: first Catholic Spain (between 1571 and 1896) and then, after a revolution and a single year as an independent republic, America, from 1898 to the second declaration of independence in 1946.

The area of the lowlands in which I worked has if anything a lower cultural profile than either the Tagalog-speaking provinces around Manila to its north, or the Visayas to its south. Although under the Spanish, Bicol had considerable economic and religious signficance, the early Spanish reports tend to contrast Tagalog and Visayan 'types' of culture in extended accounts, and pass more briefly over the lands which lay in between.[1] Its past remains full of puzzles which historians are only just beginning to unravel; why did Bicolanos ferociously resist the Spanish, but then become some of Catholicism's earliest mass converts? Why was the revolution against Spain less flamboyant and less easy to characterise in Bicol than elsewhere? Contemporary Bicol falls within Philippine Economic Region Five, the poorest in the nation, and unlike Manila or Cebu, Bicol's regional capital Naga City is not yet a boom-town of factories or Free Trade Zones. Once again, the things which are easiest to see seem to be happening elsewhere.

The Bicolano people I met, some of whom are quoted in the chapters which follow, will be described engaged in many different pursuits, sometimes tightly connected with each other and sometimes less so. I will pass

1

Map of the Philippines

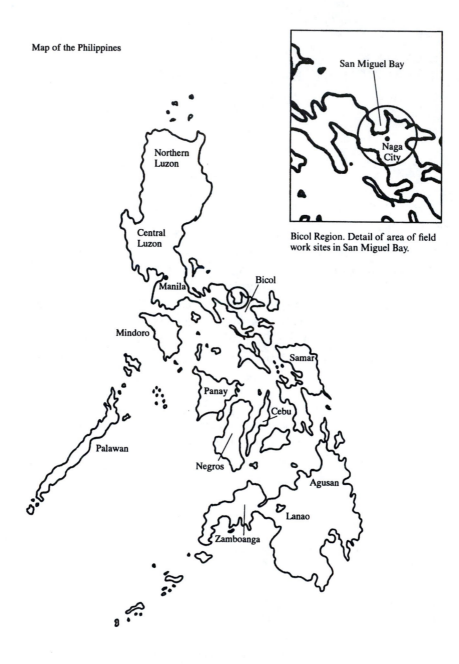

Bicol Region. Detail of area of field work sites in San Miguel Bay.

from women's stories about forced marriage and a reconstruction of their historical significance, to an account of the complex and often ambiguous forms of Bicolano spirit-mediumship, from there to an exploration of the important local Catholic cult of the 'dead Christ', and finally to one of Naga City's most spectacular events, the Miss Gay Naga City male transvestite beauty-contests. I do not want to suggest that these diverse activities can be forced into a tidy and hermetically sealed system of interpretation or cosmology, for Bicolanos themselves are comparatively uninterested in constructing and promoting a closed notion of their own 'culture'. But I will suggest that we can see a connection between these contexts nonetheless, in the attitudes that Bicolano people take to relationships of unequal power, and the centrality to poorer people of the notion that hierarchy can always be, if not eliminated, then at least mitigated, even by the apparently powerless. The rhetorical assertion that <u>submission can be turned into the beginning of a position of strength</u> is a theme which runs through every part of this book.

### Mountains and plains: the construction of the lowland Philippines in colonial history

In his ethnography of the Buid of highland Mindoro, Tom Gibson has contrasted the Buid solution to colonial invasions with that of the lowlanders. The former refused all contact and exchange with the new rulers and settlers, retreating up into the mountains and turning inwards to create a society which denies the very possibility of hierarchy even amongst themselves, while the latter entered into intensely charged exchange relationships with the representatives of the colonial powers (Gibson, 1986: 38–49).

This view of a structuring contrast between the highland and lowland Philippines is one which will inform this book. I take it that, broadly speaking, the lowland Catholic rural people, with whom I lived, have taken the opposite historical path to the Buid; while the Buid have tried to turn their backs on the historical processes of colonisation, the lowlanders have been forced to engage with them intensively, and to find ways of negotiating with the colonisers.

This contrast is of course a simplification. In reality lowland populations have alternated between the attempt to build benevolent exchange relations with colonial power-holders, the attempt to enforce a correct or tolerable form of these relations, and at times the complete abandonment of them. Lowland Filipino society has had its own movements up and down the mountains in retreat from the more intensely governed plains, in the various guerilla and resistance movements, or movements of fugitives from colonial taxes or other impositions and persecutions. The tradition of the **remontados** (Gerona, 1988b:81), or 'those who have gone back up the mountain', embraces people on the run from Spanish friars, Spanish taxes, Japanese concentration camps, American suppressions of peasant rebellions, lowland crop failures, local vendettas and the modern Philippine Constabulary. For lowlanders, the uplands (Bicol, **bukid**) have always been both a wild and somewhat fearful place, and a frontier refuge, economic and political (Owen, 1984: 22–3; 1990: 424–6; Mallari, 1983).

Partly because of their indigenous religious significance, which predates the Spanish period, mountains have also been the usual site for small 'native-syncretistic' religious communities, which make their own attempt to turn their back on, and thus radically reinterpret, colonial history. The most famous of such mountains is probably Mount Banahaw in Laguna province, site of Rizalist [2] and other nationalist cults, as well as cults based on reworkings of 'babaylanism' (indigenous spirit-mediumship) and other traditions (Elesterio, 1989; Marasigan, 1985; Cullemar, 1986).

It would be wrong, then, to picture lowland engagement in the colonial societies as quiescent. Between the later nineteenth century and the present day, there have been persistent if intermittent eruptions of 'peasant rebellions' and anti-colonial or anti-occupation movements which intercut in complex ways at different times. And recent work which takes its cue from James Scott's notion of the 'moral economy' in Southeast Asia (1985) has reintroduced the notion of 'everyday resistance' even within apparently peaceful lowland communities (Kerkvliet, 1990).

However, the Bicolanos with whom I lived are very different from Gibson's Buid. While the Buid emphasise their autonomy from these historical developments, the people I knew describe themselves and their culture[3] in some contexts as merely the product of successive colonial importations. In fact, to say (as was said to me innumerable times), 'We Filipinos are very Westernised . . . the Spanish brought religion, the Americans brought democracy', is to make a statement which indicates one's own education, since this is the view of Philippine history through primary-school textbooks, many of which have changed little since the American period (Mulder, 1990b). Of course, this kind of statement is not to be taken too literally; it was a view likely to be emphasised in polite conversation with a white foreign visitor, and it does not mean that Bicolanos never reflect on their own particularities, or think of them with pride. Nevertheless, the view of the lowlands as a layer-cake of foreign influences is an important popular orthodoxy.

**Colonialism and neo-colonialism**

Clearly, the particularity of Filipino lowland experience is bound up with the colonial history of the archipelago. Spanish interest in the Philippines was somewhat perfunctory until the late nineteenth century;[4] its main importance was in the galleon trade, in which Chinese goods passed through Manila in their way to Acapulco to be exchanged for Latin American silver (Steinberg, 1982:21–2; 35). The peninsular Spanish population in the islands was always small (less than 1 per cent of the population: Blanc-Szanton, 1990:361), although there were larger numbers of Mexican creoles and Latin-American mestizos. In Bicol, as elsewhere, ordinary people experienced Spanish rule mostly through two channels. The systems of tax-farming (**encomiendas**), exaction of tribute, labour corvees and forced purchase of produce (**vandala**) placed extremely heavy demands on the population.[5] The missions of the friars effected a rapid initial conversion of Filipinos to Christianity, and the religious orders became the main Spanish presence in most areas, with enormous influence in religion, education and a wide range of political and administrative matters. The Franciscans, who took over from the Augustinians in Bicol in 1574, claimed almost total and fervent Christianisation by 1600, and continued to be a major force in the region up to and beyond the loss of power by Spain (Gerona, 1988b: 58; Schumacher, 1981:157). Spanish was never widely spoken, however, since (in contrast to Spanish policy in Mexico and elsewhere) the friars took the decision from the first to evangelise in the various local languages of the Philippines.[6]

It is sometimes said that America colonised the Philippines almost absent-mindedly; certainly the invasion was an improvisation in the US hostilities with Spain. Once there, however, the Americans were 'tempted by the white man's burden . . . [President] McKinley eventually announced that he had no other choice but "to educate the Filipinos, and uplift and civilize and Christianize them [sic], and by God's grace to do the very best we could by them"' (Steinberg, 1982:43). This pledge to the 'little brown brother' to make a country 'in our own image' (Karnow, 1990) was pursued through a well-known and experimental commitment to universal primary school education in English – and also through a slightly less well-known but extremely brutal repression of the Filipino nationalist revolutionary movement (Goodno, 1991:33–5).

The later American colonial period was one of frustration for Filipino leaders, who saw the promise of self-rule first delayed until 1935 and finally granted only in 1946. Moreover, many people considered that the Americans used their role in disbursing capital for economic rebuilding after the war to create a form of neo-colonialism whose effects are still pervasive today. Certainly, the contemporary Philippine economy is driven by the need to spend 40 per cent of its GNP on servicing its debts to the World Bank and the United States, and by its need to attract international development capital. American pressures have been felt not only on economic issues of 'structural adjustment', but also in its prolonged maintenance of nuclear bases in the Philippines[7] and its alleged continued role in 'counter-insurgency' programmes against the communist guerillas, the New People's Army. The country's desperate need to generate foreign currency has also shaped the Philippines as the world's largest exporter of migrant labour (at least six million Filipinos work abroad), and as the US has since the later 1970s increasingly restricted Filipino immigration, closing off the 'American dream', those lucky enough to find work abroad have been diverted to other markets, especially Saudi Arabia, Kuwait and (until the Gulf War) Iraq, often in situations of considerable insecurity (Borra, 1984:16, 21).[8]

The colonial relationship with America has therefore not produced for most ordinary Filipinos the economic opportunities and freedom to travel of which they dream. Nonetheless, America is still generally regarded in the barangays, if not within nationalist politics, as the Philippines' good patron. In the minds of many people I knew in Calabanga, this idea is still vividly linked to memories of the Japanese occupation during the Pacific War (1941–46). Japanese presence was heavy in this part of Bicol, and many people I knew had family members imprisoned, tortured or killed for activities in the resistance. The US army appeared as the nation's liberators, and the possession of a US army war-widow's pension is still one of the key factors in creating relative wealth for people of this generation in Bicol.

Before describing the fieldwork setting in which these questions presented themselves to me, I shall examine the ways in which lowland culture was for many years, and often still is, depicted as broken, contentless and insubstantial, before briefly reviewing the relevance of the existing Filipino ethnography of exchange.

### The era of a negative conception of the lowland Philippines

For a period which has lasted from at least the beginning of the American period until quite recently [9] the recognition that the history of the lowland Philippines has been forcefully shaped by colonialism has been elided with something quite different; an anxious and discouraging notion in both the academic and non-academic literature, that the lowlands was perhaps nothing but the sum of its colonial parts, a culture without authenticity, or else was only to be defined in a series of negatives, by what it had failed to be.

These anxieties often took the form of a comparison between Filipinos and the American models towards which it was assumed that they should be developing. Such tropes could during the height of their fashion in the 1950s and 1960s swallow up even those who, like the ethnographer of Bicol folklore Father Frank Lynch, were deeply dedicated to the promotion of Philippine sociology and of American–Filipino understanding. Thus in the exploration of 'Philippine values' Lynch quotes from the results of psychometric testing carried out by Bulatao:

> When contrasted with the American, the Filipino is less autonomous, more dependent. He prefers a stable way of life where things . . . do not demand continual risk-taking. He will thus be more . . . oriented to authoritarian ways of thinking rather then to innovation and entrepreneurship . . .     *(Lynch, 1984a: 56)*

It was not only the Filipino's insufficient entrepreneurship that was a cause for concern, but his general cultural virility:

> . . . compared to Manilenos, American men and women are higher on autonomy, affiliation, exhibition, change and heterosexuality; they are lower on deference, order, abasement, nurturance and endurance and aggression . . .
> *(Bulatao Special Group Studies, quoted in Lynch, 1984a: 35)*

Much of the literature of the period was in fact dominated by a functionalist framework which was applied in order to find out whether Philippine society was growing healthily towards 'modernity', or, as was feared, was languishing in a state of insufficiently rational economic development (Davis, 1973), and retardation of the organs of democratic politics. Even within the national universities, the themes of 'acculturation', the adaptiveness or mal-adaptiveness of the Filipino family and other institutions to social change and cultural dysfunctionality, continued to dominate (Hart, 1977; Manalong, 1982; Mataragnon, 1984 and 1985; McDonald, 1982; Morais, 1981; Vengco, 1984). Jocano's detailed ethnographies of barangay life in Ilocos and Panay (1982; 1969a; 1969b) provided much useful analysis, but his hope that 'the presentation of ethnographic data on . . . lowland ethnic groups can assist in . . . strengthening national cohesion' (1982: iv) seemed written more in doubt than in confidence.

Indeed, much explicitly nationalistic literature has been overwhelmingly negative in its assessment of lowland culture; the call to 'cultural decolonization' in works of writers such as Renato Constantino (1969; 1976;

1978a; 1978b) being expressed with such vehemence that once again one is left with the impression that the lowlands are dominated by a 'colonial mentality' and identity confusion which can only be extirpated root and branch. Constantino would perhaps not greatly disagree with Neils Mulder's elegy for the birth of a mature Spanish-Filipino elite-led culture that, interrupted by the arrival of the Americans, was stillborn (Mulder 1991:4). 'The Filipinos were mentally recolonized in a discourse that not only extolled American culture, . . . but that also degraded the Spanish colonial past' (1991:6). American mass education, argues Mulder, created 'an undeniable measure of cultural dependency and instability . . . a "colonial mentality" that denigrated the own and imitated the foreign model' (7). Others have been more inclined to depict the lowlands as under cultural attack through foreign-oriented media, as cinema and radio have spread rapidly through the provinces since the 1950s, and as well as importing films the Philippines supports a large film industry of its own, which turns out quickly made melodramas and action films in Tagalog, the language of the national capital. Although this cinema is in fact highly distinctive, it cannot be said to fit orthodox definitions of high art, and those who claim to see its merits have often criticised its strange admixtures, its borrowings, its derivativeness and its lack of 'images of ourselves in our own reality' (Reyes, 1989:85).

While other writers would consider the capacity of the lowlands for 'resistance' an article of faith, there has nonetheless been a tendency only to measure its existence in terms external to the culture. As Coumans notes, many writers with left-wing sympathies concerned to trace events in the rural areas have taken a 'dim view of existing Filipino peasant consciousness as a means to meaningful social change' (Coumans, 1991:3).[10] Even Kervkliet's extremely valuable recent study of political consciousness in Central Luzon (1990), *starts* with the question of whether or not people in Filipino barangays 'have' the concept of class, rather than simply starting by asking what lowland 'political culture'[11] might be.

In fact, the only positive model of what lowlands society might be like was for a long time defined by the intelligent but theoretically limited writings of Lynch and especially of Mary Hollnsteiner (1973). Hollnsteiner (who, as Gibson has pointed out, basically put Mauss in the service of functionalism) proposed a society of landlord-patrons and share-cropping tenants, whose social relations were governed by the sense that the obligations which social inferiors owe their social superiors can never be completely repaid, and must therefore be endlessly acknowledged in small gestures of deference. This relation, known by the Tagalog term **utang na loob** (debt of the heart or, literally, the 'inside') was then contrasted with other obligations or contracts which were of a less permanent kind because they obtained between persons in positions of greater equality to each other (Ileto, 1979:9).

It would be absolutely undesirable to adopt an anodyne view of lowland history which denied the violent and destructive aspects of either Spanish or American colonialism, but Mulder and many other writers under-estimate the extent to which people engage with and manage the problem of dislocating historical experiences. Asking about the lowland Philippines only in terms of class or other systems of analysis primarily associated with the critique of modern Western capitalism, on the other hand, risks deepening the divide which for a long time has separated anthropological ways of looking at the Philippines from ways of looking at the rest of Southeast Asia, and therefore risks dividing the archipelago from its own pre-colonial historical context.

## Potency and reciprocity

Meanwhile, the development of anthropological and political studies of other parts of Southeast Asia, especially Indonesia, has proceeded along entirely different lines. In particular, since Benedict Anderson's seminal essay on 'The idea of power in Javanese culture' (first published 1972[12] but reprinted in Anderson 1990: 17–77) it has been taken as axiomatic that contemporary anthropological accounts of people in Java, Borneo, Sulawesi etc. both must and may assume a meaningful connection between the construction of social relations and representations in the present-day world, and a distinctive Southeast-Asian notion of power which has some continuity with even the ancient past of the region, especially with the Indic kingdoms (Anderson, 1990:19).[13] Southeast Asian 'potency' in Anderson's account is 'that intangible, mysterious and divine energy which animates the universe . . . there is no sharp division between organic and inorganic matter, for everything is sustained by the same invisible power' (1990:22). Moreover, he argues, the fundamental problem for Javanese rulers has not been the legitimacy of power, but the problem of accumulat-ing and preserving it, given that this energy always remains at a fixed quan-tity in the universe, and that a redistribution of power therefore always implies different persons gaining and losing power relative to each other (Anderson, 1990:23–4).[14]

The second key element in the re-imagining of the lowlands was the exceptional essays of the historian William Henry Scott, who put forward an original and persuasive re-reading of the Spanish missionary accounts of the Philippines at and just after colonial contact (Scott, 1985a and 1985b). Scott described lowland society as basically divided into social ranks: **datus** or aristocrats, freemen and commoners. Lowland society was never amalgamated into a single state before the arrival of the Spanish, but consisted of many small, military or (since they were often coastal) piratical chiefdoms, making war and trading with each other in conditions of relative political fluidity. But the brilliance of Scott's contribution lay in the fact that he disentangled the confusing descriptions given in the Spanish sources for the rights and duties of commoners, to show that this was above all a society which functioned dynamically on the basis of infinite gradations of debt-bondage. The power of a **datu** consisted in the fact that he was bonded to no one, and that he had innumerable dependents to whom he distributed patronage; everyone else owed some greater or lesser part of their labour to another person, who in turn often provided them with protection. Moreover, despite the existence of the three ranks of person, all these positions were mutable; a debt-slave could rise through gradually lightening relations of bondage to become a freeman or even a **datu**, and a **datu** could slip from power and descend in the other direction.

Both these analytic directions were taken up in two extremely important works on the social history of the Tagalog regions of the Philippines, Ileto's *Pasyon and revolution* (1979) on the 'millenarian' uprisings against Spain which formed part of the Philippine revolution and Rafael's *Contracting colonialism* (1988) on the nature of early Spanish Christianisation.[15] Both these outstanding works turned centrally on a revision of the **utang-na-loob** view of lowland society, and especially on a critique of the way in which it failed to consider the possibility of social conflict in hierarchical relations. Thus Ileto's study explored the use of the language of popular Tagalog religious texts, especially the sung passion-story or **Pasyon**, in 'peasant rebellions' whose leaders, wholly dependent for their sustenance and their lives on their supporters, were identified with the life and sufferings of Christ. In the search for **kalayaan** (freedom/salvation) all normal hierarchical relations are inverted; '. . . the gift is a mode of strengthening the bonds of **loob** among men. Begging and the acceptance of food, shelter and protective care create, not a subordinate–superordinate relationship, but a horizontal one akin to love . . . things are in fact turned upside-down – the debtor is the man of power' (Ileto, 1979:230).

While one might perhaps expect such inversions in the context of millenarian moments (Bloch, 1992a: 85–98), Ileto's account seems also to be exploring a potential which is always present in lowland culture for the meanings of hierarchy to slip sidewise into something else. Rafael's account of the sixteenth- and seventeenth-century period takes up this sense of slippage.

For Rafael, the main importance of the notion of **utang na loob** for sixteenth-century Tagalogs was that the **loob** or 'inside' of a person could only be created and maintained through the relations of exchange which structured all Filipino society. Thus, it is not that the 'inside' is circulated in exchanges between superordinate and subordinate, but that participation in social relationships of obligation itself makes the 'inside' (1988:122–7). Rafael offers an account of the means by which ordinary and elite Filipinos 'translated' the new demands which the Spanish church and state imposed on its Filipino subjects, so that the meaning of subjection itself was always subtly reformulated into something more reciprocal. Lowlanders, in other words, refused to 'understand' the demand that they should be absolutely subordinated to the colonial authorities, by interposing their own pre-colonial understanding of power as something which could never be absolutely one-directional, since (as was the case for Scott's indigenous **datu**) all power-holders are in a sense themselves dependent on the deference which their followers give them (Rafael, 1988:131); power is itself therefore caught in an endless loop, and rulers and subjects are merely two opposite points on its circumference.

It is perhaps the centrality to Anderson's insights of the notion of relative or *relational* power – power whose balance may be altered in any encounter between two persons since its quantity is eternally fixed – which provided the link by which both these historians connected a resituation of the Philippines in the Southeast Asian theoretical world of 'potency' (explicitly discussed, for example in Ileto's account of the amulets or **anting** with which the peasant leaders equipped themselves – most famously, those which were intended to protect men from bullets (Ileto, 1979:24–5 and 213)) with a re-reading of Hollnsteiner's functionalist account of 'reciprocity'. These works raise serious questions for anthropologists and demand a reworking of lowland power in the present as well as in the past. It will be apparent, however, that while this book in many ways defines its questions in conversation with both Rafael and Ileto, I have not generally used the terms 'potency', '**utang na loob**' (or its nearest Bicol equivalents)[16] or even 'debt' and that I do not wish to assume an exact equivalence between the historical and the contemporary contexts. Instead, for much of this book, I follow the ways in which

Bicolanos construct power relationally through idioms of speech, especially those which elaborate on the varying possible positions of power of two persons in conversation with each other, and idioms of emotion, such as pity, oppression and love.[17]

### Arriving in Calabanga

Calabanga is a modest market town, defined in 1989 as a third-class municipality. Boarding the 'jeepney', the characteristic public transport of the rural Philippines, one is about forty minutes' ride away from Naga, and a couple of kilometres from the sea at San Miguel Bay.[18] A crossroads marks the centre of the **poblacion**; to the north one immediately reaches the large fishing-barangay of Sabang; there is a characteristic pungent smell from the platforms spread with fish drying in the sun. To the east, the road curves upwards through coconut plantations and then follows the curve of the bay to arrive at Tinambac, a town whose beautiful site strangely manages to be both high and coastal, since the hills here slope so sharply down to the sea. At the Calabanga crossroads is a monumental but unlovely white Spanish church, rebuilt after typhoon damage at the end of the last century. People complain that services are often disturbed by the market which flanks the church site and laps around its edges on busy days.[19]

To European eyes, this market has a ramshackle air. Stalls are roughly roofed in galvanised iron, which rusts quickly in the heat and the rain. In this market are sold, on various stalls, fresh fish, vegetables, seasonings like garlic and **vetsin** (monosodium glutamate) and tiny packets of five peppercorns, meat in small quantities because of the high price, tin pots, lime and betel nut, single cigarettes, bright plastic slippers, brooms made from the midrib of coconut leaves, canned milk, little blocks of solid cocoa for making chocolate porridge, and all the other daily items of the rural Philippines. On market days, there are also cheap clothes, plastic buckets and sometimes bitter herbs brought by the **Agta** (the black ethnic group now reduced to a precarious existence in the uplands), and bought quietly by women desperate to induce miscarriage. The most prosperous are always those who buy and sell rice (**magtungod**), which requires capital, and they have small open-fronted shops rather than stalls. A Chinese-owned bakery is perhaps the grandest establishment, with a dark interior of wooden shelves, lino-topped tables, an electric fan blowing the sticky air in circles and a gaudily dressed Madonna on a small shelf; here you can eat 'Chinese' siopao, 'Spanish' pan de sal, and drink Coke. There are three tiny beauty-shops, two run by women and one by **bakla** (male transvestites), little eating-stalls, a pharmacy where you can buy expensive American drugs in single tablets, a popular cinema with wooden seats that shows Tagalog movies, and several photographers. Beyond the market is the town hall and the plaza, concreted in an improvement programme and thus suitable for use as a basketball court. At a distance down a quiet road, well outside the town, is the **Kampusanto** or cemetery, with its rows of tombs stacked up on top of each other like concrete filing cabinets, over-grown all year except in the week of All Souls' Day.

If you have come on the jeepney from Naga City, the provincial capital, west is now the only direction left to take. Bumping along in a passenger-motorcycle, you pass first through the central **barangays** (villages or town districts), where the houses, at least those facing the road, are usually one-story concrete 'bungalows', the homes of the town's salaried employees or substantial landowners, although just off the main route there are more modest homes, and sometimes a middle-class family still has a large old wooden house on stilts standing, not yet destroyed by the annual typhoons. Except for the very centre of the town, where there are two par-allel roads, the houses are only one row deep, and behind the swept earth yards with their waterpumps, chickens, pigsty or vegetable plot, are the brilliant green ricefields of the plain. At the edge of the town is the shrine of the **Amang Hinulid** or 'Christ laid out in death', which is roofed but open-walled, with the carved saint visible on the altar, prone as Snow White in his glass coffin. There is almost always someone there, and on Fridays, especially the first of the month when the saint's clothes are changed, there are crowds of pilgrims, teenagers facing exams, the sick, healers, members of religious confraternities, anxious lovers and worried mothers. There are people performing devotions to the **Ama** and also people who work at the shrine: the sellers of amulets and religious texts and old ladies from San Ignacio who for a small payment will choose and say with you the right novena for sickness, danger or separation from those you love.

San Ignacio is the first rural barangay just beyond this shrine and over a bridge. It is the poorest barangay in the municipality, and most of the bun-galows peter out here. Houses are largely wood, bamboo or **nipa** thatch. The little road continues westwards towards the Bicol river estuary, and houselots are arranged on either side of it, sandwiched on each side by the ricefields. Each houselot belongs to a family, and there are almost always several houses on it, belonging to a number of siblings with their spouses and children. If the old parents are still alive, they usually live in the largest and oldest house, cared for by one child, probably an oldest or youngest daughter, and her family. Houses are often still raised off the ground on poles, though they are not built so high as a generation ago. Steps lead up to one or two rooms; if there are two, both will be used for sleeping but the front room is also a living room, while the back or inner room is for sleeping and storing clothes. Floors are wood or bamboo and furniture is often limited to some home-made benches, a table, sleeping mats, a mirror and ornaments, although wealthier households have commerically made furniture. Kitchens are usually lean-tos at the back of the house, and washing is done at a pump which may be shared. Another common arrangement is for a house to have one upstairs room, and then an earth-floor room downstairs which is used as a living area.

The barangay contains a chapel dedicated to the patron saint, and the primary school which serves the surrounding area, with a concrete yard where rice is dried. Looking over the ricefields to the south, one sees in the distance the old Spanish mission of Quipayo; crossing the barangay and looking towards the north, one sees a small satellite barangay of San Ignacio, beyond which is the seaside hamlet, where men from San Ignacio often walk to fish at night, though they also fish in the paddy. There are one or two small village shops selling matches and other necessities, and there is a general air of slow village life. Little groups of women while away the afternoon playing 'Spanish' cards; children trot up and down on errands; people make their way to the several local healers (three in the barangay) with sprains and temperatures; work in the ricefields sets the pace of the day and the year. On nights when there is a full moon, everybody stays up late chatting and playing games outside to enjoy the light. Electricity reached San Ignacio in the 1970s, but not everyone can afford the supply, and it frequently shuts off as power is often diverted to Manila, and the lines blow down in storms.

Naga City is very different, although like most Filipino cities it gives the impression of being at bottom a mushroomed village, not an urban environment in the European sense. Many squatters in Naga are farmers, that is, they squat significant areas of riceland as well as house-space, and only in the railway station area is there really an urban squatter's area. Unused ground tends to sprout a hut and a vegetable patch.[20] The centre is on a rather similar plan to Calabanga, but on a much grander and glossier scale; in the main square, a church with a concrete facade is flanked by one bank and faces another. Both banks have smoked-glass doors and the inevitable security guards in sunglasses, clutching guns of dubious vintage and safety. Several glass-fronted fast-food restaurants imitate the American chains which have outlets in Manila: one is named 'MangDonalds' (**Mang** means 'old man' in Tagalog), to the rage of MacDonalds, who tried to sue the owner. These serve the local version of American food (the flavour is always Filipinised) to students, office workers and courting couples out for a treat. There are several very large Chinese-owned department stores, selling all kinds of prestigious goods such as cosmetics, canned foods, toys, music cassettes and electrical items, most of them imported. These shops are glass fronted and air-conditioned; but in the large multistory city market, and elsewhere in Naga, shops are like those in Calabanga, open fronted, darker and cooled if at all by a single fan. Some of Naga's several cinemas are also Chinese-owned, while others are owned by one of the local elite families; in contrast to the small town cinema, these sometimes show films in English as well as Tagalog. There are also a number of high schools and colleges in Naga, of which the American-Jesuit foundation, the Ateneo de Naga, is the largest.

### '*Kami mayong-mayo*' ('We who have nothing at all')

The people with whom I lived in San Ignacio, though there were certainly differences in relative income and status among them, almost all classed themselves as '**an mga pobre**', the poor, or '**kami mayong-mayo**', 'we who have nothing at all', and contrasted themselves to the rich, '**an mga mayaman**', or 'those who have something'; occasionally, someone would admit that 'we have a little bit these days', '**garo iri-igwa na kami**'.

These terms are in most instances not just modesty or affectation, although the better-off may exaggerate slightly for the sake of solidarity with their less fortunate neighbours. San Ignacio has, to a slightly worse degree than many other similar places, all the economic problems which affect the majority of people in rural Bicol. Although for centuries the plains of the Bicol river valley have been a key area for the growing of irrigated rice, they are not a region of wealthy farmers. Lynch (1973b) gave the average landholding for Camarines Sur as 0.72 hectares in 1973 (when 49 per cent of the population were sharecroppers and another 20 per cent owner-cultivators), and Barnes (in Lynch, 1974:i) comments that in the conditions of production then prevailing 79 per cent of the population had to be reckoned 'absolutely poor', meaning that their income fell short of their food requirements, and there was an average 'negative saving' (i.e. household debt) of ₱.1,200 per year. At this date, 7.7 per cent were unemployed, but a further 20.6 per cent were underemployed, and this probably underestimates the figures for women, despite a rising level of educational attainment (Lynch and Illo, 1975:1–11).

Economic conditions have generally worsened over the past twenty years, and the average riceland cultivated in 1988–89 was only 0.5 hectares (Jo Asug, personal communication) whereas local farmers say that between 1.5 and 3 hectares is needed to make a proper living for a family. Land shortage is exacerbated by population growth; between 1980 and 1990, the population of the barangay rose from 1,071 to 1,658 (Census of population and housing, 1990). Many people now only have secure access to land on alternate years, or less often, since inherited owned plots are rotated among siblings and their descendants when they are too small to be divided. Otherwise, access depends on temporary arrangements with landowners or farmers unable to farm that year, often with highly complex share-cropping arrangements. The problem is complicated by cash shortages and the need to raise loans; the **arindo** system is a kind of mortgaging-out of land for cash, with the land as security. This may be combined with a share-cropping arrangement in which the borrower works his own land but pays increasing proportions of the harvest over to the lender if he fails to repay the cash within a time limit, and people are thus easily caught in a spiral of accelerating debt in which they have the right to benefit from less and less of the product of their own labour. Other items which are means of livelihood, such as passenger-motorcycles, can also be lost in **arindo** loans. Strictly, one cannot raise **arindo** loans on land which one does not own, but in practice it is the farming rights which are often mortgaged out, the issue of rent to the landowner being treated as separate.[21]

Despite these difficulties, farming and fishing are still the main means of earning a living for people in San Ignacio. These are firstly subsistence activities, though a family will always hope to raise cash by selling fish or, in fortunate cases, a rice surplus. Buying rice used to be a rare and disdained expedient, but as access to farmland is reduced, more people are forced to buy rice regularly, which in turn sharpens the need for cash and places people at the mercy of the rice-merchants' prices. A local widow who sells rice at 50 centavos more than the rate in the town centre is widely resented, and rice-sellers are always being pushed to extend their tolerance of credit-buying.

There is a variety of small service and retail jobs with which people try to make ends meet; driving a passenger-motorbike, running a little shop and buying and selling fish are the most capital-intensive of these, and the most likely to yield a living income. Giving manicures, making and selling afternoon snacks, travelling with a **halo-halo** (sweet with ice) stall to local fiestas, holding card-games in your house for a small fee, taking in laundry or letting older children go out as domestic helps or to work in Manila factories, were all tried by people I knew. Migrant work abroad was coveted by many, but the contacts and agency fees were beyond most people, and only one family in the barangay had made their money this way.

The most important source of income therefore remains wage work in the ricefields, especially during the planting, weeding and harvesting seasons, and both male and female workgroups are employed on it. However, the income from this source has fallen with the arrival of intensive farming methods. One usual arrangement now becoming less common is **lote** in which the same workers plant and harvest a rice crop and are paid in rice. In the 1950s, this share was one sixth of the crop, and the farmer had to make his arrangements for threshing separately. In the mid-1960s, this share fell to one seventh or one eighth, and some employers asked for threshing as well,[22] but workers accepted the lower rate because the introduction of the double-cropping 'miracle rice', which at first gave better yields than it does now, meant that twice the work was available. In 1975, the mechanised thresher replaced hand-threshing, and the share fell to one tenth, as employers said the threshing was costing them too much. In 1985, the share was down to one eleventh and by 1989 it was one twelfth, except when the employer was 'someone who would feel pity for you, like your cousin'. Although the **lote** system spreads risk between farmer and workers, since the workers are not paid until after the

Figure 1 Women riceplanters in the barangay

harvest, it is now used less, and mostly among family members. The standard way of paying workers is by **tandan** or wage, and the 1989 rate was ₱.20 a day if a snack is provided, and ₱.25 if not. Full meals were always customarily provided for harvesters by farmers, but some farmers now resist even providing substantial snacks, while others (much respected by the people who work for them) regard it as shameful not to do so. The maximum number of people employed on one hectare of land would be between twenty and twenty-five.

People in San Ignacio, moreover, see themselves as poor relative to their own past. While share-cropping has been the dominant mode of wet-rice production all over Bicol for the past two centuries, the people I knew were unlike some other lowland Filipino farmers in emphasising not only the decline of paternalistic landlord–tenant relations, but also the loss of their own independence. Many people see themselves as former smallholders, whose land has been lost to debt in the last two generations, rather than as former tenants. [23]

Remarks about 'having nothing' are no doubt common in poor communities all over the world, but there is an important and specifically Filipino aspect here. Firstly, the estimation of one's poverty is always relative.[24] Secondly, the statement that one is poor and someone else is rich carries more than material implications. As Pinches notes in his article on Tondo slum dwellers, 'it is the experience of not being valued as human beings, of having to endure humiliation, disapproval and rejection, of constantly having one's dignity challenged' and of 'being shamed' (1991:177).

This experience of relative poverty is reinforced because, even for the poor, life is intermittently mobile. The generation now in their forties and upwards often did extra harvesting work elsewhere in the region when they were younger, and then as now teenagers would leave home for a few years to do domestic work, and now factory work, especially in Manila. Many people engage in small trading, bringing upland products like sweet potato and charcoal to the lowlands, or fish and shrimp to the inland barangays. Although busy married people may leave the barangay infrequently, and some have never been as far as Manila, fiestas and visits to relatives often take people travelling, and even from the most remote **sitios** (hamlets), people will walk into their local town to the market, the cinema or the cock-pit.

Women are especially active in smallscale trading, especially selling fish. Since the men catch the fish, this is of course a division of labour typical of the Filipino norms of marital cooperation (Illo, 1988: 13; 1992: 189; and 1995: 219; Rutten, 1982: 111–17 and 1990: 65), but both women and men say that men do not like to sell and are not good at it. Men are ashamed to haggle, and are also said not to know the right price at which to sell things. Usually, men only take an active role in selling in larger-scale operations, such as selling ice made by machine, larger-scale fish retailing involving buying from other fishermen (**rigaton**), or bigger business like selling rice or running handicraft businesses, though some men run market stalls, perhaps with their wives.

During the summer months, men from San Ignacio would regularly go out to catch shrimp during the night. If the catch was a kilo or more, their wives would take it in buckets and walk at four in the morning to catch the first jeepney to Naga City, arriving while it was still dark. Their only other equipment was a piece of plastic sheeting on which to spread the catch in priced piles (**atado**). Naga has a concrete market building with several stories where different kinds of goods are sold, but occasional fish sellers cannot afford a licence. Instead they climb to the 'squatters' market' – that is, the open roof. As soon as the sun rises, the heat becomes unbearable, and most people leave by 7 am.

The sellers sit on their heels with the **atado** of shrimp on the sheet in front of them, relying on experience to calculate how many shrimp to put in each. If business is slow, they will make the **atado** larger to attract customers quickly, and they may end up selling at a loss. Women from the same barangay travel together and sit near each other at the market. There is no overt competition, and selling is very low-key, although people keep an eye on each other's sales and friends exchange discrete comments on how they are doing. They might end up with ₱.15 profit on a bad day, ₱.55 on a good day, or none at all after fares are paid. Most economise on breakfast, but may pay a peso for a cup of **pamaghat**, herbal tea that prevents 'relapse' from exhaustion and sudden changes between heat and cold.[25]

The money will help to buy rice or to meet pressing school expenses, and it may be the family's only income for the day. Most women I knew reckoned that ₱.50.00 per day[26] was the minimum on which their families could survive: rice alone for a family of six would cost ₱.32.00 (4 kilos at ₱.8.00 per kilo in 1989), leaving a very narrow margin for other food, and nothing towards occasional expenses such as clothes, electric supply, etc.

To get to the squatters' market, the fish sellers pass through Naga's main squares, passing the cinemas, department stores and banks behind their glossy facades. However, they never go into them, but return straight to the barangay to see the children off to school. If they buy anything, it will be from the market, and if they go to Naga for a treat, they rarely venture

into such places. Gaudy cinema posters are everywhere, but they will not
go to the cinema here. Nor will they eat at the fast-food outlets which serve
'American' hamburgers, hot-dogs, canned juice, ice-cream sundaes and
spaghetti. Space is different for rich and poor; people from San Ignacio see
the gloss of Naga City as they pass by its windows, but they do not possess
it or partake of it; they do not consume its products as purchasers, and
they do not eat its food. The incongruity between the world of the rich and
the world of the poor, albeit superimposed on each other in the same
streets, is therefore a daily, tangible experience. It is a difference particular-
ised in a thousand material objects; canned peaches versus boiled sweet
potato, plate glass versus nipa tiles, the air-conditioned chill of super-
market aisles versus the village store.

It is suggestive that most of the food in Naga's glossy restaurants is, by
Filipino standards, not real food; that is, it is not usually served with rice,
and therefore in whatever quantity it is eaten it can only be counted as
snacks. A few office workers – from the middle classes who are most at ease
in the Americanised Filipino environment – will eat lunch there with rice,
but the rice portions are small, served in Western-sized amounts, not as a
staple, in a style which is recognisably luxurious and suggestive of the
good life of the States.[27]

It is 'those who have nothing', however, with whom I am mostly concerned in this book, and for them the experience of marginality is very
sharp. And because being wealthy is so tied up in Filipino culture with
command over the 'symbolic capital' (Bourdieu, 1977:6) associated with
colonial powers, being poor also means feeling that one has only a tenta-
tive hold on the ideas, language and gestures of America. Not being able
to afford America's canned goods, t-shirts and other products is therefore
painful twice; once because you are not rich, and once because you cannot
buy a piece of America-in-the-Philippines. Both these things threaten a
person with the shame to which Pinches refers.

The responses of people in San Ignacio to this situation are multifac-
eted, ironic and subtle. In all the contexts I discuss, there is an aspect of
challenge to dominant interpretations of the place of the poor in the
world; mediums, for instance are explicitly said to be there to help the poor
who cannot afford doctors and to be able to cure when hospital medicine
would kill (see chapter three). But practically every conversation in San
Ignacio also deals with the problem of powerlessness, especially through
the jokes and laughter which are a constant part of daily talk.

These jokes are made in a variety of ways. Although everyone in the
lowlands is known by a shortened version of their name, some people

also have a nickname of a different kind, a **bansag** which refers to some quality of theirs or episode in which they have been involved. A number of the local **bansag** involved specific jokes about poverty. One woman was introduced to me as **Maria Mayaman** (Wealthy Mary). 'It's because her house is filled with radios, fridges and electric fans', I was told. 'Yes', said Maria, 'if one of my fridges gets a little old, I throw it out, just like in the States!' Needless to say, Maria's house does not even contain an electric light bulb; it is one of the poorest houses, with an earth floor and a leaking roof. Maria has a handicapped teenage son whom she supports by selling snacks around the barangay and working in the fields. Another man is known as **Pasayan**, 'the shrimp', in reference to the poverty of his catches.

An incident which continued to amuse my friends for the entire length of my stay started when I was walking with another woman to visit her daughter on the coast. We passed through coconut plantations with cows grazing in the shade, and I wondered whose they were. 'Oh, they belong to your **Mamay**[28] Mon' (her husband's younger brother), remarked Ilar seriously. Since cows are valuable and I knew that Mon's family were in debt, I was very surprised, and asked why he kept them so far from the barangay. It didn't take me long to realise I was being teased, since when I dutifully asked Mon's wife about the mystery cows, she was torn between amusement and irritation, while Ilar couldn't stop giggling. In fact, Mon was notorious for having sold his own water-buffalo to pay for a mistress, to his wife's despair, since it had been a wedding-gift from her parents, and for extravagant boasting about his erstwhile land and herds when drunk, by which he had earned a **bansag** of 'the cow'. 'Ask your **Mamay** Mon about his cows, Nell, and why he kept them so far from home', was a line that put things in perspective whenever my questions became too absurd.

Other jokes also play on the gap between aspiration and reality; typhoon damage to houses is ironically referred to as 'air-conditioning', feet muddy from the paddy-fields as 'my manicure', worn flip-flops and housedresses as 'my dancing clothes', and so on. Although some of these jokes were addressed to me as a foreign visitor, people also made them all the time amongst themselves. Another kind of play and teasing involves acting out the same kind of message. I often saw groups of women break into the arm-movements of the **pantomina**, the wedding-dance in which money is pinned by guests onto the clothes of the bride and groom. The ideas of wealth, finery and celebration were pointed up by the contexts in which they did it; for instance, when dressed in work clothes, they were watching a barangay dance they had decided they could not afford to attend, or to tease someone who was due to have a birthday about the grand party (**blowout**) that they should provide for their friends.

Conversely, joking and teasing also take place whenever someone does dress up or offer hospitality, but the joking is never only levelling; it is always more celebratory than critical.[29] This applies especially to the offering of food and alcohol; people not only exclaim at the event on how delicious (**masiram**) the food is, comparing it to the products of those glossy Naga restaurants, but they do so in prospect and in retrospect. Three photographs of a birthday party of one of Gloria's sisters-in-law, which had happened just before I came to San Ignacio, were periodically examined by all and sundry throughout the time I was there. People told me repeatedly how there had been so many bottles of beer, they had all got drunk and started singing, how there had been two sorts of dish to eat with the beer, how delicious they had been, etc.

Photographs which demonstrate the successful carrying-off of a celebration are important and much enjoyed; people like to pose literally pointing at the food they have raised the money to buy, and have prepared for a wedding, baptism or birthday, especially if it is prestigious food like meat or expensive canned goods. It is partly the unity of those who have provided the hospitality which is being celebrated, especially if they are kin, but it is also partly the joyous success of having acquired, used and shared in some of the good things in life which are usually out of reach. Looking at the photos, as people say, one can almost consume the meal again.[30] Photographs are themselves prized consumer objects, since few people own a camera and pictures are taken by roving professional photographers and sold by the frame. But a photograph is also a kind of fetish of transformation in Bicol; it places you in a position where, in your best clothes or with the most delicious food, you have temporarily become the possessor of these things, and so escaped the threat of 'being shamed'. This is more than just 'status assertion', which, in the sense that is often given to it, implies something both trivial and aggressive; this is a joy in the transformation of the self (and one's neighbours) out of poverty.

In one house, where one of the older children had worked in the Middle East for a while, the family had put together a photographic collage made of pictures of an American-style bathroom, bedroom and fitted kitchen cut out of magazines, and pictures of the younger children placed as though playing, sleeping and eating in the shiny rooms. The pictures of the children and the pictures of the rooms were not on the same scale, so that the figures seemed much too big. 'We put the children in, because they enjoyed seeing it so much', they explained. 'When, I ask you, will they ever see it otherwise?'

This aspiration was also apparent in the way people decorated their homes. Those with more money choose the bright (floor-coverings, curtains, tablecloths) and the solid (cement floors, wooden furniture), both tastes which contrast with the lightness and plainness of bamboo and nipa houses – although everyone tends to leave their walls bare, as they were when houses were all built of hardwood. People also like to display objects, especially picture calendars and plastic dolls, and anything electrical, items which are thought of as Western goods.

Over the period between my first visit to Bicol, and the completion of this work, the Southeast Asian regional boom years had to some extent reached even San Ignacio; an increased flow of national funding had resulted in the enlargement of the local primary school to include a high school in 1992, and the surfacing of the barangay road in 1997. It also appeared that barangay captains (who received an increase in allowance over this period) were better able to raise money for certain local improvement schemes, such as the rebuilding of the barangay chapel. Those farmers whose holdings were above the viable level, those with substantial fish-trading or other well-capitalised family businesses, and those families with several adult children who were away working in Manila or elsewhere, seemed to be doing better in 1997 than in 1989, and this was most readily visible in the improvements they made to their houses, especially the replacement of 'native' building materials with concrete blocks and galvanised iron roofs, and the building of inside (but unplumbed) WCs and kitchens. More households also had televisions in 1997 than in 1989, although these were mostly bought on hire-purchase, and some were already misfunctioning before the payments had been completed. On the other hand, the many without these advantages were still living in very modest houses and the incidence of chronic TB and other poverty-related diseases was still extremely high.

As far back as the 1950s Father Frank Lynch was arguing (Lynch, 1959; 1984b) that there may be a considerable degree of historical continuity in the tendency for Filipino, and specifically Bicolano, villagers and townspeople to think of themselves as basically belonging to one of two groups: 'big people' and 'little people', or the elite and their dependents.

Such a view has been widely criticised (e.g. Ileto (1979) and Rafael (1988)) because Lynch further assumed that the relationship between these 'two groups' is therefore one of harmonious patronage rather than conflict; however, analogous self-descriptions by poor people in the lowlands seem to be widely found, see for example Illo (1985: 88). Kerkvliet, although examining the prevalence of notions of 'class' in the rural areas of Nueva Ecija, describes them as intersecting similarly constructed notions of 'haves' and 'have-nots' based on quality of life rather than the relationship to the means of production (1990: 59–63). In the very different context of contemporary urban squatter settlements in Manila (albeit communities closely tied to their Visayan barangay origins), Pinches (1991:176–83) notes the use of class-based language of **burgis** versus **masa** which is however still status-related and still constructed as a dualistic contrast.

Like Pinches, I would recognise that this notion of dependent and patron, and its concomitant notion of solidarity among the poor, 'those who have nothing' in the Bicol context, is always in tension with the more individualistic aspirations of villagers to escape from the discomforts and humiliations of poverty. Bicolano barangays are not strongly egalitarian in any generally understood sense; they do not maintain that absolute equality is a social good, or that all individual betterment is anti-social or unmerited. Yet, in the slightly improved economic conditions of 1997, it was if anything even more evident that those who benefited from increased wealth would be criticised by their kin and neighbours if they did not pursue one of two paths. Either they could share some of their wealth via hospitality, loans, the provision of work and so on, within the framework which insisted that all co-barangay members are 'siblings'. Or (much more problematically) they could themselves start to move into the position of the 'good patron'. To act as an individualistic entrepreneur and to refuse such social obligations, however, was to invite much more stringent criticism, and the accusation that one had 'forgotten one's kin' or had become 'an oppressor of one's fellow men'. The fine line between the acceptable and the unacceptable in the pursuit of individual wealth was obviously subject to continuous negotiation and rival interpretations.

One might conclude, that although the 'patron–client' relationship does not exist as unproblematic social reality, the notion – or something like it, though not necessarily derived from landholding practices – continues to have widespread salience as one model of the socially desirable. If power is to be distributed unequally, lowlanders seem to be saying, let us at least constrain the power-holders within a relationship with their dependents which they cannot entirely ignore. Similarly, if the poor are to be poor, let it at least not be forgotten that human value is not entirely measurable by wealth, and that all unequal relationships of wealth and power are, finally, mutable.

Most Bicolano houses clearly display the gap between what people have, and what they would like to have. Radio-cassette players will be kept even if they do not work, proudly displayed on shelves as objects of beauty and value.[31] In pointing two ways at once, towards what is there and what is not there, such objects act like the ironic jokes of which barangay people are so fond; they highlight incongruities as well as trying to resolve them. It is this ambivalent sensibility which belongs particularly to ordinary Bicolanos, and which, as I shall show, enters into all their 'conversations' about power.

## Preview of the argument

This book will move between different contexts in which these ways of looking at power are played out, highlighting the fact that the Bicolano view of power is of a *relationship* in which both powerful and less powerful are liable to affect each other, and in which the hope of those 'who have nothing' is always that the gap between the two parties may be somewhat lessened by what they do, and what they say, even if it cannot be closed altogether. I begin with arranged marriages, stories about which appear to be important in San Ignacio partly because they emphasise a journey repeated by many couples, from distance and a profound inequality of power, towards gradually increased equality and intimacy. In chapter two, I argue that the resonance of these stories also emerges from historical transformations in which marriage has been at the centre of attempts to create fixed and predictable social rankings – attempts which, however, were never finally consolidated, so that the Bicol model of power distribution continued to be of something which is often asymmetrical, but always dynamic and capable of change and negotiation. The relative standing of two persons or social groups, however unequal, is never seen as entirely fixed, nor is it justified in relation to some internal essence (such as aristocratic blood) or divinely ordained external cosmology as is the case in many rank-ordered societies. Chapters three, four and five explore the interactions between spirit mediums of different kinds, spirits, and their patients: a series of triangular relationships at the centre of which are the healer's melancholic recognition that, in accepting the 'help' of her spirits, she is simultaneously becoming consumed by them in a form of debt-bondage, and the play on the incommensurablity of spirits and humans which echoes Bicol's other ironic jokes and comparative reflections.[32] In the following three chapters, I address the place of Catholicism in shaping the ambivalence of Filipino relationships to the spirit world, and describe the relationship of local people to a miracle-working saint, the **Amang**

**Hinulid,** whose cult itself reveals crucial ways in which Bicolanos have resisted some of the implications of Christian conversion and the economy of salvation. Chapter ten considers the range of practices which attempt to bridge the gap between ordinary Bicolanos and the power-figures – in many ways experienced as even more distant – which are in part constructed as icons of America and the modern West, especially through women's and male transvestite beauty contests and the logic of intimacy through imitation. Finally, in the conclusion, I return to some of the themes sketched in this introduction, including the attempt to re-situate Bicol within a reading of the broader Southeast Asian literature, and the theoretical implications of the idioms of power which are traced through the ethnography. I argue that the mis-perception of the Philippine lowlands as 'culture-less' has resulted from the particular view of culture which was defined by the archipelago's colonisers, and especially from the failure to examine the ways in which large themes, such as the nature of power, are perceptible in the fine weave of daily relationships, and the sub-tleties of talk about them, as much as or more than in the transmission of 'rituals' or other spectacular practices which construct culture as 'tradition'.

# PART I

## MARRIAGE

# 1

## Marriage stories: speaking of reluctance and control

**Severina's story: 'No one talked it over with me.'**

Severina G——, mother of my exacting friend and instructor the healer Auring, was in her sixties when I met her in 1988. The story of her marriage hangs centrally on the idea – proverbially quoted in Bicol and the lowland Philippines – of a child's obedience and indebtedness to its parent, usually described in the textbooks as gratitude for 'the gift of life' (Hollnsteiner, 1973:76). This obligation defined Severina's destiny in an unusually literal way, since she was given in marriage against her will in order to repay the debt her father owed to the man who saved his life.[1]

Living in an upland barangay during the Japanese occupation, Severina's father became very ill with a 'paralysis'. Eventually, his terrified family took him to visit a distant healer, an old man with a wide reputation for the power of his **orasion** (spells). Severina's father was carried in a hammock over the mountain roads and Severina, aged fifteen, went with him to nurse him. After some weeks, the healer was successful in curing him.

But instead of accepting a payment . . . the healer said '**Padi**,[2] it would be a good thing to marry my grandson to your daughter.' My father didn't raise objections because he had recovered already. Anyway, we went back to our house, and as soon as we got there, we were married.

Severina's future husband already had a lover, a woman whom he called his 'wife' and whom he wanted to marry, and neither of the two intended spouses liked the match. Severina was not asked whether she was willing: 'At the **sungkohan** [party to set the wedding terms], they were all talking to each other, all sitting opposite each other face to face. . . . But no one talked it over with me.'

Severina resisted the marriage openly, asking to be allowed to finish school, but was told, 'Don't contradict, you'll do what you're told.'

'At the wedding,' she says, 'my feelings were very painful (**makulogon an boot ko**). He only had to lay a finger on me, and I would hit him, because I didn't want him to touch me. He couldn't get near me . . . When he came home, he had to cook his own rice, because I didn't want him to [think he could] start kissing me.'[3] According to her husband, she ran home to her mother's house every night for a fortnight after they were married.

Her submission to her parents was softened only by the fact that, as they reminded her, an obedient child in turn earns its parents' blessing and obligation. 'They said I should agree with what they wanted, and for why, because they would agree with what I wanted too. As long as he was alive, said my father, he would give me his support. So that up to now, even if I were to call him this minute, he would come here.'

Severina's marriage, it seems, has been a fairly equal battle with her husband; she says she left him in disgust on a number of occasions, and that she has always been better than he at making a living for the family; he says he has had so many women competing for his favours that it would take two days to get through the list. She says he desired her when they married; he says he preferred his other 'wife', had his grandfather been willing to allow their engagement, and that Severina's distaste was simply coy encouragement.

It might therefore seem surprising that both agree that their marriage has been successful, but their parents' choice, they say, is justified by the fact that they are still together and that they have many children and grandchildren. 'In the past,' says Severina, 'our parents were like prophets, it seemed that they could see into a person's ways (**ugali**) just by looking at them . . . because, you see, we have seen our grandchildren married.' From this viewpoint, they can see even their initial rejection of each other as part of the development of a marriage which eventually produced many spreading branches of kin.

It may be partly for this reason that, despite their own experiences, Severina and her husband arranged marriages in turn for their own children, thus helping to carry the institution forward into the generation who married in the 1970s.

### Talking about marriage

Bicolano friends in Naga and Manila were often surprised and amused when I mentioned to them that I was doing some research on arranged marriage. The most common response was 'Does it still exist? Ay, *si*

Fenella must really be living in the **bukid** ("the sticks")! There we are – she's not an "American lady", as they all think, she's a peasant!'[4]

Although in the Philippines one person's metropolis is always another person's **bukid**, San Ignacio Calabanga is, as we saw, not exactly isolated. There are many places in Camarines Sur which are further from the city and less well-served by road transport. Nonetheless, while arranged (or even forced) marriages were certainly more common in the generations born before the war, they have by no means ceased to be significant. There are still many women who were in their thirties and forties at the time of my fieldwork, and some younger people, whose marriages had been arranged. Of eleven marriages which I attended in 1988–89, for instance, one was known only to be taking place because the bride had been very heavily pressured by the groom and both sets of in-laws, and one was arranged when the young man's fiancée left him, and he accepted the substitute bride his parents favoured. The other nine marriages were mainly instigated by the young people, with parental contributions ranging from simple permission to active help, advice and taking of decisions about choice of spouse and living arrangements which reflected the interests of both generations.

It is important to note that arranged or forced marriage is only one end of a continuum of parental intervention in children's marriages, which at the other extreme tails off into complete freedom of choice for the child. Unlike, for instance, in South Asian contexts, Filipino 'arranged marriage' has at no point been the only way to get a spouse; there have always been institutionalised means to circumvent parental consent, especially by elopement. The gradual reduction in numbers of arranged marriages does not therefore represent a complete break with the past or an unprecedented plunge into 'modern romance'. Some of the possible reasons for the changes in levels of arranged marriage, their connections to ideas about kinship and their significance for Bicolano representations of continuity, are analysed in the next chapter.[5] In this chapter, however, I want to focus on this material from two other perspectives.

Firstly, I want to give some impression of the way in which in Bicol one usually hears the meaning of things only very gradually through the multiplication of individual stories which bear a subtle relationship to each other, rather than through the articulation of statements about general social 'rules'. One is not often told (as anthropologists and other visitors to different kinds of society often are), 'We Bicolanos do X, because X is the right thing to do'/'how we are'/'the way of our ancestors'/'the will of God'.[6] One correlate of the way in which Bicolanos do not often claim to have an objectified 'culture' is that social meaning remains more than usually implicit, and most often it is embedded in the kinds of stories about individual people's lives which are told in ordinary conversation, during the innumerable sweltering afternoons when one tries to find some place in the shade with a breath of air, or in the evening when groups of friends gather to chat for entertainment. These stories are moreover told with a skill and panache which is perhaps not unconnected to the local history of valuing rhetorical powers, many of which were once commonly practised in riddling games and other verbal contests which are now rare.[7]

Secondly, although almost all the stories I quote here are about arranged marriages, they illustrate one part of a more general language which people of all ages and marital situations use to talk about their relationships with lovers and spouses.[8] This language is itself in part about speaking, or, to be more precise, it is about conversations, a point to which I will return at the end of this chapter. The most common term for someone with whom one has a serious relationship is **kaulay**, that is, a person with whom or to whom you talk. In Bicol, one definition of real love (**tunay na pagkamoot**) between men and women is expressed as 'having talked to each other' (**may urulayan na**) or 'having understood each other' (**may irintindihan na**), while a lovers' quarrel or separation is 'being unable to understand each other/ agree with each other' (**dai sinda nakaintindihan**). For young people, and especially women, who are forced into arranged marriages, however, the experience is described as one of being excluded from effective speech by others; as in Severina's story, while the older people are seated 'face to face' negotiating all the details of the wedding, the young bride herself is silenced. 'No one', as she said, 'talked it over with me'. There are thus two kinds of conversational position which women can adopt in the regulation of their marital relationships, that of the speaker who commands her own choice, and that of the 'spoken for' who obeys the speech of her parents. I shall show through women's stories, however, that while some women unambiguously prefer the position of free choice (*'It's no good if you haven't talked to your husband . . . That's why all my children will choose the people they marry'*) there is an equally current and powerful construction of women's value which rests on the logic of their position in arranged marriage, as obedient but *reluctant* participants, a logic which extends beyond the context of actual forced matches to inform the notions of power and value in Bicolano relationships.[9]

### Sa gusto kan mga magurang (At your parents' will)

'In the past', says Ernea (40–50 yrs), 'if your parents wanted you to get married, it doesn't matter how much you don't want to, of course, the child would defer to the parents. You couldn't disobey . . . you'd get a beating. They'd say to you: "*Who fed you? Who brought you up? You had better make up your mind to it!*" . . . And if they didn't want you to marry someone, you couldn't.'

Marriage came suddenly for Ernea, when her parents were approached to help out friends of theirs whose son had refused at the last minute to go through with another match. 'You see', says Ernea, 'they already had the things for the expenses; they had the pig to kill, they had the rice. . . . Well, a week later, his parents came round to our house . . . you know, my mother is very kind (**maboot**), she said: "Let's have the banns called." I didn't know about it until they were calling the banns: I thought they had just come round to drop off an umbrella they'd borrowed.'

Ernea, so speedily married to Arcangel, was quite lucky in her allocated husband, for although she was forced over protests to give up her plans to finish school, at least her groom was a barangay-mate she already knew and liked.

Ideally, there was no conflict in arranged marriages between the interests of the parent in selecting desirable in-laws and those of the child for whom their elders would find a good match. In practice, however, the tensions could be extremely strongly felt by the child. Irene Mojares (40–50 yrs) remembers what happened to one of her younger sisters, who had been brought up elsewhere by adoptive parents[10]

When she was about 14 she came to visit us, and because she was angry about something she said she wasn't going back. . . . She was white-skinned, and no sooner had she arrived in our barrio than she was married off straight away. . . . Because when she had just arrived, my father's **padi** (co-godfather) said to him, 'Padi, is that your child?' and he said, 'Yes, **padi**'. And he said, 'Well, **padi**, if that girl is your child, I have an unmarried boy. . . '. So she arrived in our barangay on the Wednesday, and she was being married off by the Sunday. . .

The claims of co-godparenthood between the two men must have made this match easy to suggest and hard to refuse. But her sister, said Irene, was still very much a child and resisted her marriage long after the wedding;

The evening they came over to set the wedding terms, the parents were talking things over (**urulay**) and me and my sister were playing outdoors all the time in our petticoats. . . . Think of it, they had already held a **sungkohan** for her, and she hadn't even menstruated yet! . . . They fixed a deadline of eight months; in that time, she menstruated once, and that was it, she was married at once. But it was two years before she had any children. . . . Her husband, who was twenty-three, had to shift for himself in the house. After they were married, he would have lain down and fallen asleep already, and she would still be outside playing hopscotch in the moonlight.[11]

As Ernea remarked, parents could equally well prevent you from marrying someone whom you wanted. Adora and Emiliano are now in their sixties with grown-up children and grandchildren, but they were almost never married at all.

Adora's own father had been killed by sorcery, and she was brought up by her mother and stepfather. When she was a teenager, Emiliano's family came to live on the adjoining houseplot, and both he and his parents took a strong liking to Adora. Emiliano's courtship style, however, was not overt. 'He never said anything to to me about love or anything like that. . . . His style was to show it by doing our work for us.' Although Adora did not have to say so explicitly, Emiliano was in fact behaving like old-fashioned suitors who expected to have to pass the test of brideservice to win acceptance; a tactic perhaps all the more appropriate because his family was less wealthy than hers.

When Emiliano managed to save a field of their harvested rice from being spoiled by a storm, Adora's stepfather became suspicious and then **maimon** (selfish or jealous). He demanded that Adora allow a rival suitor, from a more propertied family, to begin to organise a marriage proposal. Even then, Emiliano's parents hung back, 'ashamed' as Adora says, because they had once been helped out by Adora's grandfather, 'Whereas, they said, we were propertied people.'

It took something else to prod them into action; Adora's cousin Heraclio was going to marry Emiliano's sister Angela. It was, says Adora, like 'an exchange of cups.'[12] 'So Heraclio told Angela they were going to **presentar** (propose), and then my in-laws hurried to **presentar** to us because they didn't want to be overtaken.'

Wisely, Emiliano's parents addressed themselves to Adora's mother not her stepfather. Adora heard a rumour that 'My husband's relatives had poured out wine for my mother and said, "Drink now, **Manay** (older sister), because we will be getting married at your house." '[13]

Adora's stepfather, however, became ill with rage, both because Emiliano was poorer than he and because he was going to lose Adora's help in the house. Nevertheless, when people objected that his 'selfishness' was extreme,[14] especially with regard to a child who was not his own daughter, he was forced to yield. Emiliano's family sold their one ricefield to cover the costs of the wedding; judging this insufficient Adora's stepfather also made a contribution 'because he didn't want his name to be defeated (**daog**) when it came to putting on an occasion'. Since the groom's family should always cover these costs alone, this must also have been a subtle but definite way of marking his view of their unsuitability as his in-laws.

### Obedient daughters

Every woman I knew whose marriage had been arranged without her participation spoke of it as been at first a source of acute shock, shame and embarrassment. Some recovered quickly, and many look back on their marriages as having gradually produced just the good partnership which their elders anticipated for them. The rewards of obedience were, in part, the help and backing which parents offered their newly married children. It was (and is) common for young women to make it a condition of their agreement that they will continue to live with their own parents after marriage, and not with their in-laws, and thus they continued to have access to the support of their mothers. But the process could be a long and painfully awkward one when the two young people were not naturally outgoing. Thus Manuelita (60–70 yrs), engaged young to Filomeno, remembers vividly both the shock of having her marriage sprung suddenly on her and the gradual acceptance of her new state. During Filomeno's brideservice, she says,

We never talked to each other. He used to play all the time with my younger brother, but we never talked; it wasn't the way then. I used to see him, but at mealtimes I wouldn't sit facing him, because I was embarassed.

Manuelita remembers that later her father would intervene if she picked a quarrel with her shy and mild-mannered young husband. 'I remember once my father gave me a wallop with a stick. He said, "Why do you keep on picking on Meno when he hasn't done anything wrong?"' Filomeno, she says, was 'a good man. Hard-working . . . and very good to me . . .' When I asked her if she found him attractive when she met him, she replied reflectively, 'Well, I liked him because he was the one my mother liked.' But, she says, had she and Filomeno not been put together by their elders to live together and sleep together as husband and wife, 'My goodness, we never would have got to be close to each other.' Independent, a little reserved with men, Manuelita didn't choose to marry again after Filomeno died of spirit-caused illness when their children were still quite young.

Manuelita is speaking of the 1940s and 1950s, but Corabel was only thirty-four when I met her in 1989, and had been married at sixteen (in 1971) to Boy. Having left school to work as a domestic helper in Nueva Ecija, she had returned to her mother's home in Tinambac, the upland town a couple of hours from Calabanga.

I was fetched by my cousin, and my husband's sister. Manay Dena's husband came to the house and said I should go to stay with Manay Dena because she was going to give birth, and she wouldn't be able to work. So I went with them to Quipayo.

Well, Manay Dena borrowed a photograph from me – a '**solo**' shot – . . . and she sent it to Boy [her brother] who was working in Manila and told him to marry me. When Boy saw the picture, he wrote back and said he wanted to marry me. But I still knew nothing about it. Then Manay Dena said to me: 'Cory, I've got a problem, because Boy has written that he wants to marry you.' I said I'd think about it, because Manay Dena has good ways and her parents are kind also, but there was someone else who was already courting me.

He was called Tomas. I was attracted to him, but the trouble was he wanted us to elope . . . I didn't want this, because my mother said: 'If anyone wants to court you, bring them here to the house so they can **presentar**.' Well, he had a pig he could have used for the wedding expenses, but he didn't want to, he wanted us to keep it. He wouldn't **presentar** at our house. I was angry. I said: '*My mother isn't difficult; it will be easy to reach an agreement with her.*'

Well you see, the way I am, I always follow what my mother wants me to do. And since Manay Dena had taken a liking to me, she went to see my mother, and said 'Let Corabel get married to Boy', and my mother liked the arrangement too. But I said, I have to see the person first, because it's different in a photo.

When Boy arrived, the first time we met, we were both ashamed: I was ashamed in front of him, he was ashamed in front of me. My cousin went to our house to let my mother know that he would **presentar**, and my mother allowed it. Then we all went together to Tinambac. We took everything we needed; there was meat, rum, sticky rice. It was easy to reach an agreement in the discussion. He went there in May, and the wedding was fixed for October.

Between the 1940s and the 1970s, marriage had become less formalised, and brideservice was not demanded from Boy. At both periods, however, it was possible for women to choose to construct themselves as 'obedient daughters' and to rest the safety and success of their marriage on the harmonisation of their own wills with those of their fathers and, especially, their mothers.

## Obligation and reluctance: parents and children

While the duty of children to obey their parents was axiomatic in marriage in the recent past (and in many other contexts, still is), however, what is most interesting and unusual about these accounts is the powerful elaboration of the idea that women may be obedient, but reluctant, and that this reluctance counts. This idea, which is one aspect of Severina's story, is also a central theme in that of her daughter, Auring.[15]

Auring was working away from home as a domestic helper when the woman she worked for decided she would be the ideal wife for her husband's younger brother, Moises.

At the time, I had a number of suitors, but no steady. I didn't want to get married, I was afraid of going through the hardships I'd gone through as a child, and I looked at my sisters who were married and saw that they were having a hard life. Married couples have to worry about where their living is coming from . . . My plan was just to go on working. I had had three previous suitors; one had already proposed (**nagpresentar na**), and I had agreed, and so had my parents, but he didn't have the expenses for the wedding and so it was called off. Another one had no money, and I told him I wasn't willing just to elope; I was only going with him if we were coming from the church . . . and so I prayed to the **Ama**[16] to give me a sign of who was my fate, and Moises was my fate, since they had the expenses for the wedding.

Auring eventually gave in to the collective pressure of her parents, Moises's relations and the saint, but remained in a state of confusion. 'They held the **presentar** at our house in June and we were married in August . . . I couldn't bear to wait around for them for a long time . . . I said, *"If you're going to marry me you'd better be quick about it, grab what you want now, because if you don't, I won't agree, and not even my parents will be able to pressure me."*

She also recalls her anger at being married under duress, exacerbated when her parents wanted to make use of some of the money set aside for Auring's trousseau. 'I had a very bad quarrel with my parents, so much so that I wasn't even slightly afraid of them . . . because they married me to someone I didn't want to marry, my thoughts were really on rebellion . . . I said, "You can have my whole salary, but you can't touch that money, it would make me ashamed."'

At our wedding, I didn't feel happy at all, I felt unhappy. I didn't want to marry him at all, I was just forcing myself . . . What I felt deep down inside me was . . . I felt angry. The priest was looking at me oddly. I said to him, 'Have you finished now sir?' 'Yes,' he said. So I picked up my train and marched outside. I didn't want to join in the photographs, but they made me be in two. Not many of my family was there, because I hadn't bothered to tell them. They brought me sticky-rice cakes, and I couldn't eat them. My wedding sponsor had to drag me to do the **pantomina**. His grip was so hard it left nail marks in my arm.

Auring and her husband Moises have a marriage which has lasted many years in more than reasonable contentment. Her sister Quering, however, has not been so lucky. Her marriage was also arranged by her parents. Her husband, a friend of her father's, is considerably older than she, and as the years went on he suffered jealous delusions. When he refused to let her replace her painful rotten teeth with a denture (in case she became too alluring) and accused her of sleeping with her own teenage nephew, she left him. Although she hadn't seen her family for fourteen years, she returned home and called in the debts, reminding them that she had married to please them. Her mother rallied to her assistance, and several months later the two women set off for the capital with the intention of running a small retail business there for a while, leaving Severina's husband at home.

### Difficult women and good husbands

Just as a woman can construct herself in marriage as an obedient or a reluctant daughter, so a man can construct his position in several ways also.[17] There is a well-developed (and rather entertaining) masculine genre of slightly rueful boasting about one's own allure, the terrible troubles one has had with successive mistresses, etc., which in some ways parallels and matches women's stories of reluctance, at least reluctance as regards their husbands. Men may therefore contradict the stories their wives tell, challenging the message if not the fact. There is also the position – obviously that taken most often by people who chose their spouses themselves – in which both husband and wife agree on their story as one of 'true love' (**tunay na pagkamoot**).[18] But there is also a way in which it is quite respectable to be the husband of a reluctant wife, and in which both spouses can share in this story about their marriage. Having won his wife round, the husband can take a rather relaxed, tolerant attitude while his wife continues to be the more flamboyant and demanding partner.

This was the case, for instance, with Manuelita's younger daughter Bea and her husband Democrito. Bea (in her late thirties in 1988, and with five children) appeared to have come to share with her mother a view of herself as chary and rather cautious in relation to men. Yet she agrees that Democrito – backed by her mother's endorsement – gradually won her over, and that he continues to deal with her 'difficult' (**pilya** – literally assertive or argumentative) character by the simple tactic of being a recognised 'good husband' – sensible, generous in conceding a point and accommodating (**maboot**).

Bea, who learned early what it meant to lose a parent when her father died young of a spirit-caused illness, adopted a fiercely defensive attitude to her mother, and hated the idea of her marrying again. She gained a reputation for standing up for herself when as child, she responded to the news that someone wanted to propose to her widowed mother. 'I said, "Where's my **sundang** (farmer's knife)? I'll chase him out of the barangay!" That scared him. He said; "I think her youngest is a bit gone in the head."'

Bea and Democrito were both from the same barangay, but didn't know each other well, and at first Bea took an unencouraging attitude towards him.

When Democrito started coming round the house, he was very ashamed, he had to bring a **balak** [intermediary] with him, a cousin of ours, as he was ashamed to come here alone. He used to bring fish, and I said; 'What do you think that's for?' He said, 'I want to hold a **presentar** at your place', and I would answer, 'Who do you think you're going to **presentar** for?' He said, 'When you answer like that, I don't think you are taking any notice of my feelings.' I didn't behave properly to him at the time.

Well, I had a previous suitor, but he was **napikon** [entrapped] by another women . . . My heart was very heavy about that. It really must have been my fate,[19] though, because just after that Democrito came to **presentar** at the house. My mother said, 'He's kind (**maboot**). He never gets angry with you. He's a farmer [Democrito's family had substantial land to farm, and Democrito was generous in his gifts of rice] . . . you won't really have to go through hardships if you marry him.'

So that was how I got married. But I said to my mother frankly, 'Mother, if I marry Democrito, I don't want to live with my in-laws . . .' and my in-laws didn't insist because my mother had a talk to them.

Bea and Democrito were married when Bea was nineteen, and have continued to live with Manuelita.

## Total escape and complete defeat

If one always has to put oneself at risk in the pursuit of happiness in love, it is not always the '**magurang**' (parents or old people) whose actions control what will happen. There is also a category of happenings referred to in Bicol as '**pikon**', which the Bicol dictionary (Mintz and Britanico 1985:424) describes as being 'hurt' or 'sensitive', but which bears the distinct meaning in these stories of being tricked, 'had' or trapped. This happens when a man who has an expectation of marriage with one woman, and who may be in love with her, is suddenly and dishonestly trapped into marriage by another woman, usually with the assistance of her relatives.

Edita (in her late twenties in 1988), who was training for her qualification as an elementary teacher, had a boyfriend who already had a teaching job. Their courtship was very intense and they planned to marry when she qualified, although his wish to marry sooner was a source of some tensions. One day Edita refused to accompany her boyfriend on a visit to a fiesta, since she had to present a term paper. She sees this as a mistaken decision which indicates her **suwerte** (fate or luck) in romance: 'My **palad** (palm) is always the same.'[20]

At the fiesta, a woman almost twenty years older than Edita's boyfriend, a fellow teacher who had taken a fancy to him, enlisted the help of her brothers in getting him drunk until he passed out; they all then swore that he had slept with her, and made a statement to the barangay captain. Within three weeks the teacher and Edita's boyfriend were married at her family's insistence. He met Edita secretly three times to explain what had happened, but was very afraid in case they should be seen by his wife's father, a wealthy Tagalog landowner. Both Edita and her boyfriend felt forced to accept events although they had been tricked because in such cases the woman's word is given legal credence over the man's, and because of the wealth, power and determination of the older teacher and her family. As she pointed out the legal system in the Philippines is slow, corrupt and expensive, and with her small amount of money she felt she had no hope of obtaining help through legal process. In these circumstances she was '**daog**' (defeated) by the superior power of the other woman. Moreover, she expected that her boyfriend would stay with his wife, and, if they had children, would 'forgive her' for her initial deception.

I was never told a story about a woman who was entrapped into marriage (as opposed to sex) by a deceptive man in this way, although it is not uncommon to hear of either men or women who have been led completely astray by love-magic (**lumay**). More common still, however, was to hear of circumstances in which the pressure of older people on a younger person had been so unbearable, and so much against their inclinations, that they had resorted to suicide by the swallowing of poison (**maghugot**). The only case I knew of directly was of a young woman in the barangay who ten years earlier had swallowed ink-removing chemicals at her wedding. She was taken to hospital, and by the time I met her seemed calm and contented in her marriage, with several children. Such attempts feature in conversation and on local radio news from time to time as the consequence of forcing the will of your child too far, so that they suffer a feeling of being completely 'defeated'.

At the opposite end of the range of experiences, many people discussed the issue of what happened when one simply defied parental wishes and decided to elope. How people feel about elopement depends both on their own character and on the importance the family attaches to complete respectability. Some women planned elopements, but never carried them out. My co-godmother Irene however recalled her decision to elope without embarrassment. She had been horrified when, working as a domestic help and aged eighteen, she learnt that her employers intended her to marry a friend of theirs, a forty-seven year old widower with several children. Knowing her to be reluctant, the family pressured her and kept a tight watch on her movements. Irene decided to run away with her boyfriend to Manila, where they presented themselves as brother and sister and lived in secret while working in a tailor's shop and saving money to get married. The marriage eventually prospered, but nearly failed after three years when the young couple still had no children, since it is children above all who cement a Bicol marriage.

Children of eloped couples moreover provide the chance for the reintegration of young people into their natal families. However angry parents may be (and they will often withdraw all support from their child for a period), it is expected that the arrival of the first grandchild will reconcile them. As Irene said;

The anger of parents whose child has run away is only at first . . . When they see their grandchild . . . hmm, you would have thought it was all the old people's idea; the baby's their pet; you would have thought they'd made it themselves!

**Learnt love, pitying your husband, and talking things over**
Women of all ages in Bicol are familiar with ideas of two different kinds of love. There is 'true love' (sometimes expressed in English, but more often in the Bicol **tunay na pagkamoot**). Then there is 'learnt love' (**pagkamoot na naadalan sana**) – almost always qualified, whether in Bicol or English, with that tag-word '**sana**' meaning 'just' or 'only'.

By using the word '**sana**' in Bicol one can stress, like Corabel or Manuelita, that during the course of a well-arranged marriage, one 'just' learns to love one's husband. Or, like Auring, one can employ the phrase 'only learnt love' to emphasise one's reservations about being joined with one's spouse; 'My love for Moises,' she says, 'is only learnt love. That's why now, when I'm angry with him because his jealousy has gone too far, it's as if I haven't got any love left for him at all.' Like many other women married unwillingly, Auring remembers a period of fear and avoidance of sex with her husband.

The first night, I slept with Manay Tiling [Moises's older sister, who had been very active in making the match], and I got away from him in the middle with all the small children . . . It's no good, if you haven't talked to your husband, then you sleep together and you don't enjoy it at all . . . I was shaking with fear . . . I thought it was going to kill me, and I was surprised when it didn't . . . It was all I could think about. Every evening I'd be wishing it was daytime, and every morning it hurt when I peed. I didn't know about it when I was still unmarried . . . I kept thinking; I suppose all married people do this. I didn't understand my own self . . .

The morning after our first night, even though he had only kissed me a bit, I was so ashamed I couldn't look at him . . . I kept thinking, that man's been kissing me. That's why all my children will choose the people they will marry.

*children*

Whichever way they look at 'learnt love', all the women I knew in Bicol regarded the birth of their first child as the moment at which they began to acknowledge a little more connection with their husbands. All their accounts contrast the time 'after we had children . . .' with the time which went before, as one of greater intimacy and freer speech between husband and wife, a new feeling born with the new child – the feeling of 'pity' or 'compassion' (**herak**)[21] for your husband. 'It used to be', said Auring, 'that if I lay down with him, I'd turn my back on him too. But then, when there were children already, my ways changed. I pitied him then, because, there were children already.'

It was only after they shared a family, that Auring was able to move from a position of solitary sexual embarrassment and anger to one where she could confide in her husband. 'Once, after we had children, we were talking and I said: "I thought it [sex] would kill me." He couldn't stop laughing. "How was that going to kill you?" he said.'

People in Bicol, as in many other parts of the Philippines, are inclined to describe many social processes in terms of a kind of mutual accommodation, usually referred to as 'getting used to it' or 'getting used to each other'; **natotoodan**. The capacities of one's body and one's consequent health may be measured by what one is 'used to'; for instance, people will often refer to their ability or inability to withstand long hours of work in the hot ricefields, to miss sleep to reach the early markets, to skip a meal, or to engage in other practices thought potentially very injurious to health, in this way. Thus Auring remembers that although her initial fear and shame about having sex with Moises was intense, 'I stopped being afraid when I got used to it . . .'

*marriage as a process*

All marriages in Bicol are thought of as a process, a transition from rather formal or even potentially hostile exchanges first, of words, then, of food (for example Democrito's rejected gifts to Bea) and finally of sexuality, which leads to the fulfilment of sharing in the birth of children. While, in a marriage sought equally by both partners, these stages blend smoothly into one another, in an arranged marriage the transition is much less easy, and the intimacy which follows the birth of children marks a greater discontinuity.

### Helen's story: reluctance and the spirits

All these strands are exemplified in the final story I wish to include here, that of Helen, who when I interviewed her in 1989 had been married less than five years (since 1984) to Agustin, and had only one child, then two years old (a consequence of what she called 'self-control'). Helen's story is interesting partly because, at a time when parents less often force their children into marriages than formerly, Helen had nevertheless been forced, but in a slightly unusual way.

I originally interviewed Helen because I knew that before her marriage she had been a healer, chosen by a spirit called Zeny (a young woman) who had become her spirit-companion. Helen had cured a number of people and had also successfully acted as the medium through which her dead father's soul spoke, among other things giving some pertinent advice to her two brothers, who were inclined to be rowdy and disruptive in the house. Helen claims that Zeny helped her to become a more confident person and to overcome her own intense shyness. Zeny also, however, put Helen through some new difficulties. Firstly, Zeny developed a 'crush' on one of Helen's cousins, which Helen found rather embarrassing. Secondly, Zeny intervened decisively in the issue of Helen's marriage.

This husband of mine, Agustin [says Helen] My love for him is just something that's been developed. Previously, I didn't feel anything for him.

This Agustin got an intermediary (**balak**) just to court me, and I didn't encourage him, because I didn't feel attracted to him . . . Then after my sister Marilou got married, this Agustin kept coming round to see my mother and speaking to her because he was attracted to me . . . he kept on courting my mother not me, because I didn't like him; I never sat down with him face to face (**Dai ko siya pig-atubang**). I didn't talk to him, they were discussing it amongst themselves, including his parents. I didn't know about it until . . . he brought a huge basket of bananas to our house as a gift.

Then people said, 'Oh, there's going to be another wedding here.' And I said, 'And who might that be?' . . . When he said that he'd had a dream about us getting married, I said, 'What did you dream that for?' . . . I told them to send back the bananas. They said, 'It would shame Agustin.' And I said, 'You can throw them out, I don't want to eat them.'

[At this point, I asked why she had not wanted to marry him.] 'I really didn't fancy him, I didn't want to marry him, I didn't want to have a relationship with him . . . [although] when you think of it, his ways were good, he was kind (**maboot**), he was hard-working . . . I just didn't want him. I went to stay with my sister in Goa for two months, and even while I was leaving I felt nothing for him. . . . While I was away, he kept on going to talk to my mother and siblings . . . and when I came back he was still coming to the house.

[Because of his good points] Zeny decided to help him. When he came round, Zeny entered my body and had a talk to Agustin. She said, 'I'll help you out' . . . I said to them [the spirits], *'Are you sure you know what you're doing, because if not for you over there, if you weren't entering my body, I wouldn't be able to get to like him . . . except for you helping me.'*

They said, 'Think about it . . . with your ways, another man wouldn't be able to be understanding to you, once he married you, you'd be sure to find yourself on the wrong end of a hard fist . . . Except that we picked Agustin out for you . . . He'll always pay attention to you, and he'll do whatever you want him to.'

I let my parents and siblings know what they had said, so they could tell Agustin. 'There's nothing to be done about it, there's no other man, it has to be Agustin for you.'

So I said to Agustin, 'Alright, I'll comply with what you want, only there are conditions . . . I don't want a husband who's always gambling, or always drinking, or smoking when there's no money for cigarettes. And what's more', I said, 'do you know what I'm like. . . ?' I let out all my really terrible ways to see how far his love would go. But it was as if he had Christ in his breast, he put up with it all . . . whatever I did, he still wanted to be at our house, so that was it, we got married.

I'm thankful when I see other couples who are always fighting . . . Whenever I have problems, he is understanding . . . if he knows there's something he's doing that I don't like much, he stops . . . If I get angry with him, he won't answer back, but even though I ask him to eat, he won't, not even coffee, then I think maybe I've gone too far . . . I take notice of that, because now that we have a family, I want to make sure that he doesn't come to any harm . . . It seems that now that we have a family, he is really a concern in my life.

While it seems that women have always taken their mother's advice seriously when it comes to deciding whether to accept a sensible marriage with a good man, Helen's relationship with Zeny expressed even more dramatically the disjuncture between the will of those advising her, and her own will. 'I just didn't want him', she says, and this flat statement became the basis on which, like many other women, she could convert reluctant acquiescence into control. I am not trying to suggest here that women stage reluctance to achieve practical goals in marriage; I do not think they often do.  But women who are reluctant may choose to shape that in such a way that their marriages become founded on the principle that it is their husband who is the petitioner, thus converting a position of weakness into a position of relative strength. Other women, like Bea, might well negotiate certain terms such as not living with her parents-in-law (women often prefer to live near their own mothers). Helen (who does live in Agustin's parents' compound although her own is nearby) addressed her reluctance entirely to Agustin, testing to see whether he would agree to all her 'conditions'. Since he did, he became the kind of husband who 'has Christ in his breast' – a phrase which I more often heard applied to long-suffering wives, although it can also refer to religious devotees. Whether Agustin will be happy to leave their marriage story cast in this way indefinitely is hard to know.

Complex trajectories of speech are involved; Helen resists Agustin's persuasions and verbally rejects him. Agustin is forced instead to approach her indirectly, using a **balak**, and speaking to Helen's siblings and to her mother instead of to Helen herself. Helen's family lend their weight to Agustin's courtship, refusing to reject him when he comes to speak to them, allowing him to enter the house and accepting his gifts of food. However, Helen is adamant in avoiding all direct negotiation and denying Agustin access to speech with her: 'I never sat down with him face to face', she says. All the talking, all the voluntary and explicit negotiation, takes place elsewhere. It is only through Zeny's intervention that Helen is forced to agree; Zeny takes Helen's position 'face to face' with Agustin, and – despite Helen's protests – brings them to an understanding with each other, cast in the terms which reflect Helen's reluctance. Zeny literally enters Helen's body and speaks through her, overwhelming Helen's own voice, and yet at the same time allowing a full expression of Helen's objections and conditions. Like old-fashioned parents – although for different reasons – spirits may be argued with, but when they are really set on something, there is no point in pretending that one can defeat them. As I will discuss in the second section of the book, spirits always ultimately have the upper hand. Helen's mother may have advanced Agustin's cause, but in this marriage story, it was the 'prophetic' insight of the supernaturals, not of the elder people, which was the final guarantor of its success. At the same time, Helen's account points to the way in which women's reluctance, the expression of which demands that both her husband and her parents acknowledge the sacrifice she is making, itself has to be underwritten by someone who is positioned as having the power to compel unwilling obedience.[22]

### 'With girls you can insist, but not with boys'

I have concentrated here almost exclusively on the marriage stories which were told to me by women, and this requires a word of explanation. The different stories told here illustrate some of the different ways to be a husband or a wife, a parent or a child in Bicol. It should be apparent that, while there are definite gendered ways for men and women to relate to each other (men are active suitors, women are resistant; men tend to be spendthrift and unreliable about fidelity; women are usually neither), the various roles taken up within marriage are not crudely gender-bound. One can be a quiet and obliging husband (given certain conditions) without being demasculinised, and one can be extremely '**pilya**' without being an unfeminine woman or a bad wife.

When it comes to relations between parents and children, however, one finds a definite and important structural asymmetry within the context of arranged marriage. Although it is true that parents in the past could force or oblige their sons as well as their daughters to marry someone not of their choice, unfortunately the one husband I knew who had been forced into marriage by his parents was still in 1992 as shy as he had been as a young man and didn't want to say much about it. His wife, however, always points out that this very shyness is linked to the fact that he has never got over the embarrassment of their early years together. One result of this is that he still avoids calling her by name (as this still feels excessively intimate), hailing her instead with a sheepish '**Huy!**' Everyone agrees however that it has always been easier to 'insist' with girls than with boys. Even two generations ago, boys were more often expected to have fixed on a girl they wanted to court, and not to change their minds. Young women have thus always been in some ways the pivot on which the system turned, the objects of persuasion both by older people and by young men.

Women's reluctance could construct largely gendered forms of value; for the man because he persuades, and for the woman because she cedes reluctantly,[23] but it is the way in which the representation of women's value is constructed to which I wish to draw attention here. As I stated at the beginning of this chapter, most women tell stories about themselves in one of two modes; either as persons who have spoken for themselves, who (like Irene Mojares) have made their own choices about husbands, perhaps with some suitable male coaxing but regardless of parental pressure. They may, like another co-godmother of mine, Mading Emma, and her husband Pading Danting, tell a joint story of how they met each other, found each other mutually attracted, and 'reached an understanding together' in a reciprocal process. Or they may tell stories about themselves as the reluctant objects of other wills and other desires.

What is important for the overall argument of this book, however, is that these two positions are logically joined. It is only because both men and women are thought of as having a volitional stake in marriage – as being persons likely to choose – and to desire – that women can construct the kind of value they do out of narratives of reluctance. These are not stories about the beauty of a seamless submission or the ideal of female self-abnegation; they are stories in which the obedience of women to another becomes a kind of forced gift of herself. However great the degree of compulsion, and however powerful the notion that children owe obedience to their parents, the acts of obedience themselves obligate others, compelling recognition, a kind of return gift. It is only when a reluctant woman has established this obligation on the part of others, which begins to balance out the inequality of the act of compulsion, that she can allow herself to 'pity' her husband in her turn, and so begin the process of sharing which is the definition of real marriage. In the next chapter, I will explore the way in which these idioms of personal experience partake in, but are not completely determined by, the history of marriage rituals which themselves elaborate notions of power through conversational exchange.

# 2

---

# Kinship and the ritualisation of marriage

*In the past, it was as difficult to marry women around here, as if they had all been princesses.*

(Florida Romualdez)

## Introduction

In the previous chapter I suggested that in telling stories about courtship and marriage, people in San Ignacio evoke a framework of attitudes to power as it shifts between men and women, and between parents and children in intimate situations. In this chapter, I attempt to excavate some of the historical factors which I believe inform present-day meanings, at the level of changes both in the economic context of marriage, and in its ritualisation. I offer an exploration of these changes through arguments about different historical periods. My own ethnographic evidence relates to the way people speak about the past of immediate memory, which dates back to 1920 for the generation still vigorous in 1989, and to 1900 for the oldest people. In addition, there are local theories about the more distant past, usually mediated through primary-schooling. Accounts of marriage 'folkways', local history and ethnography supplement this evidence, and extend the evidence back into the last century, although sometimes thinly. I also use one of the best sources on the early Spanish period, Alcina's *History of the Visayan islands* (c. 1668) to build an interpretation of the pre-colonial marriage system.

I will argue that the value which Bicolanas, however ambivalently, ascribe to arranged marriage derives in part from the fact that ritualised, virilocal, marriage has been one mechanism and one idiom through which Filipino elites have attempted to assert and to fix hierarchy at several historical periods. Pre-colonial elites aspired towards but never succeeded in creating an unequivocal rank system which predictively ascribed social positions to particular families, but the completion of each virilocal marriage itself served as an important marker of elite groups. Moreover, the competitive symbolism of the transactions between bride's side and groom's side allowed each to nod towards the theoretical equality of the other party, while simultaneously constructing themselves as the superior party through a kind of post-facto logic. An attenuated form of elite marriage ritual became a general marker of status among ordinary people in the Spanish period and, despite many economic and social changes, marriage today is still an arena in which complex and contradictory messages about power and hierarchy are played out. The bride's side and groom's side, like the bride and groom themselves in their personal relationship, are involved in a series of manoeuvres which express several alternative perspectives on the same relationship; the two sides are equals; they are like siblings; they are rivals; they are each other's debtors and petitioners; they ply each other with matched gifts. In many ways, village marriages stress the equality of in-laws, and their growing intimacy over time. At the same time, the system turns on the potential asymmetry implied by virilocality to create status for both sides. The symbolism of this system continues to be resonant for people in San Ignacio despite profound social change, and despite the fact that in practice many couples do not live virilocally.

While the detailed local histories of the Philippines which would enable a more scholarly approach are still only beginning to be written, this chapter must necessarily be highly speculative. The possible pitfalls of such an approach are numerous; in particular, I would not wish to imply that developments in lowland Philippine marriage have been geographically homogenous between regions, or simple or one-directional in their transformations over time.

It is only by making such speculations, however, that one can start to construct connections between the ethnography of the Philippines, and the well-established and fruitful work on 'kinship' in the wider Southeast-Asian region, in relation to which the Philippines has tended to be marginalised.[1] Writers on Philippines kinship in their turn have tended to ignore the more recent theoretical arguments, often remaining preoccupied with questions of the functionality of kinship networks in sharing poverty (Yu and Liu, 1980; Tagle, 1994: 152–5; Madigan, 1972:12, 137) or the now largely obsolete discussion of how to make lowland data fit the model of corporate descent-group type structures (Murray, 1973).[2] Despite outstanding work on the highland groups (R. Rosaldo, 1980;

M.Z. Rosaldo, 1980; Gibson, 1986; Beyer, 1979; Conklin, 1964) there is still a perception that kinship in the lowland Philippines is an evasive institution, 'loosely-structured' (Embree, 1950) both in fact and in conception (Kikuchi, 1991:vi).

Work on kinship and gender in Indonesian societies in particular always assumes extensive links with the political institutions of the colonial and the remote past, and this has been underlined since the discussion of 'gender' in Southeast Asia has turned to the foundational role of hierarchy (rather then 'Western'-style naturalised concepts of gender difference) in the creation of difference between persons.

The highly influential work of Errington, Atkinson and others has suggested that the Philippines can in fact be placed within the category of convenience of 'Centrist' societies as opposed to the 'Exchange' societies of Eastern Indonesia (Atkinson and Errington, 1990:55).[3] Although this formulation, like all formulations, has its limitations, we may here take it as a point of entry for comparison, since it sums up many important trends in recent ethnographic writing.

The 'Centrist' view of Southeast Asia sets out a series of connected propositions about the relationship between kinship and notions of power. Gender differences are considered as *relatively* unmarked in such societies, because although not indifferent to the construction of contrasts between male and female, nor to their recognition through genital and other bodily markers (Atkinson, 1990: 61; Tsing, 1990:118), it is argued that these are not the primary or unrivalled arenas for the construction of the authentic ('natural'; sexualised) self as they appear to be in many Western societies (Atkinson and Errington 1990:5). This different view of the relation between the body and human identity is associated all over Southeast Asia with the possibility of seeing men and women as more the same than different. Although men usually hold more power positions than women in such societies, it appears to make at least some difference that persons are not defined first and foremost in terms of the determining possibilities of male and female 'essences'; women can in fact 'beat the odds' (Atkinson, 1990:83) to hold any power position, although they do so in lesser numbers than men.[4]

Errington and Atkinson have pointed to a connected tendency also observed by anthropologists working in a different tradition (Carsten, 1987) for the importance attached to siblingship to be extremely high, and for paradigms of gender difference to be based as much on brothers and sisters as on husbands and wives, with the two often being treated as transformations of each other (Atkinson and Errington, 1990:47). Errington in fact defines 'Centrist' societies as those in which (following Benedict Anderson's early and seminal formulation of the idea of power as 'potency' in Southeast Asia (Anderson, 1990)) power is regarded as ideally having one unified source. While 'level' societies (including those classically referred to as the 'hill tribes'[5]) often locate this power outside their own society, enacting dramas of travel or active capture through which it is acquired (Errington, 1990:46; 1989:33, 49–51 and passim), those which belong to the 'Indic kingdoms' with developed ideologies of monarchy, elaborate the ruler as the possessor and still cosmological centre of a power which is already within the boundary of the realm. Such rulers are supposed to cast themselves as the site and origin of unified power, which in its purest form is identified with the perfectly still power of the ancestors (Errington, 1989:272). Yet, for the living, unified power always passes through processes of division and reunification (which Errington calls 'institutionalised unity haunted by duality', 1989: 269) and these processes are often epitomised by the division and reunification of brothers and sisters, especially cross-sex twins. Royal rulers may make symbolically incestuous marriages, approximating themselves to the gods, for whom absolute unity is possible (Errington 1989: 244–5).

These connections between siblingship and hierarchy have further been explored both by Errington and by anthropologists such as Carsten, Waterson and others (Carsten and Hugh-Jones, 1995; Waterson, 1990; Hoskins, 1990; Boon, 1990; McKinnon 1991; Macdonald, 1987) through a re-thinking of Lévi-Strauss's concept of 'house-based societies' (Lévi-Strauss, 1983a; 1983b; 1984; 1987; 1991) applied to the 'Centrist' area of Southeast Asia.[6] While Errington focusses on the ways in which aristocratic ideologies in Southeast Asia may be constructed by elites as endogamous Houses in which they are placed at the centre through strategies of marriage and genealogy (Errington, 1989:257), Carsten has commented that in localities where communities are strongly egalitarian in ethos (and are also endogamous), the tendency is for the house to feature not in the way predicted by Lévi-Strauss as something which transcends or unites opposing principles of kinship, but as an arena in which such principles succeed one another *through time* within a kinship which is more 'process' than 'structure' (Carsten, 1995: 127).

**The shifting context of marriage and livelihood in Bicol: the 'Age of the Father' and the 'Age of the Child'**

Marriage in rural Bicol is described as a cooperative partnership, the sharing of work and of children; 'the two of you, helping each other out'.

The value placed on lifelong monogamy and Catholic marriage is strong, but mutual reliance and shared children are even more important; unofficial unions are widely tolerated, and it is thought understandable that bereaved spouses might need to remarry.[7]

The claim that gender patterns show a relative lack of elaboration in terms of fixed oppositions in this area seems to be borne out within the occupational divisions of Bicol marriage, where, in a pinch, men and women will perform most tasks associated with the other sex; for instance men will cook and wash clothes when their wives have just given birth, or if their wives are away making money for the family. Women regard themselves as even more capable of taking on 'male' tasks which make a living for the family, and this is one reason given for that fact that widowers remarry more often than widows.[8]

This flexibility is however in tension in some contexts with what might be called a 'patriarchal bias'. This is usually ascribed to the influence of the Spanish; and not wrongly, for the Spanish did indeed expect and encourage the authority of fathers in relation to wives and children.[9] However, the reception of Spanish influence in these areas was far from simple, and I will argue that 'patriarchal' tendencies were already clearly discernible in the pre-colonial period, as known from early Spanish accounts.

A consistent statement made by lowland Philippine couples in many provinces is that it is the business of men to 'seek a living' (Bicol **hanap-buhay**), while women are 'in/for the house' (Bicol **sa harong**). This apparently conventional statement conceals the almost infinite extendability of the kinds of work which can be considered to be 'for the house'[10] and for which, as Jeanne Illo has shown, the term 'housework' would be quite inadequate (Illo, 1995:222). Indeed, until the 1950s, Bicolana 'housewives' located production (rather than consumption) 'in the house', weaving **abaca** cloth on looms set up under the raised houseframe, both for home use and for sale (Owen, 1984:153–4).[11]

Nevertheless, people in San Ignacio associate a particular form of gender complementarity with what they call 'Spanish manners', and which they evoke both by the reputation of the Spanish for being **maisog** (aggressive) and 'strict', and by memories of the generation who were born around the turn of the century, that is, the parents of those people in their sixties when I met them. People agree in thinking of the fathers in this generation as more given to a certain kind of male behaviour which involves the 'jealous' restriction of the free movement of their wives beyond the house,[12] authoritarianism towards their children (in which mothers also joined) and strategic violence against their spouses.

This image is partly connected to a past–present contrast, which is usually phrased as the difference between the past 'Age of the Father' (in which parental authority was paramount) and the present 'Age of the Child' (in which it is not).[13] But it is also a contrast between foreign or '**mestizo**' and Filipino conduct, and between the habits of the wealthy and those of the poor. In this latter context, 'Spanish manners' are often associated with formally conducted weddings between prosperous persons, and with a tendency for the new couple to fulfil the requirement (which is otherwise often ignored) to live with the groom's parents after their marriage and at least until the birth of their first child. All these factors are considered in some ways a mark of elite forms of behaviour.

During the Pacific War and the Japanese Occupation (of which, it will be recalled, people in San Ignacio had direct and terrifying experience), it seems that despite the complete disruption of agriculture, which prevented the proper celebration of weddings, some parents took steps to protect their daughters from the attentions of the soldiers by marrying them early (aged fourteen or fifteen) to reliable young men; these marriages were arranged. In the late 1950s, the life-cycle of a moderately prosperous farming household was still largely directed by the decisions of the parental generation about the deployment of resources, and this would have tied marriages closely to parental preferences (Lynch, *c.* 1956). During and after the destabilising economic and technological changes of the 1960s and 1970s, however, the loss[14] of land and property by many households in San Ignacio meant that parents had less to give their children in inheritance or at marriage. The chronic shortage of jobs and cash also meant that the flexibility of Bicolano definitions of marital complementarity had to come into play; women moved into many areas (such as selling fish) which were formerly defined as men's work, while men moved into a few (such as planting rice) formerly defined as women's work, but failed to make changes to the same extent; one correlate of this is the considerable male under- and unemployment in Bicol barangays.[15]

At present, while some parents are still able to realise the widely held aspiration to provide their children at marriage with enough land to support themselves, most are not, and even the wedding expenses themselves often draw heavily on the contributions (**ambag**) of the groom's wider kin-group, rather than his parents' finances alone. The reduction in bridewealth and brideservice therefore appears to be connected to the loss of parents' financial control over their children. This financial independence may be somewhat illusory for children in Bicol, however; while the scarcity of resources at home often forces them out to Manila or elsewhere to work in the service sector, the general lack of solid financial opportunites in the region[16] and the harsh conditions of life for the capital's snack-sellers and sweatshop workers often end up forcing them back home again. In the barangay at least their parents will find them room for a houseplot, but there too families are thrown back upon dividing what little they have to make it stretch as far as possible, enjoying those rare occasions on which there is enough.

## Spouses and siblings

The general exclusion of the lowland Philippines from the discussion of Southeast Asian kinship seems all the more striking when one considers the ubiquitous Bicolano (and Filipino) preoccupation with siblingship as the paradigm of relatedness. As in other parts of Southeast Asia, human generations are thought of in layers of siblings, and sibling-sets can be considered in this sense as all the same. However, within sibling-sets, it is just as possible to concentrate on age and sex differentials. The sibling-group can thus encompass images of both sameness and difference, both within one generation and over time; this latter as marriages disrupt a sibling-group, and the disruption is eventually closed over by the birth of children to the couple, who are the shared grandchildren of their two sets of parents (Errington, 1989:302–17; Carsten, 1987; 1991).

People in San Ignacio continually focus on the importance of siblings (**tugang**); the desired unity and harmony of the barangay is described by claiming 'We are all siblings here: we are all of one stomach,' or, 'We here are all cousins, that is, we are all siblings.' Two people trying to trace their relatedness will do so by referring back to the first set of antecedents they know of who were either each other's **tugang** or (nearly as good) each other's **pinsan** (cousin). There is some considerable technical latitude when it comes to claiming that so-and-so and such-and-such were actually 'like siblings'. Nevertheless, it is easy to find such connections, because kinship is cognatic. Being in theory infinite, it relies at the margins on maintenance by contact and proximity.

Like other such cognatic systems, the scope of Bicol kinship is thus highly susceptible to manipulation, which Bicolanos talk about in the idioms of 'remembering' and 'forgetting' kin. 'Remembering' is very important when issues of class are involved; a returned migrant back with greeting-gifts (**pasalubong**) from a job abroad, or a member of the barangay who has a US widow's pension and a little money to lend in an emergency, will please those they acknowledge and wound those they 'forget', especially if they seem to be neglecting one side of the family

systematically. Wealthy people anxious to shake off their village obligations will sometimes try to take leave of the whole dilemma by moving
weddings and other functions out of the barangay and into an urban
Chinese restaurant. On the other hand, one may voluntarily 'forget' links
which entitle one to, for example, a share in the devotion of a family saint
if one is not especially interested in taking it up.

Siblingship in Bicol is both unitary and divisible. Siblings, the paradigm
of harmony, are often discussed as a unit without regard to age or gender.
Serious quarrelling between siblings is profoundly deplored. On the other
hand, terms of address for siblings invariably (and terms of reference
optionally) distinguish between sisters and brothers, and between those
older and younger than the speaker. While some of the more well-known
birth-practices (from Malaysia and elsewhere) which extend siblingship by
treating the placenta, amniotic sac, etc. as ranked 'siblings' of a newborn
child are not found in Bicol, there are some aspects of Bicol midwifery
which recall this theme; for instance, one midwife told me that she kept the
umbilical cords of each of her adult children, dried them (this is common),
mixed a little of the dust of each together, and added it to her children's
coffee if ever they argued, instantly re-uniting them.

In these ways, Bicol recalls siblingship in both the aristocratic and hierarchical kingdom of Luwu (Errington, 1989:232–72) and the endogamous
and egalitarian fishing-community of Pulau Langkawi (Carsten, 1995). As
both Errington and Carsten have elegantly demonstrated, one of the
important aspects of 'Centrist' siblingship is that it can always be viewed
as *both* differentiated by age and sex *and* internally undifferentiated, and it
transforms dynamically between the two possibilities. This duality belongs
to siblingship whether in a ranked kingdom or in an egalitarian fishing
village, and it seems that it also persists in societies more directly structured by class (Dumont, 1992: 152–9).

In such societies, marriage tends to be seen as the coming-together of
two groups of siblings, which at first disturbs each set, but gradually
allows for the absorption of each spouse into the sibling-group of the
other. This absorption is usually hastened by the birth of children, who as
cousins are all 'like siblings' to each other, covering over as it were the
breach made by affinity.

In Bicol, this process can be viewed for example through ways of
talking to and about brothers- and sisters-in-law (Jocano, 1989: 179).
Bicolanos, like other Filipinos, refer to spouses' brothers and siblings' husbands as brothers-in-law (**bayaw**) and spouses' sisters and siblings' wives
as sisters-in-law (**hipag**) and also use a term for Ego's spouse's sibling's

spouse (**bilas**). Cognatic kinship in Southeast Asia has often been regarded in older literature as mysterious, arbitrary and explicable only by function, and therefore these Filipino terms have usually been cast as useful 'lateral extensions' of ego's kin network (Jocano, 1989:188–9). However, it is easier to see them as ways of describing the spousal connections of a given sibling-set (see diagrams). **Hipag** (women) and **bayaw** (men), distinguished by sex, are thus the whole sibling-set of your spouse, *or* all the spouses of your own sibling-set, while **bilas** (not distinguished by sex) describes all the spouses of your spouse's sibling-set, considered as a group.

These terms could therefore be seen as describing affinity in terms of its relationship to a given sibling-set. However, in most referential contexts and always in direct address, Bicolano people will repress these terms in favour of those which do not distinguish between siblings-in-law and siblings. Similarly, the reciprocal term for co-parents-in-law (**balayi**) tends to be replaced by the less formal term for co-godparenthood (**padi/madi**), and the reciprocal terms for parent-in-law/child-in-law (**manugang**),[17] are used quite easily in reference, but in address are always replaced by the terms which apply to parent and child.

Therefore what emerges is a sense that in Bicol kinship, too, a stress on the marriage-links of sibling-sets can alternate with a stress on the absorption of affines as siblings within the set of siblings. Again, this process is moved on with the birth of children, which unites both sets of parents-in-law symmetrically as grandparents of the child. Grandchildren and great-nephews and nieces, too, are often 'borrowed' back and forth between the houses of their older relatives (Carsten, 1987; 1991).

This is also linked to an apparent oddity of Bicol marriage, the **magribay tasa** or exchange of cups; described as the way in which two sibling-sets (or people in parallel positions one generation above or below, or less close cousins) 'exchange' siblings, i.e. a brother and a sister from one set marry a brother and a sister from another. This is marked as

Diagram 1 *Hipag/bayaw* as 'lateral extensions of an ego-centred kin network'

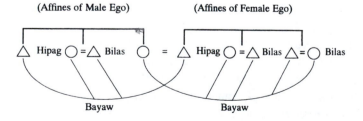

(Affines of Male Ego)          (Affines of Female Ego)

special in Bicol accounts (see, e.g. Adora's story above, chapter one), partly I would suggest because it intensifies the aspect of equality and mutuality between two sets of affines via intense play on substitutability of spouses and siblings.[18] It is possible that the 'exchange of cups' is also linked to the the myths of permitted incest as a divine or aristocratic practice in other parts of Southeast Asia areas. If this is so, then the flirtation with incest may also be a play with the definition of the limits of endogamy. Although San Ignacio is not actually endogamous (people may 'marry close' or 'marry far', expressions which have both a geographic and a genealogical implication), people are always interested in the boundary between incestuous and permitted marriage; a boundary which sometimes has to be adjusted by post facto discussion amongst the older people when close cousins become partners.[19] The barangay however is marked by the fact that, while people say on the one hand, 'we are all siblings', they also emphasise the idea that the barangay is composed of 'two surnames'

Diagram 2a *Hipag/bayaw/bilas* envisaged as (partly gendered) relations between sibling-sets of spouses

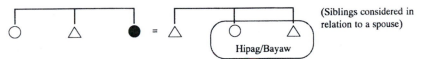

(Siblings considered in relation to a spouse)

Hipag/Bayaw

Diagram 2b  Spouses of a set of siblings

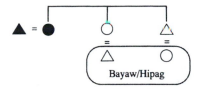

Bayaw/Hipag

Diagram 2c  Considered as a set of spouses in relation to a sibling-set

Bilas

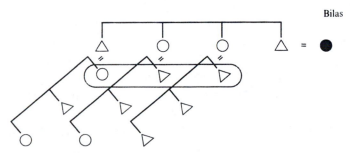

(Guiro and Gavez) and to say that 'We are all Guiro/Gavez here' is to say the same as 'we are all cousins; we are all siblings'.[20] Yet Guiro and Gavez are usually permitted to marry, and in some respects are treated as the paradigm of affinity, any wedding between them being accompanied by a special frisson of enjoyment. San Ignacio therefore seems, although in a very different context, to bear out Errington's description of systems of 'institutionalised unity haunted by duality' and (by reason of the same features) Carsten's account of kinship as a continuous process of transformation over time between spouses and siblings, as those who are affines become, over time, 'brothers' and 'sisters'.

This alternating perspective is interestingly illustrated in a text which pushes this formulation to its logical conclusions, by explicitly equating spouses with siblings.

Popular printed texts in Bicol were published in great numbers in Naga from the 1850s onwards, and circulated in the towns and barangays. One such text still in print in the 1960s is a **hulit**, or little homily, on the subject of marriage.[21] Perhaps intended as a model for formal speeches, or to be given as a gift, it addresses the bride and groom as if at their wedding, exhorting them to become the ideal husband and wife. The putative speaker is an authoritative older person addressing his juniors or children. Clearly in this **hulit** we are in the more prosperous world of 'Spanish manners', the woman 'for the house' and the man 'seeking a livelihood'. The couple are advised on marital cooperation; 'In getting a living, it is you two helping each other' (12) and 'There are two heads but only one body' (12).

In the light of the stories of arranged marriage, it is interesting to note how much of this text is given over to the problems of getting the two young people to adjust to each other, to form a stable marriage, and not to retreat to their own natal families. The man must remember to nurture his wife, must refrain from excessive jealousy and must not beat her, 'or she will leave you out of hurt feelings' (18). The woman must always welcome her husband's relatives when they visit, and must not keep running back to her mother's house. Above all, the writer of the **hulit** tends to agree with Bicol women who seek to set terms with their husbands; a man must be as grateful to his wife as to his mother, 'and do not oppress her **(dai oriponon)** *because she is not your wage-worker*' (7; emphasis added).

The language of spouses as siblings could not be clearer in the **hulit**; 'Your spouse', says the speaker as he urges conjugal closeness, 'is the sibling that you get as an in-law' (8) (**si agom mo tugang na panugagnanon**), and

Out of you two spouses, groom and bride,
There is neither a youngest child nor an oldest child,
Only that it is you, groom, who is like a sort of father. (13)

To some extent, indeed, the patriarchal tendencies of 'Spanish manners' and the egalitarian reading of the couple seem to be at war in the text of the **hulit**; a similar tension between egalitarianism and gendered asymmetry is I think a structuring factor in many contexts in Bicol kinship, and not necessarily only in those which can be ascribed to the Spanish. In order to see this fully, we will need to consider changes in the ritualisation of marriage, and their implications.

### The ritualisation of courtship and marriage in the recent past – the *bahon*

I have already mentioned that courtship formalities have not completely disappeared, but have been reduced in scope. There may well be informal sounding-out between families at first. A formal proposal (**presentar**) with discussions on terms by the two sides, and the sharing of special food, is still always used in the barangay, but things are often not formally elaborated beyond that. As one barangay expert put it: 'They still do it, but you can't say they give it its full value.'

I will describe for comparison the more elaborate version of the negotiations which still obtained in the 1960s.[22]

One should bear in mind that the attempts of young men themselves to win over the women they wanted also had more formalised aspects at this time. Notably, the **harana** or serenade was still used, the objective of which was for the young man and his friends to coax the girl to open the window and give them a song in return. This pattern – an attempt on the house of the girl and an attempt to draw the girl into verbal interchange – seemed to anticipate the form of the negotiations between adults which might follow it. The negotiation of marriage too involved a wide range of formal rhetorical techniques and a series of visits to the girl's house, which can be visualised as a gradual approach to it, and a final triumphal entry.

The bride's side was first alerted to the intended proposal by a preliminary **mapaisi** (lit. 'to let it be known'), giving both sides time to back down if the match should be unwelcome or impossible. The main event was (and still is) the **pagpresentar** (presentation or proposal). The groom's side would approach the question of marriage indirectly, and at first the bride's party would pretend not to understand the groom's party, and would refuse the special offerings of food. As the evening wore on, the exchange of ceremonious language would give way to the sharing of food and the reaching of agreement. However, the details of the wedding, the timing, the scale of the entertainment and bride's trousseau to be provided by the groom were often set at a third meeting, again with a meal, the **sungkohan**, provided by the groom. Intermediaries were always used by both sides.

The degree to which the two families were already well known to each other, and the practical need to arrange things quickly, might modify the formality with which these arrangements were followed. However, the most formal kind of **pagpresentar**, the **bahon**, was quite widely used here and in surrounding barangays.

The **bahon** was recalled for me by one of its skilled practitioners (**parabahon**), Mamay Etring, who had last performed it in 1978 for the wedding of one of his nieces. The **bahon** vividly dramatised the image of the marriage proposal as a process in several stages, in which the groom's side was only gradually allowed to approach the house of the bride.

The wooing party would set out for the bride's house, led by the **bahon** expert. As they moved nearer, they would be fended off by the **bahon** of the bride, each side debating verbally with the other. The rhetoricians of each side would draw heavily on the language and imagery of popular religious texts and verse for their improvisations. A debate in which one side celebrated the marriage of Adam and Eve as the origin of humankind, while the other denigrated it, was a set piece.[23] As Mamay Etring remembers it:

If the **parabahon** are clever, it's like putting on a play.[24] There downstairs, outside the girl's house, is the boy's side, and they'll say:

'*My sibling, let us sing you our verse. We have come here to beg from you the thing we would like to be given. If you won't let us come up, we will have nowhere to go . . .*'

The people upstairs will say: '*There's no place for you here! You are not needed here!*' Then those downstairs will reply: '*Please, take pity on us, and listen to the words of Almighty God. We will only ask to be included in your pity! Even if you won't let us in, open the door just a little bit!*' (See – it makes you pity them, doesn't it?) '*We will beg for just a little bit of daylight.*'

If they are allowed up, everyone goes rushing after them: ay, there are so many people up there! There are the big cooking pots, there are the young girls carrying them . . . They've brought the food for the **dulok**.[25]

Says the person representing the young girl: '*My sibling, it seems we are afraid to eat this, perhaps it contains a bomb!*' (But no one is laughing, everyone is serious.) The boy's side then replies: '*We have brought this offering[26] here, siblings, as really coming from our hearts, and in order that things may turn out well. There is nothing to be afraid of; these are just our girls bringing food to set before you, the "approach".*'

The **bahon** would begin the process of negotiations over the marriage, and the agreement of conditions, with the two parties seated, as Severina described them, 'face to face and opposite each other' sharing the food of the **dulok**. If the bride was in the know and consenting, she might hide behind the door to listen; in an arranged marriage as we have seen the woman might not even know the negotiations were for her.

Until the war, a common condition of marriage was brideservice. Called **magbantay** (to stand guard), this consisted of months or a year in which the young man served in the house of his future in-laws, carrying firewood, drawing water, and so on. This period was marked by extreme embarrassment and tension between the future married couple, and by quietness and obedient endurance on the part of the young man, as well as by a quasi-parental protectiveness on the part of the in-laws to both children, for it was especially associated with marriages in which both partners were very young and/or with marriages directly arranged by the parental generation.

Property transactions were also agreed. The 'brideprice' might consist in different kinds of fees and levies according to the locality, and in San Ignacio was perhaps not as high as in other parts of Bicol. However, in the past as in the present the groom always paid for the wedding, and for the bride's **entregar** or trousseau. In addition, the groom's side must match whatever dowry gift the girl's parents made to the young couple; this joint gift was called the **endono**.

### The ritualisation of courtship and marriage in the recent past – the wedding

Apart from the absence of these **endono** gifts, which often included water-buffalo, pigs and other matched pairs of animals which were displayed for the guests to view, weddings today are very similar to those of the recent past.

Whether or not the marriage has been arranged, the wedding ritual itself is structured around the same symbolic themes. The man builds a **tuytoy** – which is an extension of the bride's house by means of a canopy and poles, built with kin labour – and provides pig(s), rice and all the other components of a meal, cooked by his kin. Contributions towards the cost (**ambag**)[27] are made by all of his kin who are able, or who have received contributions for their own weddings in the past. A man who built a **tuytoy** at his own parents' house instead would look, I was told in 1989, 'as though he wanted everything for himself'.

The bride and groom are married in church, and then return to the **tuytoy** to take part in the wedding meal, in which they are formally seated on decorated chairs, and later eat together/feed each other and dance together. Both parties, and especially the bride, generally look embarrassed, and this is most striking where marriage has been forced. The wedding sponsors arrange a **pantomina** or wedding dance, in which money is given competitively; the bride's side pins money on the groom's clothing, and vice versa. This money goes to the couple, although if funds are very low some may be used these days to cover the wedding costs.

After the wedding, the couple in theory will reside with the groom's parents at least for a short period, although after the birth of children they will probably live neolocally.[28] This removal to the house of the groom's side has been quite heavily ritualised in the recent past in the lowlands, for instance in Cebu, where the couple would initially return to the bride's house but be prevented from having sex, thus making the implications of their arrival in the groom's house even more obvious (Quisumbing, 1965:45).

In contemporary San Ignacio, it is just as common for the couple to live near or with the bride's parents as with the groom's, although they may perhaps make a short courtesy visit to his parents first. As was evident from their stories, many women make conscious efforts to live with their mothers, not their in-laws.

The new couple generally lives with one set of parents until the birth of children, when they move to their own house. However, one child plus spouse of any sibling-set (the oldest or youngest) will continue to live in the parental house to care for the old people and inherit the house. In this

Figure 2  Bride, groom and guests at a wedding-feast

case, the child-in-law is likely to be thought of as the special favourite (**padangat**) of the old people.

The pattern, very reminiscent of that described by Carsten for Pulau Langkawi Malays (Carsten, 1987; 1995: 116) is therefore one of movement from social distance between bride and groom and their families, with even a hint of possible hostility, through formal ritualised reciprocity between spouses and affines, towards the gradual increase of sharing between both marital partners and affines which is consolidated by the birth of shared grandchildren. The sibling-set of each partner, meanwhile, is at first disrupted by the marriage, but gradually stretches to include the new spouses, and is recapitulated in the birth of cousins who are themselves 'like siblings'.

*[handwritten marginalia: process of marriage]*

### The ritualisation of courtship and marriage in the distant past

The early Spanish accounts of the Philippines give considerable detail on the conduct of marriage at the beginning of the colonial period, both because the moral condition of the 'indios' was a central area of concern, and because the priests began almost immediately to adjudicate in disputes arising over inheritance, property transfers and divorces, and therefore required an understanding of their subjects' ordering of these issues. One of the most useful of these accounts is that given by the Jesuit priest Alcina (1668).[29] Alcina's account focusses almost entirely on the marriages of the elite, but he is one of the most astute, comprehensive and un-condemnatory of the contemporary observers. It should be noted for the purposes of this argument, however, that there are some reasons to suppose that Visayan society had a more elaborate rank system than the Tagalog regions at the same date (see especially W.H. Scott 1983: 145; 1985a: 123) and although Alcina's base in Samar was probably quite similar to the Camarines and Ibalon (Bicol) of the same date, it is also possible that it was more hierarchically structured.

Social structure at the time of the arrival of the Spanish was not constructed around largescale states or formalised kingships. Instead, the best historical accounts of lowland society see it as hierarchical, but fluid. It will be recalled from the introduction that the most important differences were between the **datus** (local warrior or pirate aristocrats), the freemen (who served them in raiding), and the slaves, who entered into service through birth, capture or debt-bondage (W.H. Scott, 1983:138). Debt-slavery and the ability to command human labour were in fact one hub of the system, which did not depend on a command of landed property until significantly after the arrival of the Spanish (W.H. Scott, 1994b:144–5);

slavery however was an 'open' system (Reid, 1983:163; W.H. Scott, 1983: 141–3), in which many persons classed as slaves lived with only comparatively moderate demands on their time and labour, and might otherwise work for themselves.

Although Spanish sources complain of the ease with which persons were pushed into slavery through the structures of loans, fines for offences against the elite and debts, e.g. for brideprice, which favoured the power-holders (W.H. Scott, 1983: 142–3), a slave or his children could also labour or buy his way out of bondage, or be freed, as the bondage could be lessened by degrees within one lifetime, or gradually reduced over several generations by marriage to persons who were not bonded.

A similar fluidity characterised the upper ranks, where the possibility always existed for new **datu**s to rise to prominence and eclipse the old (W. H. Scott, 1985a:102; 1983, 149). It is not clear whether the elite ever attempted to reinforce their status by developing any notions of exclusive qualifications of 'blood' or other physical symbols of heritage. Certainly, however, the system was fluid enough for the child of a bonded and an elite person to be able to rise to **datu** status in one generation. One consequence of this was that although women were independent and often wealthy, high-ranking families apparently sought to control sexual access to their women and to direct their marriages, 'as an essential part of the initial efforts to consolidate rank' (Blanc-Szanton, 1990: 356).

The symbolic and existential importance of debt-slavery to this system, as well as its practical significance, is clear even as mediated through the Spanish priests. The status of slaves as both property (of a kind)[30] and person must have informed all other notions of personhood by contrast. It seems that slaves formed a kind of currency of life;[31] a slave was sacrificed when a datu died as a protection for the chief in the afterlife. Mourning was avenged by the taking of a life from an enemy group. Slaves were sometimes intimate members of elite households, and were referred to by names which evoked their place inside the house (W.H. Scott, 1994b: 88–9, 91). In a society in which power depended ultimately on the command of personal followings, a **datu**'s dependents literally constituted his power, status and protection from rivalry. Slaves were quintessential valuables in all life-cycle transactions, along with a class of other inheritable valuables such as ceramics, gongs, gold and textiles,[32] and constituted wealth, especially in marriage transactions. The value of slaves in bridewealth was further inflated in the early colonial period because, as Alcina records, the Spanish efforts to repress native slavery were already succeeding in limiting the supply (Alcina, 1668: Part I, Book 4: 194, 213).

It is striking how Alcina's account of courtship and marriage in the seventeenth century follows a formal path of development which is clearly recognisable in the present-day rituals, and still more so in the more elaborate versions of the earlier twentieth century. The non-Catholic elements of the wedding itself have powerful echoes in present-day practice, as they included the building of a canopy by the groom at the house of the bride; feasting; the linking together of the abashed bride and groom in various ways including the sharing of food, and so on.[33] As a Spaniard from a dowry-giving country, Alcina is struck by the institutions of brideprice and brideservice, and gives an exhaustive account of the negotiations between the two sets of parents. He stresses the way in which the groom's side must gradually approach the bride's house step by step, assisted by intermediaries. As in the **bahon** of recent memory, the parties of the Visayan grooms needed to use high powers of rhetorical persuasion to gain entry to the bride's house for the first discussions, although in this period the language of war and assault seems to have been much more explicit than it later became.[34] Once inside the house, the two sides sit opposite each other, share refreshments and talk property, and this is the stage on which Alcina concentrates.

Although, given his own biases, Alcina may have underplayed the role of siblings in the negotiations (about which we hear nothing), he is very clear in stressing above all the role of the girl's father, who was highly demanding in setting the level of brideprice. They asked, says Alcina, 'as much as they gave when they were married with the mother of their children' (Part I, Book 4: 187). This demand was then symbolically reiterated almost endlessly in the number of additional compensatory payments which had to be made before the son-in-law can end brideservice, which at this period was conducted after marriage and not before the wedding as in more modern times. Only after its completion could the groom take his wife to his own parents' house.

The demands made on the groom were clearly susceptible to strategic manipulation; if he was in a weak position, or failed to make all the payments agreed, he could be kept in an indefinitely extended state of brideservice in the house of his father-in-law.[35] If he were a highly desirable match, the actual terms of the brideprice could be made lighter, although in all cases the two sides would initiate negotiations by publicly advertising the agreement of a huge settlement 'for honour' (Alcina, 1668: Part I, Book 4: 188).

The elements of brideprice were extremely varied, and included compensation to the bride's mother and grandmother for their labour in bringing her up, and many payments to the wife herself, for instance to induce her to set foot in the boat which would take her to her husband's home (Alcina, 1668, Part I, Book 4: 210). But perhaps the most interesting class of payments were those made, not to a particular person, but to the house of the bride itself. For instance, a groom who wished to take his bride away must first gift a slave who was called **sa saliliocodan** (p. 209) 'to sit by the side' – a slave whose human presence was taken to replace the bride herself within the house. Moreover, '*the son-in-law also paid for the void in the bocot which is the room or retreat from which he had taken his wife, because it remained wasted and without an inhabitant. They called this* **paggubatsabucot** *(for the abandonment of the room)*' (p. 209). The equation is further driven home by the fact that the secluded women of the elite were often known as **binukot** – literally 'wrapped up' – which partly referred to their being covered in public from the covetous gaze of other men, and partly to the inner room of the house (**bucot** or **bokot**) which was their particular domain.

However, even the considerable degree of property exchanged in these transactions did not make the Visayan women unilaterally the property of their husbands and their families. On the contrary, not only did these women retain considerable property rights of their own after marriage; it is also the case that in cases of death or marital separation, slaves, children and property could all be resumed in large part or shared (depending on circumstances) by the woman's family. The women described by Alcina retained the right to return to their parents' home after marriage, and frequently did so, whether as a strategy or in case of urgent need (Watson, 1985: 122–4 and 135–6). Bridewealth and brideservice, so-called, therefore, did nothing to establish the completely transferred rights in women said to be typical of patrilineages in China, India or elsewhere (Watson, 1985:125; Parry, 1986). Instead, marriage with its prolonged, expensive and reversible transferral of the bride from one house to another seems to have been a gradual and step-by-step affair in the seventeenth century as indeed it is in the twentieth.

Moreover, although Alcina seems to be describing a system in which the fathers of young women (and perhaps of young men too) had a disproportionate amount of power in the arrangement of marriages which were clearly involved in largescale property transactions (Part I, Book 4: 193–4, 214), the women of the 1680s seem to have been as unlikely as those of the 1980s to consider themselves as volitionless and sexless instruments of their families' politics. Philippine women were noted with varying degrees of approval or disapproval by the Spanish for their positive attitude to their own potential for sexual pleasure (Loarca, 1582: 116–17 and Pigafetta, 1524: 43 quoted in Reid, 1988:149), and the idea of erotic love and volitional courtship was a favourite theme of epic song in Alcina's time.[36]

This co-existence of relative political powerlessness in marriage with an ability and willingness to express dissent in self-conscious ways made itself known even (or perhaps particularly?) to Alcina as the resident priest. He records that a well-known elite convert lady had 'often' (Part I, Book 4: 258) told him that she had been married against her will, and that although she had born him many children, 'in all her life she only had one hour's pleasure with her husband'. She had stayed with her husband out of duty, but she knew herself to be short-changed in the entitlement to voluntary sexual union which clearly belonged not only to the realms of poetry and secret affairs, but also to the realm of real life marriages.

### Hierarchy and 'the house' in the seventeenth-century Philippines

The notion of 'the house' (Lévi-Strauss; 1983a; 1983b; 1984; 1987; 1991) has been invaluable for students of Southeast Asian societies. Lévi-Strauss's insistence that this institution persists through time precisely because it unites and transcends principles of kinship previously thought to be in opposition (especially 'descent' and 'alliance') permitted a way out of the confusions which had arisen from attempting to isolate strictly defined corporate descent-groups in the region, and which had given rise to the somewhat despairing conclusion that all such societies were indescribable except as 'loosely-structured'.

Recent work which has moved from Lévi-Strauss's original emphases to focus on the ways in which 'opposing principles' might not so much be united, as *succeed* one another processually over time, has been especially illuminating and it will already be apparent that a similar perspective informs the present analysis (Carsten, 1995: 125, 127).

Within 'Centrist' Southeast Asia (rather then Eastern Indonesia) the most striking anthropological explorations of the relationships between kinship and power have tended to centre either on extremely hierarchical societies such as those usually referred to as the 'Indic kingdoms' or on small-scale communities with explicit (although highly diverse) ideologies of egalitarianism.[37] A useful synthetic statement of the argumentative direction of a wide range of different ethnographies was given by Atkinson and Errington when they suggested that 'in hierarchical situations, the tendency is for power to be imagined as coming from the inside, whereas in marginal situations the power is imagined as obtained from the outside' (Errington, 1990: 46).

The sevententh-century Philippines however do not fit neatly into either of these two dominant models, since they are characterised both by a social fluidity much greater than that of the 'Indic kingdoms', and by institutions of rank far more hierarchical than those of 'egalitarian societies'. By no means all of the parameters of this situation are clear. We know that people calculated the degrees of free and unfree status inherited by the children of mixed-rank marriages, for example, but we do not know whether the elite ranks asserted their nobility in terms of a language of 'blood' or any other metaphor of physical inheritance which would serve to build more rigid barriers between themselves, commoners and slaves. What is clear from accounts such as Alcina's, however, is that the contemporary marriage-system is best viewed in terms of the tensions between elite attempts to increase hierarchy on the one hand, and the still-considerable potential of the system for movement between social ranks on the other.

Perhaps the most convenient point of contact with these arguments is to consider the 'fetishisation' of the house in the Lévi-Straussian sense, through Alcina's text. For I would suggest that in this account of seventeenth-century kinship one certainly sees a house which appears to take over from its inhabitants, to be accorded a kind of animate status, and to take an almost agentive place in marriage exchange.

If houses in the Lévi-Straussian sense seek to perpetuate themselves through time via a language of relatedness, without distinguishing greatly between adoption, descent and alliance, the Visayan material allows us to view any single marriage as an extended process of competition between the house of the bride and the house of the groom for the eventual possession of the newlywed couple and their children. This competition turns on the close association between the bride and the other most important valuables of the house, since she belongs to that central room where members of the house are born and die, and where gold, ceramics, cloth and other heirloom objects are kept. The bride can in fact be taken to epitomise these valuables, within a currency in which the interchangeablity of persons and things is predicated on the importance of debt-slavery. Each single marriage then permits of at least two possible outcomes; either the groom will succeed in replacing the bride within her house with sufficient substitutes (first his own labour and presence, then payments of objects and slaves) to enable him to take her to live in his own house, or else he will be unable to do so, and will remain with his wife and children within the other house. Thus, at one level, either one house or the other will have 'won' the struggle to absorb its heirs.

This simple statement of course takes account of only one marriage at a time when what is actually involved is a dynamic which continues indefinitely and, within the minds of the actors, encompasses several generations. While Alcina does not supply enough information on the role of the wider cognatic kingroup in marriage to provide a complete picture, it is clear that the economy of persons is complex and far-reaching. The fact that the bride's father, for instance, seeks to gain a brideprice equivalent to what he once paid for her mother suggests an attempt, at least at the symbolic level, to hold steady the quantity of 'valuables' in the house over time, while the groom's side too is involved in the claiming and paying out of contributions towards brideprice for many other family members beyond its own sons, and must remember obligations which date from the marriages of their fathers at least (Alcina, Part I, Book 4: 230–4).

The marriage system as Alcina describes it, however, is not founded on a complacent realisation that in the end all gains and losses between houses will balance out in an orderly fashion, nor on a collective recognition that the same people will always come out on top, but on a tense process of emulation between houses in each particular marriage, which leaves one with the indelible impression that the destination of each married couple really counts.

There are in fact two opposing principles at work here. The Visayan courtship and marriage rituals have in common with 'egalitarian' contexts the notion of the equality of affines, and like many other Southeast Asian societies past and present they represent this equality as moving with the passage of time in a marriage from a highly competitive and emulative stage, through a stage of balanced exchange and reciprocity, and finally to a stage in which blending and sharing are emphasised more than separateness and opposition (Carsten, 1987; Errington, 1989:256). Although competition may have become muted with the establishment of the marriage, in this case it appears never to have died down completely.

What they have in common with the most extremely aristocratic forms of society, however, is a stress on the asymmetry of the marriage process which runs along the pathway of gender. It is not perhaps that the women of Alcina's time were defined (like nineteenth-century Europeans) as being different in 'nature' from men, but that women were different at least among the elite by virtue of occupying a particular structural position within the processes of exchange; elite women were in fact the pivot on which the marriage system turned.

Alcina tells us that, like the brothers of contemporary Luwu (Errington, 1989: 260–2) with their aristocratic sisters, Visayan fathers made every attempt to prevent their daughters from marrying men of lower rank. Of course, the children of an elite woman and a lower-rank person (even a slave) would be mixed in status, but they could also rise socially and threaten the ranks of the datus. Elite men preferred to treat their daughters as the location at which the status of their house was preserved, not dispersed.

Ritually speaking, however, the spectacle of elite marriage was played out as an endless drama of upward mobility. Although affines were equals, the logic of courtship and brideprice suggested that the bride's side were in fact superior to the groom's side. This double-think allowed for the aggrandisement of both parties, the bride's side demanding an immense sum which would be publicly seen as maintaining its status at at least the level it had acquired in the previous generation, while the groom's side paid both the bride's house and its own the compliment of meeting these demands. It is as if the notion that the elite bride can only marry a man of her own status worked in the Philippine case with a kind of post-facto logic, rather than acting as a literal principle for the selection of suitors whose exact rank was already known in advance; the groom and his house *became* the equal of the (symbolically elevated) bride and her house through the processes of marriage themselves. Both sides can thus be seen as playing with the ambiguity between equality and superiority, in order to give themselves the pleasure of enacting the acquisition of an enhanced status through alliance.

Practical politics could be nicely accommodated under such an arrangement, for a groom whose status claims were weak could be kept in the bride's house, where she remained under the shelter of her father's status; but a groom who was actually of higher status than the bride would simply be allowed to take her away more quickly, having in effect elevated the standing of her house through marrying her as an equal.

The focus on a contradiction between virilocality and the equality of affines is not confined to the Philippines. The Merina of Madagascar, for example, place great importance on the equality of free Merina persons[38] within the endogamous deme, and attempt to compensate for the affront of virilocality by a ritual courtship process not dissimilar to those used in the historical and contemporary Philippines (Bloch, 1989a: 103). In this courtship, the groom's side engages in a series of rhetorical battles with the bride's side, in which they are systematically humiliated before being allowed to take the bride away. While the formal properties of the systems are very similar, however, their political intention seems to be almost inverted. The Merina try to cancel out virilocality in order to preserve an

ideology of equality. The Visayan elite deliberately elaborated the potential of virilocality for carrying the meanings of social asymmetry, and in
doing so were probably limited by the still-fluid and mobile dynamics of
their own society. They were also constrained by the countervailing value
of notions of equality, if not among all members of the society, then at
least among those of the same rank who might become one's affines. For
if, on the one hand, the play with asymmetry served to enhance the status
of both sides through competition, on the other, too much attention to the
'winners' and 'losers' in the competition between houses could only
advance some members of the elite at the permanent expense of the
others, creating a powerful ranking, not just in relation to commoners and
slaves, but within the group of the datus themselves.

Another way of describing this process of emulation might be to say
that if, as Errington has claimed, in 'Indic kingdoms' the raja constructs
himself (with a royal spouse/sibling) as the still and unified origin of power
and thus creates himself at the centre of a cosmological House, while in
'egalitarian' societies power is located 'beyond' and not 'within', in
Visayan society, with its rivalrous elite families, it was impossible to be
absolutely sure over a long period which 'house' was the definitive house,
nor which among many rivalrous houses has best captured a power which
might still in part be thought of as gained through the journeys of piracy,
raiding and trade, with their associated influx of captives and marriage-
able women (Scott, 1985b:140; Blanc-Szanton, 1990: 355).

What seems to underlie the Visayan marriage system, at any rate, is a
different paradigm of the flow of power. For while Errington has rightly
pointed out that in 'Indic kingdoms' one ideal aspiration is that the
power/potency emanating from the centre should be unanswerable (literally allow of no reply and thus no contradiction),[39] one of the arguments
of this book will be that, at least for the (rather subordinated) people with
whom I worked, but probably also for Filipino societies including other
ranks or classes and at other historical periods, *there is almost no such
thing as speech which is without contradiction.* I would argue that in
Alcina's account, even though we are dealing with the assertion of hierarchy by elite groups, these assertions are not built around 'unanswerability',
but on the contrary are paradigms of power *which always includes a reply
or resistance.*

Although many if not most situations in both the historical and the
contemporary Philippines involve profound inequalities of power, therefore, these inequalities always retain the potential to be both re-created
and modified through acts of verbal negotiation – and if they are not,

there will always be someone (possibly a woman) who thinks that they should be.

**Past into present**

Spanish sources suggest that this version of 'the house' and its rituals was confined in the seventeenth century to the elite, and that marriage among the commoners was celebrated more simply, or not at all (Loarca, 1582: 153–61).[40] Whether or not this was so, it seems clear that by the end of the nineteenth century, and most probably much earlier, ordinary people were celebrating courtship and marriage in ways which bore a close formal resemblance to those of Alcina's **datu**s (de Mas, 1842: 291; Fee, 1910: 232–43).

The rituals which I have described as belonging to the recent past (and which perhaps stretch back with some considerable degree of continuity into the 1800s) are still clearly articulated in the language of the house. The negotiation of brideservice and brideprice is a key moment in the gradual approach, via the **bahon** and other formal rhetorical devices and the use of intermediaries, of the bride's house by the groom. The **tuytoy** is built in compliment to the bride's house because at least in theory the bride will be taken away from it. The young couple, whose alliance has been directed or approved by their parents, is only gradually brought to blend together, and affinity is only gradually converted into the continuity of the house.

The reason for this, I would suggest, is that the social reproduction of farming families within a context of considerable economic and political limitation by a national colonial government, found part of its expression through the status-elevating symbolism of the house which had formerly only served the rank aspirations of an indigenous elite. Nevertheless, it is likely that nineteenth- and early twentieth-century farmers' weddings ritually stressed aspects of the equality of affines within the barangay more forthrightly than the **datu**s had done, and the actual inflexibility of demands for property transactions in marriage must have varied with the local context of wealth and class structure.

Both the control of property and parents' powers of compulsion over their children which form part of this system of marriage, have been considerably undermined in this century among the formerly more established farming families of Bicol. At the same time, some aspects of symbolisation which centred on the house have been reduced; for instance, the generation born around 1900 retained a number of practices linking the harvest, the spirits, the fertility of the house-hearth and the health of its family, which are now not practised and not usually discussed; since these involved traditional strains of rice, the technological changes of the 'green revolution' seem to have been decisive in wiping them out.[41] The architecture of the house and its relationship to status assertion have moreover been complicated by the influence of American styles of house-building which were deliberately introduced as models from the first days of colonial education,[42] as well as by the exhaustion of the hardwoods with which high-status houses along traditional lines were built.[43]

However, even these changes have been by no means total and, as I indicated earlier in this chapter, parents and children still engage in rituals of a similar structure, even if, as Mamay Etring put it, 'you can't say they give them their full value'. Moreover, there is a continuity of the house at a less apparent level, and that is at the level of kinship, especially as expressed through the importance of siblingship and its transposability of spouses and siblings. For, as Janet Carsten has ably pointed out, this itself constitutes one way in which Lévi-Strauss's notion of 'the house' (with its stress on the unification of principles of descent and alliance) can be understood. While Carsten claims that (as in Langkawi) where social groups wish to emphasise egalitarian values, the language of the house may take the form of siblingship rather than of architecture (Carsten and Hugh-Jones, 1995:25), we might deduce that where the ability of those using it to assert its more hierarchical implications has been reduced by historical change, its strongest survival might be in the language of equal co-godparents, and unified brothers and sisters 'who are all cousins, who are all like siblings'.

Thus in San Ignacio, the parents still like to have their children 'marry close', and if they have any way to envisage making a living, they value having their married children and grandchildren building smaller houses in the same compound, behind the major house of the senior couple. The in-marrying child-in-law is still the 'favourite' (**padangat**) of the couple whose house she (or he) has joined and continued and she (or he) will care for the parents-in-law in old age and inherit the main house with her spouse, while the **tuytoy** must still be built at the bride's house by any groom whose family is not making a different kind of upwardly mobile move – that is, one which will employ the logic of class to make at least a partial exit from the obligations of barangay society.

**Marriage stories, the house and the power of talking**
In San Ignacio, the marriage stories women tell suggest a continuity which may appear to be at odds with the degree of economic change in the barangay (although even this has not produced a radical severance of

continuity). In fact, it is only through the internal coherence of the marriage stories told by women of all ages about reluctance and control that
the relationship between contemporary Bicol and the Southeast Asian
'house' becomes apparent or relevant.

Women's language of reluctance is partly constructed in relation to men.
It is noticeable how, as if echoing the ritual structures which emphasise
active approach by the groom to the bride's house, one important strand
of masculine behaviour in Bicol is concerned with movement, with active
approach. The woman, on the other hand, derives her power not by movement, but by immobility and reluctance. This is a spatial register for the
construction of gendered roles in courtship, of which an example in the
Philippine highlands has been brilliantly described by Renato Rosaldo
(1980: 180–6).[44] The connection between Southeast Asian masculinity and
movement has been widely noted (Freeman, 1970: 222–7; Metcalfe, 1982:
213–23; Tsing, 1993: 123), although few have described a complementary
feminine power located in immobility. This axis of gendered asymmetry
could easily be played out in different ways despite the changes in marital
economics, and therefore there is no necessary reason to suppose that
women's language of reluctance in relation to men is on the verge of dis-
appearing.[45]

Reluctance is also, however, partly constructed on the basis of relations
of authority between older and younger people, and on the pivotal position of young women in the system of arranged marriage.

If the arguments which I have put forward about the probable historical
interpolation between marriage, hierarchy and 'the house' are reasonably
well founded, and lowland Philippine marriage historically institutionalised a tension between the hierarchical aspirations of the elite and the
notion of equality and, even more, the potential of marriage to join
together and make a unity of two (unequal) parts, then this tension is still
reflected in certain ways in contemporary marriage stories.

Bicol women's attitude to changes in the courtship system in arranged
marriage are ambivalent. While there are many factors which could proxi-
mately affect their responses including, of course, education and shifting
views on women's economic roles, I would argue that their attitudes res-
onate with a way of viewing courtship and marriage themselves as constituting people in power relations in ways connected to my historical
exploration. Women can value themselves as acquiescent transacted
persons, and regret the curtailment of courtships which made them 'as
difficult to marry . . . as if they had all been princesses' because that
difficulty relates to a real history in which women form the turning-points

in transactions through which houses value themselves, and each other, and compete for status. On the other hand, the possibility exists for poor women in contemporary Bicol, and probably always existed in thought if not in fact, even for elite women in the past, to value oneself through the pursuit of ones own marital and erotic choices, in a way more proverbially associated with men.

More than this, those women who concur with parental or other preferences about their marriage may do so in a number of different ways, each of which is honourable; they may act through obedience, aligning themselves with the strategies of their wider family. Or they may act with honourable reluctance, a possibility on which I have dwelt both because so many of the women I knew tended to stress it, and because it seems to me the most intriguing position to adopt and the least understood aspect of 'arranged marriage'.

Clearly a woman who tells her story as one above all of honourable reluctance is partly appealing to the rhetorical value of reluctance and resistance which is also part of courtship ritual; the groom's side advances and the bride's side resists, creating a drama of two wills (or two potencies) in confrontation with each other. Women may exaggerate their reluctance, and men may understate their wives' reluctance for very understandable reasons. But because reluctance has a rhetorical and strategic value does not make it less signficant or less felt; to judge at least from what women say (and men address) about their sexual and emotional reactions to marriage. Reluctance needs to be taken seriously.

The point I would argue is that the celebration of reluctance implies that power relationships are not simple, that they must be seen from multiple perspectives, that the location of power is not quite certain even when it seems to be – or at least, that one cannot divine it for sure from seeing one single stage in relationships which are in fact always in process. Parents can force children, especially daughters, into marriage – however, they cannot discount their daughter's sacrifice of will, which places the parents in turn under an obligation, and which can make a groom a semi-permanent suitor within his own marriage. Even though a reluctant young woman starts from a position of disadvantage, from her own point of view, which is somewhat shared by those around her, her acceptance of the will of others in itself converts into a kind of power, not extinguishing her own, but indebting them. It is only the long, transformative processes of union in marriage and the sharing of children which will accommodate the will of bride and groom progressively to each other, in the course of which both will be changed.

In the chapters which follow, I will pursue the theme of the connection between apprehensions of power and intimate relationships, and expand ethnographically on the particular value of speech in Bicol and the place of ritual in people's imagination of the past, the present and the value of continuity. For the purposes of the marriage stories which began this section, however, one point of interest concerns the relation of speech and ritual in marriage. It seems possible, although not proven, that although marriage and courtship rituals are considerably truncated at present, the aesthetics of feeling and ways of describing relationships with which they are historically intertwined may maintain at least a partial life of their own. Through the aesthetics which inform Bicolano marriage stories as a genre, ways of talking about power and reluctance in relationships (that is, about kinship) may persist even longer than either the rituals or the economic relationships which historically defined their meaning.

# PART II

---

# HEALING AND THE SPIRITS

# 3

Introduction: healing and the 'people who have nothing'

**Healing in Calabanga**

At 11.00 am on an oppressively hot Friday morning, I was surprised to see Joseline arrive at her sister-in-law's house with her six-year-old daughter Aisa. Joseline lived three kilometres away in a barangay with bad roads; nevertheless she made the same trip on foot every Friday for a number of months. Having recently had a Caesarian delivery which had left an unhealed wound, she found it painful and exhausting to walk in the heat. The reason for her trips was Aisa's persistent illnesses; a visit to Riko, Aisa's favourite out of the three practising healers in San Ignacio, had confirmed that the child was often **naibanan**, or 'accompanied' by the **tawo na dai ta nahihiling**, the spirits or 'people we cannot see', and especially by the dwarfs (**duende**) who are known for wanting to play with children and making them ill. In addition, she had been affected by her father's **usog** or 'influence' (see below). When Joseline didn't have the strength to bring Aisa with her, she took some of her clothing which Riko used to counter-act the **usog**. On the way back from Riko's, Joseline would fulfil a religious promise she had made for her own and her daughter's recovery by calling in at the shrine of the **Amang Hinulid** on the corner to kiss the feet of the image among the other pilgrims. Like healing, this devotion is known to be most effective on a Friday.[1] If her family was short of food, Joseline would call on her wealthier in-laws to raise a loan of rice or cash against the future income from the pig she was rearing, and then walk home again unless she had to catch the jeepney to Naga to attend the public hospital for treatment of the septic wound.

Joseline's trips are entirely typical of the way in which people in Bicol spend a great deal of energy and travel considerable distances in order to obtain help from the different specialists thought capable of promoting healing. This applies to men and women, but as women are concerned with the running, care and finances of the household, the care of sick children (like the raising of rice loans) falls specially to them.

Travelling to and consulting healers takes up a good deal of time in Bicol; it is also the subject of lively interest and frequent discussion. I have said that in San Ignacio there were three practising healers and two former healers in 1988–89, and many more in adjoining barangays. People regularly consult trusted local healers, but are eclectic and willing to travel to visit a healer whose reputation is growing, or who has a particular specialism. Itinerant healers are also employed on recommendation, and may sometimes be sent for from nearby towns or barangays they are passing through; it is my impression that, with the exception of visits made to healers who are relatives living at some distance, journeys to see non-local healers tend to be made more to relatively spectacular practitioners and specialists (e.g. counter-sorcerers), while the most low-key and trusting relationships between healers and patients are those conducted locally.[2] It should also be made clear that, as the example of Joseline's Friday journeys illustrates, the search for healing involves not only mediums but also Catholic shrines and devotional practices. Bicolano healing practices, although highly variegated, all involve Catholic syncretic elements. Although the relationship between healing and Catholicism is a richly complex one, almost all healers clearly identify themselves as Catholics, and many in the Calabanga locality are themselves devotees at the shrine of the **Amang Hinulid**, talking care to attend the 'first Friday' ceremonies when the image of the saint is washed and changed, and to take away little phials of the water used, and pads of cotton wool, to use in treating their patients.

Healing (**pagbulong**) is said by healers (**parabulong**) and their patients to be the 'help' which is given to the poor, to 'those who have nothing'. Although many wealthier people in Bicol and the Philippines generally use healers, they can do so to supplement or complement the Western hospital medicine which they can afford. Poor people feel excluded from hospital medicine by its prohibitive cost, and yet in life-threatening emergencies they need to resort to it. Doctors are for the rich, I was told, and healers are there 'as a help to the poor'. Healers often initially expected me to disparage their practices, and thought of the West as being, like the world of the rich, a place where physical sufferings were eliminated by the surgeon's knife; people often commented that the wealthy were spared the pain of childbirth, for instance. American women, they thought, were simply 'sliced open' and then sewn up again after a caesarian, to save them the trouble of labour.

The attitude to this is very ambivalent, however. Such evasion of natural processes is also thought of as somehow less than human, and as slightly ridiculous. The expense of doctors is often unfavourably contrasted with the 'help' of healers, who are not allowed by the spirits to ask for any fixed payment. Patronising attitudes from doctors are hurtful, while healers and their spirit-companions are often 'understanding' and 'good' (**maboot**). And while people desperately want access to life-saving medicines, they equally argue that however rich you are, you cannot buy life; both God and the people we cannot see can control whether you live or not, despite all the doctors in the world.          *syncretism?*

Healers often coexist fairly peaceably with doctors; most healers define some ailments as within their remit, and others as purely physical and best treated by hospitals, although the definitions vary from one healer to another. Just as some priests recognise that healers have what they define as exorcistic powers to cast out 'demons', so some doctors recognise a healer's competence too. They may admit the value only of 'rational' treatments like **hilot** (traditional massage), or they may acknowledge the existence of the people we cannot see. One healer in San Ignacio was on good terms with a local doctor, and even healed several patients with spirit-caused afflictions in his waiting room while going to have her blood pressure checked. One noted healer in Libmanan lived just outside the public hospital, and was often called in by patients' families.

At the same time, there are conflicts between the treatments of doctors and of healers. Bicolanos distrust injections, which can make an illness fatal if it is caused by sorcery,[3] and know that surgery and pills will not cure illness caused by spirits. Because of expense and lack of information, people often buy prescribed drugs like antibiotics in single pills and do not complete a course, while fear of various 'side effects' is also a factor, and is a strong reason for many women rejecting contraceptive pills.

In practice, these conflicts are usually dealt with by the order in which treatments are sought (if spirit causes are eliminated, the person moves on to a doctor), or by the attribution of illness or deaths to several different kinds of causes; at the funeral of one infant that I attended, for instance, three women helping at the wake said the baby's death was due to being 'played with' by the invisible people, being 'pitied' by the soul of its dead grandmother, malnutrition because its mother didn't suckle it properly, and TB. None of these explanations contradicted the others.

Aetiology is complex in Bicol, as in other lowland areas (Tan, 1987: Magos, 1978; 1986) and I will not provide a full account of disease typologies here. However, as a generalisation one can say that definitions are based more on the disease-causing agency than on the symptoms. These agencies include 'humoral' and 'environmental' causes (especially **pasma** – the effect of sudden changes between heat and cold on the **ugat** or body vessels), 'contagion' theories such as the effect of corpses polluting the blood of menstruating women,[4] sorcery (**kulam**) in the form of small objects introduced into the body by people motivated by spite and the unspecific desire to dominate others, illness caused by the pity of dead souls (**kalag**), especially of grandparents for grandchildren, and illness caused by the spirits or people we cannot see.

Besides these, there are instances of illness which concern the involuntary effect of one person on another more vulnerable person, including **usog** and **daog**, although I must stress that I and not my informants am responsible for categorising these two things together. **Usog**, which Aisa suffered from, is sometimes defined as a mystical 'contagion' (Tan, 1987:19); it occurs when a tired or stressed person unknowingly gives another person stomach pains by talking to or touching them, especially by cuddling babies or young children.[5] If someone is **paradaog**, on the other hand, it means that they exert an effect on people closely linked to them which will be fatal if the weaker person is not protected. One sibling can often be **paradaog** to another, and if the vulnerable one continues to get ill despite wearing amulets and protective prayers, their mother may try to separate the two; in some cases this may even result in the **paradaog** child being fostered or adopted by other relatives (Illo, 1988: 61).

What is noticeable about these forms of illness is that they are akin to what is called elsewhere 'soul competition' (Magos, 1986:89). Sorcery (**kulam**) too involves a process in which one person, the sorcerer, exerts influence over another, but in this case deliberately and maliciously, with the aid of material magic. Sorcerers are always said to be motivated by the wish to 'oppress their fellow men' (**uriponon sa kapwa**), and often 'experiment' on victims they do not even know. I knew a family of orphans whose father had been killed in just this way, by sorcery inserted into his food by a stranger at a wedding.

In the introduction, I argued that the idioms of oppression, reluctance and submission in which relationships are made in different contexts in Bicol are related to a broader Southeast Asian literature on the self. I also mentioned that although many Bicolanos describe processes very similar to those which have figured in these other Southeast Asian ethnographies – possession, soul-loss, shaming and so on – Bicol is unlike these other cultures in that it doesn't use a single word for the 'self' which undergoes these processes. Instead, Bicolanos may refer to the **kalag** (dead soul) the

**espiritu** (soul or self), **buhay** (life) – both these latter terms are frequently referred to in healing contexts – the **boot**, meaning feelings or inner emotional self, or simply use the personal pronouns in conjunction with verbs expressing processes like 'defeat', 'oppression' and so on. Elsewhere in the introduction, I suggested that Bicolanos are usually hesitant about making cultural assertions and laying down rules, and that they are disinclined to exegetical explanations of things, a preference which may itself be a significant feature of their culture.[6]

I note 'soul competition' forms in Bicol definitions of illness, since it seems likely that they are connected to the theme of unequal power, the idioms of oppression, reluctance, etc. in which it is expressed, and the management of its effects, which I am pursuing. In this chapter and the following one on healing, I will be considering the negotiation of relative power between people and the spirits, especially between healers and their spirit companions, and then exploring the claim made by people in Bicol that healers have become weaker, and that in particular they have lost the ability to talk with the spirits 'in their own voices'.[7]

### The 'people we cannot see'

Like other Filipinos, Bicolanos think of the world of ordinary people as being co-existent with the world of the spirits, or 'people we cannot see' (**tawo na dai ta nahihiling**), who are often abbreviated or euphemised by the simple terms **tawo** or **tawohan**, meaning 'people' or 'the people'.

The **tawo** are said to live wherever ordinary people live. Some parts of the lowlands, such as Panay (Magos, 1986:87–102), retain a highly specific cosmology, built on four sacred mountains, caves leading into the spirit world, rivers leading into the world of the dead, and layers of the heavens and earth. In this system, the **tawo** are divided into different classes with precise characteristics and locations (spirits of the air, land, water and earth). In the Tagalog and Bicol areas, people rarely propose such a complete and consistent picture, although the evidence suggests that historically their cosmologies were similar. However in Bicol certain themes recur which appear to be linked to these earlier cosmologies; these especially include sacred mountains and caves, where Bicol healers sometimes experience 'shamanistic' journeys (Eliade, 1964). There is some association in Bicol of different kinds of **tawo** with different spheres; fishermen often encounter the people of the sea, for instance, who are known to have a powerful king (**hadi**); women cautious about miscarriage know that the **patianak**, which causes abortions, belongs to the people who live under the earth and are powerful at dusk; children are attractive to dwarfs, and there are three kinds of these, the aggressive red ones, the possibly malevolent black ones and the kindlier white ones. Another typology is that of dumb spirits, who are frequently encountered in seance, where they pose a special communication challenge; as everyone knows, **masakit kaulayon an mga pula** ('the dumb ones are hard to talk with').

In addition, people still recall stories of themselves or their parents seeing particular creatures, known as **engkantos** – enchanted beings. These include monsters such as the **laki** (which is half-horse) and the **baloslos** (which turns its face inside out), as well as a range of other beliefs of apparently ancient origin, such as the belief in snake-twins, which I will not discuss here. Like death beliefs and beliefs in the **aswang** or viscera-sucking witch (which will be further discussed in chapters seven and eight), people's willingness to mention the **engkantos** is contextual; most people in San Ignacio say that they left the barangay when the last uncultivated area of forest was gradually cut down in the 1940s and 1950s; people in Bingkay, Libmanan, seemed more willing to assert that various 'kings' of the **tawo** and **engkantos** stayed in the vicinity. They are also more precise than people in Calabanga in linking local sites (streams, boulders, etc.) to particular known and named **tawo**. Partly this is perhaps because there is more 'lonely' virgin land in Bingkay; partly also people seem to modify their thoughts according to what healers they are intimate with, since it is the healers who can most often see the invisible **tawo**. A healer in central Calabanga had seen a 'king', a 'mermaid' and other **engkantos** near an iso-lated waterway close to the town centre, and her patients, who may dis-cover in seance that these precise beings are responsible for their illnesses, will take this on trust. But adults, especially those who are self-proclaimed **pilosopo** or sceptics, will often dismiss such possibilities as mere children's fairytales, or at least as things that only happened in the past.

Though people may sometimes dismiss the more monstrous and threat-ening beings of the spirit-world, there are few who would question the existence of the spirits as such. The **tawo** are the counterpart of 'people like us'; 'it seems that there are as many of them as there are of us', I was told. Like ordinary people, they are male and female, adults and children, and most importantly, as people frequently repeat: 'the **tawo** are just like us; some are understanding (**maboot**) and some are aggressive (**maisog**)'. Their world is co-existent with the visible world, but is also misaligned to it or is an inversion of the world we see. What we see as ricefields may be a road for the **tawo**, and they may have their houses (which are often said to be palatial) where we have our water-pumps or pigsties; sometimes a house and the **tawo**'s houses actually partly overlap. From this arises the main inconvenience which causes illness, for unwary ordinary people are forever bumping into them, treading on them, or most unfortunately, urinating on them. Gradually, people get to know the unseen geography of the area, but it is still wise to say **makiagi po** ('may I pass among you, sir') when in doubt. Because children play and run around outside, they are specially likely to have these accidents.

When bumped into, the **tawo** become annoyed and are likely to **balos** – to pay back the injury. Thus, a pain in the knee will often turn out to have been caused by inadvertently kicking the knee of a **tawo**, who has kicked you back. This is the most common form of spirit illness; the person becomes **naibanan** ('accompanied'); he shows symptoms of the fact that his soul has gone with the **tawo** to their world. Simultaneously, the injured **tawo** sometimes seems to be thought of as being constantly near the sick person, and may ultimately possess them.[8]

In the most common kind of seance I saw in Bicol, the healer would first establish the identity of the spirit causing the illness, and where and how the encounter happened. This is done either through forms of divination, or possession by a spirit companion and the injured **tawo**, or both, depending on the working methods of the healer concerned; divination followed by possession is most common. The purpose of the seance is then to talk to (**urulay**) and calm down the angry **tawo**; if the case is difficult, it is understood that a food offering (**tulod**) of some kind is required. The main business of the seance is for patient and audience to hear out the **tawo**'s grievance, build up a rapport by talking to them, apologise, and persuade them to 'pity' (**herak**) the suffering patient, in words such as these:

Please heal him now, you can see he is suffering; we are sure you are very kind. He says he is sorry for injuring you, but you know, you can see us, but we cannot see you, and that is why it happened.

The phrase 'you can see us, but we cannot see you' occurs again and again in seances and when talking of the **tawo** generally; it reminds the **tawo** of their superior position, and nudges them towards 'pitying' their less powerful victims.

If the seance is successful, it will have achieved **bawi**, which literally means 'to take back what you say' (Mintz and Britanico, 1985:248). When the **tawo** is persuaded to retract, it will return to the world of the spirits and the sick person's spirit will return to their body from the world of the people we cannot see, a process partly indicated by the strengthening of the pulse and other physical signs, as well as by divination. Divination methods vary considerably, but one of the most common is **santiguar**. In

**santiguar**, a plain white plate is marked with a cross or three crosses in oil (usually holy oil from a church), and then passed over a candle, so that the soot forms patterns in which the healer can read the site and cause of the patient's encounter with the **tawo**. Food offerings (**tulod**) are undertaken when simple methods do not achieve **bawi** and the patient does not recover immediately. Another method often referred to as **bawi** is to release one or two white chickens into the wild for the spirits to raise, as a swop for the soul of the sick person.[9] Once the patient has been treated, his newly restored soul will be protected by a variety of techniques which include references to the Catholic repertoire; the use of crosses marked on his pulse-points, and **orasion** (prayer-spells) written in dog-Latin, which can be tucked under the pillow, marked on clothing, tattooed on the skin, recited or dissolved as ashes in water and swallowed. Each healer knows a number of these spells.

Those for whom the **bawi** is not successful, are lost to the living because their souls remain permanently in the land of the people we cannot see. They seem to be dead, and are remembered with the other dead at All Souls' Day and on their death anniversaries; however, their relatives know that they are living with the **tawo**. Mothers especially tend to think of little children whom the **tawo** have 'taken' as growing up invisibly, playing around the houselot. It is always clear when someone has been 'taken', because however dead they seem, their bodies do not stiffen with rigor mortis, but if all efforts have been made in seance and the **tawo** still will not release them, there is nothing to be done.

The **tawo** can cause serious problems; Nana Pilar has for many years known there are three spirit siblings living in her house. They have told her that they moved there when her aunt inconsiderately cut down a tree which had been their parents' house. Pilar is now on good terms with them, but there were difficulties when her son and daughter-in-law were found to be living on the site of another **tawo** mansion. They became ill so often that they had to move their house to a smaller and hotter plot by the road while the original lot stands empty.

**Tawo** may also approach people without being bumped into, for three main reasons; they may 'pity' (**herak**) someone's sufferings and wish to cure them; they may 'pity' or be attracted to a person and want to become their friend, co-godparent, or spouse; they may 'pity' a person and wish to help them by making them a healer. The third possibility is the subject of the following chapter, but the second deserves mention. Offers of friendship from the **tawo** are dangerous, but hard to turn down. The negotiation of the relationship depends very much on the discussion conducted in seance; a child befriended by a **duende** may receive certain kinds of help and protection, but his mother will be concerned to keep the child and the **tawo** far enough apart. The child will be subject to periodic illness such as headaches, which will signal the need to 'remember' the **tawo**, hold a seance and perhaps make a food-offering.

Love relationships with **tawo** are even more dangerous, and are likewise essentially beyond human control. Many healers say that they have felt the spirits have sex with them on the sly, and it is well known that women can have children fathered by spirits, and they will not be considered at all to blame for such encounters. Men can also be made love to by spirit women who bear their children in the spirit world. There are two dangers here; one is that half-spirit children will be 'taken' from their human mothers to live in the spirit world. The other is that a spirit will prevent their spouse from marrying another human, and out of jealousy will cause them severe illness and even death, unless a healer can convince them to release their husband or wife. As with illness, the healer's persuasions are vital, but in the end it is the spirits who decide whether escape and recovery is 'allowed' or 'not allowed' (**togot/dai togot**).

# 4

## Spirit mediums and spirit-companions

*Q. Why did the spirits choose you?*
*A. They chose me because I do not oppress people, but instead I*
*am oppressed by my fellow men . . . and this oppression is always*
*that: money!*

(Nana Alastia)

In this chapter, I will examine how some of the people I know came to be healers, and the crucial relationship between the healer and her **saro**, a term which literally means 'one (more)' or 'another (person)', but which I will usually translate as spirit-companion.

Despite the great diversity and even idiosyncracy of styles of healing in Bicol, almost all healers tell similar stories about the development of their relationship with their **saro**. This companionship, both intimate and uneasy, is expressed through the several meanings of the words which indicate 'oppression'. Mediums who are asked by the anthropologist or by friends to tell how they came to be healers will always begin by defining themselves as **apihon** 'oppressed'; and especially they say that they are **uripon, inuri, urihan**, variants on the word which literally means 'enslaved' or put into bondage. (Mintz and Britanico, 1985:548). 'I do not enslave people but instead I am enslaved by . . . my fellow men . . .' would be a correct if somewhat startling alternative translation of Nana Alastia's definition.

Literal enslavement by 'Moro' sea-raiders from the south remained a threat in this region of Bicol as late as the mid nineteenth century (Mallari, 1990:453), and although the popular religious dance-dramas which commemorated the attacks are now less frequently performed, the 'Moro' (like the Japanese of the Occupation period) remains a byword for cruelty. Together with Judas in the Passion story, these are the comparisons people reach for to condemn those who wield power abusively. A landlord who squeezes his tenants, a male boss who sexually exploits his household's homehelp (**katabang**)[1] or his wife who holds back her wages, a farmer who provides poor rations to her wage-workers; all these people might be described as **kuripot** (stingy), **masakit** (difficult) or **maisog** (aggressive), elements of the syndrome locally known as being **[para]uripon sa kapwa** – an oppressor of your fellow-men. In this chapter, I follow the narrative by which healers receive the gifts of the spirits as 'help' in the face of the oppressions they and their patients suffer from their fellow-men, but thereby acquire a relationship with the **tawo** which can itself be felt as 'enslavement'.

## Becoming a medium

Spirits are said to be first attracted to healers by the feeling of 'pity' (**herak**) for their difficult lives. As elsewhere in Southeast Asia, a period of suffering triggers and signals the start of a healing career, but in Bicol it takes a specific form. Healers experience a period of loss of consciousness when they appear to 'die' for three days, and this explicitly or implicitly associates them with Christ's passage from death to resurrection.[2] During this time, the healer may be possessed for the first time by her **saro**, who will announce herself by recruiting patients and curing significant numbers of people. When the healer regains her own 'personhood', she will remember nothing, and friends must describe for her the activities of her new spirit-companion.

The healer's first encounter with her **saro** is therefore an indirect one. Being able to see one of the 'invisible people' face to face is a skill only of real adepts, and many established healers have only seen their 'companion' in their dreams. But they feel the **saro** in and around their body, talk to them whenever they sense their presence, and after the initial shock of possession has diminished, a relationship of intimacy with their supernatural 'other person' is thus acquired little by little.[3]

## Elsa and Alastia

I begin this account with Elsa, who in 1988–89 was one of three practising healers in San Ignacio. A busy and entrepreneurially minded woman in her thirties, whose husband is the local policeman, Elsa was also the healer who 'consecrated' the second woman healer there, Auring. Elsa's father was a healer too, but this is not something which she emphasises in her story.

Elsa begins her story of how she came to be a healer with this statement:

How I began was, beginning from the time I was born it really seems you see that I was oppressed by those around me[4] . . . I was oppressed, because if something good happened to me, for instance if I had something nice to play with, they all got envious of me, like that, until the time that I was a young girl.

When she was fourteen, Elsa was sent to work as a **katabang** (homehelp) with an 'aunt' in the northern province of Ilocos, who promised to send her to school. It was there that Elsa says she first began to feel that her life had a difference to it:

'If I moved to do something, you would have said it wasn't just me who was shifting themselves. You would have thought it seemed as though I had someone helping me (**may katabang ako**).' Piles of washing and other tasks would be finished astonishingly fast by the **katabang** with a **kata-bang**.

After two years, Elsa's family claimed her back, but in Bicol she began to suffer terrible headaches, which the doctors warned her might be a brain tumour. These opinions put Elsa into what Bicolanos call a state of 'nerves'; 'I told my mother: "Mamma, I must be going to die" . . . and she said, "Elsa, we might as well find some healers."'

Despite numerous consultations and the praying of many novenas however, Elsa's symptoms persisted until she was twenty, and meanwhile she began to dream at midday (a time when the **tawo** are strong) of healing people, and of journeying in mysterious mountains with the **Amang Hinulid** and Saint Teresa. Finally an older healer friend of her father visited the barangay, and made his diagnosis:

There is nothing wrong with her, only there is 'somone with her', 'someone who wants to stay here together with your child'; you should accept them, because your child will be put through suffering by this one, and they will even go so far as killing her, because they want to 'take' her [with them].

At her father's urging, Elsa was 'consecrated' by the visiting healer, and allowed the spirit to come into her. A food offering of betel, ricecakes and alcohol was made to welcome the **saro** and 'Seny' introduced herself and set the terms of Elsa's healing.

Elsa did not begin healing at once, however. The old man had told her that she should not marry if she was going to heal, but she was as she said 'already getting married' at the time to her husband Martin. Elsa's solution was to set healing aside, but after the birth of her first child the imperative reasserted itself. Elsa was washing clothes when a sudden lightning stroke[5] startled her spirit out of her, and her spirit-familiar entered her body, and began a spectacular phase of healing, attracting patients from as far away as Cavite.

Acceptance of this new career, however, involved acceptance of the logic of the spirits which demands that healing should be a gift for the poor. With a few untypical exceptions, the healers I knew in Bicol did not make any great sums from their vocation.[6] Average payments to a healer ran between P.5 and P.10 in 1989 (approximately the price of a kilo of rice), with the occasional windfall gift of between P.30 and P.100. Since the income is not regular, at best healers like Elsa might achieve a modest competence. While in this cash-starved context every little makes a difference, I observed that when healers made money, their family and neighbours would also increasingly turn to them for 'help' with small loans and subsidies. Elsa's **saro** 'Seny' was as particular as most spirits that her healer should not accept large sums of money, even when they were offered in the proper way, 'not as a payment, but as thanks'. Elsa refused a sum of P. 5000 from a Chinese businessman because:

My **saro** didn't want to . . . she said, they were coming here to the earth beneath . . . so that they would be able to help my fellow-men . . .The people they approached, they said, were the people who really knew how to pity their fellow-men, those are simple people . . . Because the payment to the doctor now is really dear . . . Someone who is suffering needs to be healed, so do not ask to be thanked by demanding money.

If she was greedy, she said, '*who knows what might happen to me?*'

Alastia is a decisive woman in her sixties, living in a spotless but spartan plank house in the next barangay. Elsa's husband, of course, has a salary, while Alastia relies on agricultural work and fishing. Alastia was unusual among the healers I knew in Calabanga, because of her willingness to discuss and make definite prescriptions about the performance of different kinds of seance and food offering.[7] She had been healing for three years in 1986, with a multinational cast of **saro**s including an **agta** ('negrito'), a Japanese, a Jordanian and an American.[8]

On the issue of monetary reward, however, she spoke for all the healers I met:

If you will study to become a healer, you must call on God the Father, and ask him for help, for you to be given health for your fellow men, that you can help them . . . Then, after your healing, you must be first with your 'amens' [i.e. thanks] that you have been helped by the Almighty so that someone will recover when you have healed them. Then, when you are given money, that's the thing, you mustn't think of getting a lot, just a little. Then, you mustn't make slaves of your fellow men . . . if someone calls you, you should go with them.

Alastia stresses that patients will desert a healer who tries to overcharge them, and that a healer must accept whatever money her patients offer her gratefully: 'If you are just given a little, and then a little again, you'll find you are happy.'

Alastia also made explicit a comparison which I think is implied in all the statements made by healers I know in Bicol, between the gifts of help made by spirits to healers and thence by spirits and healers together to their patients, and the qualities of meanness and ingratitude which are opposed to them;

Harelips, lame, blind, broken legs – whoever calls you, go with them, as long as you can manage it, you mustn't complain, press ahead if you're not too unwell and you'll find when you get home that you [also] have no illness . . . That's why they say, before you give to your fellow men, give your thoughts to the Almighty, because then their thoughts will be given back to you as thanks, yes that's how it is. So you should always be grateful, if you manage to complete your healing, turn your thoughts to God again, you see?

This chain of gifts is contrasted with the behaviour of ungrateful and selfish people (Alastia, who was perhaps in a slightly rhetorical vein when I talked to her, only admitted a little later to including tight-fisted patients among her list of the grudging and ungiving):

You can get money any old way, but not people's grateful feelings (**boot nin tawo**). . . . Some people these days, if they are a little bit well off, start to look askance at you . . . but in fact, you should look at people all the same whether or not they have a lot of money or a lot of rice . . . It's like when you borrow money from someone, and you haven't yet given it back, they get angry with you, but if it is you who lends them money, you'll never get it again.[9]

## Auring

Auring was brought up in a coastal barangay as the daughter of a small fisherman.[10] She was used to helping her parents in the boat as well as selling fish from an early age – an experience which, she says, taught her 'how to talk with all sorts of people'. She is somewhat more in control of her economic circumstances than some of her neighbours, but is certainly not wealthy. Rather, she and her husband have the sort of modest income which allows her to raise a pig or otherwise put a little by; but this in turn means she is often called upon whenever anyone in her family needs cash.

Auring feels that she has suffered 'oppression' in a number of contexts including the arranged marriage to Moises described in chapter one. It was after she was married with children, however, that the crisis occurred.

Moises was ill with a spirit-caused 'paralysis' and unable to work for several months. Meanwhile, the healer who treated Moises had seduced Auring's sister Salud (possibly using a love-potion), and had to be pressured to marry her. When Salud's new baby as well as two of Auring's own children became seriously ill as well, Auring, herself suffering from TB-like symptoms, found herself without any more money for medicines, and completely exhausted. She sat up dosing her family with herbal infusions, and as she says: 'I was pitied because by that time it was an emergency' and the **saro** Clara made her first appearance.

My mind was all over the place. Where I could get money for treatment. Because Moises couldn't sell [fish] because of the pain. Perhaps about nine in the evening I was entered by Clara. You see I had lain down and had . . . folded my two hands over my face. My feet were terribly cold. I was very pale . . . and I was wet with sweating . . . Then I was lifted upwards . . . and that was Clara who had come in . . . [Q. What did you feel?] It didn't feel bad, I didn't feel anything except I was scared because my chest had lifted upwards . . . my back was high off the mat, I couldn't stand up. But I didn't forget [what was going on, i.e. lose consciousness] . . . She didn't come in entirely because I was frightened . . . [Q. Did you know who it was?] I didn't know her name . . . but I just remembered what Moises's uncle had said, that there was someone going to **sanib** to me [lit. 'cover' me, i.e. possess me] [11] . . . Because in the past, before I started to heal, I was ill all the time, and I didn't recover wherever I went, whether to the doctor or the healer . . . [Q. What did you feel?] . . . My chest always felt tight, and my head hurt . . . then I spat some blood . . . [Moises's uncle] is a healer in D–. He told me to be a healer so that I would recover. I said I didn't know how. Then when Moises had this fever, that's when Clara arrived.

Thus Auring had made a classic entry into mediumship; propelled by the 'oppressive' experiences in which other people's wills overrode her own, she was eventually pushed into the spirit-caused illness which fore tells a closer relationship with a **saro**. Like other healers, Auring experienced the moment of crisis as a quasi-death, lying brooding, cold, pale and sweating – symptoms which Bicolanos recognise as dangerously close to the loss of the soul, and which also always recall for healers the death and resurrection of Christ.

Clara's 'kindness' and 'pity' were immediately signalled by the tact with which she avoided 'entering' suddenly and shocking her new medium. Even so, says Auring, '*when Clara arrived, I was terribly scared . . . I said "I'm going to die straight off, I can't recover from this, see I'm stiff already."*' Still, Auring recognised the 'help' that was being offered. She called Elsa, who spoke to Clara for the first time and performed the food-offering and 'consecration', and then she 'accepted' the will of the **tawo**. Clara began by healing Moises and the sick children, then a neighbour with head pain, and thus Auring's career as a **parabulong** was launched.

## Auring and Clara

As I know her, and from her own self-descriptions, Auring is someone who regards herself as competent, able and resilient, but who also feels she has often been forced unwillingly into situations. She is an attractive person, both perceptive and pragmatic, but she says emphatically that she can become very angry when people behave badly to her, and that once angry she broods and finds it difficult to 'forget' – a mood her family and friends would prefer not to evoke too often.

Auring's **saro**, on the other hand, was only eighteen in 1989, a gentler younger sister to Auring's forcefulness. Auring describes her as 'kind (**maboot**) – she's pretty, but her gestures are just simple[12] . . . she doesn't have any . . . pretensions. . .' When I last saw her in 1997, Auring had still only seen Clara in dreams; 'I've never seen her to talk to face-to-face as we are talking now.' Clara has suggested she should show herself to Auring, and towards the end of 1989 Auring was considering whether to agree. However, she then became pregnant again, and in that more vulnerable state felt it would be unwise to expose herself to such a powerful and potentially dangerous direct encounter.

Like other healers, Auring says she experienced intense 'shame' (**supog**) at the outset of possession. While some people simply state, 'I really didn't want to take on healing because I was ashamed', specifying especially the exposure of performing in seance in front of a crowd, or travelling round visiting patients, Auring evokes her shame as an elision with Clara's initial bashfulness:

After Clara had arrived, they say . . . I clung to the house-posts, hiding down there at the side . . . Because the first time she came in to me she was really terribly shy . . . Then . . . Elsa . . . asked her name, how old she was, so that way they were introduced to each other . . .

When it comes to healing, though, Clara has the upper hand. Auring complains that her **saro** is too kind-hearted, and that even when Auring is feeling unwell or busy she will pester her with a headache until she agrees to heal someone. Auring constantly stresses that it is Clara and not she herself who knows how to heal. Although she comes from a line of healers, Auring insists that she could never heal 'by myself' (**sa sadiri ko**) and that the making of diagnoses, selection of medicinal plants, or choice of the foodstuffs for an offering is always prompted by Clara even when Auring is not actually possessed.

At first, Auring experienced the relationship with her **saro** as one of intense loss of control. She remembers that as soon as she saw anyone who was ill while she was out,

I would feel afterwards that Clara was going to come into my body and I would . . . have to run back to the house and climb up and she would come into my body. Then she'd have the sick person called so she could heal him. Whether you will pay or not, you'll be healed, that's what she's like . . .

On occasions, even now, Auring will return home from a shopping trip to find she's bought something unsuitable (a girl's cute culottes and blouse instead of a woman's housedress, for instance); then she'll know that Clara has been nearby, exercising her consumer choice. However, over the years healer and **saro** have, as Bicolanos say, 'become used to each other', and a gradually increasing intimacy has made their encounters better coordinated and, from Auring's point of view, more negotiable and better under her own control. As she says: 'It's a strange feeling when you're being . . . when she wants to enter . . . Nowadays, it seems it's not like that; it seems we've come to an understanding . . .'

With the establishment of this understanding, the healer can begin to look on herself as the conduit of a benevolent patronage which passes both to her patients and to herself. The spirits, after all, are motivated by 'pity' both for the individual they choose as medium, and for the whole of the poor. While the farmer coughing blood, the old lady with an intolerable skin-rash, the child with a worrying fever, can look gratefully to the spirits for the alleviation of sickness, the medium can also expect signs of 'help' in his or her life; he or she can expect a degree of protection from the worst crises of health, emotional pain, poverty and overwork. But the 'help' the mediums receive, despite all their protestations of passivity, also has the special quality of including them as the givers of that help by association.

This benevolent view of healing is perhaps most vividly enacted during large-scale and more formal seances, especially those involving food-offerings, which the patients share after the spirits are finished since they are said to have medicinal value. At such times, the healer who gathers her grateful patients together around her to celebrate the gift of healing can be said to have become vicariously a kind of patron herself, the means through which the **sakop** or 'dominion' of people gathered under the spirit's protection is actualised. For Clara and Auring, these moments would occur during the making of a **tulod** for a patient who is being successfully cured, or during the annual celebration of Clara's birthday, the date at which she first became Auring's **saro**.

There is however a much darker side to healing which can never be evaded. It is an ingredient of every medium's relationship with her spirit-companion that the **saro** would like to take the medium back with her permanently to the spirit world. The **saro** will argue that she 'pities' her medium so much that she cannot bear to see her suffer in the visible world any more. **Saro**s are known to disapprove when patients or family make their healer unhappy, but this protectiveness can easily become coercive. Clara becomes restless when Auring has one of her black moods. As Auring says:

At times when I am like that and it seems you have hurt feelings and are thinking about your problems all the time, it seems that you'll just [find yourself] there, that you'll go back [with the spirits] to their place. She says to me sometimes, 'If you like . . .' – she tells me I'll be taken there. There are times also when I'm afraid.[13]

There is therefore an acute ambivalence about the relationship between Auring and Clara. Clara is younger than Auring, refers to her respectfully and is a gentle, kindly character. Nevertheless, Clara is also a spirit and in this sense her will can and does overwhelm Auring's.

Q: Did you ask how long you would heal for?
A: I didn't ask her, Nell. . . .You see it's as if, enough to say that it's as if it doesn't concern me. When they invite me to go with them, I will always go, never mind where (**sige ko sanang iba**). I won't separate from them, saying 'No, I won't go with you.' I always accompany (**maiba**) them. I don't ask how many years I am to heal for.

The power the spirits exert over the medium is thought of in one very important sense as absolute and inescapable. There is a suggestion in all discussions I have heard of mediumship that it is at least possible to see the death of every medium as their being finally 'taken' by the spirits, the people whom we cannot see.[14] Sometimes this is implied, and sometimes it is directly stated, as it was by Auring:

There are times when . . . I have a lot of problems . . . I don't feel like crying, but my tears are pouring down there. I don't know really, because all my understanding is that I am being helped by them, but at the hour that the time for you to die arrives, it is only they who will kill you. Yes. Because it is they who will take you away. It seems it's something like that I feel.

And in another image almost universal in the language of healers in Bicol, Auring describes her healing as a 'sacrifice', in a way which obviously overlaps with the language of Catholic sacrifice:

. . . In the talks I have with them (**nakikiulay sainda**) I don't go on about that [being afraid]. I said my body is just an instalment in my payment to them.[15] If they want me to be made a sacrifice of, then I will sacrifice as long as no one else has to pay. But that's what she says. Enough that it seems that she doesn't oppress me, she doesn't want to.[16]

This sacrifice which the medium makes is not only their potential translation to the spirit world: it is also the sacrifice of their service to their patients. Auring, like most healers, has good days and bad days with the payments she received for her services. Her emphasis in the context of talking about healing, though, is that she often makes almost nothing.

I sometimes feel angry, Nell, because there are times when I heal many people, and after I have finished healing I have only a very little money, but I am exhausted . . . It hurts my feelings very much . . . afterwards, I don't speak a word, just sit and look out of the window . . . On other days, I heal other people and . . . I also get a lot of money. Because we do not set a price; how much is up to the person's wish from their heart. (**voluntad nin boot**) . . . It's very tiring. . . . And in Lent I had a dream of a woman who came to me to be cured; but she said, 'I can only give you thanks, because I don't have any money', and I said 'Yes madam.' So you see, I don't take any notice no matter how much they drop there. Because I may not ask for what I want, not at all.

For Auring, then, as for other healers, there are two elements to the idea of their 'sacrifice' or 'enslavement'; one is that the spirit is ultimately in control of their life and death, and that in one sense prolonged contact with the spirits is felt to lead almost inevitably to being overwhelmed by their greater power and 'taken' out of this world and into their world. Meanwhile, the healer is subject to the wishes of her spirit-companion. Secondly, the healer's life is one of sacrifice to other people who present themselves for treatment. While no healer should expect to grow rich from her calling, what she may hope for is a compensatory return of 'gratitude', part of which will be expressed as appropriate payment for her labour. But patients are prone to be disappointing. Auring had not recovered in 1989 from the chagrin of a whole year before, when she and Clara had successfully cured a small businesswoman in the nearby fishing barangay. The patient was about to be admitted to a private hospital (where it was understood the fees were ₱.1,000 per night) and was afraid of surgery. But though admitting a complete cure, she gave Auring only ₱.50. The disproportion, rather than the amount, offended Auring. Worse, the patient had promised to bring for Clara's birthday-party the one thing she asked for in seance – a small, pink, iced cake with seventeen candles, from a bakery. She was expected at the party, but never arrived, and Clara was extremely hurt.

**Healers and the 'other person'**

Through the stories of these and many other healers I knew, the somewhat elusive shape of Bicol healing begins to emerge.[17] Just as the range of local therapeutic practices is neither completely 'oppositional' to Western medicine, nor completely devoid of oppositional messages, so one can see in healer–**saro** relationships a range of what one might call sociological referents whose meaning is unavoidable but which however do not seem centrally explanatory of the significance of the practice. Some **saro**s, such as Nana Alastia's Jordanian and Japanese for example, appear to have a clear ethnic identity which is relevant to the life of contemporary Filipinos. Others seem to belong more to a traditional cosmology of Filipino enchanted creatures traceable in historical accounts. Some have a cross-gendered relationship to their healers which is partly implicated in sexual and family life; others have a same-sex relationship with healers whom they address as their 'siblings'.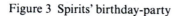

Similarly, a few healers in Bicol (not those described here) establish themselves as 'cult' figures, usually by building themselves a small 'shrine' on the model of a saint's shrine, and setting out to attract pilgrims or to build a group of devotees. Although the possibility of any directly political implications for most of these cults seems very remote, such healers could be described as claiming a position of charismatic power for themselves,

Figure 3  Spirits' birthday-party

and therefore occupying a position closer to the shamanic leaders of egalitarian communities or popular movements more familiar from the literature.[18] These healers, however, are very much in a minority, and the relationship between healing and any form of direct local leadership or influence is almost always as remote as it is for someone like Auring.

Although all these aspects are themselves interesting, it is true of healing in Bicol as elsewhere[19] that attempts to see it as an epiphenomenon of anything else (whether individual psychology, politics, or the process of 'culture-loss'[20]) will stumble over the vast number of cases which seem to be *directly* determined by very little at all, except the logic of the way mediumship is experienced and described as one kind of relationship, with its own risks, rules and particularities, among the range of relationships which human beings have. The **saro** really is a 'companion' of her healer, the 'other person' who 'accompanies' her even when she is not actually possessing her.

The force of this can only be imagined when one knows that Bicolanos (and other Filipinos) talk constantly in the idiom of companionship and accompanying (**kaibahan; mag-iba**). Anyone taking a journey, however short, is asked at once not 'When will you get back?' but 'Who will go with you? Who will be your companion?' Companions may be your peers, elders or juniors, but they are needed in some form for eating, occupying a house and sleeping, all of which it is abnormal to do alone, and people who do these things together are said to influence each other in all sorts of ways. A pregnant woman's unborn child will be imprinted with the features of the people she often sees; a bereaved aunt will be visited by the dead child who used to keep her company during her afternoon nap. Companions[21] facilitate everything in organisational terms in the Philippines, acting as go-betweens, mediators and performers of introductions, so that it is both peculiar and impractical to go to find someone you don't know on your own, however valid the reason. Even the gestures people use when walking or standing around seem (as Sally-Ann Ness (1992:123) has also noted for the Visayas[22]) to emphasise companionship, a man draping an arm lightly across another's shoulders, or a woman taking a friend's hand loosely at the wrist.

As companions, however, it is clear that a **saro** will always be seen as a potential rival to the healer's human intimates. Spirit-marriages present an obvious conflict of interest as would any adulterous 'second family', but much more common are the cases like those of Elsa and Auring, where the **saro** is not a sexual partner, but a sibling.[23] Even so, mediums automatically try to avoid the coincidence of periods of intense closeness to their

**saro** with those in which they are newly married, pregnant, with very young children, or recently bereaved.[24] In pregnancy, there is some thought that possession might cause miscarriage, as Auring told me, but in general it seems that there is an inappropriateness to the healer and **saro** 'becoming used to each other' at a time when the healer needs to be 'becoming used to' someone else, especially a husband or wife (see chapters one and two).[25] Moreover, every healer (male and female) worries that the predatory aspect of the **tawo**'s gifts might be deflected, and that their children rather than they themselves will be at risk of being 'taken'.[26] Thus, Auring noted that the risk of being made a 'sacrifice' of herself was better than that of anyone else being harmed by her **saro**.

For most healers, the process of 'becoming used to' a **saro** is strongly marked with feelings of shame and reluctance. Many people (men and women) fear the risks and are especially scared of possession, which some think 'stretches' the body. People will try to fob the spirits off with excuses or to satisfy them with a simple food-offering before they 'accept the will of the **tawo**'. The healer Tiang Delia[27] had four **anting** dropped in her lap at different times, and being 'hard-headed' ignored the first three until the spirits finally got her attention with a ferocious back-pain. Even then, she claims that healing in her special costume made her feel 'terribly ashamed' and 'trussed up like a performing monkey'; she was also worried that people might think she neglected her children to pursue her vocation.

If this is reminiscent of the ways in which people talked of forced marriage, it should be no surprise. Healers too use their (real) reluctance rhetorically, to regain some negotiating room in a relationship which has been thrust upon them. Both marriage and mediumship involve the creation of intimacy out of distance; and as with forced marriage, mediumship must cross a vast gap. One could say that in both cases 'shame' is the emotion one feels on being suddenly forced into intimacy with 'another' who is very distant, and in an unequal power relation. But while even a forced marriage with an undesired spouse can slowly proceed towards a joining of equals, the extreme, exaggerated intimacy of mediumship, in which the spirit enters her medium's body, can never eliminate the asymmetry between the two companions.

The 'sacrifice' which healers make could therefore be seen another way, as the suffering which results from intimacy without equality, and from attempting, on behalf of oneself and others, the impossible; that is, to close the gap between the two. The healer straddles two worlds which cannot be made equal, and in order to reduce 'oppression' in one, she or he takes the consequences of exposure to 'oppression' in another, because with that oppression, and indistinguishable from it, comes a certain kind of gift.

**Debt and healing – healing and money**

During my fieldwork and later, I would often puzzle over the final flourish which Nana Alastia gave to her definition of healing – her claim that the 'oppression' of healers always came down in the end to matters of money. We have seen that the point of healing is not commercial enterprise (healers rarely get rich, nor try to). We have also seen that at one level healing is presented as a precious gift which belongs specifically to the poor, and which in that sense could be said to constitute resistance to the values of the rich. Nevertheless, healing is said to be a *compensatory* gift to the poor, rather than an unambiguously preferable *alternative* to money and the medical care it can buy – and with the exception of a few specific techniques which they regard as dangerous, both healers and their patients may decide to include such Western medicines as are accessible to them in their treatment regimes. While poorer people may sometimes wish to stress that they are more moral, less greedy and more compassionate than the rich, this does not translate into a rejection of the dream of prosperity. What, then, does Alastia mean?

In his important reassessment of Mauss, Jonathan Parry has argued that salvationist religions, and in particular Christianity, tend to innovate and elaborate an ideology of the 'pure gift' (alms-giving, for example), and simultaneously to denigrate an opposing category of purely interested commerce (Parry, 1986:467–8).[28] The realm of spiritual interchange between the soul and God, aimed at the ultimate salvation of the soul after death, is represented as superseding and transcending worldly exchange relationships, as well as less 'pure' or 'disinterested' exchange with super-naturals. One reason why Christian missionaries and priests criticise spirit-beliefs is because, as well as being 'idolatrous', they are viewed as forms of bargain, and Christianity posits a single deity with a monopoly on spiritual power who sets his own terms for interactions with mortals. Bargaining with God is not encouraged by the Church, which considers it strictly speaking pointless, and certainly vulgar.

As we have seen, however, although Bicolano healers are perfectly conversant with the idea of disinterested Christian action, and although they sometimes draw on this rhetoric to explain why their life is a calling worthy of respect, they are not committed to the notion that exchange with God in anticipation of the world to come is the only exchange that matters, nor to the notion that the Christian God is the only supernatural being with whom relationships have to be sustained. Indeed, they seem more interested in reconciling these kinds of exchange than in choosing one at the expense of another.

The argument for which Parry's article on Mauss is best known does not concern the effects of salvationism, but the effects of capitalism, or as Parry puts it, 'an advanced divison of labour and a significant commercial sector' in 'state societies' (Parry, 1986: 467). Parry argues that we can best understand *The gift* (Mauss, 1990 (1950)) as an exposition of the strangeness (in a comparative context) and the perniciousness (in a moral and political one) of the Western insistence that 'gifts' are one thing and 'commodities' are altogether another. Salvationist modes of thinking may accompany and interact with the changes in economic relations which both draw on and enable such radical ideological separations.

In the introduction I outlined some aspects of the complex economic changes which affect San Ignacio and other Bicol barangays, and which are driving many former smallholders into an increasingly precarious reliance on agricultural wages. While some better-off people are withdrawing from village obligations into an explicit espousal of 'capitalist' values,[29] the effect on most has been to force them to be increasingly entrepreneurially inventive on the one hand, and increasingly reliant on formal and informal resource sharing on the other. One symptom of this pressure is that networks of debt are sometimes strained to the limits, and the complexities of doubly mortgaged properties and assets, as well as the extra-legal mortgaging of rights of cultivation or use of those assets, are the cause of many disputes and even violent confrontations.[30]

In other parts of the Philippines, as Mark Johnson has shown,[31] similar global economic pressures have been locally interpreted by the adoption of perjorative meanings for the term **utang** (debt), which Johnson argues is locally contrasted with the term 'remembrance' and which takes on nuances of alienated labour as opposed to the category of objects which are intended to be kept and inherited.

What appears to be the case in Bicol, however, is that rather than elaborating such a division between what is kept and what is abjected, the financial dealings between **saro**, healer and patients enact a refusal to make certain kinds of division, especially between money which is owed and gratitude which is owed (**boot nin tawo**), and between healing for sale and healing as a gift. Although part of the rhetoric of the good healer is to claim to be content with 'thanks alone', in practice, as we have seen, healers interpret the omission of payment as a hurtful lack of proper gratitude. The efficacy of a good healer is demonstrated by the unforced flow of both thanks *and* gifts, as inseparable signs of gratitude and tribute to her ability. Conversely, she will decline any payment which exceeds the sums proportionate with 'deep feeling', and which therefore threatens to become a mere pay-off. [32]

It is not only within healing that poor barangay people attempt to retain debt (**utang**) as a socialised category and to resist its escape into the realms of unfettered economic logic. Barangay members who have a little capital to lend, will do so to make a profit, using conventional rates of interest such as '5/6' (i.e. 20 per cent) which are often much higher than those used in commercial banks. This is locally acceptable, and it is also expected that lenders will make practical calculations about which potential borrowers will fulfil their obligations. Close family may be too inclined to take a loan as a gift, but it is reasonable to expect repayment from friends and co-god-parents.

When I returned to Bicol in 1992, on my first visit to Auring I was surprised to find her house filled with sacks of unmilled rice, and wondered if she had acquired rights to farm a field. Seeing my speculative look, she remarked with a kind of wry pride: '*You would have thought I'd harvested it myself, wouldn't you, Nell?*'

It turned out that what she had 'harvested' was the profits from her neighbours' fields, lending at standard rates: ₱.100 before harvest for a return of one sack of **paroy**[33] worth ₱.150 after harvest. She was proud of the fact that she had gathered enough to see her family through most of the year, as each real farmer aims to do. However, among those whose loan repayments had left them with 'only the husk' – that is, with none of their own harvest at all to eat or sell – was her co-godmother and 'guard' during seances, Leonor. Leonor bitterly regretted the situation, but she did not see Auring as exploiting her, but as offering 'help' on locally standard terms. Auring was only one of her creditors, and perhaps the least exigent. No doubt, she would also be able to ask for an emergency gift of Auring's rice later if need be.

The key contrast which people make is not between 'good' cheap loans and 'bad' expensive ones, so much as between loans 'on the inside' (**sa laog**) and 'on the outside' (**sa luwas**) which imply two different kinds of lender–borrower relationship. In the first, the key factor is the sense of the possibility of 'talking things over' with the lender if an extension or change of terms is needed; in the latter, which people associate with bank loans and government projects within land reform, the terror is that of foreclosure without negotiation. One woman remembered the repayment of a farming bank loan as the worst time in her life; the 'strictness' of its demands forcing

her family to eke out their rice with maize (considered a food of the desti-
tute) and reducing her to tears of shame and hunger. Better then to have
debts to those who are not 'difficult to talk to' and whose demands might
take more account of the basic decencies of human existence.

It is perhaps not surprising to see that in Bicol, where (as Kerkvliet has
remarked of people elsewhere in the lowlands) 'contending values' of economic relationships are at work (1990:243) and 'individuals can be of
mixed minds' (1990:252) about what constitutes proper conduct, one finds
a rhetoric of the identity of gift and commodity persisting against the
pressures of partial capitalist transformation. **Utang** pushes at the seams
of social relations, but people work hard to keep it from bursting out. Like
everyone else, healers must live with the stress which these tensions
produce, but even more than most people, perhaps, they are given the task
of directing the flows of money and gratitude so that they can continue to
run together through the same channels, even if to do this they must
expose themselves to the unpredictability of both patients and **tawo**, and
to all the contradictions which such an effort entails. The 'sacrifice' of a
healer's life consists not only in laying themselves open to the dangers of
the spirit-world, but also in shouldering the burden of a double mediation;
between the 'predatory' and the 'benevolent' aspects of the **tawo**, and
(which is not identical) between the hope of properly conducted exchange,
and the spectre of a world in which 'business' and 'altruism' have been
completely severed from each other.

### Debt and healing – patrons, pity and oppression

It is as a political as much as an economic category, however, that the
Philippine literature has considered **utang**. Indeed, Mary Hollnsteiner's
classic American-school formulation put the 'debt of gratitude' or **utang
na loob** at the centre of lowland social structure. In a model based on a
somewhat uncritical and unconflictual view of 'patron–clientage', she proposed that lowland society is held together by the workings of a range of
rules of reciprocity, short and long term. One of these, the 'debt of gratitude' or 'debt of the inside' existed only between unequals (in age or, crucially, status) and was thought of as an immense debt which the
subordinate party could never pay off, but which they would acknowledge
through constantly repeated little acts of deference. The limitations of this
model in excluding a notion of social conflict have been well analysed both
by Gibson (1986: 45), and by Ileto, who pointed out that normal representations of **utang-na-loob** deference could be and were inverted during
popular revolutionary uprisings (1979:9–10).

It was Rafael (1988:121–4) however who reread the meaning of exchange and the **loob** (lit. inside) through an application of the meanings of 'debt' in an earlier period, that of the sixteenth and seventeenth centuries whose debt-bondage society had been brilliantly analysed by William Henry Scott (1985a and 1985b). In this reading, it will be recalled, the 'inside' of the person is made and remade only through constant social transactions with others to whom one is indebted, or who are indebted to oneself. There are thus now two classic models of the political meaning of **utang** in the lowlands: one connected to twentieth-century patron–clientage model, and the other a model of the existential implications of precolonial debt-bondage. Ironically, given the much greater historical distance, it is Rafael's model which is in the end more useful for the argument of this chapter and of the book as a whole.

Rafael argues that the old pre-colonial elite constructed itself as the new, colonial elite by becoming the broker between old forms of power which tied people into positions within the cycles of debt, and the newer forms which insisted on reference to an external source of power, the Spanish king or the Spanish God (1988: 166). Looking at Bicolano healers, we see people who still represent themselves as constructed in some ways through cycles of 'indebtedness' to superordinate powers of various kinds, although these have perhaps now become more numerous. These are not elites, however, but people who themselves say they 'have nothing' and who feel themselves to be in a painfully subordinate position, without thereby seeing themselves as having no rights, or no claim to dignity.

In Bicolano healing, we can see a complex and multiplicitous response to this situation; healers in fact do not think of their relationship with their **saro** in any single way (as, for instance, a kind of patron–clientage); they think of it in at least three ways at once. From one viewpoint, it *is* patronage, a benevolent gift. From a second, it is its inverse, a relation of inevitable exploitation. From the third point of view, it is a relationship of intimates in which **tawo** and human 'become used to each other'. All these possibilities are held within the healer's sights. The general superiority of the power of the spirits is a given, but the outcome of any particular encounter with them is not. And the notion of intimacy with the spirits is perhaps the most intriguing moment in the dynamic, holding out as it does at least the ghost of a chance that the sacrifice which healers make straddled between two worlds will succeed both in calling 'help' into the world, and in eliciting a recognition of the equal value – if not the equal power – of those who request it. It is this dimension of uncertainty, of different possibilities held in tension, which is missing from Hollnsteiner's tidy categorisations of types of social contract (for she implies that most relationships will fit neatly into one category or another) and which is not incompatible with, but is inaccessible to, Rafael's interpretation of the seventeenth-century written evidence.

Although the stories of Bicolano healers presented here are in many ways engaged both by this literature and by the questions raised by Parry's reading of Mauss, I have preferred not to give an account which is organised from the outset through the language of 'exchange'. The theoretical importance and intellectual genealogy of the term tend to produce their own momentum, creating the risk that both author and reader will leap too soon to the conclusion that they know for any given context what is being talked about, and in what ways people consider it important. Those local usages which appear to correspond most closely to the market-metaphors of exchange with which we are familiar, or to the gift–commodity pairing, may be misleadingly privileged over other ways of speaking. If the primary focus on 'exchange' in the Philippines has been on **utang na loob**, it may be as well to remember that neither **utang** nor **loob** (for which there is in any case no single Bicolano correlate) dominate the terms in which Bicolanos talk of their relationships with the people we cannot see. Bicolanos equally define these encounters through the idioms of experience and feeling which we have already traced in their accounts of marriage, especially those which emphasise pity, reluctance, oppression, affection and desire rather than debt, reciprocity or exchange. Healers' stories evoke what happens when human and **tawo** meet. In these encounters, the powers of each party can be allied, or they may be balanced in combat with each other, or one party may elide, dominate and overwhelm the other. At other times the relationship seems to be imaged in physical terms. The spirits are seen as pulling people who cannot 'manage' (**kaya**) them into the invisible world with an almost hydraulic force, an almost audible suction.

As Danilyn Rutherford has pointed out, a reading of *The gift* in a different tradition to Parry's might also choose to emphasise a different side of Mauss's arguments, that is the extent to which Mauss himself is interested in the 'dark side' of exchange (Rutherford, personal communication). Much of the force of Mauss's arguments in fact relies on evoking both its sometimes extreme burdensomeness, and its emotional effects; aggression, fear and anxiety are as much a part of the potlatch as the destruction of goods (Mauss, 1990 (1950): 37–42). In Bicol, a healer's **saro** is her 'companion', her 'other person', her 'sibling', her workmate, her patron, but also commands her life and ultimately her death. 'Exchange' here has to be understood as an emotional economy as much as a political economy. The stories which Bicolanos tell about healers and **saros** are about the relationships between one person and another, and the ways in which they are constituted.

# 5

## Spirit mediums and seance forms: changing relations to the spirit world

**'Talking to the spirits, Nell, that's the right thing to do . . .' ('. . . *Makiulay an mga tawo, Nell, iyan an marhay . . .*')**

I have said that healing in Bicol is an intense and varied activity which daily absorbs the attention both of educated people and of the poor, but especially of the poor, for it is they who must rely on the 'pity' of the spirits in the absence of other resources. In this chapter, I turn from the intimate power relationship between medium and **saro** as it is conducted in terms of pity, oppression and debt, to examine in more detail the range of Bicolano healing practices, or seance forms.

It would be almost impossible to give a comprehensive account of Bicol healing, since virtually every healer has his or her own variation on the theme,[1] and for some time I regarded this over-abundance with a certain amount of confusion. Firstly, like many other anthropologists (Lewis, 1986:78–94; Thomas and Humphrey, 1994:3) I was inclined to regard any absolute distinction between 'shamanism' and 'spirit possession' as highly artificial, but people I knew in Bicol often seemed to be insisting on a contrast between a category of active, voluntary, non-possessed healing, and a category of inferior, more passive, possessed healing in a way which almost seemed designed to echo Eliade's original categories (1989 (1962): 347). Yet this simplistic description did not fit the diversity of healing forms and, as I shall argue, it was in many ways misleading. It was therefore necessary to account for both rhetoric and practice. Secondly, as a student in the anthropological traditions (Leach, 1983: 76–7; Bloch, 1994:136–8; Atkinson, 1989:297–324) which have pursued the connections between changing forms of interaction with the spirits and the evolution of political power (whether in the form of the growth of hierarchy and 'central cults', or of egalitarian popular uprisings) I was troubled by the lack of any neat and coherent correlations between variations in Bicol practice and crystallised political movements.

Bicol healing is not constructed around a central orthodox theory, and the most coherent account which could truthfully be given of it is one which sees countless variations placed along a range, which itself represents many possible ways of reconciling different sources of power. One thing which all healers have in common is that the 'solutions' they individually offer to this conundrum are all cast in the idiom of 'voice' and 'conversation'. While I will suggest, at the end of this chapter and in chapter nine, some ways in which these discussions about power in healing may relate to lowland popular politics, I would also argue that to concentrate on these rather infrequent historical conjunctures is to disregard the way in which Bicol healing is resonant with many experiences and areas of life which are not reducible to formal politics.[2] To push these sometimes elusive connections too far would be misleading. It may be important to see the coherence in variety, but it would be a curious picture of Bicol which thereby discounted the significance of that variety and confusion itself. The other concern of this and the following chapter, therefore, is to evoke a little of the richness of imagination which characterises the healers I knew. It has been recognised by several writers on spirit mediumship that the interaction between medium and spirit allows for a relatively loose (though not free) play with identity. I will suggest that in Bicol, where one mode of social contact which people greatly value is that of a balanced conversation between two sides, possession can be seen as something more like a pun, a *double entendre* or an ironic double-take, eliding the voice of healer and **saro** without extinguishing either. Moreover, it is the nature of the 'people we cannot see' to be themselves figures of a kind of power which is not fixed, but is always [Anderson] mobile, elusive and wilful, their resistance to equal conversation like their invisibility guaranteeing their advantage in relation to human beings. Spirits retain the ability to move across boundaries, and to surprise, and in doing so they offer an arena in which other kinds of ambiguity and transformation remain thinkable by association, and in which power itself can be thought of as something mobile and prone to change, and not as something defined and fixed.

### Voice, unequal conversations and the Bicol seance
Although much is debatable in Bicol healing, everyone I talked to agreed that the central duty of a **parabulong** is to know how to talk to, and 'talk

round' (**urulay**) the spirits. Negotiation and hospitality go hand in hand. As Fred, a Libmanan healer, put it:

It is necessary to understand how to talk to the people you cannot see. It's as if you had a visitor to the house; you have to know how to talk to them, or they will go away unsatisfied . . . But if you know what to say, you will be able to reach a satisfactory conclusion . . .

Words, as everyone also knows, are followed whenever necessary by food as an alternative means of engagement:

If the spirit didn't answer when you performed **santiguar**, then you would make a food offering . . . with chicken, alcohol, betel nut and so on . . . What they call **anito** is when you make a food offering, and you have a conversation with no human person there, saying '*Approach now, all of you, because now you will eat.*'

(Florida Romualdez)

This focus on the voice is carried through in the most definite statement that people are prepared to make about seance forms; that is, that the difference between healers who are weak and those who are strong is to be explained by a difference in technique which is also often locally identified as a decline from past standards. 'Strong' healers, it is said, are those who 'heal in their own voices' or who 'do not keep changing their voices'. It is 'they themselves who talk to the spirits', and they are associated with verbal powers of summoning and command, and with impressive techniques of persuasion. Stories of healers from the 1940s and 1950s emphasise their calm verbal management of even the most ill-intentioned of spirits. This is contrasted with most present-day healers, who let their **saro** speak instead of themselves, and who lie down and allow the **saro** to 'enter the body' in possession.[3] As Zelda, in whose house I first stayed, put it: 'I don't believe so much in the healers these days, like Auring and Elsa. They cure by sleeping. In the past, there was none of that, and the healers then didn't lie down and go to sleep. They tapped a spoon on the side of a glass and called the spirits, and then they talked to them.'[4]

Although there probably has been some real shift from the techniques of 'healing in your own voice' to those of healing with a **saro**, Zelda's picture of decline is in several respects misleading. It should not be assumed that calling a healer 'weaker' implies a loss of therapeutic efficacy, for instance; on the contrary, healers who 'lie down' are only rarely disadvantaged in bringing about a cure. In almost all cases, they continue to convey the healing 'pity' of the **tawo** to people to their patients' general satisfaction and nobody suggests that net healing power in the world is becoming any less. What is more in question is the way in which that power is accessed and the formality with which it is managed. Nonetheless, there are a number of healers working in the immediate area of San Ignacio and even in Zelda's family who still work in the way she attributes to the heroic practitioners of her youth, although it was not until a return visit in 1992 that I witnessed healing of this kind.

Mamay Lino, the father of my co-godmother Emma, had become suddenly ill with an alarmingly painful, swollen and blistered face, and a high fever. He lay prone all day, 'singing his pain'.[5] His care was entrusted to the healer Nana Nening,[6] who had already ascertained that the illness was caused by contact with spirits near a neighbour's house. However, since the **tawo** were proving resistant to hints, Nana Nening decided to hold an offering and address them directly. In the sufferer's darkened house she prepared a deep bowl of water, a saucepan-lid of live coals with two kinds of incense to burn on them,[7] a tee-shirt belonging to Mamay Lino and an offering-plate containing silver coins,[8] betel-nut packages, a candle and three 'sweet' cigarettes. Children and bystanders were warned to keep back and especially not to obstruct the doorways, through which the **tawo** were expected to pass, for, as Nana Nening tartly remarked, 'If they pay you back one for that, it'll be no laughing matter.'

Taking another coin, Nana Nening rang repeatedly on the side of the deep bowl, several single chimes and then little runs of three or four. She called out in a commanding tone, as though to unruly children;

Apong Omoy, Apong Omoy, approach now all of you; all of you who were in front of Leonor's house . . . Apong Omoy and Pontsio Pilato,[9] approach now all of you, for here is some betel-nut, for those of you who would like to chew betel. And for those of you who might want to smoke cigarettes, there are some. Come, and we will talk to you . . .

All the time, Nana Nening was sprinkling incense on the coals, and she directed her remarks first towards the smoke, and then, when the **tawo** (whom only she could see) had arrived, towards Mamay Lino. Addressing the **tawo** as they tasted the offerings, she described Lino's plight and asked for their help, adding:

Perhaps you have finished now, and so Apong Omoy and Pontsio Pilato, go to the place . . . and fetch whoever was responsible . . . because you know that you can see us, but we cannot see you . . . You are the ones who should talk them round . . .

The two named **tawo** were clearly acting as intermediaries for those who had caused Mamay Lino's sickness, and who Nana Nening knew to have arrived in their turn:

Just heal him now, because if he has caused you any offence, he begs pardon, but we want to talk it over with you . . . You should heal this Lino, because look at him! His eyes cannot open and his face is swollen. It is you who should pity him and you who should make it better, who should heal him, because . . .

While exhorting the spirits to let Lino go, Nana Nening also addressed Lino's soul, assumed to be off wandering in the invisible world of the **tawo**. Passing his tee-shirt repeatedly through the incense to summon back his soul, she called to him too:

Aquilino, Lino, Lino, come back home now, come back to your body. Don't you keep on letting yourself be beguiled by those ones who keep on trying to beguile you, because you should not be there; you should be here. Lino, Lino, Lino, come home now![10]

Once the transfer of Lino's soul was assumed to be completed, Nana Nening took care to seal it and to encourage the spirits to do likewise, by marking betel-nut juice crosses on Lino's wrists and other pulse-points to keep his soul in place. Then she let the spirits go, sending after them an offering of betel and cigarettes, set to float on the bowl of water and then tipped cautiously out of the house window into the dusk. Advising Lino to keep his tee-shirt on at all times and to apply a herbal poultice, she used **santiguaran** divination with plate and candle to read the traces of the spirit encounter. 'There you are,' she remarked. 'It's a case of young girls [i.e. girl spirits] – two of them, what's more. One's sleeping with you, but she'll get tired of it, then she'll leave you alone. But it won't happen in a big hurry.' Adding that he could take ampicillin along with other remedies if he felt very bad meanwhile, she left with a promise to return in three days' time.

Nana Nening's style of healing made sense of the many accounts I had been given of 'healing in your own voice', although I very much wished that there had been some less painful occasion for this illumination. Nana Nening could apparently 'see' in seance the 'people we cannot see' (although healers usually leave this slightly ambiguous), thus temporarily overcoming the disadvantage which marks all human dealings with spirits. Control over visibility went with control over the movement of spirits and souls through the voice; Nana Nening like other such healers can summon both to cross the barriers between worlds, and can persuade, cajole, send named **tawo** on errands to act as intermediaries to others, and thus restore the proper boundaries between this world and the invisible one.

This emphasis on command is especially striking when, as in this case, the whole structure of the seance corresponds to what Florida Romualdez called 'having a conversation with nobody there'. The healer sees, and the healer speaks, but the spirits and their response are visible and audible only to her; her voice is authoritative, and the audience witnesses the conversation with the **tawo** only at second hand, taking it on trust. When patients actually become possessed by the **tawo**, though (as often happens), the healer must engage with an embodied and vocalised spirit, and her authority is tested within an even more difficult conversation. When someone is plagued by a possessing spirit who comes and goes, the healer must in fact be able to induce it to talk through the body of the patient in seance, in order to reason with it. Thus for instance the well-remembered healer Doro Munoz, who was still working in the early 1970s, explained his patient Helen's condition to her. 'I was only there by fits and starts . . . [because, as he told me] . . . there was really a different spirit that was in my body.' After an initial attempt to send back the spirit and summon her soul without possession had failed, Doro realised that 'we would have to repeat it if the **tawo** that was entering me wanted to be able to have a talk'. He summoned the **tawo** with incense and placed a protective rosary round Helen's neck.[11] As she remembers, 'I lost consciousness . . . it seemed I suddenly lost all my strength, and . . . then the spirit said '*Papasok na!*' [Tagalog: 'I will enter now!'] . . . and I felt myself growing completely numb.' Doro then addressed the spirit confidently. 'What's your name? You know we want to talk to you! Your comings and goings have been causing a terrible disturbance . . .' As soon as the spirit gave her name (which was Zeny), and stated her intentions, Helen was on the way to a short healing career, and a cure.[12]

The same basic processes of disengaging humans and spirits from the kind of inappropriate intimacy which is dangerous for 'people like us' apply whatever kind of healing technique is employed. Whether healing 'in their own voice' or 'just lying down', **parabulong** are always concerned with redirecting persons back across the boundaries to their respective worlds and securing the gates, and of achieving this through the use of summoning, banishing, arguing, persuading, seducing and gradually reaching a negotiated agreement.

Healers who act as mediums must work within different kinds of conversational seance forms, since they construct their authority and their 'voice' as the voice of another, the **saro**. A spirit-companion is not only the initiator of the healing relationship, but is also regarded formally at least as the only one of the pair who 'knows how to heal', as Auring says of Clara. Possession in Bicol is not 'ecstatic' in the sense of employing either hallucinogens or techniques such as chanting which are designed to alter consciousness dramatically, although the **paraanitos** healers (whom I discuss below) may include music and rhythmic dance in their seances. When deliberately preparing for healing, Auring will lie on the floor and breathe deeply, allowing Clara to 'enter the body' through the crown of the head or the soles of her feet, and one can see Clara arrive by the lifting of Auring's ribcage. Usually possession is even more undramatic, being signalled by quite subtle alterations in body movements and sensations, especially by the repeated tapping of a foot, or the rapid cooling of the hands as the healer's spirit withdraws to make way for that of the **saro**.

Healers differ in the ways that they envisage the presence of the **saro**: while Auring certainly feels her 'enter the body', others see their **saro** as hovering somewhere near or on their shoulder, and the vocabulary of mediumship in nearby areas suggests both an imagery of the healer as house and the **saro** as a visitor, and of the **saro** as a kind of layer, like a layer of clothing, which is thrown over the healer for her to wear.[13] This last image is perhaps especially useful, since all healers including those like Auring say they often feel their **saro** nearby, not quite possessing them, but close to them and sometimes guiding their actions. Possession is thus not an absolutely either/or experience in Bicol, and despite what they say about their passivity in relation to their **saro**, neither is the healer absolutely distinguished from her **saro** at all times. In fact, it was not uncommon for me to find myself having a conversation with both a medium and her **saro**, the spirit flickering in and out of focus in the medium according to which of them could most appropriately answer my question.[14]

The main activities of a **saro**, or of other spirits when possessing a medium, are talking, eating and drinking – or refusing to talk, eat or drink. Mediums who eat or drink in seance are hungry and thirsty afterwards, since it is the spirit and not they themselves who has been nourished, and similarly they do not know what has taken place in the seance until told afterwards by an attendant, or told in a dream by their **saro**. The following is taken from an account of a healing session like many others in Auring's house, in March 1989.

Clara had been treating patients for about an hour in a busy healing session; a long queue of children had come and gone. Everyone here is used to Clara; since she is a young girl and known to be friendly, no one uses respect language to her or treats her with special deference. While Auring is possessed, a **bantay** or guardian sits near her, to take care of her. This is usually Auring's co-godmother and neighbour Leonor, but when she is busy Auring's sister-in-law or some other close female relative can take over. The 'guardian' helps the course of the seance along, by asking questions of Clara and any other spirits who may 'arrive', together with the patient and the patient's relatives.

Clara had been asked to take a look at Lydia, one of Auring's husband's nieces, who had come down from the uplands to stay with her mother while her baby was born. Lydia had been warned by the doctor that she had high blood pressure, and was also concerned about dreams she had been having of a snake on the roof, which she thought suggested the **tawo** might have an interest in her unborn child.[15] Taking one look at Lydia, Clara confirmed[16] that she was 'accompanied'. Auring lay down on the mat, and her back arched as Clara left to search among the **tawo** for the one responsible for Lydia's illness. Auring arched again as a new spirit 'entered' to the sound of a deeply indrawn breath. Lydia fumbled trying to get the newcomer to talk to her; she appealed to Auring's brother who was nearby: 'You do it.' 'I don't know how', he said, embarrassed at this unaccustomed role, but he tried: 'Are you the one whom Clara's fetched?'

After a few questions, the **tawo** began to speak in a voice like a speeded-up tape recorder. 'Dwarfs!' everybody told each other. This was what Lydia had suspected; she told the dwarf that her husband had warned her that there were dwarfs behind their house, but that being very pregnant, she had been caught short on her way to the privy. She begged his pardon, she said, but since one cannot see the invisible people, surely he would excuse her for dampening him: 'You are kind, (**maboot**) I'm sure?'

'Unkind! (**maisog**)', said the dwarf. Lydia looked dismayed: 'No, no, my husband said you were kind **tawo**. You are kind, aren't you?'

The dwarf, refusing to be drawn as to his temperament, said he wanted to be made **Ninong** (godfather) to Lydia's child. Lydia looked very uncomfortable. 'As long as you're the kind sort . . .' People around began to suggest: 'If you become co-godparents . . .' '. . . *we'll help each other out'*, said Lydia bravely. '*Won't you help me?'*

The dwarf remarked sourly that Lydia's husband did nothing but sit around the house. Lydia laughed; 'My husband's a fisherman; there's no work for him at the moment. Won't you help me, so that I don't have a difficult birth?'

Somewhat grumpily, the dwarf began to heal Lydia by pressing hands over her belly, then suddenly laughed when the child kicked. 'Thankyou', said Lydia. Auring lay down again on the mat, and the dwarf left her body, to be replaced by Clara, who cured Lydia by blowing on the top of her head, mixing water with the ash of an **orasion**, giving her the water to drink and marking ash crosses on her pulse points. Next day, Lydia felt a real improvement in the headache she'd suffered from for weeks, although she wondered if the child would be premature, it was kicking her so much.

Another example from December of the same year:

My co-godmother Emma was acting as Auring's assistant. The client, sitting next to Auring on the wooden floor, was a forceful woman from a nearby fishing village; she and her nine-year-old daughter had both been made ill, it seemed, by the same **tawo**. Clara had already been sent to fetch the spirit responsible by the time I arrived; since these patients had been before, they already knew the **tawo** was a child, and the mother had brought an apple to coax her with.

The child-**tawo** in Auring's body was nibbling slices of apple down to the peel, which she twisted restlessly in her hands. The neighbourhood children, who rarely taste apples which are imported and expensive, watched with a kind of patient fascination. The mother was questioning the **tawo** in a robust sort of way: 'What's our name, now? How old are you? Won't you cure me because I have this rash all over my body, and it's very itchy.'

The **tawo** seemed too young or shy to speak, but at the mention of itching she began to roll about on the floor, scratching her head. 'Have you nits?' prompted Emma encouragingly, but she still wouldn't answer or open her eyes. Still, the reflection of the sick woman's itching was helpful; it showed that this was a case of 'paying back' (**naigo**) an inadvertent injury. Although exceptionally coy about giving her name, the spirit eventually responded to people's questions and guesses, recounting in a complaining lisp how the fisherwoman had accidentally spattered her with **balao** (small, salty shrimp), which caused rashes, and had indeed been 'paid back' with rashes. As soon as this was determined, the **tawo** was persuaded to heal mother and daughter, blowing on the crowns of their heads to restore each soul to its proper body. Clara then returned, and concluded the treatment by writing out a spell/prayer for the woman on a slip of paper.

Clearly, although both kinds of seance construct a conversation, healers like Auring adopt a very different position within it; their acting as mediums renders visible and audible for the whole audience what is invisible and inaudible except to the healer in Nening's treatments. While 'healing in your own voice' relies on an evocation of command, healing 'lying down' relies for its authority on the direct manifestation of the **tawo**. In theory, a **saro** like Clara simply substitutes for a healer like Nening, in directing and conducting the seance. Yet we have seen in the previous chapter that, however close the relationship between a healer and her particular well-intentioned spirit-companion, humans and spirits must always remain incommensurable. The **tawo** never lose their ambivalence or surrender their potential for predation and excess. Substitution is therefore never a matter of replacing like with like. Moreover, while healers like Nening are present throughout the healing session, their voice a constant interlocutor of patients and spirits alike, a **saro** like Clara is not, but disappears each time her medium must accommodate another spirit, relying on the 'guardian' and audience to manage the interrogation. When people draw a contrast between these two styles of healing, then, they are attending to a contrast which implies, not a loss of supernatural power or of access to it, nor a reduction in the provision of healing, but a shift in the forms through which the spirits are engaged in conversation with decorum.

//social power?

The link people make between these contrasting weak and strong conversational forms and the healer's use or avoidance of possession however, is in fact a misleading simplification. For while healers who work 'in their own voice' have the ability to cure without possession, this does not mean that they themselves never voluntarily act as mediums. At least some 'strong' healers will occasionally cooperate with another healer who acts as questioner, while they become the medium through whom a spirit speaks.[17] Other kinds of healer who unequivocally work with a **saro** may frequently allow their own spirit-companions to 'enter the body', while however generally avoiding being possessed by the spirits of their patients, and definitively refusing to act as medium for powers which they consider dangerous or demonic. The form that a seance with such a healer can take will be illustrated in the next chapter, in the account of the **birthdayhan** of Aling 'Gnesia.

Rather than regarding this as a simple case of healing 'with possession' and healing 'without possession', therefore, these Bicol healers can more properly be seen as those who have both possession and 'healing in their own voice' within their repertoire, and those who have possession only. The implications of this were brought home to me on one of the very few occasions on which Auring and everyone in San Ignacio declared that her use of a **saro** actually compromised her ability to heal. The circumstances were regarded as quite bizarre, for Mamay Luis, the husband of my friend Nana Ilar, had been suddenly revisited by a spirit which had troubled him in his youth, when he like many other people in the area had been a healer for a few years. This spirit, a large and aggressive male, was notorious for having insisted on flamboyant seance techniques involving duelling[18] and for inspiring Luis to beat himself, and was thought by Luis to have 'used up' the lives of several of his young children. Its reappearance was therefore a cause for alarm. Everyone agreed that this was not a case for Auring. The spirit himself forbade people to call her; '*Poor thing*' he said '*she would not be able to manage me* (**Dai niya ako kaya**)'. Auring later echoed this in almost-identical terms: '*I couldn't manage that one*', she said, '*and Clara couldn't manage him.*' In fact, in the absence of a someone like the healer Pitong whose words had soothed and controlled him twenty years before,[19] the **tawo** wandered disruptively around in Luis's body for a couple of days, before prescribing himself a kind of hot-water baptism,[20] and managing to leave of his own accord. In this case, as in the case of a raging madwoman who paid a visit to the barangay for treatment, it was clear that neither Auring nor Clara could answer the spirit voices or match these **tawo** effectively, and all agreed that Auring would be 'defeated' (**daog**) if such a spirit entered her body.

Auring of course would have been able to 'manage' the violent spirit better if she had the option of avoiding possession. But the reference to Clara as being also unable to 'manage' him suggests a further point which in Bicol is never stated and remains completely implicit, although an explicit elaboration of it may be common in healing in other parts of the world, and even other parts of the Philippine lowlands, which are known for their 'shamanic' idioms. While local talk focusses on a contrast between possession and non-possession, in practice it is known that some people's **saro**s offer more powerful protection to their healers than others, and are capable of testing their strength against more violent and obscure powers. So some types of 'healing with a **saro**' are more powerful than others, depending on who the **saro** might be. What seemed like a straightforward local deprecation of the spread of possession techniques as a weakening or decline in healing actually forms part of a more complex attitude to the location of power. And while a small third category of healers, whom I will describe below, do self-consciously avoid possession under any circumstances, it is the healers 'in their own voices' who have the full range of techniques at their command, who are most flexibly equipped to deal with any challenge from the spirit-world.

### 'Temptations', 'baptised spirits' and the 'reach' of God's blessing

People who want to undermine the reputation of a particular healer in Bicol will sometimes say, or hint, that her spirit-companion is an evil spirit, a **tentasion** or **maligno**. This suggestion will be indignantly rejected by the healers, the **saro**s and their loyal patients, but it always provides food for thought, and for conversation. Attitudes to the spirits in Bicol, as in all parts of the former Spanish Empire, are of course heavily marked by centuries of the Church's struggle to control the definition of the orthodox and the unorthodox. The early missions in Bicol attempted to reclassify the **tawo** as false gods or demons, and the carved statues representing them as idols (Gerona, 1988b:49–58). They also sought all over the Philippines to extirpate the local supernatural practitioners of all kinds, but especially to eradicate the influence of the many women mediums and healers (whom they labelled 'priestesses' or 'witches') and of the male transvestite mediums called **asog**, replacing them with male Catholic priests, lay confraternities and catechistical groups (Rafael, 1988:186; Castano, 1895:29; Alcina, 1668: Part I, Book 3: 212; Guerrero 1996:2). The missionary preoccupation with extirpating 'demon-worship' in fact led to a possible overemphasis in Spanish accounts of the part which possession played in indigenous healing methods. The image of the possessed healer, foaming at the mouth as a supposed agent of Satan enters her body, was the defining one for contemporary missionaries, and less flamboyant aspects of healing tend to be less clearly described, making comparisons with the present more difficult.[21]

While conversion created fundamental changes in local practice, there is no evidence that even in the few areas best supplied with missionaries it ever succeeded in suppressing it. Indeed, local sources complained about Filipino tendencies to treat Catholic saints as equivalent in kind to already-existing indigenous supernaturals, and to refuse to recognise the difference between statues of saints and pagan 'idols' (Hislop, 1971: 154; Ness, 1992:74; Rafael, 1988: 111–2). Contemporary Bicolanos, however, do inherit four hundred years of clerical suspicions that their healing may conceal the work of Satan, as well as the complex attitudes of the post-Vatican Two church, some of whose churchmen favour the more secularist rational humanism which would dismiss dealings with spirits as superstition, while others draw on the 'inculturation' movement which seeks to re-appropriate all aspects of local spirituality and render them fruitful in the service of Catholicism.

It would not therefore seem surprising that people in Bicol discuss the **tawo** with some degree of ambivalence and, in the case of those who are most concerned with Bible Study and other church revival activities,[22] with a perceptible anxiety about the right place of the spirits in the order of things. Among ordinary people, all of whom will have at least one close relative who is a healer, there is a widespread hesitation about whether (as Catholic teaching, though not all contemporary priests would have it) the **tawo** are all unChristian beings, or whether (as many healers maintain) some spirits are unChristian and others, epecially the healer's own spirit companions, are Christians on their own terms.

The story which is often told about the origin of the **tawo**[23] illustrates this:

When God created the world, he blessed all the people in it . . . [the story-teller makes a gesture like a priest sprinkling holy water] . . . But the **tawo** were hiding among the tree-trunks of the forests, and so they didn't fall within the dominion[24] of the blessing. That is why we cannot see them. But if the blessing at Mass reaches one of the **tawo**, we will see them and they will not be able to go back to their own place.

This is the reason many people give why healers do not wait for the end of Mass; if a healer were to be possessed during the blessing, the spirit-companion would be unable to leave the healer's body, and the healer's spirit (**espiritu**, the term generally used for a living person's soul) would remain stuck in the world of the invisible people.

It is an awareness of this ambivalence which more than anything else perhaps makes sense of the variations in healers' practice, as healers position themselves in relation to what they are told are the contrary pulls of God and the spirits.

Healers are of course aware of the frisson created by the suggestion that they might be consorting with 'demons', and occasionally one meets someone who exploits this rather than shying away from it. Luis, whose bad-tempered **saro** was mentioned above, often hinted at some such thing, and at least one healer in Libmanan (also male) made no bones about it, although his definition of 'demons' was still somewhat at odds with his disapproving priest's visions of Satan and his works. Some people draw the line at, say, visiting a healer who uses firewalking, on the grounds that it indicates a dubious reputation, but this is a matter for individual judgement.

Much more often, healers will attempt to distance themselves from any such implication. Given the questionable nature of possession, one way to do this is to refuse to act as a medium, restricting one's practice to those acts (divination, sending back, blessing, protection) which mesh best with Catholic notions of the acceptable. Indeed, some more open-minded priests express a professional curiosity about the use of **orasion** to heal the possessed by banishing the **tawo**, especially since they are themselves not infrequently called on to perform exorcisms.[25]

In this vein, Auring's mother Severina and her sister-in-law Oling both explicitly contrasted their own styles of healing with Auring's, to me and to other people. 'I don't have a **saro** like your Manay Auring; I just rely on God.' In terms of techniques, both women combine **santiguaran** divination with the use of **orasion** and the restorative blowing on the crown of the head, and like many other healers of all kinds they make constant use of signs of the cross, amulets, clothing with prayers written on it, and other integrated Catholic apparatus, whose main function is usually a 'disjunctive' one, keeping the spirits out of the body of a patient. Neither woman would consent to be possessed either by a **saro** or by other spirits.

To underline the affinities of her healing with good Catholic practice, Severina also had an impressive (if eclectic) collection of saints' statues, and she arranged these at home into a shrine much more elaborate than the usual little figure or religious calendar which can be found on a niche in every household. Other attempts to appropriate the power of saints may be more flamboyant. Marita, a healer in Calabanga town who likewise avoids possession, centres her healing on a tiny piece of wood shaped like Christ which was given to her by a mysterious old man who came to her house looking for something to eat. When it proved efficacious, she knew her visitor had been the **Ama** (the 'Father', i.e. Christ himself). Another woman, Zenobia, who had experienced episodes in which very powerful and possibly demonic spirits and spirit-snakes had tried to possess her, resisted with the aid of an entire living-room filled with saints, in which she held frequent prayer-sessions as well as healing.

Such things may reconcile the conscience of those among a healer's clientele (especially church-going middle-class people) who feel that possession may be dubious, but most patients of all classes draw the line further along, reasoning that while of course *some* spirits and **saro**s are unChristian creatures, those favoured by their own healer are perfectly Christian in their own terms. This would also be the position of most healers, who sometimes go to considerable lengths to insist that *their* **saro** is a force for good, and even that it has been baptised or attends the full Mass (which of course is supposedly impossible for the **tawo**).

An attachment to and insistence on proximity to saints, therefore, is not only a characteristic of non-possessed healers, but is as general as the use of Catholic symbolism in the treatment of patients. All the local healers I knew, for example, frequented the nearby shrine of the **Amang Hinulid** or 'Christ laid out in death', whose importance in Calabanga is described in the following chapters. Items bought or begged from the shrine were prized for use in treatment, and for healers, as for all local people, the near full-size image constantly on display in its glass coffin was what they meant whenever they talked about Christ.

This desire for nearness to the saints can sometimes lead to gestures which don't quite work, as in the case of Riko, a young man who practiced healing betwen 1988 and 1990, and who during an afternoon divination session suddenly took up a position as if transfixed on the Cross. Though it is not unknown for people to be possessed by saints, his unspoken claim to be possessed by Christ was met with a certain scepticism. Nonetheless, it was only the excess of the attempt which invalidated it, not the under-lying logic of identification with Christ (and in San Ignacio, specifically with the **Amang Hinulid**), for that identification is made in numerous ways by all Bicolano healers.[26] Above all, it is made in that period of each healer's first vocation when, like Auring, the healer undergoes a near-death experience; her soul journeys to the world of the people we cannot see, and her **saro** meanwhile occupies her body and inaugurates her healing career. These experiences are always described in ways which recall the death and resurrection of Christ; they often last three days, they may well begin on a Friday and end on a Sunday; the language people employ is resonant of popular religious texts such as the Bicol Passion story. Thus Nana Ilar recalls her uncle, Apolonio, whose most spectacular feat was to die and come back to life each Good Friday, dramatically recapitulating his initial calling.

. . . He would say, 'As I watch over you, so let you now watch over me . . . I won't be healing you now that it's Passiontide.'

He would then lie down in the barangay chapel and would 'die' at exactly eight o'clock. His relatives and patients had to keep vigil as at a wake until he 'returned to life' the following morning.

This identificatory logic provides access to one source of power, and this power is used in various ways for the management of relations with the **tawo**; Zenobia simply employs it to fend off spirits in their 'demonic' guise, insisting that if she were to become possessed she would be irredeemably 'defeated' (**daog**) and would turn mad.[27] Healers with a **saro** reject this notion, but still call on items from the **Ama** and props such as holy water to help them control the movement of the **tawo** in healing, while relying on their own and their 'good' **saros**' 'closeness' to God and the saints to strengthen them and guarantee their own protection as far as possible. Thus they become more able to 'manage' (**kaya**) encounters with difficult spirits.

It is important to recognise that Bicol healing also envisages what might be called a 'shamanic' idiom, fragments of a genre which stresses deliberate, voluntary searches for power, and movement between the human and the spirit worlds. Every healer, after all, begins her vocation by a voyage which takes her to the dwellings of the **tawo**, and then brings her back transformed by the crossing. Many healers have been given objects as gifts by the **tawo**, which they use in seances. Doro Munoz had a medallion, others have pebbles or coins which mysteriously appear; healers in nearby Canaman I am told still collect herbs and roots on Good Friday and preserve them in holy oil (Tito Valiente, personal communication), while in San Ignacio people say that healers used to bury a cat alive secretly on

Good Friday, to dig up its bones later when they would be filled with power. All these objects belong to the class of **anting**, or charms, which take related forms in other areas of the lowlands (Ileto, 1979:22–7; Demetrio, 1990: 220; Natividad, 1979: 97; Chirino, 1604: 164–5; de los Reyes, 1909:181–4; Kayne, 1907).

**Anting** are associated with the deliberate search for power, whether as healers or, sometimes, as political or sexual influence over others. Marcos is often said to have had an **anting**, and in Bicol in 1988–89 the mayor of Partido was widely held to have an **anting** which protected him from his enemies and enabled him to attract scores of younger women, including a beautiful American.

In healers' stories, there seems to be a loose genre which focusses, like Marita's story, on the gift of an **anting** brought by a stranger, and it makes little difference for these purposes whether that stranger comes as a saint or as a more 'traditional' figure from among the **engkantos**. But one may also acquire **anting** on a journey which (in the best shamanistic traditions) one initiates oneself, deliberately seeking out power rather than waiting for it to be dropped into one's lap. Although I met some healers who had themselves undertaken these voyages, they are, like 'healing in your own voice', mostly thought of in San Ignacio as something which was more common in the recent past, in the generation born around the turn of the century of whom few were still alive in the late 1980s, but many were remembered.

When for instance I asked Ilar about changes in healing practice, she expanded on the contrast between Auring and her same uncle Apolonio whom she had been taken to see as a child. His techniques included taking the pulse, **laway** (healing with saliva) and the use of **orasion**. These were in a little book or **librito**[28] which Ilar described as *'full of things which are not explained to people'*, and which *'he got in a cave'*,[29] along with his other 'bits of medicine'. Like other possessors of such books, he is supposed to have eaten it when he died.

Apolonio had obtained his powers

... because he went into a cave on Good Friday ... in the uplands, the forest. If you are given healing (**bulong**) there, they say ... that it is put on a sort of table at the entrance of the cave. But the problem is your steps are made of the hanging tongues of snakes ... there are so many vipers, the floor looks like rubber bands ... Ay, if they don't want you to be given it, they're ferocious, those ones ...

Apolonio's vocation began when, after he had been ill off and on for some time, he met an old man he didn't recognise:

The old man called him, 'Come here, because you'll learn something . . .' [Apolonio] had a talk to him and he said: 'If you want me to heal, help me', and so he was helped . . .

and given the protection which he needed in the cave of snakes. It was that same cave, he said, which he revisited each Good Friday during his 'death', to bring back healing for the barangay.

These stories of voyages in search of **anting** and **orasion** are not uncommon, and there is a certain amount of agreement about the range of powers of the formulae. Florida Romualdez remembers her father's **librito** included formulae 'for snakes', 'for riding', 'for the bones of the dead' (keeping them as guards of the house) and so on. Others enable the possessor to walk vast distances in a few steps, while a different arcane book known as **De Mica** was said to make you invisible when you opened it. Many people in San Ignacio said that such **libritos** are not used nowadays, or that they have been lost, though whether accidentally or through their owner's consumption is difficult to say. These books of spells, however, are not a phantasm, for I was once shown the **librito** of a healer in Libmanan, and it was exactly as described: a tiny printed book with exorcistic and other magical formulae in dog-Latin.

Some people who were not practising healers acquired power in similar ways. Zelda's father, for instance, who died in the 1970s, is one of several other people I knew or heard of who claimed to have travelled to a mysterious cave. He assisted women in childbirth, but did not heal otherwise. Zelda gave this brief account:

Dad knew how to keep away 'temptations' and how to recognise these things, because he had gone to a cave on Good Friday . . . First, he went to Tinambac [an upland town], and then to Sipocot [further to the north] – places where there is virgin forest . . . He met an old man who said he should go inside the cave because he had something very important to show him there. Once he went inside, he said, all manner of things came to meet him; first snakes, and then all kinds of terrifying things. The old man said that whatever he saw he must take no notice but just say 'Let me pass among you, sir', and make his way through them. When he emerged again he found himself at Naga Cathedral and it was Holy Saturday. The old man had given him a belt (**habay**) and said that he mustn't take it off, or else he would lose the powers he had acquired. So after that he was able to see the hidden people – he would be growing vegetables at the back of the house, and you would hear him call out 'Eek!' because the hidden people were teasing him. He said they had a road that ran along the irrigation ditch and a tricycle went on it. So when he was guarding a woman giving birth, he could also see if there were any **abay** ['bystanders' – hovering bad spirits] and the belt taught him what prayers to use. But once they went to the mountains and they were bathing, and he forgot and removed his belt and so he lost his powers, but by that time he knew how to use the prayers anyway.

Zelda added that her mother's father had owned one of the books, '**De Mica**', which, when opened, caused you to fly up into the air, but when he died he ate it. '*He died eating something*', she added darkly, '*and so did Dad.*'[30]

Elsewhere in the contemporary lowlands, the characteristics of 'shamanic' forms of healing, are also associated with access to, and reliance on, 'ancestral' power. In Panay, for example, the **ma-aram** ('knowledgeable') healers described by Magos (1978; 1986; 1992) are assisted in their travels through the unseen universe and in their encounters with spirits by spirit-companions who protect them. These spirit-companions are usually an ancestor (often male) of the shaman (also often male), and the calling is thought of as inherited, although significantly it is also possible for someone to be 'called' by a non-related local ancestor (Magos, 1992: 60, 88). In **ma-aram** areas, there is much more consensus than in Bicol about what should constitute healing practice, and there also appears to be more agreement and certainty about types and statuses of spirits, and how to map the cosmology of the spirit-world. Panay, in short, is in comparison to Bicol a site of greater orthodoxy and more homogeneous expertise. The definition of a 'right' kind of knowledge and practice is linked to some emphasis on lineal ancestry and inherited status which, as many authors have pointed out in various contexts, inherently exclude some people and include others, thus providing the potential for the development of increased hierarchical tendencies.

In Bicol, these links are more loosely forged. Healers telling their stories do not stress the inheritance of their vocation, but the will and choice of the **tawo**, or occasionally their daring searches for these gifts. In practice, however, it often emerges that the future healer's career was predicted when they were a child by some aunt, uncle or grandparent with special powers, and sometimes the older relative will even make the younger the present of a healing-aid or **anting**. Similarly, Bicol healers stress the ways in which they have acquired their techniques through direct inspiration of the spirits, and many emphasise that (in contrast to the 'knowledgeable' **ma-aram**) it is not really they who 'know'. Yet healers clearly do also consciously teach each other skills, and every new healer needs another one or two to 'consecrate' them by establishing through seance what the terms and duties of their relationship with their **saro** are to be. As healers become 'used to' their **saro**, the line between the two is less clearly drawn, and many mediums as well as healers 'in their own voice' act in seance with considerable authority and aplomb.

The Bicolano healers who come closest to the Panay model are those known as the **paraanitos** or **paradiwata** healers. Apparently very common in the region in the 1950s and 1960s, they were famous for firewalking, which Bicolanos associate with the Visayas. **Paraanitos** healers are also unusual in present-day Bicol because they form groups or associations, who have agreed healing styles from which they should not deviate. Such healers are known in Calabanga, but have declined in numbers and tend to be elusive, and some people say they work only in distant rural villages. In the event, I had to travel to a hamlet outside the nearby town of Libmanan, before I met the **paraanitos** healer Tiang Delia, whose seance I refer to in the next chapter.

Part of the reason for my pilgrimage to meet Tiang Delia was that **paraanitos** and **paradiwata** are loaded terms in the Bicol language. Although many people cannot now say what they mean, other than to link them to this particular style of healing, the literal sense of the words is 'by/for the **anitos**' (ancestors/spirits) and 'by/for the **diwata**' (deities). Tiang Delia's practice does in fact have a tinge of the 'ancestral' about it, since one of her **saros** bears the same name as an older sister who died before Tiang Delia was born, while another is referred to as 'grandmother'. She is conspicuously more interested than many Bicol healers in the notion of things being done in the right way, and explicitly appeals to the need to do them in the way that they have always been done, in order to please the spirits. Tiang Delia is confident of the status of the spirits who regularly speak through her in a way which is quite distinctive, and refers to some of these spirits as 'the high ones' – elevated personages worthy of the term **anito** or **diwata**, even if in contemporary Bicol those terms do not carry the unequivocal meaning of 'ancestor'. After all, as the patriotic bibliophile and **ilustrado** Isabelo de los Reyes noted, in the history of Bicolano and lowland religion generally 'the classification of the gods is inexact' (de los Reyes, 1909:122; my translation),[31] and one part of that inexactitude is precisely that the dividing line between ancestors and high spirits/minor gods is blurred or non-existent. The protective companions of healers, it appears, may receive slightly different ancestral or spirit colourings depending on the history of a particular locality. But any **saro** who is called an **anito** is likely to be a supernatural of considerable consequence, able to 'manage' more than a spirit such as Auring's companion, Clara.

It is at this point that we arrive back at the complexity and difficulty of relationships with the **tawo** which so dominates the lives of healers that they stand in need of protection from the **saro**'s enslaving gift. Whatever the explanatory force of the interventions of the Catholic church through history, it is clear that ambivalence about the **tawo** predates the Spanish invasion of the lowlands. At the time of the conquest, it was recorded that there were both good and evil spirits, but that all were varyingly dangerous to deal with, challenging the capacities of the healers. Moreover, as well as being ambivalent, spirits were also ambiguous; for it is impossible from the evidence of even the earliest Spanish texts to draw a clear line between the **tawo** and the souls of the dead, then called respectively **nonos** and **anitos** in Tagalog and **divatas** and **anitos** in the Visayas. The souls of the dead were also regarded as having a benevolent and a harmful side, the former of which was cultivated as a household guardian, and the latter distanced from the living as soon as possible. Alcina records a further ambiguity between good souls who protected the living, and two guardian souls, one good and one evil, with which every person is born (Alcina, 1668; Part I, Book 3; 194–260). While it is not clear from the Spanish accounts how historically healers related to these supernaturals, it seems entirely likely that they too made use of spirit-companions who were either powerful **nonos/divatas**, or powerful **anitos**, or perhaps both at the same time. Such powerful supernatural allies provided one form of protection, but with conversion to Christianity, the possible ways of handling the **tawo** were multiplied, without the original method being abandoned. Like almost every other healer I knew in Bicol, Tiang Delia insists that her **anitos** are exemplary Christians, but they still retain the aura of high indigenous supernatural patrons and allies.

I have argued that rather than being literally concerned with the distinction between possession and non-possession as local discourse would have it, Bicolano healing practice is most coherently accounted for as a range of 'solutions' – some more generic, some more idiosyncratic – to the problem of control in dealings with the spirits. Historical conditions, especially conversion to Catholicism, increased the layers of ambivalence towards the **tawo**, by suggesting that they might be 'demonic', while simultaneously supplying in the Catholic saints a new repertoire of possible allies in healing which added to but did not replace the existing spirits and ancestors on whom healers could call. Meanwhile, the existing ambiguity about the character of **anitos**, who could be seen as either protective ancestors and/or protective non-ancestral spirits, was increased by a further elision between **anitos** and saints. In present-day Bicol healing practice, therefore, one sees a range of differences between healers about the best way to 'manage' threatening encounters with **tawo** (through avoidance, 'exorcistic' banishment, protection, or engagement and confrontation with the healer's **saro**) combined with a range of ways of understanding the status of the **saro** and the derivation of its power, as non-Christian, exclusively Christian, or (in most cases) a combination of the two – **anitos** who have received Christian baptism, for instance. As I have argued in this chapter, this combination of powers may be regarded as the ideal, but it is nonetheless difficult to sustain, and the variety of Bicol healing practice reflects the tensions which this engenders.

There is clearly a sense in which Bicolano nostalgia for the decrease in the numbers of 'healers who talk in their own voices' also partly conceals a nostalgia for the decline of the number of healers whose spirit-companions could be seen as truly powerful agents, of **saro**s with claims to power such as those who are called **anitos**. And yet, the source from which such spirit-companions actually derive their power remains ambiguous in Bicol. Bicolano **anitos** are not unambiguously local ancestors, like the spirit-companions of shamans in Panay, but they are tinged with ancestrality; they are not aggressively 'indigenous' deities, nor are they certainly Catholic figures. They may attempt to be all three, but no one is quite certain whether or not they have succeeded. The discussion of some of the implications of this quality of irresolution for the interaction between healing and political events in Bicol must be deferred until the end of chapter nine. I would argue, however, that this lack of closure is in one sense the most important fact about Bicol healing, for it is in the environment created by that uncertainty that the most characteristic 'conversations' of seance practice take place, and these conversations are, in the end, their own point.

# 6

## Coda: the birthday-parties of the spirits

*We have come here to the house, we have arrived,*
*Because they say there is a celebration*
*In fulfilment of the occasion . . .*

### The *Birthdayhan* of Aling 'Gnesia

I want to conclude this account of the world of the spirits with two brief scenes from a special kind of seance, the birthday-party, which is held not for the healer, but for her **saros** on the anniversary of the healer's 'consecration' and the arrival of her spirits.

'**Birthdayhan**' in the Philippines are occasions for the provision of hospitality, rather than the receiving of gifts, by the person concerned, and anything more than the most simple sharing of a few beers carries a hint of high society, wealth, and a **blow-out**. The alternative to the English term is the Spanish one, **kumpliaño**, which with its associated verb, **magkumpli**, also suggests 'observing' an occasion in an almost religious sense. Both these meanings attach to a spirit birthday, which also provides an opportunity for a display of the powers of the **tawo**, who either through the gifts and payments of attending patients, or through some other means, are supposed to help their medium to provide the costs of the refreshments they require. The food is both a **tulod**, or offering to the spirits, and a gift from them, a self-fulfilling circle.

The **birthday** can be held within an elaborate and 'traditional' seance format, or within a looser one. Thus, the most vivid experience I have of healing with a powerful **saro** is from watching and learning from Tiang Delia, the Libmanan **paraanitos** or **paradiwata** healer, and her two **saros**, Aling Agnesia and Don Alejandre, who were, they informed me, not only good baptised Christians, but 'high ones' second only to 'that famous **engkanto**, Maria Clara'.[1] These Libmanan healers, like other **paraanitos**, convene as a group on important occasions, and use music, dance and special 'protective' costumes which in Tiang Delia's case comprise an 'archbishop's' hat and bands, decorated with pink spangles, gifted to her by her predecessor who had 'consecrated' her. Over a period of several months, I visited Tiang Delia many times, for at our initial meeting she had diagnosed my arrival as indicating that the **tawo** were asking me to learn certain kinds of healing. She kindly undertook to oversee the process of introducing me to these spirits (who turned out to be a sort of **duende**), which she eventually did.[2] But before that business could be completed, she invited me to attend the birthday-party of her own **saros**, together with her patients, the other **paraanitos** healers of the area, and the various spirits who comprised her other guests.

Having spent all the previous day preparing a complex spirit-meal, Tiang Delia started the occasion with prayers, welcomed her family, patients and the two other healers (one man, one woman) who would also bring their **saros** to the birthday. She then rose to call the spirits into the house from all the directions of the compass, using incense, guitar music

Figure 4  A healer possessed during a seance

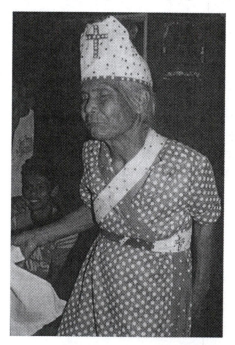

and ringing on a plate with a dagger. '*Enter! You have also come to the occasion . . . you, ha! you have been felt now!*' Once invited, the **tawo** began to 'arrive' in sequence, starting with the **saro**s of Tiang Delia's deceased mentor, spirits which played an organisatory role, and proceeding to a cast of characters all of whom were easily recognised by the audience of her patients. Each spirit tossed back some alcohol or chewed on betel, the 'food' of the **tawo**, and greeted the guests including myself in his or her own style. Soon one spirit, Buterawan, began to urge the **anitos** of the other mediums to introduce themselves and to 'eat'.

The male healer was showing signs of the arrival of an **anito**, staring fixedly and tying a red headband round his forehead in preparation; though by some oversight both the two guest healers were without their full protective regalia, which caused them some problems. As the guitar reached a one-note crescendo, the male healer began to chant in a strange hybrid Tagalog.

'*Hey! . . . my humble self . . . my humble self . . . will say farewell, now farewell . . .*'

'*Well, I don't know!*' exclaimed Buterawan, annoyed. '*I am not saying farewell yet, why are you? . . . You were asked your name already . . . what sort of person is this?*' [Several of the guests started laughing]. The spirit replied with something garbled which seemed to mean '*Your own body you see is joined to you very weakly.*' This was greeted with a collective 'Mmm!' of enlightenment from the healers. '*He's having difficulty*' said Delia/Buterawan in Bicol. '*Who are you by name?*'

'*I come . . . from the edge of the sea.*'

'*Aaah, from the sea!*' murmured the woman next to me. '*That kind are fierce.*'

'*Who are you? Don't take so long about it!*' commanded the other healers and their **anitos**. '*Why have you come here? What is it you want?*'

Obviously feeling himself the target of some criticism for his hazy appearance, the spirit murmered a greeting, and added an explanation: '*You know, all the equipment belonging to my humble self is still at our place; all the things relied on for protection are there.*'

'*Well, I don't know, I'm sure*', said Delia/Buterawan. '*Didn't bring it, that's it, didn't bring what you depend on for protection.*'

'*My humble self did not . . .*' said the spirit, and faded into the realm of the non-verbal. As if to make up for this dereliction, the woman healer Tiang Obing's spirits arrived with reasonable formality, the guitar playing to accompany their declamation.

'*How are we, now?*
*How are those who have become my siblings?*
*There is a foreigner arrived here in our town!*
*Excuse me, you who have become my siblings,*
*The life of my humble self has come to a state.*
*My outward body is sometimes very weak . . .*
*I did not bring all my equipment*

*So I cannot manage to dance*
*[Without the gear to] protect my outward body*
*Do not be unhappy about my humble self . . .*
*We have come here to the house, we have arrived,*
*Because they say there is a celebration,*
*In fulfilment of the occasion . . .'*

The other **anitos** accepted this gentle apology, and indeed there was little to apologise for in the party, at which were generously entertained in turn Salve '*the Castillian*', Estrella '*from Catanduanes*', Terri ('*fliratacious with a sharp tongue*') who teased the ladies on their beauty, Jerry ('*an unmarried man with four children – now how did that come about!*'), a number of dwarfs who had business with me, instructing me in healing, and the imposing and shadowy Maria Clara, '*come from the very top of the mountain near to Pasascao*'. As the evening closed in, these guests began to depart, and Tiang Delia reappeared in her own body to divide food and mark crosses on her community of patients. It was Don Alejandre, however, who, as it grew late, insisted on courteously accompanying me at a pace abnormally fast by Filipino standards along the muddy paths and rickety plank bridge, holding my hand in a powerful grip for which I will be eternally grateful, but gruffly avoiding extended conversation, and returned me to the town centre, where the cinema was showing a movie with Barbara Hershey.[3]

Contrast with this the birthdays, equally generous and entertaining, of the San Ignacio **saro**s. The year before my arrival, Clara had had her 'debutante' year (her seventeenth), at which one of the visiting healer's **saro**s, a mermaid, had enchanted the barangay children by dancing on her tail. Clara's 1989 party was festive and well attended by humans and spirits, but appropriately a little less extravagant, although the **bakla** (male transvestite) **saro** of one of the healers (not himself **bakla**) fascinated everyone with his elitist tastes. The barangay birthday I want to recall here, however, is that of Elsa's **saro** Seny, as related by my co-godmother Irene, who was working for Elsa at the time.

It was . . . a few days before the birthday of Elsa's **sanib**, the one we call Ate Seny . . . when Elsa was taken on a visit to Ilocos by her **sanib** . . . and the spirit that was left here in her place was a **bakla** . . . It was really amazing to see it Nell . . . In the evening, Elsa went to sleep and her husband Martin hadn't yet left the house to go on duty when Talen [a child] came running to me . . . '*Manoy Martin is calling for you, because Ate Elsa is already stiff!*' [i.e. like a corpse] . . . I went running!

Irene found the house in uproar and Elsa completely unconscious. At midnight, she recovered consciousness, but 'Elsa's spirit wasn't there any more, it had changed with that of a **bakla**'.

The **bakla** was to remain in Elsa's body for twenty-four hours, and behaved in all the ways characteristic of **bakla** among the humans:

He never smoked a "Hope"[4] cigarette down to the end; he lit them and threw them away . . . "Ho!" I said. "Your husband Martin's bed is over here, see?" "*Ay, my gracious!*" he said; "*I'm not going to get into bed with him! I don't even know him yet!*" Well, I said to myself, that's certainly not Elsa. It's Elsa's body but it's not her spirit . . .

(The next morning early there was a high-stake cockfight at the Nordia cockpit in Naga; women do not go to cockfights.)

The **bakla** said: '*I'm off to the cockfight, but I haven't any money at all. Ate Seny's about to have her birthday.. and Elsa hasn't got any money for the expenses, and I haven't any money whatsoever . . .*' So Joy [a neighbour] says: 'Ho, I'll lend you ten!' '*Ay, my goodness!*' says the **bakla**, '*I'm not taking your money, I wouldn't win with it.*' 'Hmm, well, up to you'. says Joy. 'If you want to go cockfighting with no money, you can sort out where you get hold of it from.' Well, the person he took a fancy to borrow it from was Manoy Kikoy [an old married man who runs a small shop]. '*Hoy, come here*', he says . . . '*can you lend me ten, because I'll be sure to give it straight back to you this afternoon, its a certainty*'. So he went off, dressed as a man.

The range of talents of the **bakla** spirit was revealed when he came back with more than P.300 worth of supplies for the **birthdayhan**, including sugar and sausage, and more money in his pocket. He had won P.400 at the cockfight and had not even had to spend on the fare, because (as one of the people we cannot see) the drivers of the tricycle and jeepney hadn't noticed him. The **bakla** announced that he was off, but that Ate Seny would be there soon, and fell asleep, waking up again as Elsa.

Elsa's own spirit, meanwhile, had been entertained by her **saro** for five spirit days in Ilocos, and had celebrated the birthday in a house so beautiful and with such lavish food 'You would have thought you were in Paradise.' The spirits had tried to persuade her to remain with them, but she had told them she had to return to her children, and had avoided eating the enchanted black spirit-rice (**palagayon**) which prevents humans from returning to the visible world. Back at home, Elsa celebrated the birthday party for her **saro** in San Ignacio, using the ingredients bought by the **bakla**.

In one sense, the contrast between these two stories strikingly illustrates the kind of differences in ways of thinking about and accessing power which I discussed in the previous chapter. To leave the analysis at that, however, would be to miss the point. Bicol healing is not just a formal structure or a logical problem, but a series of episodes in the lives of characters – human and **tawo** – tied in complex and subtle ways to each other. The conversations of each seance are anxiously focussed on finding an agreement and a cure for the patient, but mediumship or its avoidance is also its own point, both funny and serious. The alternation of gap and elision between the identities of healer and **saro** works like a pun, or like the gently sly Bicol jokes I recounted in the introduction, focussing on the ways identities are both combined and yet uncombinable. The 'voice' of the medium is above all perhaps in conversation with the 'voice' of her **saro**. And the sudden transformations of mediumship – within which switches in gender and other aspects of the person are echoes of the primary transformation of power – serve as a reminder that, whatever one might wish, it is the essence of the **tawo** to escape containment, and to continue to have the means to take one by surprise.

*ambiguity*

Perhaps it is partly for this reason that people in Bicol are in the end philosophical about changes in healing and seance styles. They may worry about the decline of the techniques of formally courteous speech, but they are not overly astonished, for it is the nature of the **tawo** always to elude complete definition. Mamay Etring is perhaps an unusually reflective older man – in his youth a musician for the **paraanitos**, but in his maturity an enquiring reader on religion and an active Catholic – and when I asked why the **paraanitos** had declined in numbers, he gave me a careful and religiously responsible answer.

All healing comes from God, and healing which comes 'direct' from God is the best, it's what people ought to use. But God also made all creation, including the 'temptations' and the 'malignos' and all those . . . These are also powers, you see, and God allows them to have their power and to give it out in healing . . . Now these **paraanitos**, these things that are called **paradivata**, these **saro**s like your Manay Auring's . . . God allows first one of them and then another to have their day[5] . . . and that's why some of them are 'finished' now, and now you will see others that are walking around.

# PART III

SAINTS AND THE DEAD

# 7

## The living and the dead

### Death and mourning in Calabanga

In this section, I will consider the idea of death and the processes of burial and mourning in Calabanga, and also local Catholicism and devotional relationships with the saints. The one must necessarily precede the other, since so many popular religious practices in Bicol and the lowland Philippines generally are concerned with Lent, and especially the period between Good Friday and Easter Sunday, the period of the death of Christ ending with his resurrection. In Calabanga, which is a minor pilgrimage centre for much of the Bicol area, many religious practices and experiences centre on the local shrine to the Christ **Hinulid**; that is, the recumbent figure of Christ taken down from the cross and laid out in death. The statue of the **Amang Hinulid**, whose shrine adjoins San Ignacio, has healing and other miraculous powers.

In San Ignacio, as in any barangay in Calabanga, funerals are a regular and public event. Most of them seem to come in the winter before harvest, when food is shorter and the old and frail perhaps a little weaker; but infant mortality is high and children die at all times of the year. If you do not know the family of the deceased person, the funeral will be announced by the mournful, squeaky marches of the little brass band which plays at every town funeral, always the same tune. The procession of band, car or cart, the distraught family clinging to the coffin and the neighbours following at a distance can be heard approaching and receding down the long road which comes from the river estuary to the west and passes towards the centre of town and the church. It is a neighbourly duty to walk in a funeral procession, since it shows that the dead person had many friends, and as I will describe, it is a duty too to attend the wakes. For if the dead person were at all known to you, by the time of the funeral you will already have visited the wake at least once, to help out, to look at the corpse, and to gamble. Even as a visitor, I attended more than ten funerals during my first fieldwork, and viewed many more in passing.

In discussing death, funerals and bereavement in Calabanga, I am immediately forced to confront again the complex and often ambivalent tone of Bicol culture, shaped by the colonial history of the Philippines. The understanding of death was, according to historians, one key arena in which battles were fought out between Filipinos and their colonisers. Pre-colonially, it appears, Filipinos thought of the dead as passing into an undifferentiated afterlife, represented as being located at the end of a long river journey in an integrated sacred cosmology (see, e.g., Magos, 1986:86–105; Alcina, 1668: Book 3: 181–95). Rafael (1988: 167–9) argues that the central event of the Spanish conversion process was the intrusion of the idea of sin, confession, heaven and hell. While reconstructing the notions of sin and penance that the religious wished to foist upon them, argues Rafael, Filipinos were partly drawn to accept Catholicism because of its promise of a good afterlife, achieved via a good death. Heaven itself was given an indigenous reinterpretation in early Filipino-language devotional texts, becoming a place of perfectly realised exchange relations. Yet, says Rafael, the idea of heaven itself created a central change in thinking, since it promised an escape from the possibility of endless predation in the afterlife by **aswang**[1] and other spirits. The integration into the Filipino cultural repertoire of texts such as the **Pasion** (the Passion story in verse in Filipino languages), which, as Ileto's landmark study (1979) records, were woven into the idioms of Tagalog peasant uprisings, began with this acceptance and appropriation of the Christian concept of death.

Syncretic development was not in this case, if it ever is, homogenous and complete, however. It will emerge in this chapter that 'pre-colonial' ideas, such as the desirability of cultivating and propitiating dead ancestors in their benevolent aspect, still form a strand of thinking at present even in Bicol, which is less notable for this than parts of the Visayas. In addition, although it is not my intention to examine Rafael's admirable argument in great detail here, I will suggest that my findings in Bicol do not quite square with the stress he places on the adoption of an unequivocal idea of the afterlife in Filipino popular conversion.

Moreover, the second, American colonial period and the present construction of Filipino–Western relations have rendered the Spanish/Catholic as well as the pre-Spanish/non-Catholic aspects of ideas about death more problematic. I have already argued in the previous section that Bicolanos have a complex attitude to what they believe and what they will say they believe. As I show in the ethnography which follows, in the context of a death, people would sometimes emphatically reclaim beliefs (in the **aswang** for instance) and observances (such as **palihion**) which in daily life they ignore or even deny, and which when talking about what happens at a death they will not say that they do.[2] Peoples' awareness of what is considered 'superstitious' by the lights of Western values (as filtered through primary school teaching especially) may have contributed at first to their inhibitions in talking to me about death-practices. However, the gap between what people did and what they were able to say they did persisted even with people I was close to, and who knew all my odd interests; I am sure that I reflected this ambivalence about belief rather than provoking it.

In this, as in other aspects of the ethnography, I have therefore tried not to smooth away too much of the uncertainty and the 'ad hoc' feel of actions and opinions that I remember, since in itself this seems an important characteristic of the situation.

If the people I knew maintained a somewhat difficult relationship with customs and beliefs, however, they were in another sense much readier to talk about death than people in European/American cultures. Another aspect of the material which I wish to bring out is the Bicol treatment of grief as an emotion, and its proper expression.

Except for close relatives during wakes and funerals, Bicolanos do not value the dramatic expression or reliving of grief, but they do think it natural for the experience of bereavement to be often talked about and asked about. The questions I asked people about their bereavements were almost never reluctantly answered; but they were answered with calm, sometimes even with smiles; the strong emotions they described were usually conveyed not so much by tone of voice as by the content of the story itself, and by the idioms of mourning and mediated separation between the living and the dead which I describe here.

I will not be discussing here in detail the subject of deaths caused by the people we cannot see, since these were treated in the previous section. However, it should be noted that spirits played a part in many of the deaths I talk about here; the **tawo** 'took' Ilar's son Toto, for instance, and also played a part in the death of Catalina Dominguez (see chapter eight). Seances to talk to the dead are of course conducted by local healers.

Because of the complexity of these attitudes to death and the Christian saints, I have divided this section into three chapters, which cover the way death appears at a number of different moments. In the first, I describe funerals and discuss the relationship between the living and the dead. In the second, I explore the particular identification which is made between Bicolano funerals and the death of Christ, and describe the cult of the **Amang Hinulid** which centres on Lent devotions, the 'reading' of the **Pasion** and the passion-play. In the third, I view healing devotions to the **Ama** and the saints somewhat more broadly, considering the ways in which identification with the **Ama** is extended through kinship and patronage idioms which incorporate an idealised reciprocity.

The most immediate context in which death must be seen, however, is that of the poverty of these people which so often causes it, and it is with this that I shall begin this section.

## Death and 'those who have nothing'

My three children died . . . of too much neediness.

Many people in Bicol die early because they are poor; they live in a country which is economically marginal in the world, and within that country they are themselves in a marginal position. In small towns like Calabanga, the fragility of people's position is highly visible.

One aspect of this marginality is that many known murders of poor people never come into the courts. They are arranged (**areglado**) unofficially by the parties concerned. In many cases, an extra-judicial agreement will be drawn up by the local police or the fiscal general (public prosecutor), in which the complainant states that he or she does not wish to proceed with prosecution, providing that certain conditions are kept by the person accused. Where murder is concerned, this is almost always a compensation payment to the widow and family. These vary somewhat according to the circumstances of the death, but much more according to the wealth of the dead man. If he was someone with a little education and a regular income, the payments would be quite high (₱.20,000.000–₱.50,000.000.) But if he was a poor man with low earning potential, and his killer a rich man, his family would be expected to settle for derisory amounts of a few thousand pesos. The poorer the family, the more desperately they will need the money to pay for immediate expenses. A decent funeral might easily cost ₱.6,000.00 in an area where a family of six often survives on ₱.50.00 per day, besides which the family must pay for a burial plot in the cemetery (**Kampusanto**). As a friend put it:

The relatives will be told by the rich man's representative – 'Have you got a lawyer? – who is going to fight for you down there?' – and the poor family will think of the expenses of the lawyer, and they will give up . . . (Bea)

Consequently, for the rich and unscrupulous there is little legal or economic disincentive to killing a poor and powerless person if they have
some reason for doing so, and I heard of at least three cases of this kind
betwen 1988 and 1989; no doubt there were many more.

In addition, people's limited ability to raise cash loans often delays or
prevents their attendance at hospital, even in the most serious emergency,
since they know that the burden of debt placed on their family in paying
for treatment may be ruinous. Being admitted to hospital is often an experience of financial as well as medical fear and shame, while communication problems between staff and patients whose categories for disease may
be widely divergent mean that many barangay people die or watch their
relatives die without even being certain of the scientific diagnosis.

Like most mothers in the barangay, Nana Sining has lost several children. On the death anniversary of her son, who died aged five, she remembered what had happened:

He was taken by the people we cannot see because he was handsome and full of
chatter (**madaldal**). He got a fever . . . Lino [her husband] and I had taken him to
hospital in Naga City. When he died, Lino picked him up and carried him cradled
against his shoulder (**kulkul**), and took him out of the hospital . . . I wanted to go
after him, but this nurse stopped me . . . she took me into her office and kept on
interviewing me about how I was going to pay . . . The child had just died and she
wouldn't stop interviewing me . . . I saw Lino outside, so I ran out . . . Then none of
the drivers would let us ride the jeepney when they knew the child was dead,
though it was already evening . . . So we said he was still breathing and we were
taking him to the healer, and we wrapped him up so no one could see his face . . .
When the two of us got down at the corner, we couldn't do anything but cry . . .

## Funerals in Bicol: calling the dead, embalming and the *aswang*

At a funeral, it's as if you pity the dead, and your feelings are heavy . . .

Wakes and funerals in Calabanga, and with some variations throughout
Bicol, follow a fairly set pattern. Most people die at home. If the crisis is
foreseen, relatives will be sent for, and the house will be full of the person's
family at the time of their death; otherwise, telegrams will be sent immediately to summon home children working in Manila, or other close relatives
who are not at home. Meanwhile, in all but the poorest of families the
body will have been embalmed and laid out with hired funeral furniture in
the upstairs of the house by a commercial embalmer. Bamboo poles and
tarpaulins are used to form a temporary roof which extends the house at
the side or the front, and a black sign bearing the dead person's name is

written up on a prominent part of the structure. From this point, when visiting begins, until the corpse is buried, the house is referred to as **sa gadan**, the dead person's house, and not by either the name of the deceased, or the name of the living relatives. Gambling tables are set up under the tarpaulin, and family, friends and neighbours have an obligation to visit the bereaved to keep them company, and to gamble (an otherwise illegal activity), since a tenth of the winnings goes to the bereaved family as a contribution towards their expenses. The possibility of legal gambling is one of the great attractions of wakes, but people in the barangay emphasise that in performing these duties, and later walking in the funeral procession, they are 'helping each other out'.

As people arrive at the wake, each will approach the coffin, which is partly open, to look at the deceased, and often to drop a small money contribution into a glass or jar. Much importance is placed by Bicolanos on the appearance of the corpse and the expression on their face (see below); they fear to find a frightening-looking grimace, and the interpretation of the facial expression is the subject both of open discussion at the wake, and of private gossip and dark insinuation after leaving it. The body itself is usually embalmed, and is always made up and dressed in formal clothes, to present the best possible appearance.[3]

In theory, a wake demands an all-night vigil, but in practice when wakes extend over as much as a week, the close relatives will snatch a few hours' sleep each night. Even so, I have never seen the last guests leave a wake before one or two in the morning, and in fact there is a strong if unverbalised imperative not to leave the bereaved family alone with the corpse for the hours of darkness, but to fill the house with light, noise and activity, while the visitors in turn must be sustained with drinks and snacks. Inevitably, though, the family will be grey and exhausted by the day of the funeral.

A death will almost always provoke property disputes. If a parent has not allocated a property division during their lifetime, the regulation of inheritance should be settled by harmonious discussion (**urulay**) among the group of siblings (**magturugang**), guided by the eldest. However since property should be equally divided between siblings, and the conventions governing how this should be done are fairly fluid, in many cases acrimonious disputes concerning land smoulder on throughout the funeral period. These undercurrents of potential fissure of the sibling group exacerbate the atmosphere of loss and mourning for the parent.

The last night of the wake always draws the biggest crowd of people; even those who have paid one visit already should pay another if the dead person is close to them. On the following day, the funeral car and the musicians will arrive at an arranged time. The car is usually an imitation of the white American Cadillac, often somewhat battered, but the musicians are local, and almost always drunk. They comprise saxophone, trumpet, a Bicol variant on the trombone, and drum, always playing the same sad but pompous march tune for every funeral. In the case of a more expensive funeral, the funeral car will have a tape recorder in it with American-style funeral music of the 'choirs of angels' type playing loudly, and so the result is complete cacophony until the funeral car draws far enough ahead of the musicians.

Funeral processions (**dapit**) walk from the barangay to the town centre for the Requiem Mass; this takes about three quarters of an hour and is a slow, hot business. After the Mass, the procession then walks again to the **Kampusanto**, which is situated outside the town, for the burial. Unless given a special fee affordable only by the wealthy, the priest never comes to the burial.

The key emotional points of the ritual thus all take place without the priest, for there are three moments at which weeping and calling the deceased (**manambitan**) takes place. These are: at the moment of death, when eerie wails are likely to resound round the barangay; at the moment when the dead body is brought out of the house and put onto the funeral

Figure 5 Closing the coffin for the last time

car; and at the moment when the coffin is put into the waiting tomb. If the close relatives do not weep at these moments, there are two possible interpretations: either through some fault of their own or the deceased's they are not grieving, or they are known to be upset, but they have 'hard tears' and are unable to weep. Failing to weep in this way is thought to be quite dangerous for the health, and to result in swooning and other ill effects.

Embalming is now standard for all but the poorest families. Bicolanos say that it has the advantage that the body can be kept for longer, the wake extended, and relatives far away can be sent for in time, but there are also probably other advantages, not only in terms of status, but in relation to traditional beliefs about the fate of the dead (see below). In the recent past, and in the case of very poor families today, the coffin will be made not by a commercial firm but by a local carpenter, the corpse will be deodorised with flowers or coffee, and the wake will only last one night before the burial. The inclusion of the Requiem Mass also used not to be a matter of course, but in any barangay within reach of a parish church it is now expected.

After the burial, some of the guests will return to the house for a meal. In theory, all the closely connected guests are expected for this meal, but in practice whether people attend or not will depend partly on their assessment of their status relative to that of the dead person.

The case of Teresita's funeral which follows illustrates some of the ways in which an actual death precipitates observances which are otherwise ignored or denied. It also addresses the question of how much tension there still is in ideas about the afterlife, and how far they depart from Catholic orthodoxy.

In this connection, the question of belief in the **aswang** is of great historical significance. Sixteenth-century Bicolanos were said to believe in **aswang** as the source of all evil and sickness, especially prone to consume the entrails of little children and sick people, and also to torment them after death (Castano, 1895:30–5). The **aswang** belief was considered by Lynch as particularly Bicolano, and was reported by him in 1949 in similar terms; the **aswang** feeds off the mortally ill, especially their phlegm, and off the flesh and blood of the newly dead (Lynch, 1949:402). While Castano describes **aswang** as a spirit with monstrous assistants, Lynch's informants thought of **aswang** as a witch-like condition of persons, subdivided into 'walking' and 'flying' types.[4] In both the historic and modern accounts, much stress is placed on the fact that **aswang** consume their victims by sucking their entrails, usually with a pointed snout and through cracks in the house floor (Castano, 1895:22; Lynch, 1949:403).

Most pertinent to this chapter are two points concerning the ways of protecting the dead against **aswang**. Firstly, it is to guard against the consumption of dead bodies by **aswang** that the living are enjoined to keep vigil over the recently dead.[5] Secondly, the bodies of important chiefs in pre-Hispanic practice were protected from the predations of the **aswang** by the removal of their viscera. These were placed in a jar guarded by a slave and hidden, so that they could not be consumed (Gerona, 1988b:33–4). This form of embalming was also intended to preserve bodies while a feast was prepared, and the bodies, at least in the Tagalog regions, were also decorated, perfumed and dressed in their best clothes as a mark of respect (Rafael, 1988:188).

In Calabanga, people were usually reluctant to talk about **aswang**, although they would be mentioned spontaneously when events seemed to point to their activities. I was told that they seek out the dying, especially those with tuberculosis, and anyone who takes a long time to die, and 'sniff' them (rather than suck them).[6] As to what effect this produced on the dead, people wouldn't – or couldn't – say; it was something vague, but horrible. The living assaulted by **aswang** might, it was clear, be killed or made **aswang** themselves, but the fate of the dead 'sniffed' by the **aswang** seemed to be literally unspeakable for my informants.[7] The possibility that **aswang** might attack the dead was strongly denied at those times when a wake was taking place, and people considered my questions about it either silly or unseemly. As the discussion of Teresita's, Calixta's and Loreta's funerals show, however, the spectre of the **aswang** seems still to be acknowledged in practice if not in words, in a number of ways.

**The death of Teresita: customs relating to death**
Teresita was in her late eighties, and living with her son and her daughter-in-law, Auring. After some months' decline, she became bedridden, and was put on a wooden frame bed to one side of the main room of the house. When it was clear that she was near death, Teresita's elderly spinster sister and her niece arrived from Partido to pay a last visit. The crisis came very quickly. However, she did not lose consciousness, nor did her eyes roll upwards in her head in the way Bicolanos find so frightening at the moment of death.

During the period after Teresita had taken to her bed[8] Auring had been dropping hints to the effect that she had seen or felt **aswang** approaching the house at night. Her neighbours, who often said there were no **aswang** any more in that area, were surprised but not openly sceptical to be told that there were several around.

When the old lady stopped breathing there was an immediate **sibot** (commotion). First Auring rushed down the steps out into the yard. People told me it was no good for a healer to be in the house when someone dies: the healer would be 'startled' and 'the blessing will leave/be lost' so that her patients would never recover, I was told, but nobody could be clear about why this was. Neighbours and family ran towards the house where mourning cries were going up. Then Teresita's relatives washed her, and at ten that evening the professional embalmers arrived with their bottles.

Whether because of the influence of Teresita's elderly sister, family tastes, or because of Auring and Clara, many more **palihion** (taboos/ beliefs) were kept and spoken of than one usually observed in San Ignacio. From the moment of Teresita's death all mirrors were turned to the wall,[9] and everyone was told not to wash or comb their hair until at least a night after the funeral. Children did not perform **bisa**, the usual way of showing respect by pressing an older person's hand to your forehead: and during the endless washing-up which accompanied the feeding of the visitors, plates could not be stacked up to drain. As usual in Bicol, no one was allowed to sweep the house while the body was still inside.[10] All these things were to prevent there being 'others following after'; i.e. to prevent other deaths within the same house.

While a body is in the house, all the living relatives will take naps crammed together on one sleeping-mat, keeping a light burning. Despite this safety in numbers, the children still felt nervous. Noel, Auring's youngest, feared that his dead grandmother would visit him and refused to look at her body until just before the funeral. Then, seeing the old lady arrayed in her make-up and best dress, with her religious medals on a ribbon round her neck, he declared with relief that 'Inay looks beautiful now with her lipstick on.'[11]

Teresita's daughter Florida arrived on the second evening of the wake with a large number of women from the coastal barangay of which she is captain. Florida poured out gin and encouraged her companions to drink from the circulating glass, and soon two of them began entertain themselves and the mourners with a **sara-sala'on** – a ribald variation on Bicolano riddling games:[12]

Interrogator: What colour's your underwear then? [lifting a skirt].
  Reply: Red!
  Int: And whose underwear is it?
  Reply: It's Manay Gina's of course . . .

Int: How many did you manage when you got in?
Reply: Managed three! [raising three fingers, the centre one protruding phalli-
cally above the other two].

The funeral was held after several days. The musicians and the funeral
car arrived at about one in the afternoon. As always, the removal of the
coffin from the house to begin the funeral journey produced an outburst of
emotion. As the coffin was brought downstairs, Auring collapsed inside
the house amidst all the crying, and when people rushed to revive her, it
was her **saro** Clara who spoke, asking to be taken downstairs and out of
the house. *'What's the matter with Aurelia, that's an unchancy thing that she
should be possessed when there's a dead person in the house'*, cried out her
sister-in-law. Clara in Auring's body came down the steps looking
annoyed, and went off on her own for a little while, and the alarm passed.
Later, people had put things together; Clara must have wanted to pay her
respects to the dead woman too; Auring said that she had felt pains in her
legs just before she collapsed, and other people agreed that they had too;
in some unspecific way these were attributed to proximity to the dead
person.

As the coffin was brought down the steps, a woman from a nearby
barangay who was a sister-in-law of Teresita[13] started fainting in the way
that mourners are said to do when they cannot let out their grief in crying.
Several people reached out to pull her hair on top of her head in order to
stop her passing out.[14] The general impression was that everyone was
exhausted from the vigil of the wake, and overwrought.

During the mass, the priest as usual conspicuously sprinkled the body
and coffin with holy water several times, and passed clouds of incense
from the censer over it. This 'blessing' of the body is important to
Bicolanos,[15] and is quite likely to be mentioned by them as a feature of the
funeral, whereas I never heard anyone discuss the standard Catholic
orthodoxy of importance of the Mass in speeding the soul's passage
through Purgatory.

At the burial (not attended by a priest), all of Teresita's children wept in
the **manambitan**, and some of her grandchildren. Her second son Lino
kept asking her, 'Mother, pardon us please . . .' while his wife held up the
smaller children to look into the coffin, saying, 'Mother, are you leaving us
behind now, mother?' The coffin swayed back and forth towards the tomb
mouth, and was finally placed inside.

After the funeral was concluded, people talked it over, and one of
Teresita's small great-grandchildren recalled the priest censing the body:

'He blessed it, didn't he', the child said to his aunts, and then, mistaking the word for smoke (**asohan**), 'He "**aswanged**" it . . . ?'

The child's mistake I think indicates something about the partly unspoken view of death which persists in Bicol, as a time of the application of beliefs, understandings and practices which are normally denied or forgotten. Naughty children may be disciplined with stories of the **aswang**, but at times like this it becomes a present reality for even those adults who class themselves as 'sceptics'.

### Embalming, the look of the corpse and the moment of death

They've been putting lipstick on her, but she still looks miserable!

I have said that in pre-Hispanic practice, embalming was apparently connected to protection against the **aswang** and involved evisceration, body decoration and perfuming. This also enabled the wake to be prolonged, and a status-enhancing feast prepared. The treatment of dead bodies in the lowlands has always combined the aspect of preserving them with that of deodorising and decorating them, making them beautiful. Thus, sixteenth-century Tagalogs used body decoration as a way of paying respect to the dead (Rafael, 1988:188). Although I cannot make any judgements about actual historical developments in burial practices, it is interesting to note that contemporary embalming as practised by the poor has some similar motivations.

When I asked people why embalming was important, they gave me a variety of replies. The most obvious concerned status; embalming, they said, used to be confined to the rich[16] and had only recently become something the poor feel obliged to afford. It allowed the body to be kept longer, and hence meant all the members of a sibling-group could gather together even when they had to come from far away. Another sort of reply was given to me less often and in lowered tones; some people, they said, claimed that embalming prevented the dead soul from coming back to the body, 'although of course dead souls did not usually come back in any case'. A third sort of reply was borne out by all the activity surrounding the corpse; embalming allowed the body to be 'set right'; it made it more 'beautiful' and allowed it to look more as if it were 'only asleep'; it dispensed with the need for a binding cloth to tie shut the mouth.

All these replies are important, and their implications will be drawn out in the remainder of this chapter. Bicolano embalming is at present carried out by commercial funeral companies which also make up the corpse and hire out hearses, make carved and gilded coffins, etc. The embalmers remove the blood of the corpse with a crude hollow skewer and hand pump, pumping the blood from the body into one jar and from the 'stomach' (abdominal cavity) into another. Formalin is pumped in as the blood is pumped out, and if the wake is a specially long one they also remove the viscera. The relatives then take the blood and bury it secretly somewhere on the houseplot. Concern about the removal and hiding of the stomach blood/viscera therefore plays a part in contemporary as well as[17] historical practice, although in Calabanga people did not wish to connect this directly with the **aswang**. I will suggest, however, that these ideas may still be linked indirectly as part of the way in which people react to death.

If the removal of the stomach is one important aspect of embalming, the other is the appearance of the corpse and especially the expression on the dead person's face. This attentiveness to facial expression is itself linked to the idea of the moment of death.

The state of being near death is called in Bicol **agaw-buhay** (snatching at life), a phrase which conveys something like 'at his last gasp' does in English. The moment of death seems to be imagined as the process of struggling for breath before it leaves the body, and of the turning up of eyes in the head or other physical signs. For Bicolanos, the stiffening of the body is of great importance in establishing that someone is really dead; a dead person who does not stiffen may be merely suffering from soul-loss and be recallable from the spirit-world (see below).

As well as fearing to look at the dead person in their coffin, many people are also afraid to watch the moment of death; what is it, however, that they fear to see?

Two contrasting cases help to answer this question in part. The death of one woman in the barangay, Loreta, was regarded as a particularly peaceful one. Loreta had taken the last rites (though it is common for Bicolanos not to do so). The relatives and female neighbours at her bedside heard the beating of wings as she died. The dying woman had also heard it, and the women attending her, despite seeing her eyes turn upwards, knew therefore that she was only following the flight of the angel taking her soul to heaven. Loreta's wake was well attended but decorous; her children, grandchildren and great-grandchildren all gathered together, and large numbers of neighbours walked with the funeral procession.

At the wake, it was conspicuous how everyone agreed that the dead woman in her coffin looked peaceful and unfrightening, as though she were only sleeping (**turog sana**).

Loreta's death seemed to be viewed by everyone as unthreatening; she was old, and her death had been neither unexpected nor preceded by long-drawn-out or gruesome illness. She had put most of her affairs in order, and her husband was still alive so no major quarrels over property ensued (although see below for an account of tensions over her jewellery). She was liked and respected, and known to be good and sympathetic to others, and so she left no terrible resentments in the barangay.

People noted with satisfaction that she had seen all her children married before she died. This is important; there are a number of stories in Bicol of mothers who came back from the dead because with a child, especially a daughter, unmarried, they had undischarged duties troubling them. The only problem was her youngest daughter Margie, who lived on her parents' houseplot. Margie and her husband Salvador were a stable couple, with their third child due when Loreta died. But problems in Salvador's own family had prevented them from ever celebrating a church wedding or living with his parents, and the family relied a great deal on Loreta for moral and practical support.

This was the background to the one element which disturbed Loreta's peaceful funeral, Margie's violent display of grief at the **manambitan**. She had attended the funeral although it is often said that pregnant women should avoid them, and at the burial she had to be carried away from the tomb, to which she was clinging, refusing to let go of her mother's coffin. She was hoarse with weeping, and was howling barely comprehensible words of grief:

Inay . . . I won't leave my mother here . . . surely we will go hungry now, mother . . . who will cook rice for us now . . . who will be my companion to the cinema . . . Mother!

It was noticeable that Margie shunned her husband and children; it was her brother who eventually half-dragged her away from the tomb. As she was pulled towards the cemetery gate, she shouted out angrily: '*Mother! If Salvador leaves me, who will look after us now?*'

As we left the **Kampusanto**, people were watching Margie; 'Now, that's what you'd call emotional', commented one of the men, between disapproval and sympathy. Everyone knew that Margie's situation was the reason for her terrible grief: although poor Salvador showed no signs of leaving her, the loss of her mother's guaranteed protection made her 'incomplete' marriage seem suddenly precarious.

In strong contrast was the death of Calixta, the second wife of the former barangay head. The whole barangay was awakened during the small hours by the wailing of her niece Pacita, who had been looking after her, and by the concerted howling of all the local dogs. The next morning, everyone assumed that the dogs had sensed an **aswang** passing down the road, and several people who earlier had blankly denied the existence of such things, said they had been afraid to open their windows, in case they should let it in.

Since Calixta had lingered paralysed for two years before dying, the presence of the **aswang** was thought especially likely. This long illness was for some a sign of her own misdeeds; perhaps she had swallowed mercury (**asuete**) which magically impedes death. Perhaps God was punishing her ungenerous words and deeds to her poorer neighbours by refusing to let her die; for if one '*oppresses one's fellow-men . . . it's as if you've run up a debt, and now the time has come when you have to pay it back again*'.

Others less hostile to Calixta argued that it was her husband's failings rather than her own which were the long-outstanding debt that had kept her in this world. He had abandoned his first wife before she died, and he neglected his second during her illness also; many said he was already seeking a replacement. The lavishness of the funeral arrangements, and the sudden (and temporary) piety of the widower certainly suggested an uneasy conscience. Nonetheless, Calixta's appearance in her coffin was not judged satisfactory: '**Dawa piglipstican na, garo mamundo pa**' ('They've been putting lipstick on her but she still looks miserable') was the verdict of those who went to pay their respects to the dead woman. After the funeral, there was a special mass 'to take with her',[18] and an unusually elaborate set of mysteries sung for Calixta.[19]

So far, then, it appears that what the Bicolanos are afraid to see in the face of a corpse is an expression of someone who has parted from life with their obligations to others, or others' obligations to them, unmet, with ties or debts of resentment or loving anxiety still binding them and the living together. They also fear to see the marks of struggle and suffering which result from a long illness which can often be associated with a sinister supernatural penance, the payment of debts before one is 'discharged' into death.

The way in which the **agaw-buhay** is envisaged seems to bear the marks of Spanish Catholicism, at least in the more pious interpretations which are offered. The image of Loreta's eyes following the upward path of the angel which will take her soul to heaven is compatible with many standard Catholic textbooks on the good death.[20] However, the bad death of Calixta is less clearly compatible with Catholic orthodoxy, attended as it is by **aswang**. Moreover, the idea of Calixta as suffering for her sins not after death, in Purgatory, but before she is able to die, as well as the similarity of ideas current in stock stories in Bicol (the wicked rich man who was seen dragging leg irons as he worked his ricefields, etc.), suggests a somewhat different ordering of the relationship between this life and the afterlife, and of the notion of sin.

If Teresita's death brought out the Bicolano ambivalence over **palihion**, Calixta's and Loreta's illustrate the complexity of attitudes to the moment of death itself. Although people in Calabanga reject a direct link between embalming and the **aswang**, they appear to connect them indirectly. Embalming prevents the dead soul returning to the body, and makes the appearance of the corpse less frightening to the living. But a prolonged death is frightening both because it suggests notions of wrongdoing and unpaid debts, and because it suggests the presence of **aswang**. Moreover, it is the visits to the living of those who died uneasily which are most feared. The return of dead souls and the fear of **aswang** thus seem to be more blurred than people's overt statements would suggest.[21]

In the remaining part of this chapter, I consider in more detail encounters between the living and the dead, ranging from the controlled to the uncontrolled and the feared to the sought-after.

### The problem of the next world, and the ability of the dead to come back

You never see **kalag** face on and they cannot speak.

Unlike European Catholics in Portugal (Pina-Cabral, 1986:228–9) or Spain (Christian, 1972:138–45; Catedra 1992; 289–91) rural Bicolanos rarely mention, or elaborate by anything they do, the question of the destination of the soul in heaven, hell or purgatory.[22] In fact, I never heard anyone mention Purgatory spontaneously, and only one woman in the barangay, a former catechist, responded to the notion when I put it forward. But the same woman told me that the dead:

. . . are out there in the darkness (**kadikloman**) they say; they cannot speak and cannot see anything . . .

I have argued that Bicolanos think of God punishing the living and not allowing them to die until they have paid their debts; although I was rarely able to persuade people to speculate openly about what happens to the dead in the abstract, this notion of 'the darkness' is one which recurred explicitly and by implication. A person who is asked straight-on about what happens to souls, will usually say that they go to heaven immediately (or to 'wherever they are going' – a euphemism which includes hell); people often add that if it rains after the death this is a good sign, since the heavens will be open and it will be somehow easier for the soul to fly upwards. But if someone spontaneously imagines the dead without being asked, the idea of heaven or hell almost always seems to be absent. Thus Irene Mojares, quoted above, told me how each All Souls' Day she (like all families visiting the **Kampusanto**) will light candles on the shared tomb of her three children so that they will be able to 'see their way back' to the world of the living; otherwise they will remain in darkness, this rather amorphous **kadikloman**. Another possible location for some of the dead is, as I have explained, the world of the spirits, which is similar if only in that it is amorphously imagined and evasively spoken of.[23]

I am focussing, then, on one aspect of the notion of the afterlife which presents it as a vague darkness, and of the helpless dead unable to speak or to see (both connected with Bicol idioms of power and the ability to negotiate among the living) except in seances or through dreams. This seems to fit suggestively with the facility shown by the Bicol dead for crossing back into life.

Death is often described as a reversible process; the moment of death itself can be uncertain and deceptive. Irene Mojares described the death of her first husband in these terms:

You know, he was **agaw-buhay** three times and recovered; three times he came back to life . . . three times we changed him, because he was dead already, we matched his feet together because he was really already dead, but he still lived . . . he overcame it . . . Then, the fourth time, yes now, the final death . . .

This image of death as uncertain and reversible is extended by the idea that the dead return to the house of their living family on the third day after burial.[24] Although many people will say out of context that they do not believe that the dead return, there are equal numbers of people prepared to discuss instances. One local schoolteacher, who had been suddenly widowed, described how her daughter had heard someone rattling the door-latch on the third evening after the funeral; she instantly realised it was the **kalag** (dead person's soul). '*Husband*', she said, '*don't come back here to visit us; I will look after our children; go back to wherever you are going to . . .*'

Another woman, Maria, described how she had been her father-in-law's favourite when he was alive, and had seen him visit the house after his death. 'I was alone in the house and I saw Dad climb up the steps out of the corner of my eye; I screamed and ran out onto the road.' Maria also saw him for months afterwards in dreams, and he several times gave her numbers to bet on in the **Jueteng** lottery game.

**Kalag** may want to help their living relatives, but in almost all cases contact with them is dangerous, which is why they must be firmly instructed to keep away. Asing remembers talking to her beloved maternal grandmother when she was about to die: '*I said: "Old one, when you die, don't come back, because we'll be afraid of you." "All right, I won't", she said. So we weren't afraid and we were even able to use her blanket on the night she died.*'

In most cases, though, the visits of the dead to those they love cannot be prevented in advance, and they are always likely to cause sickness and death. Babies wear amulets to guard against the inappropriate attentions of their dead grandparents and great-grandparents. Anyone, adult or child, can be made sick by the 'pity' of their forebears, and anyone who struggles or cries out in their sleep should be wakened at once, as they may be suffering from **om'om**, a dream in which a dead relative asks you to go with them, which can prove fatal.

Florida's son Jaime, an eighteen-year-old who dived for seashells as a living, suffered danger when a close friend, another novice diver, died suddenly.

The beginning of Jaime's illness was, he got a shock . . . the two of them had been out on a bike together on the afternoon his friend died . . . He was a kind-hearted lad . . . They were friends . . . If [the dead boy] didn't have enough to eat, he would eat with us . . . If his father was angry with him, he would come here to let it pass . . .

Possibly weakened by the strains which diving without equipment places on even young bodies, Jaime's friend turned cold and breathless and collapsed without warning of a heart attack. Jaime was elsewhere, and Florida steadied herself to break the news to her son, who at first didn't seem to be affected.

Then little by little he began to think about it . . . in the evening, I was cooking small shrimp, he said his chest hurt and he was very cold, and he felt very weak . . . He was terribly pale, so I slapped him to bring him out of it, but he didn't come back to himself at once . . .

Florida took Jaime to all sorts of medical specialists and healers. She discovered that he was affected by a spirit as well as by a **kalag**.

But the first thing that accompanied him was the **kalag** of the dead boy . . . We called a medium and held a seance with food offerings. I talked it over with him, I said, '*Don't make Jaime ill, he's a friend of yours . . . It's true that you were not long for this world; well at least you won't wear yourself out in a life of diving . . .*'

Jaime's friend agreed to relinquish his old companion, asking in return only that '*he didn't want us to summon him by name all the time, because formerly we always named him when we told his story*'.[25] One should always be careful in naming the dead, but there is something especially sad in the prematurely dead teenager unable to resist the lure of the living calling his name. Once they stopped, Jaime began slowly to recover, though he is still 'nervous' of the places where he used to dive with his dead friend.

### Controlled encounters between the living and the dead

There are three contexts in which encounters between the living and the dead are controlled and voluntarily sought by the living; these are seances, the prayers and observances for the dead after the funeral (including the **Pistang Kalag**), and in the rather rare continuing instances of the practice of keeping bones in the house.

Seances with the dead, conducted through the local mediums who most often deal with illness caused by the people we cannot see, are held quite often in the area of Bicol where I lived. I never however witnessed one directly, because they tend to be rather private family affairs and I did not live with a recently bereaved family. Seances may be held for two reasons: either because it becomes clear that an illness is partly or wholly caused by **kalag**, or because the family needs to speak to their dead relative.

During my stay in San Ignacio, Marilyn, a teenage girl whose father had died prematurely some eight years before, became seriously ill with liver disease. As well as being taken to the doctor, she was treated by a healer, who discovered that her illness was partly caused by her father pitying her; this was confirmed by the fact that a drunk had seen her father in the plot behind her house where she had been sitting on the evening she became ill. A **tulod** was held, for the **kalag** as well as for the spirits, and her father was also asked to leave her alone so as not to make his daughter ill.

It seems likely that illness caused by ancestral **kalag** is less often diagnosed by healers now practising in Calabanga than it was by their predecessors; in the recent past, divination for **kalag** was quite widely used, the method involving reciting the names of dead relatives, while letting a pair of scissors hang over a winnowing-basket; if the scissors moved, the name of that **kalag** could be added to the list of those causing illness. People say that they sometimes asked for masses or mysteries, but I have no examples of this happening at present or in my informants' recollections. In this as in other respects, there is a contrast between Calabanga and Libmanan, where ancestral **kalag** still crop up with some regularity.

There are many cases in Calabanga, however, of seances held to establish communication with a dead relative. This may often be because relatives want to know why someone has died; in the case of Manuelita's fisherman husband, who died when their two daughters were tiny, for instance, it was only through talking to him in seance that she was able to learn that the **tawo** of his fishing-grounds were responsible for his death, having taken him to the invisible world. On the other hand, the voice of the dead may be needed to restore harmony among the living, especially among siblings. After the funeral of Loreta, described above, it became necessary to contact the old lady's **kalag** in a seance in order to sort out a problem over inheritance. Loreta had left some items of jewellery to her son's wife; however, her daughter-in-law feared that by accepting them she would provoke bad feeling among Loreta's daughters; in a seance, Loreta apparently told her daughter-in-law to take the earrings without worrying, and asked her daughters not to resent the gift or quarrel over it.

### *Pistang Kalag*

The observances relating to death are not completed with the funeral. For nine days afterwards, the immediate family should attend early mass every day, and hold a mystery for the dead in the evening. Another mystery is held one month afterwards, and then each year on the anniversary of the person's death.

These **misteriohan** are small, family affairs, and the priest is never involved. A number of the older women in the barangay know how to sing the different novenas, including those for the dead, adults and children; these women are not catechists or in any sense officially connected to the church. They have simply learnt the prayers, amassing dozens of the little paper booklets which contain the different texts in Bicol. They often make a little money saying rosaries for a small fee at the local shrine of the **Amang Hinulid**. A family about to celebrate a **misteriohan** for the dead will usually ask whichever of these women they are most closely related to – although in a barangay where so many people are related, this is some-times a moot point. They will pay the woman (or several women if the family has means) a small fee of about P.10 or P.20 each.

On the first and last day of the novena, and the conclusion of the month (**kataposan**), as well as on death anniversaries, the family will prepare snacks to offer to those who come to join in the mystery. The elaborateness of the preparations depends on the family's means at the time, and on the significance of the particular occasion, and the number of people (for instance, children and grandchildren) who might expect to join in the pro-ceedings. Often, the death anniversary involves only the closest relatives and only the sound of singing and the candle burning inside the house indicate that it is taking place.

The celebration of the **Pistang Kalag** or **Pistang Gadan** (lit. Feast of the

Souls or Feast of the Dead, i.e. All Souls' Day) is in many ways similar to individual death anniversaries, and I will describe this major festival in detail.

Bicolanos say that the **kalag** revisit the living each 1 November. Some people give quite detailed accounts of how this happens, saying that the **kalag** return to the world at about four in the afternoon, guided by the candles lit on the tombs of the **Kampusanto**, and stay until the early hours of 2 November. During this time, the living will visit and keep vigil at the tombs of the dead, and the dead will also visit the house of their living family.[26]

Preparations for the **Pistang Kalag** are made during the week before, when the grass and weeds are cut from the **Kampusanto** and the graves and tombs cleaned, tidied, whitewashed and so on. The **Kampusanto** looks very different at this time, for during the rest of the year it is bleak, overgrown and desolate, and is a place rarely voluntarily visited by Bicolanos. Its location outside the town centres, sometimes a half-hour's walk away, emphasises this avoidance. During the **Pistang Kalag**, the normal situation is reversed, as the **Kampusanto** is made gay and inviting, and people make every effort to travel home to the provinces to attend.

In the afternoon of 1 November, preparations are completed by a trip to the **Kampusanto** to buy candles and flowers and arrange them on the tomb. Then, during the evening, the family or at least one member of it will visit the **Kampusanto** and sit by the tomb. If a family's dead relatives are buried in several different places, as is often the case unless a family is wealthy enough to buy its own plot, then it is most important to visit and light a candle at each one. After dark, the cemetery is very pretty, with glowing red and white candles, a soft hum of conversation, fresh or paper flowers on the clean graves, and stalls selling peanuts and other snacks.

There is a constant press of people passing to and from the tombs in the inner recesses of the **Kampusanto**, which is deep and narrow. In the crowd, the flimsy plywood sticks and crosses marking the earth graves, usually the graves of children, often get crushed underfoot. These graves, crammed along the edge of the footpath, contrast brutally with the elaborate (and, to my eye, often ugly) concrete and wrought-iron structures erected by the richest families and by the police and other organisations. The contrast is not lost on barangay families: '*That's what it is to "have nothing at all"* . . . *the plots for those harong-harong [lit. 'sort-of-houses'] cost 3000 Pesos or more* . . .' Sometimes, the bones of the poor come up through the shallow earth graves and lie about the cemetery.

Besides the visits to the dead, visits are also made among the living, as people circulate between tombs to greet their friends, relatives and neighbours. Wealthier families will bring a supply of sticky-rice cakes (**ibos**) and other foods to give to visitors, and the men will often gather in groups to drink beer or rum. In these respects, the evening in the cemetery echoes the annual fiesta day of the barangay patron saint, when visitors move from one house to another, calling in to eat and pay their respects to the household.

Another kind of activity takes place during the evening back in the barangay. Every house will prepare a food offering for the **kalag**, which is left in front of the family altar, or on a table specially arranged with candles, a crucifix and any other saints' images the family has in the house. The offering consists of a plate of betel-nut makings, a plate of **ibos**, and a plate of sweet biscuits (bought), as well as a glass of water or coffee, and perhaps some alcohol. The precise nature of the offering depends upon whom it is intended for; if the **kalag** visiting the house are children, they will want biscuits, while the betel is primarily for old people, and the alcohol for men.

In 1989, I attended a **misteriohan** held for all the dead of the house belonging to Manuelita and her daughter and son-in-law. Besides the food-offering, they had prepared snacks for their visitors from their own sticky rice. Manuelita had a handwritten list of all the **kalag** whom she wanted to have mentioned in the mystery; her father Severo is still alive, so they started with her mother Estrella, her husband, her uncles, her grandparents, and her son-in-law's mother. With two women leading the mystery for adults, everyone sat on the floor and sang the responses to the lilting, four-line tune imploring the Virgin to pray for them and the dead; then prayers with the names of the **kalag** were read out, before everyone was urged to eat **ibos**, and the candle was left to burn down on the altar table.

Throughout the day, people visiting another house would say jokingly, '**Makikalag**; **Makikakan**' (May I join in with the **kalag**; May I eat too), which is an invitation for the householders to press their visitors to taste the **ibos** or other special food. Jokes are often made about the visits of the **kalag**; one woman would greet each arrival at her house by declaring, 'It's the **kalag** of my grandfather', or, 'Surely that's my cousin's **kalag**!' But this does not mean that the visits of the **kalag** are taken lightly; many people say they are nervous of being near the offering-table after dark. When I asked whether the **kalag** eat what is set out for them, I was usually told that they 'just sniff at it'; although some people think that the leftovers have no flavour the next morning, they can be eaten rather than thrown away.

As well as eating in the house, the **kalag** will often want to sleep next to the living on the family sleeping-mats. You can tell that a **kalag** has slept next to you when you dream of the dead and wake up chilled by them in the morning. This happens very often to mothers who have small dead children, as well as to widows and widowers.

The third way in which controlled contact with the dead may be sought by the living is much the most infrequent, at least at present; this is by keeping the bones of the dead.

In Calabanga, I sometimes heard stories of people who had kept the bones of someone in their family in the house. Since most Filipino tombs are in fact rented from the Church, many people will eventually re-entomb the bones after decomposition in a small, permanent niche called the **restos**. I assume that bones to be kept in the house are taken home at this stage instead of being re-interred, but this is not quite clear to me.

The immediate reaction of Bicolanos to this subject is split; some are puzzled or embarrassed, dismissing it as something which was only done by their parents and grandparents 'when people were different'. But a sizeable minority reply 'that it is very good guardian for the house'. They recall that where bones are kept in the house, no one who is not supposed to be there will be able to enter it. The whole family can go out, leaving the house empty, and a thief who climbs the house-steps will find himself unable to enter, and will perhaps be terrified to see a broom sweeping the floor entirely on its own.

Although there was one household in the barangay which kept bones in the house, most of my information about this practice comes from outside Calabanga. One family who told me they still did this were relatives of people from Calabanga, living in Partido (Goa). The old lady told me that her sister lived in a house where bones were kept in this way: the bones of her mother-in-law, together with the cloth that used to be used to bind up the chin, were kept in a box made of glass, she said. Her sister had been accustomed to it:

When she went out, she would say: 'Mother, just mind the children.' Then she could leave them alone in the house . . .

In this family, food from the evening meal was set aside for the dead mother-in-law each evening, since her **kalag** was felt to be still present. But in order to keep bones in this way as a 'guardian' it is imperative that you 'keep to an observance', which consists of saying an **orasion** (like those used by healers) to the bones, generally daily.

One of the loyal patients of the Libmanan healer Tiang Delia knew of one household who kept bones (albeit apparently rather casually in an outhouse!), and another who had been prevented from using them by their owner.

Roberto was still a bachelor, still young . . . and he had a sister who was an old maid . . . What happened was, he killed a bat with a sling, and at the same time he fell ill with pains in his stomach . . . they took him to hospital, but he died within a short time . . . [My companion prompted her: 'So the bat must have been a pet of the people we cannot see'.) The **tawo**, yes. What happened, they embalmed him after a few hours, even though his skin wasn't yet stiff. After that, the old maid was the one who kept feeling things; she got possessed, and she was only herself by fits and starts . . . So, they called for Tiang Delia . . .When Tiang Delia was possessed, they found out a lot of things . . . The stomach pains had been the 'paying back' of the people we cannot see, and if he had been healed by a medium, Roberto need not have died . . . Both the spirit and Roberto possessed Tiang Delia . . . The people we cannot see wanted to have Roberto as a swap for their bat . . . The **kalag** was angry because he said: 'If you hadn't slit my body open and embalmed me at once, probably you could have talked to the spirits, and they would have let me come back!' So he was angry, and that was why he kept bothering his sister.

His parents-in-law . . . wanted to keep his bones in the house, but he didn't want it . . . He refused, he was very angry, because he didn't want to accept that he was dead . . . So they weren't able to get his bones . . .

I do not know of any case where someone had wanted to stop observing the **orasion** of the bones, but I was curious about what would happen if this occurred; the reply seemed to suggest the vivid presence of the dead person's power in the house: 'I suppose', I was told, 'that you would have to bury them all over again.'

The counterpart of the stories about the dead who trouble the living are stories told by the living who have been to the land of the dead and come back. It is not at all uncommon in Bicol to hear stories of dead people who returned to life, and I have already described the way in which healers often equate their journeys in the spirit world with a death and resurrection. Stories of journeys to the spirit world and to the afterlife have resemblances of form and incident, and it will be recalled that the distinction between the two is not entirely clear. However, some non-healers say that they have been, not to the land of the **tawo**, but to somewhere like paradise. One old lady in San Ignacio told me the story of her twenty-four-hour absence from her body as a teenager. Her soul wandered a great distance before coming to a church full of candles and heavenly music, but although she wanted to stay, she was sent back by a tall man, who told her that her own candle had not yet burnt down. Returning to her body, Juanita found her relatives weeping for her, convinced she was dead. 'It's my belief, it was my own grave I walked through', she said.

**The language of bereavement**

. . . if you have a child who dies and you are always thinking of him, it will make him fall down from Heaven . . .

One further way in which the living can be ensnared in impossible relationships with the dead, is through the experience of intense bereavement.[27]

During wakes, the way in which someone died is constantly enquired about and repeated. The story of the person's death, developed in this way, informs the content of the **manambitan**. We have seen, however, that while it is important to express violent grief at the funeral, and to commemorate the dead, the emphasis is on the need for the living to 'forget' the dead, to avoid their attentions and to separate from them except in occasional controlled encounters.

Ilar described the loss of her three dead children in this way;

When my children died one after the other, Nell, then my mind was broken. I didn't want to talk to people, I just wanted to stay here. I didn't want anyone near me, I wanted my peace. Keep my thoughts to myself . . . At that time, my mind was really no more. That's really how it was. I had already taken to my [death]-bed . . .

Ilar's grief, the fact that her mind was broken, caused her to neglect her other children. One daughter lost two years of school. One son took up gambling. Ilar also gave up all the services she normally performs for her neighbours, since she never went out of her house. She never took part in sociable drinking with her sisters-in-law or co-godparents, and never sang the Passion at other people's houses, although she is an expert in this with an extraordinary voice.

The way in which Ilar began to recover her mind is interesting. Her husband, Luis, invited their co-godparents to drink at their house.

. . . Just so that I'd go, he said to my co-godmother: 'Saling, let's drink together.' So there it was . . . 'Manay Iling, come on, let's drink.' I didn't even taste that sort of drink at that time, I didn't even go drinking. . .

Eventually, Ilar's co-godmother and husband forced her to drink a little with them by making her hold her nose so that she could swallow it without tasting it, since she said it had become bitter to her.

Grief makes the living adhere to the dead and can pull the souls out of the living, so the living must take care to pull back, even when mourners have lost their taste for the pleasures and duties of ordinary sociality.

'That's when I began to take some care of my life so that I got better again.' Relatives and neighbours also urged her to stop forgetting her living children by always thinking of her dead ones, and to think of how many people she could still serve. When she started to 'read' the Passion again, 'Manay Francesca said to me, this Ilar here is really too much; what do you think you're doing, keeping on neglecting that life of yours?'

Her constant remembering, like that of other Bicolanos suffering grief, suggests a comment once made by Nana Asing, talking about things that old people used to believe in Bicol:

The old people say, that if you have a child who dies and you are always thinking about him, it will make him fall down from heaven, and you will have to have mysteries sung to put him back up again.

### Conclusion: the living and the dead

There are three conclusions I wish to draw out from this chapter. Firstly, I have argued that an exaggerated ambivalence surrounds death beliefs in Bicol at present. People perform customs which they do not describe when asked about death in the abstract, and refer contextually to beliefs which they otherwise deny.[28] Some aspects of death and bereavement seem to have become literally 'unsayable'. It seems likely that this 'unsayability' is connected to the history of Filipino colonialisms, that the focus on death emerges as one arena for conflict between Filipino and non-Filipino understandings. The relative lack of interest which Filipino Catholics show in heaven, hell and purgatory, sin and punishment, suggests that Rafael is right in stressing the degree to which the messages of the Spanish conversion were modified and 'contracted' by Filipinos. However, if as he says the idea of paradise was a major motivating factor in popular conversion, it is interesting that at least in the late twentieth century the prospect of heaven is so unstressed and still competes with unCatholic ideas of death to such a degree.

Secondly, if what Bicolanos say about death is not clearly focussed on the afterlife, it is focussed on relations between the dead and the living, the permeability of barriers between the two, and the problem of achieving a correct separation. In a number of ways that I have described or referred to, the dead are felt to threaten the living with their proximity; deaths can 'follow each other' and many people are said to have died on the death-anniversary of someone close to them.

The dead attend the living people to whom they were close, seeking their companionship, but this can only be safely offered in controlled conditions like those of the All Souls' Night observances, where the dead are offered prayers and food, visited in their tombs and invited into the house. At the same time, the living make clear that the participation of the dead cannot be real or permanent; the dead can only 'sniff at' life and not consume it, and by morning they must return to their voiceless realm of darkness.

However, the recently and closely related dead may attempt to stay with the living on other occasions. The 'pity' of the dead for the living, especially of grandparents for grandchildren, results in the **kalag** 'accompanying' their descendants and making them ill. In **kalag**-caused illness, as in spirit-caused illness, the person shows the symptoms of soul-loss. Specifically, when the illness is caused by **kalag**, the person becomes cold and sleepy, a little like the dead themselves. The 'pity' of the living for the dead is equally dangerous to the living; at funerals when people say they pity the dead most strongly, mourners faint and have to be pulled by the hair, a gesture which restores the soul to the body. Similarly, those who are mourning a child or other person they cannot forget become a little like the dead too, and will not eat or speak. The dead pull the living towards them, and the living must resist.

Various aspects of funeral practice are designed to separate the living from the dead, including **palihion** and, crucially, embalming which prevents the dead from returning to their bodies.

The whole process of the funeral also separates living and dead in another way. I argued that unfinished business and unsettled obligations make the dead more likely to come back. Moreover, people cannot even die until they have 'paid back' the debts they have incurred by acting badly to others. Death should mark the moment when the debts of the living and dying person to each other are settled.

The funeral can be seen as the first of a series of attempts to make a kind of final payment to the dead. The dressing and embalming of the dead, which is associated with the wealthy, was historically a way of paying respect, and the same can be said now. The dead person's face is made up and made beautiful, partly it seems in order to cancel out the idea of a long death and the association with the **aswang** which this provokes. But the dressing-up of the corpse also has something in common with the dressing-up of beauty queens or bridesmaids in a Bicolano barangay; it marks them out as special; it confers glamour. The typically American-style trappings of the funeral companies emphasise this. The big white car, the gilded coffin and electric lights, the elaborate props and heavy make-up, contrast with the clothing, bearing and houses of people around it much as the stage of a fiesta singing contest does. The act of walking in the **dapit** also enhances the status of the dead person, because as people say it shows that he or she had many friends or many followers; that is, it makes the dead person temporarily like a wealthy and politically important patron. The extension of the house with a canopy for hospitality during the wake and in the funeral meal can also be seen in this light, for throughout this time the family house is referred to as 'the dead person's house', making the deceased a kind of retrospective host at a large gathering. All these acts can be seen as a kind of gift or tribute to the dead person.

The **manambitan** usually refers either to unfinished business between the dead and the mourners, or to the notion of cancelling debts and obligations. Margie's cries to her mother Loreta were of the first kind; the cry of 'Mother, forgive us' at Teresita's funeral is of the second kind, since the word used, **patawad**, also means the discount a vendor gives to a customer at the market. **Tawad** implies a concession on what is owed, something from which you are 'excused'. While **herak**, pity, draws the living and the dead together inappropriately, **tawad** implies a cancelling, and a separation.

*[margin note: social dynamics ·/· living & dead]*

A Bicolana friend assured me that in her childhood in 1950s Iriga this element of **manambitan** was highly explicit, and that the stereotypical cry for mourners was, 'How can we ever repay you now?' (Jeanne Illo, personal communication). The moments of burial that I have seen all stress the reluctance of the living to part with the dead, as the living cling to the coffin and scream that 'I will go with you' or 'I will not leave you here.' The coffin has to be ritually pulled out of the hands of the chief mourners by the bearers to be placed into the tomb, and this reluctance is also surely both a form of tribute to the deceased, and an indication of the struggle between the feelings of indebtedness to kin and the necessity to separate from them.

The offerings which are made on the day of **Pistang Kalag** provide opportunities for the living to continue to make gifts to the dead in a controlled form, while seances allow any demands the dead still have to make of the living to be heard and reconciled. They also allow the living to discover what happened to people who died violently or in mysterious circumstances.

The third conclusion to be drawn from this chapter, therefore, is that the ambiguity which Bicolanos express about the afterlife may not be only a matter of uncertainty produced by the historical and economic situation. It may also be that for Bicolanos the process of exchange and separation between the living and the dead is as important as the imagination of destinations for the soul.

In the next chapter, I will consider funerals from a different point of view, as an integral part of the cult of the **Amang Hinulid**.

# 8

## The funeral of the 'dead Christ'

*'Pity the poor **Ama**, he looks so pale and wan.' 'Yes, for he's dead now.'*

(*'**Herak man si Ama, garo malungsi, ho.**' '**Iyo, ta gadan na.**'*)

**The dead Christ**

In this chapter, I will discuss the cult of the **Amang Hinulid**, the dead Christ whose almost full-sized statue lies in the local shrine in Calabanga.[1] The **Ama** is made of wood, carved and painted with great detail.[2] Like all Filipino saints, he is European, or as Filipinos say, mestizo in appearance, with pale skin, bony features and a 'high' nose, and long wavy brown hair.[3] His eyes are almost closed and fringed with heavy lashes. Usually, he is dressed in splendid outfits which are frequently changed, and wears wigs of real hair, both of which are donated by the numerous pilgrims who visit his shrine. Beneath these clothes, however, his arms, chest and legs are painted with the most pathetic bloodstains, for the **Ama** is Christ taken down from the cross and laid out in death, but not yet buried.

The shrine of the **Ama** is also being enlarged and rebuilt with donations, and is open-sided. Large cupboards hold the scores of outfits, complete in all details down to the underclothes. The **Ama** lies in a glass coffin above the altar, and the procession of people shuffling past his prone figure on Fridays very much resembles the line of visitors who come to see a dead person laid out at a wake.

In fact, it is my argument in this chapter that the entire cult of the dead Christ is constructed as and emotionally identified with a Bicolano wake and funeral, and that participation in the events of Lent is felt, like participation in a funeral, as an experience of **herak**, pity.

### The funeral of Catalina Dominguez

In order to make this integration clear, I want to return for a moment to actual funerals, and describe the burial of a young woman who died in the wet season of 1989.

Catalina was only twenty-eight when she died after giving birth to her second child. Apparently she died from undiagnosed high blood pressure, although her family had discovered that both sorcery and the spirits had also played a part. Catalina was a cheerful, efficient person, and her prospects had been unusually good; she ran a small grocery shop in the town market, and lived with her husband's parents, who buy and sell rice.

Catalina's funeral was held on one of the first days of rain, with heavy clouds hanging dark over the green of the ricefields. There were six jeeps, four motorcycles and two private cars in the **dapit**, as well as a contingent of about forty people who would have to go on foot to the more distant of the two churches serving Calabanga.

Catalina's husband appeared worn out by grief. 'They say I should cry', he explained, 'but I've used up all my tears'. Her two chief mourners were her mother-in-law, a large woman with the permed hair and formal clothes typical of prosperous Bicol matrons, and her mother, a slight girlish figure in a black tee-shirt. Catalina's mother talked in a flat, emotionless voice as she arranged practical matters, the taking of a final group photograph with the open coffin. Meanwhile, Catalina's mother-in-law had begun to make little yelping noises from her seat: '**Aray ko! Suss Ko!**' (My pain! My Jesus!). Then she suddenly leapt up to weep in a high-pitched chilling tone as she bent over Catalina's coffin, beginning the **manambitan**:

Aaaaay! Why is it that you never saw the 26th? You had so many plans . . . My Jesus! Because you said you would have your child baptised on the 26th, because that's your birthday. You said, let me have a pig to kill, because all my friends will come to the house. Aaaay, you had so many plans and now you are no more. You were always such a fighter when you were a young girl, and now . . .

After a little while, as her screams became more sharply pitched, someone pulled her away from the coffin because Catalina's natal family were waiting to group for the last of the pictures. The moment came for the coffin to be closed and taken out: a large crowd was waiting inside the house, but some withdrew as if to avoid being drawn into the violent expression of grief. I saw Catalina's mother being held by the arms as she struggled to reopen the coffin and screamed: '*My child, my child, I will go with you.*' She followed the coffin out of the door, suddenly furious, and screaming: '*I don't want to, I won't, I won't put my child in the cemetery.*' It was several minutes before the bearers were able to wrench her hands from the coffin and place it in the car.

The **dapit** was completed in increasingly heavy rain. In the church, the priest gave a standard address on the transience of earthly life, and we set off again for the cemetery, which was heavily overgrown with most of a year's worth of weeds. It took a long time to walk through the grass to the open tomb. The party stopped, the coffin was reopened for the last time, and Catalina's mother and mother-in-law, neither being clearly the chief mourner, both began to grab at the coffin and hold open the lid, as the bearers tried to close it and finally slide it into the waiting tomb. The two women began a kind of antiphonal, keening declamation:

M-in-law: Aaay, why didn't you reach that date, the 26th, all your plans . . .
M: Aaaay, my child, my child, your sufferings . . . these heavy stones, these too-heavy stones . . .
M-in-law: Aaaay, because if you come back, where will you stay? If you come back, what house will you come into?
M: Why is it that you said that on the 26th, there would be so much happiness, but now there is so much sorrowing . . . After you leave, I feel your pain, after you go into there, I feel your pain, my child.
M-in-law: If you come back, when it is evening, you will have no companion. If we are all in the house . . . if you come back, who will watch over you, who will stand guard over you . . .
M: Why are you no more?

The less closely related mourners drew back as soon as they had seen the **paglaog**, the moment when the coffin is actually put into the tomb. Although their eyes may fill with tears at the **manambitan**, most people will turn away almost angrily to hide them. Ritual weeping at the burial is necessary, but it is also deeply disturbing. A close friend of Catalina's, herself painfully bereaved and shocked, later told her mother: 'The way Catalina's mother was weeping', she said, 'it was too much; it was frightening'.

## The funeral in the *Pasion*

The central moment of a funeral in Bicol is the placing of a dead body in a tomb, while the mother or other mourners exclaim over the body, and try to pull the coffin back from the brink of the grave. This moment of ritual has a textual resonance too obvious to be ignored in the Bicol **Pasion**, a resonance of which I am sure Bicolanos are aware.

The **Pasion** is written in Bicol, in verse, and tells the story of the sufferings of Christ, beginning with the creation and ending with the resurrection, but with the emphasis on the trial, scourging, crucifixion and burial of Christ. The text is punctuated by **hulit**, or little sermons, which consider the message of the story for Christians. The current Bicol **Pasion**, printed in Naga and sold throughout the province, is apparently derived from the 1826 Tagalog **Casaysayan**, the most influential of the Tagalog passion-texts. This was originally derived from the **Pasyon** of Gaspar Aquino de Belen of 1703, the first Tagalog passion, which was in turn based on Spanish religious texts dating back to the sixteenth century (Javellana, 1988:11–20; Rafael, 1988:194). The Bicol **Pasion** is dated 1866,[4] and a dedicatory letter to its commissioner Archbishop Gainza states that '. . . until now we Bicolanos only knew of the Passion in Tagalog; those who could understand it, did, and those who couldn't, didn't'. (Hernandez, 1984:6; my trans.). This accords with what habitual **Pasion**-readers in Bicol told me. However, though the **Pasion** was the second-earliest translation of the Tagalog text (Javellana, 1988:235), other Filipino-language Passion traditions had developed independently prior to the nineteenth-century dominance of this version, and more research would be needed to assess exactly what existed in the way of earlier Bicol religious popular texts.[5]

The performance of the Passion is always by chanting, known as 'reading' **(pabasa)**, but the forms this takes vary widely in different provinces and between provinces (Javellana, 1988:6–7) as do the tunes and improvisations used, especially for the **hulit**. The Passion-play (Tag: **sinakulo**, Bicol: **tanggal**) is now based on the Passion texts, but they may or may not have evolved from the text itself (Javellana, 1988:6). The immense popularity of text and play increased in the nineteenth century, though their earlier history is less well understood.

The Bicol **Pasion**, like all Passions in the Philippines, was associated with the didactic efforts of the Spanish church, but long ago took on a life of its own as a popular religious text. It is never used in a formal religious or church context. Instead the entire text is sung in the **pabasa** ritual held by one or more households within a barangay on each Saturday night of Lent, and during Holy Week. The readings are performed in fulfilment of religious vows, usually associated with healing. A reading of the **Pasion** involves an all-night vigil, to which friends, neighbours and relatives are invited. A small altar is set up inside the house, with a cloth, a cross and candles on it and sometimes a small bottle of rum to 'warm' voices made hoarse by the night-time chill. Depending on the vow, some people prepare supper for the readers, and others breakfast, but all will serve snacks at midnight, with **salabat** (hot ginger tea).

In Calabanga, **Pasion**-singers always perform in pairs. Though the arrangement is flexible, habitués of **pabasa** usually have a singing partner of their own sex. In Lent, many people practise the **Pasion**, trying to make their voice perfectly suited to their partner's. Good readers will say proudly that 'the fit of their two voices cannot be equalled', blending together to produce every word clearly.

This is a skilled matter, since the technique demands that one voice lead and the other (harmonising a second part) follow as smoothly as possible, emphasising and ornamenting the line in certain places. Moreover, the **Pasion** is 230 pages long, and consists of four-line verses fitted into a complex metrical form which cuts across the ends of the lines. Some readers also know a range of alternative tunes or forms, especially for the **hulit**. The combination of skill, voice, endurance and coordination with another which reading the **Pasion** well involves makes it a source of pleasure to the readers and admiration from others, which is enhanced because to read the **Pasion** often is both a mark of a mature householder, and an enactment of the best kind of neighbourly service. People sing the **Pasion** with relish as well as with duty and emotion; I have often seen pairs of women or men, seated sturdily in front of the altar and working through some long section of the text, suddenly come to a part which requires

Figure 6 Reading the passion-text

special skill and, catching each other's eye, time the change of rhythm or tune with the pleasure which comes from a degree of mastery complete enough to enable improvisations. This is, after all, a text in the Bicol language, read in people's own homes in the context of vows they have made with the saints, and it has little to do with the priest, the government, the schools, the landlords, or any other party in confrontation with whom they are vulnerable. It is a text which is closely familiar performed in a way which is confidently understood, and which (in contrast to many other areas of Bicol life) is not appropriated or mediated by other authorities.

Although the bulk of the **Pasion** is sung to one tune, there are shifts in the music during key moments in the story. Among these, the episode which recounts the burial of Christ with Mary and the other women looking on is the most poignant. Because of the timing of the vigil, the burial episode always comes during the early hours of the morning, when everyone is most exhausted. Neighbours in the houses adjoining that where the **pabasa** is being held will be awakened by the haunting tune of Christ's burial suddenly swelling up out of the night, and those at the vigil who have dozed off uncomfortably on the narrow wooden benches will be prodded awake to sing the interlined unison parts. This is the section of the **Pasion** which was always chosen when I asked people what the most significant passages were; as they say, it is **pinakamakahibi** – the part most likely to move you to tears. Roughly translated, it reads like this:

When the mother of sorrows
Almost would not let go of
The coffin of her child
As she thought even more intensely
Of these pangs and sufferings

To so much pain, pity is added too
For the bereaved mother.
Her breath was almost extinguished
And it was the same for those two,
John and Magdalena.

Kneeling and moaning
Those holy two
Have opened up the coffin now
And placed carefully in there
That holy flesh.

They nailed it shut, O.
The coffin of Jesus Christ.
It had a true fragrance

Of sabanas and sudarium,
A fragrance which spread everywhere.

The angels in heaven
Longed to join in the funeral procession
And walk along the path
Where they saw
The coffin of Jesus passing.

Many and numerous
Were the women who went with them
Each one had tears in her eyes
A grief without equal
Was their deep feeling.

[Three verses omitted: they go to the tomb]

... When they arrived there
At that dear tomb
They put in very gently
That dear body you see
Into the gloom and darkness.

Into the grave they put him
And nailed it up
And sealed it
With a stone called marble
Which is clean without a blemish.

*(Hernandez, 1984 (**Pasion Bicol**; 1866):178–9. My trans.)*

This account of Christ's burial is apparently conventional, but it seems at the same time to belong to the world of Bicol funerals. Partly it is the choice of language which connects the two, particularly the emphasis in Bicol life which we have already seen on the feeling of **herak**, or pity, for the dead. The mother who cannot let go of her child's coffin, the weeping, the mourners who want to show respect by joining in the funeral procession, the sealing up of the tomb and the consigning of the body into the dark, all take on a particular meaning simply because they are sung and understood by Bicol people.

Bicolanos, familiar with the **Pasion** which they read several times a year, are accustomed to drawing comparisons between the sufferings in the story and their own sufferings. As I show in the next chapter of this section, the **pabasa** is intimately connected with devotions performed by parents for their sick children's recovery. The emotional charge of this passage of the **Pasion** and the experience of mourning and attending funerals, especially for one's own children, as Catalina's mother and mother-in-law had to do, enter into each other for Bicolanos. The Bicol funeral forms a context for the **Pasion** and the **Pasion** in turn becomes part of the context of a Bicol funeral.

However, in Calabanga, the Christ whose story is sung and experienced in this way is, as I have indicated, not an abstract Christ, but a particular known Christ, the **Amang Hinulid**, the Christ laid out in death in his shrine. It is the **Ama** who prompts the devotions which involve the readings of the **Pasion**, and which heal the children of the people in San Ignacio.

I will now look more closely at the identity of this particular Christ, and at the events which take place at his shrine. I will suggest that the main religious event of the year can be seen as a form of wake and burial for the **Amang Hinulid**.

### The funeral of Christ

Almost all images of saints in the Philippines are owned by individual families, who sponsor their devotions, and the **Ama**, although the most famous and publicly displayed of local saints, is no different in this respect. The family which now owns the **Ama**[6] is the third to do so. Partly because of this change in ownership, it is difficult to reconstruct the factual history of the image, but the mythology of the **Ama** is much easier to discover.

The first owner of the **Ama**, it is said, was a childless woman. The **Ama** was washed up on the beach of the nearest fishing barangay to San Ignacio, where she found it. At first the image was only a formless piece of wood with a rough swelling where the head should be. The woman, however, realising it was an important and possibly sacred object,[7] wrapped it in blankets as though it were a baby, and gradually the wood began to take on human form. She started to carry it on the Good Friday processions, holding it **kulkul**, that is, cuddled against her shoulder as one carries a baby. Anyone who has a saint which they sponsor is said to be **pig-aataman an santo**, that is, bringing up or taking care of the saint, in the way that one brings up a child, but in this case the equivalence was made much more explicit. The woman adopted a human child, but meanwhile the **Ama** was becoming entirely human-looking, as it is now, and began to work miracles of various kinds, which are not directly relevant here except for one. Tiang Genny, a woman who now takes part in the annual Corpus Christi performance of the passion play at the Hinulid shrine, remembered what happened to her uncle when she was a child. A young mestizo man had come to call on her uncle, saying he was looking for carpenters to rebuild his house, since the rain was dripping right through it. He left his address and went away. The uncle and an assistant set out for Calabanga with their tools, but when they called at the address the man had given them, an old couple came out and said they were the only people who lived there. 'We have no mestizo child', they said. The carpenter was angry: just then, he was seized with a terrible need to urinate, and the old woman said he could use her privy. As he walked through the house, he saw the **Ama** lying in the old couple's bedroom, and recognised the man who had come to see him. He then spent a week building the first shrine, or 'house' of the **Ama**, as it is usually called, for pilgrims to visit in more comfort. This shrine has since been replaced by the present concrete structure, which was paid for by the donations of two wealthy families in Naga City.

Tiang Genny was clear about the point of the story concerning her uncle: 'The **Ama** is very miraculous . . . as he grew up, so his house got bigger too.' It was at this period, I am told, when the **Ama** had his first house, that it became known that he had literally grown, to his present near-life size.

The **Amang Hinulid**, therefore, is even more than other Filipino saints in some ways a person, who has not only been seen and spoken to by living people, but has been nurtured, adopted and literally brought up by Bicolano families, and who lives in a house with a family and eventually acquires his own house. Knowing this makes it easier to interpret the principle devotions held on his behalf or at his house, the Hinulid shrine.

*[handwritten margin note: duty/ obligations of the [owners?]]*

The first of these with which I am concerned here is the **pagparigos ki Ama**, or bathing of the **Ama**, which takes place on a Friday, usually the first Friday of alternate months, and during Holy Week. Pilgrims are always numerous on Fridays, but the bathing of the **Ama** attracts a specialised crowd of pious women and men, and numbers of healers and mediums from the surrounding area who feel a special connection with the **Ama**. They all come to collect little bottles of the water used to wash the image, or to rub scented cotton wool over it; to use in healing. Some people also write letters to the **Ama** explaining the problems with which they need help, and tuck them under the pillow and mattress on which he lies. These are referred to ironically as **'love-letters'**, using the English phrase.

The bathing of the **Ama** is an elaborate process. As many people as can crowd around, lift the prone image complete with bedclothes from the glass box in which it lies, and place it gently on a table nearby. Layers of wraps are removed, and petition letters fall rustling to the ground. A new outfit is selected for the **Ama**, from his wardrobes full of donated clothes. The **Ama's** outer clothes are removed, revealing the image, with its realistically painted wounds and pallid skin. The women bathing the image sponge down his whole body carefully but rather proprietorially, changing his underwear discreetly beneath a towel. When they finish, the **Ama** is replaced in his swept-out glass case with fresh sampagita perfumes.

When I first saw the bathing of the **Ama** the attendant women made a strong impression on me, for it seemed that they handled the statue with just that mixture of respect and possessiveness with which dead bodies are washed to be laid out. Although none of my informants ever said as much, the washing ritual that occurred during Holy Week made me sure of it. On Holy Wednesday and again on Good Friday, the **Ama** is washed and dressed in purple robes, his chin bound up with a bandage, just as Bicolano corpses were once prepared before embalming became so widespread.

The most important religious activity at the shrine of the **Ama** takes place during Holy Week. Lent is in fact the focus of the religious year throughout Bicol, perhaps even more so than in the recent past, since religious celebrations in Advent and Christmas seem to have been more raggedly maintained in the post-war period than Lent and Easter observances.[8]

Figure 7  The **Ama** bathed and changed

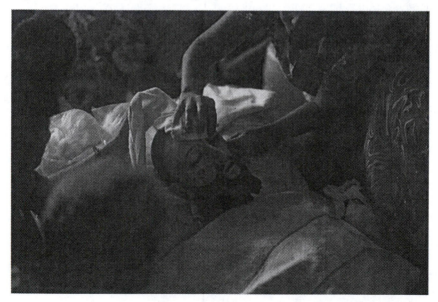

The readings of the **Pasion** will have been taking place in the houses in the barangays since the beginning of Lent, but at the start of Holy Week activity intensifies around the shrine. During 1989, the first noticeable preparation was the large canopy which was erected in front of and around the open sides of the shrine, supported by bamboo poles two stories high, and spanning the street between the shrine and the houses opposite. On the same day, the **Ama** was bathed, attended by an enormous crowd, all eager to touch the body. Instead of being replaced in the glass case above the altar, he was left on a lower table uncovered. Large numbers of people came to kiss the image's bare feet with their visible nail-marks and bloodstains. At one corner of the extended area, which was now covered by the canopy, an altar was set up with a large, reversible painted board, called a 'calvary'. One side represented the crucifixion, the other side the descent from the cross. Gradually over the week, the shrine became full of pilgrims from remote parts of the province, including many healers. Those who came from farthest away were actually camping out in the 'house' of the **Ama** in order to fulfil religious vows by taking part in the Good Friday observances. Meanwhile, local people were coming and going as they kept track of the different events at the shrine, at home and in the main church in Calabanga town centre.

Holy Week is marked in Calabanga by two public processions, on the evenings of Holy Wednesday and Good Friday. On Holy Wednesday, eleven saints owned and sponsored by different families in the town are carried in a procession which represents the last episodes of the life of Christ. The saints assemble at the church at the east end of the town, and then process along the north road to the Hinulid shrine at the west end of the town, before returning along the south road to complete the circuit. The images, all of which are quite large and some of which are nearly life-size, are all mestizo in appearance, like the **Ama**. People constantly point to the white skin, wavy brown hair and 'high' noses of the saints and apostles, the 'beauty' which they say makes them feel ashamed of their own Malay features. Each saint has been dressed in the house of its sponsoring family in velvet and satin robes, and placed on floats glowing in electric light; surrounded with flowers and pushed by devotees, the saints seem to hover luminously in the darkness just above the heads of the ordinary people.

There are also many other lesser saints present at these processions, lining the route together with the human spectators, for each household and each barangay chapel takes out its own statue and places it, on a suitably decorated altar, by the road where it can watch Mary, Veronica and the Jesus of Sorrows passing. The barangay saints keep guard just in front of their chapels, which like that of the **Ama**, are known as their 'houses'. It is as if a different geography is revealed by the progress of the procession, in which the dwellings and movements of the saints temporarily overlay the familar outlines of the town.

On the Thursday before Good Friday, activity intensifies at the Hinulid shrine. Pilgrims have travelled in small and large groups from all over the province, to fulfil a promise to 'read' the **Pasion** for the **Ama**. Some start earlier in the week and 'read' over several days, some 'read' without a pause, but by Friday morning everyone is reaching a conclusion, and the shrine is full of dozens of Passions, and many different local styles of tune and presentation.

Some of the pilgrims arriving at the shrine have vowed to perform more extreme and unusual penances. The most common of these is to carry a heavy wooden cross from the pilgrim's home barangay, perhaps ten or twenty kilometres away, to the shrine of the **Ama** on Good Friday. The pilgrims go barefoot, and do not eat or drink, and they frequently collapse several times before completing their journey. Even more physically extreme are the flagellants. The coastal barangay of the town has a famous group of flagellants who beat themselves at noon every Good Friday before plunging into the sea to wash their wounds. But there are also flagellants who come to the shrine, some of them from the large town of Pili, and in 1989 there were two such groups. I have not seen this form of penance, as in both instances I was involved in proceedings elsewhere, and I have only heard a few stories about why flagellation is practised. One man who whips himself each Good Friday is supposed to have committed some terrible but secret crime. He says that the whipping lets out the 'bad blood' and that the more blood he sheds, the happier and more at peace he subsequently feels. Like all the wounds occasioned in religious devotions, it is said to heal quickly and painlessly, leaving only clean scars. These stories accord well with accounts of the logic of blood-shedding devotions from other parts of the Philippines (Zialcita, 1986; Barker, 1994). I am in agreement with the point made by both these sources, that repentance and contrition are a relatively minor part of these devotions, and that they may be performed by people who see themselves as having committed no crime or sin, for their healing and empowering effect. However, in Calabanga, blood-shedding is performed by only a small minority of people. The predominant forms of devotion, which are even more focussed on healing and not on sin and expiation, are discussed at greater length in the next chapter of this section. It is enough to note here that most people feel that spend-

ing many nights throughout Lent in vigil in readings of the **Pasion** is a
significant and sufficient sacrifice. These devotions culminate in the
process of 'joining in' the funeral procession of the **Ama**.

On the afternoon of Good Friday, a large crowd gathers in front of the
shrine of the **Ama**. Although women are active in all stages of the Lent
activities, at this point the crowd consists mainly of men and the women
hang back. This is because the men will, as is always the case in the procession of a miraculous saint,[9] jostle to gain a good position from which they
can help to push the bier of the **Ama**. In this way, they stand a chance of
securing some of the ornaments and flowers from the bier as tokens of
their participation, and hence to provide some of the saint's protection for
their families in the coming year. The crowd is awaiting the musicians,
those same brass band players who attend every funeral in Calabanga.
When the musicians arrived, the bier was drawn up to a shrine, a glass-
sided, carved wooden case, freshly repainted every year and covered in
flowers. There was an expectant pause, then a pressing forward of bodies
and shouts as the **Ama** was passed into the bier from the interior of the
shrine and people rushed forward to take places pulling the bier. The head
of the **Ama**, with the bandage tying up his chin, the purple robes and white
covering cloth, was clearly visible as he was place in the bier, and people
around me remarked to each other;

Figure 8 The **Ama**'s bier carried in procession

'Pity the poor **Ama**: he looks so pale and wan!'
'Yes, for he's dead now.'

The huge crowds which fell into step behind the bier in the hot afternoon sun were, people commented, another year's proof that 'The **Ama**
has many friends'.

Along the route eastwards, the processsion paused several times for
saints to leave their sponsors' houses and enter the **dapit**, but the main
group of saints was waiting to join at the church. The saints then accompanied the **Ama** on an entire circuit of the town, followed again by groups
singing traditional hymns and holding candles, and again watched not
only by a human audience, but by other minor saints from their altars at
the side of the roads. Dusk fell, and then complete darkness. When the
procession with its multitude of followers reached the church for the
second time, the saints were taken back to their homes, and the **Ama** was
carried back to his own house at the Hinulid shrine and replaced on the
low table beside it. The 'calvary' board had meanwhile been reversed to
show the scene of Christ taken down from the cross, because as people
said, 'The **Ama** is now dead.' At this point, there were two separate focuses
of activity. One was a secondary procession, in which the image of the
Mater Dolorosa is taken searching for the tomb of her son, which is eventually discovered hidden in a secret location known only to those who have
been chosen to make it that year.[10] The other centre of activity was at the
shrine itself, where there were still lights and crowds of people, and the
sound of the **Pasion** being sung, and where several people were preparing
for the **pagtapat**.

The **pagtapat** can be regarded as a special competition between two
sides in rhetoric and knowledge of sacred matters, based on knowledge of
the **Pasion** text itself, and a corpus of other popular religious arcana. It
begins when a group which has passed from singing the **Pasion** to asking
riddles connected with the **Pasion** amongst themselves makes a formal
suggestion that they should go and take places for a contest of wits and a
'holy discussion fitting to the occasion'. This suggestion, and the whole of
the **tapat**, is sung in the same tunes and metres as the **Pasion**, but with
words which are improvised as the players go along. What is even more
remarkable is that, as in all **Pasion** singing, the **tapat** players sing in duet
with a partner, who therefore has to anticipate what is being said in order
to sing the harmonisation. Although many stereotyped phrases and arguments are employed, it seems to me that this is still a striking form of
coordination and virtuosity. When the **tapat**-players take their places at
the table, an opposing pair take up their challenge, and the ensuing debate

is presided over by a **sentencia**, or judgement-giver, in a way which it is said is meant to recall the trial of Christ before Pilate, although what actually happens has little relevance to the episode beyond the image of a legal hearing.

One team sets an initial challenge or question, such as 'What is the significance of the seven leaves?' and the others then do their best to answer this from the texts, and to elaborate wittily and with well-crafted metaphors on the meaning of the reference (in this case, the seven sacraments), setting out other questions and challenges in their turn until one of the parties is declared defeated by the judge. This form of riddling and debate continues throughout the night until dawn, or as long as there are any challengers.

To sustain the crowd of pilgrims, many local people make a promise to go to the shrine with cakes and other snacks to give away, of the kind provided at **Pasion** vigils and wakes. In the past, the family which owned the **Ama** would provide full meals, using fish caught in paddies dedicated to the upkeep of the saint; thus, the **Ama** could be said to be providing food for his guests to eat. It is whispered that this land has now been put to more commercial uses.

In the morning after Good Friday, although most of the crowds will have gone home during the night, there are still numbers of pilgrims, including many healers, at the shrine. Women who normally spend a great deal of time at the shrine, including members of religious organisations, will sweep out the rubbish from the night before and make the house of the **Ama** tidy, as neighbours do when a human corpse has left the house for burial, sweeping with the broom which helps ward off the **kalag**'s attentions to the living. But in the morning after Good Friday, the 'body' of the **Amang Hinulid** has not left the house forever to be buried in the **Kampusanto**; on the contrary, it has 'returned home' from its procession and visits to the other saints and is reinstalled in its house in a permanent state of wake, a vigil which is only brought to its full expression during the Holy Week events.

Although the celebration of Easter has not yet been completed, the emotional high point of the celebration in Calabanga is ended with the culmination of the Good Friday processions and the reading of the **Pasion**. The Sunday-morning **tontonan**, the ritual of the meeting of the risen Christ and his mourning mother, is enthusiastically attended at the local parish churches. Little children with chronic illness are often given the parts of attendant angels singing a celebratory hymn, and this is a matter of some interest partly because it is believed to help cure them, and partly because places in the **tontonan** are won through competitive charitable donations to the Church. But contrary to Lynch's observations (c.1956), I never found people to be so intensely involved with this, from the liturgical point of view the climax of the Easter period, as they were with the proceedings of Lent. In this part of Bicol, at least, the dead Christ arousing pity as he lies wanly on his bier, is more familiar and more important that either Christ crucified or Christ risen.

One further element of the cult of the **Ama** needs to be considered here, which is the **tanggal**, or Passion-play. At the time of my fieldwork, this was performed in June, although in the past it has been included in the Lent activities. However, the current group of players, all of whom come from an agricultural 'squatters'' area in Naga City, are engaged to play for sponsors throughout the province during Lent, and therefore made a promise to play for the **Ama** on Corpus Christi, a date they described to me as the real 'end of Lent'.

The play is performed in and outside the Hinulid shrine, and lasts three days and two nights. It comprises a large part of the sung **Pasion**, with some additions and elaborations which are taken from other Bicol religious texts, some of them obscure. The arrangement of the sung text, as well as the choice of gestures and direction, are the responsibility of Mr Jose Santiago, the founder and leader of the group, who for many years also played the part of Christ. Mr Santiago also recruits his actors from among his neighbours, prompting people when sickness in their family suggests they should be thinking of performing a devotion.

Mr Santiago bases his **tanggal** on those he knew as a child, and it is at once evident as one watches the play how closely the tableaux and the costumes (which represent a considerable outlay for the actors) are modelled on the scenes and illustrations of the printed Passion text.

The reasons the **tanggal**-players gave for taking part in the play were focussed on the notion of sharing in the experiences of Christ and the other figures in the story by becoming like them. For example, the young man who played Christ in 1989 was said to have suffered very much when his wife deserted him for someone else. According to his fellow-players, he had endured all this patiently; 'it seemed he had Christ in his heart'. He himself said: 'Since I've been put through sufferings like Christ, it seemed I might as well imitate him' (**aarogan ko lugod siya**). This idea was echoed by other members of the group, who said that the **tanggal** was a matter of imitating/being like (**mag-arog**) the events of the Passion. Perhaps it is also relevant that words for acting or representing figure very little when people talk about the roles they take. Mothers who put their children into the

**tanggal** always say, 'I had him be the Word' or 'I had her be Mary' (**pigpaVerbo/pigpaMaria ko siya**), literally 'I Worded him/I Mary'ed her', while the players themselves simply say, '**NagMaria ako**', 'I did Mary.' While this is partly an effect of Bicol grammar (which has no verb 'to be'), I think it may also reflect the close engagement with which people approach their parts.

Zialcita describes the blood-shedding devotions of the Pampanga and Tagalog areas as incorporating an experience of 'becoming Christ's intimate', and reports that the devotees embark on this task in order 'to help Christ and share in his ordeal' (Zialcita, 1986:59) – using the Tagalog word **damay**, to feel with someone. In the case of the Calabanga **tanggal**-players, and all the participants in the Lent observances, there is a very similar sense of entering into the feelings of Christ and the other saints. But in the cult of the **Amang Hinulid**, it takes a particular form, being centred around the emotions of pity which are awakened by death and mourning.

It is clear that just as the death of Christ as recounted in the **Pasion** is experienced as the context of all Bicol funerals, so the practices connected with the cult of the **Ama** are in effect a Bicol wake and funeral. The readings of the **Pasion** in individual households are like a wake without a corpse, in that the whole text can be seen as answering the customary question 'Why did they die?', and in their recreation of the exhausting vigil and the comforting and sharing presence of kin and neighbours who are meant to help the bereaved. The emotional effect of the **Pasion** is linked up with that of the **manambitan** or ritual weeping, since both evoke strong feelings of pity (**herak**) for the dead. As I have already argued in the contexts of marriage and spirit mediumship, pity is the emotion which draws you closer, either when you pity or when you are pitied, and pity for the dead is dangerous for the living.

Even more, the Good Friday procession is like a funeral. The ultimate readings of the **Pasion**, the ultimate wakes for the **Ama**, have already taken place on the preceding nights in the shrine which is the house of the **Ama**, and which, like every house where there is a dead person, has been extended with a canopy which accommodates all those drawn together to mourn as one group of friends and followers. The proceedings of Good Friday are initiated by the bathing of Christ in the manner of bathing a body, though in this case the body is not a corpse but an image. The pilgrims who keep vigil before Good Friday in front of the statue are keeping a form of wake at which food is donated and distributed by some of the **Ama**'s devotees, while others sweep out the shrine on the following morning, in exactly the ways that kin and neighbours offer help to a household which has suffered a death. All those who join in the procession, both human beings and saints, can be seen as taking part in the **dapit**, which shows respect and acknowledges gratitude and obligations to a dead person. Moreover, the key moment of the procession, like that of any other funeral, is the taking down of the body of the **Ama** from his house to be placed on a bier.

Between Good Friday and Easter Sunday, the **Ama** is said to be dead, as the second procession of Mary's search for the grave indicates. However, the image of the dead **Ama** is not actually buried, but is returned to the shrine, stripped of the decorative flowers which have healing properties. The **Ama** of course is no ordinary dead body either for ordinary Bicolanos or for the Catholic church which teaches that Christ has overcome the grave. The differences are in many ways marked in the celebration of Good Friday; the removal of the body from the shrine is not accompanied by the anguished **manambitan** but by excited shouts from the crowd positioning themselves to walk with the image. And the pity that one feels for the **Ama**, unlike the pity the living feel for the dead, is not dangerous and does not need to be cut off.

Indeed, the whole tone of the devotions is centred on drawing closer to the **Ama** and identifying with him. This process is common to both the procession and the **tanggal**, but in the latter the idea of sharing experiences with Christ is given an extra aspect. It is not only a process of a devotional contract, as described by Zialcita, in which the sharing of suffering produces the return gift of healing; it is also a process of **magarog**, of becoming like Christ, Mary and the other figures, taking on their clothes, gestures and words, and so transforming oneself.

Perhaps this explains one strange occurrence. Two weeks after Corpus Christi, I was invited to visit the **tanggal**-players at home and record some of their music. Yet the performers whose haunting and accomplished singing I had so recently witnessed, found themselves suddenly unable to reproduce more than fragments of their parts. They themselves were perplexed that they could have 'forgotten' them so soon. But perhaps it is not surprising in terms of the identificatory logic we have been tracing. For only when one's identity is actively merged with that of the holy figures, it seems, can one become the 'voice' of Mary or of Christ.

In the final section of the book, I will discuss imitation and self-transformation in very different kinds of performances. However, in the last chapter of this section, I will first discuss some aspects of the devotional relationship with saints, including the **Ama**, which have not emerged from this account of the Lent devotions.

# 9

## Kinship, reciprocity and devotions to the saints

*The acts of exchange energizing the fishcorral ritual apparently renders a social process built on a personal reciprocation of deeds bound up with a 'supernatural mercy'.*

(Polo, 1988:53)

I have argued that the funeral of the **Ama** and the funerals of ordinary Bicolanos are identified with each other, because people treat the **Ama** in many ways as one of their own dead. In this chapter, I will describe other ways in which the **Ama** is integrated into Bicol kinship in the context of religious vows (**promesas**) such as the vows I have already mentioned to 'read' the **Pasion** or to perform some other religious devotion in return for the recovery of a sick person, especially a child.[1] I will expand on the nature of identification with the **Ama**, and will also look at the notions of reciprocity involved in these devotions, suggesting that they are quite similar to lowland practices such as the Binalayan fishcorral ritual referred to above, which are usually defined as 'animistic'.

### The saint as child and parent

The intensity and intimacy of the relationship with the dead Christ are connected to the way in which he, like other Bicolano **santos** and **santas**, is adopted by and raised in a human family. This is especially clear in the case of the **Ama**, who literally transformed himself from a block of wood into a baby, then into a vigorous youth walking round performing miracles, and eventually into a householder with many guests. The **Ama** does not only grow up; he grows old. People often remark that since the **Ama** is now a little elderly, he doesn't walk around as much as he once used to. It is

183

not only the **Ama** who has a life-cycle, however, but many other miraculous saints in the vicinity, including some smaller and less important Christs.[2] This emphasis on transformation is central to the significance and distinctiveness of Bicol holy figures, and I will return to it in the conclusion.

It should be clear how any saint is situated as a child in relation to the family which cares for it, dresses it and tends it. It may be less obvious that these same saints are each also in the position of parents to their families. One way to see this is through the mechanisms of land-inheritance, in which saints play a part.

The key element in inheritance as in Bicol kinship generally is the sibling-group or **magturugang**.[3] All siblings have equal rights to their parents' property, though services such as caring for the couple in old age should be recognised. In practice, both the parents' wishes and the discussions of the sibling group determine division of resources.

Ideally, each child receives sufficient land to farm.[4] Where there are not enough fields, the land is divided into strips. But if this would result in impractically small strips, the whole field will be rotated between the siblings each year or each harvest. Clearly, where families are large, a child may only have the use of the land every few years. Land rotated in this way is called **paralibot** ('for circulation').

This division of land also applies to subsequent generations; if six siblings rotate land between them each harvest, then each farms it once every three years.[5] But if one sibling dies, her children as a group also have a claim on the land only once in three years. How they manage this is up to them; they may farm the land as a group, or they may themselves take turns, so that eventually the land comes round to them only very rarely, but in either case their access is defined by the original division of land between the sibling group.

These arrangements have special meaning for the relationships of parents and children. While parents are alive, their land may not be divided up **paralibot**, but must be farmed by all the children together, or whichever of them has need of it at the time. **Paralibot** land therefore goes with the death of the parents, but as it circulates among them it also reinforces the idea that the sibling group is bound together as (sharing) equals. This sibling solidarity itself indirectly commemorates the couple who were the parents of the **magturugang**, although memory of them is usually only active over two or three generations.

While parents are alive, the ideal way in which land is cultivated involves a different kind of sharing, that is **gusi** or share-cropping. In this arrangement, all or some of the children (according to circumstances) work the land, and divide the harvest with the parents who are still reckoned its owners. Children are often hesitant to press for favourable rates of harvest division in **gusi**, out of 'shame' towards the parent to whom, proverbially, Bicol children owe un-repayable gratitude for bringing them into the world and raising them.

Thus the norms of land division promote two different kinds of sharing: an unequal form (**gusi**) in which parents are seen as making a gift to their children in the use of their land, and the children return part of the harvest in grateful acknowledgement, and an equal form (**paralibot**) in which every sibling has the same share as every other sibling. Yet both these forms seem to share an emphasis on the centrality of the sibling group, first in relation to the parents of the **magturugang**, and second in relation to the descending generation, the children of each of the siblings.[6]

While in the recent past share-cropping arrangements such as **gusi** were quite common between paternalistic landlords and tenants, in the present one is unlikely to receive such reasonable conditions and good security from anyone except close kin and friends. Now more than ever, therefore, **gusi** suggests the protection that parents (as some of the few remaining good patrons) will try to extend to their children.

The relevance of forms of land inheritance is that saints in Bicol are also inherited. Moreover, in the past when land was in better supply, most saints were endowed with land, typically a ricefield and a fishpond. The land and the saint were inherited together, and were when necessary rotated among siblings using the **paralibot** system. Siblings took turns both in holding the devotions for the saint and in farming the land which went with it. During that year, the saint was cared for in the house of that branch of the family.

The only exception to the circulation of saints among the sibling-group is when the saint was originally acquired on behalf of just one child. For example, the San Pedro in Calabanga (one of the saints which takes part in Lent public processions) was being sponsored in 1989 by the Bandong family. The statue had been bought on behalf of Mrs Bandong's paternal grandmother Caridad, by her parents. In theory, therefore, only Caridad's children need have maintained the devotion, and they would have circulated the saint among them. However, the heirs of Caridad's own siblings had wanted to join in, and the saint was therefore rotated among the descendants of her own sibling-group after all.[7]

The saint in Bicol is always described as the owner (**may sadiri**) of the endowed land. Moreover, Bicolano families with devotions of this kind describe themselves as being in a **gusi** relationship with the saint; they farm his land, and share the harvest with him. A part goes to pay for the costs of the devotion, and the rest is used by the family. Bicol saints have thus been integrated into both the patterns of equal circulation of land which marks siblingship, and the parental or patron-like model of share-cropping.

The way in which the saint is like a parent or patron becomes even more evident during the devotion itself. Bicol devotions can be held by individuals, families or a whole barangay or town. They also vary in what they involve. Sometimes a folk-dance or sung drama is rehearsed and staged for the saint in a private house.[8] Other saints must be dressed and decorated to take part in the public processions of Holy Week. However, all devotions have common elements; prayers are said and hymns sung before the saint over a novena period, and on the feast day itself, a meal is offered to all the participating kin, and to any other devotees and volunteers. The food may vary from **ibos**, noodles and ginger tea in modest houses to a fiesta-type spread of rice, different meats and sweet dishes in wealthier families. During the novena of a barangay patron-saint, several families each evening will undertake to supply snacks for the singers and the village children who attend at the chapel.

The meals given as part of a devotion are remarkable for the way the saint seems literally to preside over the occasion. This is all the more visually striking when processions form part of the devotion, since these mostly take place after dark. On the last night of the novena of San Ignacio, for example, the patron saint is carried around the furthest extent of his barangay, on a little wooden platform lit with kerosene lamps. The people of his **sakop**, or dominion, walk before and behind him, singing the old (partly Spanish) devotional hymns; everyone knows the tunes, but the words are prompted line by line by one woman who carries a worn written copy. Partly for this reason, there are pauses at the end of each phrase, and the alternation of pause and raw but ethereal two-part harmony can be heard for a great distance over the ricefields. The procession passes with difficulty along unlit paths for several kilometres until (getting hoarse by now) it reaches the most distant hamlet, where the families take turns to entertain the saint and procession. In 1989, it was a very modest bamboo house without electricity. The saint was set down in brightly lit splendour on the ground, and everyone was handed rice and noodles in half-cylinders cut from the banana tree, for the family did not own many plates. We ate in the dark under the glowing gaze of the saint. We did not get back to the chapel until two in the morning, the fields by then under an enormous moon.

This procession illustrates several features of the saint as patron. Firstly, the saint seems to preside over a meal, or distribution of food, made in his or her name. The saint is therefore a kind of host. This is specially clear when the meal is held for a barangay saint in front of his chapel – for like the shrine of the **Ama**, such buildings are always known as the 'house' of the saint.[9] He is therefore entertaining at home, the patron providing food for his guests. When the devotion is held in a family house, the saint in a sense takes over the house of his family – he is, after all, a kind of family member. A **paralibot** saint is always said to be 'invited in' (**inalok**) to the house of the sibling who has the devotion for that year. He is given hospitality, but is also seen as giving it (as was, I argued in Part I, also the case with spirit birthdays).

The sense in which the saints give food and act as hosts is very clear in some of the stories told about devotions. Alicia, asked by the **Ama** in a dream to hold a **Pasion** reading as a devotion to him, was without any food to give a meal to the readers. Her mother lent her rice, but she had no fish. On the day of the devotion, her husband went out to the pond, and came back with an extraordinary catch: 'There were great big **puyo** and **talusog** and **hito**, lots and lots of them.' What is more, the food was medicinal, prompting her sick baby to begin to eat again. The **Ama** had himself supplied the food necessary for his devotion.

The **Ama** is exceptional in that he has relevance to the devotions of a circle of people much wider than the family who care for him. However, all the saints endowed with land can be said to provide the necessities for the meal and costs themselves, especially as saint's fields are said to grow well, unless the saint disapproves of the lives of the family who are sponsoring him.

In practice, the direct link between saints and the food they provide has been attenuated by the problems of land shortage and water contamination in Calabanga. Fishponds give low yields because of commercial pesticides, while some families have pressed saints' fields into their own use, or even alienated them, although this is locally disapproved of. Several saints in Calabanga do retain their fields, but where they do not, the family usually maintains the devotion using earned income or whatever money is available to them. Patronage remains only in the sense that families attribute their economic success or at least survival to their saints.

With or without their land, Bicol saints can in fact be seen as a kind of inherited property which creates and maintains kinship at the broadest level, when those who are distantly related as 'siblings' gather together again to participate in the devotion. It is important to remember that there

is nothing fixed about the largest level of kindred which Bicolanos sometimes call a **tribo**; indeed, people frequently forget or neglect (and sometimes rediscover) their potential membership of such gatherings. But like a
'family reunion', a devotion offers the opportunity to claim that 'we are all
siblings', and even when the couple who were the parents of the original
**magturugang** has been long forgotten, the 'siblings' remain connected, as it
were, under the gaze of the saint, who guarantees their relatedness in the
present without reference to a specific ancestrality.

Beyond the group of siblings some saints may act as patrons to a wider
circle. Both the processions and the meals gather people together under
the protection of a saint – as his **sakop** or following, just as the funeral of a
distinguished person or the birthday-party of an **anito** does, making
visible the extent of his influence and the number of his supporters. But it
is on the basis that he is parent as well as child to their families that people
appeal to the **Ama** and other saints; since he is family, they do so with a
certain confidence and sense of entitlement, and even more so because
they appeal to the holy figures above all on the basis of a shared experience
of the love between parents and children.

## The pity of mothers

. . . never mind if I feel pain, if only my child doesn't.   (Alicia)

**Promesas** are vows to perform a particular devotion or 'sacrifice'
(**sacrificio**) to Christ. They are made when someone is ill; they may be
made by a sick person on their own account, or on someone else's.[10] In
Bicol, they are made especially by parents for sick children, and although
the spouses will discuss it between them, everyone agrees that the main
burden falls on mothers because 'it is women who look after the sick'.
Women who keep devotions are clear about their purpose. As Alicia says,
'My **promesa** is for my family.'

When a child is persistently sick, the family will start to consider a devotion. This may be as simple as attending mass seven times at the **Ama**'s
shrine, but often it means deciding to hold a reading of the **Pasion**. For
those involved in the **tanggal** I described in the previous chapter, the idea
of promising the child to play a part suggests itself. Mercy, the woman
who played Mary in 1989, became involved in this way. As her mother
Tiang Genny recalls: 'My child was ill all the time. She had measles, and
already it was serious and she couldn't speak. So I said, only let her
recover, and she will do Mary.'

Such intentions are often confirmed by a dream or sign from a holy personage. In Tiang Genny's case, this was a mysterious woman who might have been Mary.

I was taking Mercy to the doctor every Sunday, and once when I was riding in the motor-tricycle there was another woman riding with me who I didn't recognise, and she said, 'Where are you taking your daughter?' I said, 'To the hospital, madam.' And she said, 'Your child is looking for a remedy, she is looking for a devotion.' And so my elder daughter said, 'Mother, let's have a reading, and I will see to the expenses, so that the little girl will live.'

In Calabanga, these signs often come from the **Ama**. Alicia, whose baby son Teofilo seemed as though he would not recover from diarrhoea, had laid the little boy to sleep next to her on the mat when the **Ama** came into her dream. Dressed in purple as the Nazarene, he told Alicia exactly how he would like the reading held, with a white altar-cloth and people singing throughout in pairs, then told her 'I'll go now, because you know my errand and it's up to you to carry it out.' These signs encourage people to carry out devotions, making of them a personal compact with a known saint.

Just as people identify Bicolanos funerals and the funeral of Christ, so women with devotions find an identity between their experience of their

Figure 9  The **tanggal**: Mary with the dead Jesus

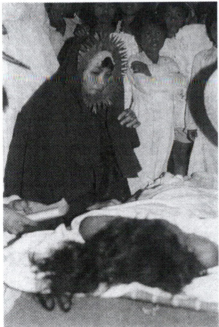

children's sufferings and Mary's pain for the suffering of her own child. One of the passages which many people picked for me from the **Pasion** text as being most important, as a moment when 'your thoughts really pain your inner feelings', is the episode in which Christ meets Mary on the way to the cross. '*Your eyes dear mother, see my flesh*', he says. '*This pain of mine, this heavy Passion, oh, only see it.*'[11] Ilar explained this passage to me:

What her child wanted, was to show his mother, just for her to see his Passion . . . But his mother, she was so pained, so unhappy. But he insisted: 'Look at your child suffering this pain!' That's where you will really weep, when Mary replies: 'Oh my dear offspring, my most beloved child, my delightful new being', she says. Why has her child to suffer? She says her pain is the same as her child's and she begs that she might climb up there instead of him.

Ilar and many other women see in Mary's pain their own pain at the sickness and deaths of their children, and stories about the making of devotions include almost formulaic remarks to this effect. As Ilar says, echoing the reaction of Mary that she finds so touching: 'Never mind if I feel pain, if only my child doesn't.'

Of course, as Catholics, these women are aware of the instructive intention of the **Pasion,** and to some extent they endorse it. Included among the passages people picked out for me were many of the **hulit,** or sermons, which invite people to repent and mend their ways.[12] Yet it was striking how little the discussion ever turned to sin and punishment, or centred in any way on the afterlife, heaven or hell. Instead, people suggested that, hearing the **hulit,** those contemplating aggression against others would think again. The one concrete example they suggested was that badly behaved young men might feel sorry that they had wounded their parents, to whom they should be grateful. The general tone of these comments was summed up by Ilar. 'If you're already going grey, and haven't yet become a well-ordered person (**tultul**), then it's a waste of those grey hairs.' The **Pasion** should make you think of right behaviour in this world, but your fate in the next is comparatively underplayed.

Similarly, while many women wove echoes of Mary's suffering freely into their accounts of their own children's sicknesses, few made use of the parallel to point a deliberate moral.[13] Mary was never put forward as a model to follow by Bicol women in the way that some authors have suggested occurs in European Catholicism.[14] The emphasis, as in the case of funerals, was more on what was shared between Mary's experience and their own.

In the previous chapter, I argued that this sense of shared experience (shared 'pity') drew participants in the **Pasion** and Lent devotions into the experience of Christ, and hence also into a share of his power and healing. This is very similar to the logic of blood sacrifices, flagellation and nailing as described by Zialcita (1986). Devotees in Pampanga who have themselves nailed to a cross do not fear illness or permanent injury, says Zialcita, because 'By becoming Christ's intimate, the flagellant believes that Christ will grant his request' (1986:59).

What the women who undertake devotions for their children are doing, it seems to me, is to read their sufferings as already constituting a shared experience with Christ and Mary, which ultimately leads to sharing in the healing power and help of the holy persons. This is strongly suggested in the way the moment of crisis, and the making of the promise, are recalled. Leonor vividly remembers her fears for her youngest daughter's life.

> The illness she had, probably if not for the Almighty she would have been under the ground by now. She had a terrible illness, I was already weeping over her, because I didn't think I would be able to bring her back here alive. The doctor even asked me if I had put her name in the death-register yet . . . My mind was confused, and I couldn't sleep. I begged the dear God for help, I made a promise,[15] and after that evening her fever really did come down. The doctor was astonished . . . but it was really from God, you see. I had no other hope but God.

Even before they volunteer to take on a formal sacrifice, the women already know what sacrifice means. The **promesa** in a sense merely converts this suffering into a form in which the help of the **Ama** is actively solicited. But the way in which that contract is made needs to be looked at more precisely.

### Begging for help

. . .you will ask for help from the dear God . . . [and say] . . . what it is you are going to give back to the dear God . . . (Leonor)

('. . . **mahagad kang tabang sa mahal na Dios . . . [masabi ka] . . . kun ano an iba- balos mo sa mahal na Dios . . .**')

Leonor's account of making a **promesa** is typical of the way women presented such moments in several ways. The promise is made during a moment of extreme crisis. The person calls on the help (**tabang**) of God or the saints – often it is the **Ama** – and promises something in return. This help is given, usually in the form of the recovery of a child, before the promise is fulfilled. Devotions are thus a kind of conditional or proposed exchange with the **Ama**.[16]

The story of Alicia's vow for her daughter Cristabel, mentioned above, illustrates this aspect of conditionality. The doctor had said that the child would probably die from bronchopneumonia. As a last resort, Alicia sent her older son to buy Vick's Ointment blessed at the shrine of the **Ama**.

I said to the **Ama**, for there was no one else there: 'Alas now, my **Ama**, teach me what will make her well, for she's not suckling any more.' I said we'd make a penance to him, mother and child. And that's when it passed through my mind to massage her with the Vick's. I said to the **Ama**, 'Teach me, Holy **Ama**, what should be the suffering of the mother and child.' I talked it over with the **Ama** (**kinaulay ko si Ama**). 'Never mind if I sacrifice', I said, 'as long as my child lives'. And so it came into my mind that we would go round, mother and child, and ask for alms, and so send a mass to the **Ama**.

These encounters are always described by Bicolanos as 'asking for help' (**maghagad tabang**): '*Ama, tabangan mo kami!*' ('**Ama**, help us!') is the summons which begins everyone's prayers. This word, tabang, has two key implications. Firstly, to ask for help is to place oneself in a dependent position, to throw oneself on someone's mercy, to admit need. Secondly, however, it is to do so with a degree of confidence both in one's right to ask, and in the likelihood of the request being met. **Tabang** is what one can expect from those closest to you; it is the assistance of those who should not abandon you and who cannot disown you. It may come from your superiors, who have plenty to give, or your parents; it may also come from your good neighbours, if on some particular occasion they have something and you do not, and in that case they will expect you to return the favour later, 'helping each other out'.

Although the making of a promise consists in offering something in exchange for the help of the saints, it is always implied that the material means, and physical and emotional strength needed to carry out the **promesa**, come from the **Ama** as part of the help that he gives. As a young woman struck down with a severe attack of TB, Ilar began to have dreams of a statue her parents had once kept, of Christ crucified, but she saw that it was broken:

I said (to the **Ama**): 'Why have you shown me this. Did you want to be mended? But the trouble is, I'm ill now, you see that I can't even get up. Only, you just go to my father's sibling's place, because they've got money.'

The next night, the cross appeared again intact, and helped Ilar to stand up, signalling the beginning of her recovery. Once she had recognised the request being made of her, the **Ama** was willing to fulfil it on her behalf, since she was unable to do so.

Another way in which a person performing a devotion feels **tabang** is in the ability to endure physical hardship. At the simplest level this includes the ability to stay awake all night in the vigils of the **Pasion**, which is said to strengthen rather than exhaust those who take part. The passion-players must stay awake even longer, for the **tanggal** takes three days and two nights, and the man who plays Christ will also fast for the period 'of Christ's death' between the representation of the crucifixion and resurrection.

Everyone who performs devotions says that they do not feel tiredness or pain after they have finished, but on the contrary feel lightness, healing and happiness.[17] Any self-inflicted or accidental wounds rapidly heal. Again, this is an aspect of sharing in the experience of Christ's suffering and hence in his power and healing. As Jose Santiago said: 'Once, it seemed that the **Ama** was about to sit up, and they say he nodded at me . . . it seemed that he saw our sufferings.'

Jose Santiago, after a lifetime of involvement in the **Pasion**, sees his life shaped by the **Ama**. 'I have been helped, there are signs', he says. 'My children all passed through the Holy Passion, and so they had luck come to them.' Although Jose has lost his sight, he does not regard this as a failure of the **Ama**'s help. Instead, he says: 'It seems like a miracle that was given to me. Because I can't work any more, but my children earn for me. That you see is the return the **Ama** has shown me, because I accepted the penance in the past.' As Alicia says, 'it seems that the help of the **Ama** is hidden'; but it is revealed when the recipients and their families name it and interpret it as such.

I have argued that the religious **promesa** is made in a context which stresses the kin-like relations between saint and family. In devotions, people take on some of the suffering of the **Ama**, and by sharing in this way in his sacrifice, they also share in his powers of healing. Pity and help thus flow from those engaged in devotions to the **Ama**. But they also flow in the other direction, as people beg for the help of the **Ama** and experience their ability to complete the devotions as itself due to his help.

There is an ambivalent aspect to the **urulay**, the negotiation, in which the **promesa** is made. By 'begging for help', people cast themselves in the role of dependent petitioners. But they also ask with a certain confidence; in moments of crisis it is sometimes almost as if they demand the appearance of the **Ama** with a certain peremptoriness; he is, after all, kin, and one should be able to rely on the assistance of one's family.

**The nature of exchange with the *Ama*, and the effects of Christian conversion**

It is often said that the stereotypical representation of Christ in Philippine Catholicism is as a divinity to whom an unpayable 'debt of gratitude' is owed (Hollnsteiner, 1973:65; Zialcita, 1986:57). In the making of **promesas**, however, the prevailing idiom is not one of **utang** or debt, but instead one of **tabang**, or help. In the context of everyday secular life, the contrast between these two terms is clearly made by barangay people: do not lend money to close relatives if you need to get it back, they say, for kin will be inclined to treat your loan as **tabang** rather than as **utang**; they may thank you for it, but they may also forget about it, subsuming it under the category of family sharing and support. The casual meaning of the term **tabang** as applied to the **Ama** looks similar; he gives his devotees assistance, it seems, while not expecting them to provide him with anything in return. In fact, the contrast between 'help' and 'debt' is not so clear-cut.

In discussing the relationship between healer and **saro** in chapter three, I commented that **utang** does not carry a simple negative meaning in Bicol, either in dealings with supernaturals or in business between humans. 'Debt' can in fact be understood as a kind of 'help' even in monetary transactions, where the key fact is not the absolute standard of interest charged, but the willingness of the lender to 'talk to' a borrower in difficulties, and to avoid foreclosure on the loan. For poor people in Bicol, the category of 'debt' remains socialised, although at some cost, and the relationship of healer and **saro** turns on this ambiguity.

If 'debt' can be a form of 'help', then the example of religious **promesas** suggests that 'help' is also inseparable from 'debt' and obligation, even when it is the 'help' of the **Ama** which is under examination. As I have argued, **promesas** which the devotee initiates contain more than a hint of the contractual: on the one hand, the devotee usually does not begin his 'sacrifice' until after the 'help' requested (such as the recovery of a child) has been delivered; on the other, there is the notion that one should say at the outset, 'what it is you are going to give back to the dear God' and even the possibility of divine retaliation if, having made the bargain, one defaults on the terms. Despite the best efforts of the local priests to emphasise the duty of unconditional worship and gratitude to God (acknowledged in the references people make to the need for giving thanks to God), 'bargain' is in fact not an entirely inappropriate term here. Bicolanos sometimes refer to other people's **promesas**, if not to their own, as **negocio**, a business deal. For his part, the **Ama** tends to be fairly specific in the instructions he gives his petitioners through dreams about the type of **Pasion**-reading or other service he would like them to perform. The distinction of **tabang** is not that it comes without any demands or obligations; it is that when the **Ama** asks for a devotion to be carried out, he himself provides the resources to fulfil what he asks (fish or money to feed guests at a **Pasion** reading; strength to sing to the end of the text), and thus the means to acknowledge his own gift. While the melancholy of Bicol healers is produced by the anxiety that the 'help' of the **tawo** may turn into unstoppable demands which devour the healer's life, the devotees of the **Ama** know that they will always be provided with the means to give satisfaction to their benefactor.

At this point, the Bicolano idea of the **Ama** as a God who always credits his own debtors seems surprisingly close to attitudes among new Tagalog converts to Christianity in the seventeenth and eighteenth centuries, at least as these are reconstructed by Rafael (1988:167–209). Rafael argues that the mass enthusiasm for conversion to Catholicism among ordinary Filipinos could only be accounted for by the seductiveness of the Christian idea of heaven. As Tagalog people understood it, says Rafael, heaven came to represent an entirely unprecedented possibility in relations between ordinary people and supernaturals. For while most lower-ranking Filipinos were constantly caught up in cycles of demanding and anxiety-provoking debt and obligation both to other men and to the **anitos**, heaven promised a state of continual radical fulfilment of one's obligations to superiors, and 'definite expulsion of any state of loss' (Rafael, 1988:173), in which one is utterly protected by God and thus forever preserved from 'the consequences of exclusion from divine patronage: the unrelieved sub-jection to the assault of everything one fears' (Rafael, 1988:179) which is itself Hell. The power of the innovation, Rafael suggests, was reinforced because before conversion only the elite could ensure protection against predation by spirits after death, by providing themselves with slaves who were sacrificed with them as a substitute offering (Rafael, 1988; 192–4).

While Rafael's argument that conversion to Christianity worked through the modification of ideas of exchange and obligation seems extremely persuasive, however, I would suggest that there are also certain difficulties in assuming that conversion totally and permanently re-ordered Filipino social relations. One problem arises from the fact that the self-fulfilling contracts with supernaturals which are apparently very similar to those between the **Ama** and his devotees, also occur in non-Catholic parts of the present-day lowlands. Polo (1988), for example, describes the Binalayan fishcorral ritual in Leyte terms which are reminiscent of this idea of promesas. The fishermen summon the spirits of the sea with a food-offering (including fish, and sweets) in the **pananampit**. They appeal humbly for their mercy, but also invite the spirits to remember the gifts and payments they have given them, and to respect their right to fish in order to live.

Come eat,/ And I will pay you/According to our belief/ You Datu Lawron because you are the Datu of the seas/ I need your help . . . (Polo, 1988: 49)

In both kinds of appeal for 'help' there is an expectation that the offerings given will be enough, and that the claims which are made will be recognised. At certain moments, then, and in certain contexts, the ambiguous **tawo** can be treated with relative confidence as givers of 'help' who will be satisfied with what ordinary people are able to provide, and with what, in the end, like the fish and the money for sweetmeats, is derived from the bounty of the supernaturals themselves. It is not that spirits are never good patrons; it is only that the saints are more reliably so. Admittedly, it would be possible to argue that contemporary lowland 'animism' has been constructed through ideas of 'help' which actually derive from Christian models. On the other hand, it is difficult given the historical evidence to be sure that no such **Ama**-like 'gift' processes existed in religious or secular contexts before Philippine conversion.

The second difficulty with Rafael's argument is of a slightly different kind; that is, if he is correct to argue that the radical appeal of 'heaven' was what drew the seventeenth-century masses to Catholicism, it would appear that (as is perfectly possible) some fundamental changes and reversals have taken place in the intervening centuries. For, as I have argued in the preceding chapters, Bicolano Catholics in the late twentieth century are not especially concerned with the ideas of heaven, hell, purgatory or the relationship between Catholic notions of sin and the fate of the soul. They do not appear to use the idea of heaven, even a re-interpreted heaven, as an important metaphor for ideal forms of social relations, and self-fulfilling contracts of the kind reminiscent of Rafael's Tagalog Paradise are invoked not so much in the context of discussions of the afterlife, as in the context of access to healing power in this world.

One might in fact wish to consider both the blurring between **utang** and **tabang** and the Bicolano indifference to heaven as a kind of refusal of the logic of transcendence which is supposed to accompany the advent of Christianity, and perhaps other 'salvationist' religions (Parry, 1986; 1994: 251–71). As we saw in chapter four, Parry points to Christianity as one precipitating factor in the creation of ideologies which oppose a category of 'pure', 'altruistic' gift-giving to one of desocialised commodity exchanges. The material on both healing and relations with the **Ama** shows, however, that while rural Bicolanos are not unaware of either a language of capitalism or a language of disinterestedness ('thanks alone'), they tend in both speech and action to focus on ideals of exchange which maintain the continuities between 'help' and 'debt' rather than allowing them to fracture irredeemably apart. What is one to make of a local form of Catholicism which lacks interest both in the idea of 'altruism' and in the imagination of Paradise?

Discussions of the problems which Christianity poses for people in ordinary life have a long pedigree which (although few anthropologists seem inclined to claim the connection) was probably first articulated by Hegel as the ʻunhappy consciousnessʼ which is the fate of humanity when power is seen to withdraw from immanence in the material world to a transcendent world beyond, leaving mortals, as it were, orphaned (Hegel tr. Knox, 1975:301). The same problem was rephrased in more familiar works by Durkheim (1984:231) who claimed that '. . . it is only with Christianity that God finally goes beyond space: his kingdom is no longer of this world. The dissociation of nature and the divine becomes so complete that it even degenerates into hostility', and again by Leach (1983:75), who emphasised the need for mediation in Christianity.

An influential discussion of these issues in European peasant Catholicism is provided by Pina-Cabral (1986).[18] The Portuguese of the Alto-Minho, argued Pina-Cabral, are faced with the logical difficulty inherent in the other-worldly focus of Christianity, which promises access to transcendent divine power, but only at the cost of a privileging of the 'life after death' over the life of this world, and the future life of the spirit over the present life of the flesh (Pina-Cabral, 1986:234–6). Since it is impossible for persons other than celibate religious specialists to renounce their involvement in the present world, peasant communities seek to tap divine power through various unorthodox forms of mediation and to reintroduce it into the world.[19] Minhoto mediators include a cult of the dead souls in Purgatory, 'non-eaters' (who live off the Communion wafer alone) and the cult of incorrupt bodies. These persons, known to have led a religious life, are popularly acclaimed as saints if their bodies do not decay, and are eventually displayed with the acquiescence of the Church.

The idea of keeping bodily relics of the saints, or displaying preserved or mummified flesh, is one which provoked horror or amusement among those Bicolanos to whom I suggested it. To Europeans, incorrupt bodies seem to be a central symbol both of a truimph over time (Dahlberg, 1987) and of a kind of truce in the battle to determine whether this world or the bodyless world beyond is more important. Bicolanos, by contrast, wish to prevent decay only *before* the renunciation of the body by the family, and are thereafter concerned only with bones and not flesh as objects which could be kept and re-appropriated.[20] The **Ama** is clearly a different kind of 'body'; like all Filipino saints, he is an image, not a cadaver. His participation in the nature of humanity resides not in the halting of the normal rules of fleshly corruption, but in conjoining the qualities of the inanimate (wood) and the animate (a growing child) so that the differences between them become null. I would argue that this is subtly but distinctly different from the (finally impossible) attempt to re-unite immanent and transcendent power towards which the logic of European incorrupt bodies seems always to be straining.[21]

When the **Ama** returns to his house from his own funeral year after year to lie in state in his glass coffin, what is enacted is a permanent drama of liminality of which the Lent celebrations are only the most explicit manifestation. As the dead Christ, he is presented as continuously occupying the time between life and death; he is not ascended into heaven; he is not resurrected; he is in fact in the mysterious, suspended state similar to that which takes hold of Bicolano healers when they lose their 'personhood' as their soul journeys elsewhere and before the arrival (if any) of their **saro**.

While the Minhoto incorrupt bodies re-introduce some of the power of the transcendent world above (the spiritual world) into the world beneath (the world of flesh), and set up other oppositions (played out for instance in anti-female gender symbolism in a way which also differs from Bicol contexts), the movements of the **Ama** seem differently ordered; he continuously crosses back and forth between the visible and the invisible worlds, which (in so far as the invisible world is not exactly heaven) are not in the relation of hierarchy to each other which is the hallmark both of orthodox Christian teaching and, apparently, of European popular Christianities. The indistinct **kadikloman** of the Bicolanos may be a world of beings more powerful than ordinary mortals, but it is not necessarily a location of moral superiority, of a 'life' which is 'better than' this life. The **Ama**, then, is not the same kind of 'mediator'.

In fact, while Bicolano healers cannot always 'manage' the **tawo**, and risk becoming lost in the world of the invisible people, the **Ama** is never lost and always returns. He is, in other words, continuously performing something that I have described as the idiom of shamanism in Bicol, the ability to cross between the world of the living and the world of the dead or the **tawo** (the two as I have shown not being very clearly separated) and to return unscathed many times over, resisting the tendency of any other power one might encounter to overwhelm, annex or destroy you. The **Ama** is of course Christ and everybody knows it; it is simply that the Bicolano

Christ is imagined as being in this respect like the most powerful and exemplary of shamans.

### Bicolano healing and the absence of political event

This interpetation suggests a possible answer to some of the questions raised at the end of chapter five. If the **Ama** is the most accomplished of shamans, it is entirely appropriate that he should be so well attended by healers at his shrine. It will be recalled that those healers themselves attempt in this and other ways to imitate Christ and so share intimately in the power and protection he offers. Each healer then attempts, in many different and often idiosyncratic ways, to effect a perfect combination of these powers with those which issue from relationships with the **tawo**, either through the agency of a **saro** or through the use of **anting**, 'healing in your own voice', and so on. The huge variety of Bicol healing may be viewed as indicating the lack of any single, definitive version of the best management of the rapports between healer and **tawo** and **tawo** and Christ. Yet at certain moments in Filipino history, it appears that people have felt that such ideal combinations were possible.

Writing about the 'millenarian' peasant uprisings of the 1898 Filipino revolution, Ileto (1979) has remarked that the Tagalog provinces, on which he concentrates, took a different route from the related traditions of uprisings in the Visayas; while the Visayans tended to group behind **babaylanes** – that is, mediums and shamans who emphasised their inspiration by the **anitos** rather than by Christianity – the Tagalogs found a language of revolution in the Passion story, originally of course a text of colonial conversion. What is of interest here is that the Tagalog peasant leaders described by Ileto clearly identified themselves with Christ, and with the stages of his life and final sufferings; they also, however, availed themselves of **anting** and other sources of power associated with the gifts of the spirits, rather than with even an unorthodox reading of Christianity, and most possessed **anting** which were thought to ward off bullets in battle.

It seems, then, that at a moment of intense political activism, the Tagalog leaders (and possibly in a different way the Visayans, for even the most 'traditional' of Visayan healers integrate references to Catholic liturgy into their rituals (Echauz, 1978:109–11)) successfully combined the possession of arcane magical power with the profound 'sharing' with Christ which would strengthen them and allow them to deploy it with greatest effect and safety. It is therefore possible that there is a correlation between the two phenomena, and that the florescence of organised forms of healing which tightly combine the power of the spirits and intimacy with Christ are characteristic of periods of popular political activity; it is even conceivable that some such explanation might account for the multiplication of **paraanitos** groups in Bicol in the turbulent period after the war, of which people in Calabanga spoke. Meanwhile, however, it seems that the relative political quiescence of the present period may be one factor which is correlated with the bewildering diversity of Bicol healing styles, and the multiplicity of solutions which healers propose to the problem of finding the best way of talking to the **tawo**; and it is in this context that the image of the dead Christ itself remains for the present the best shaman.

I began this section by stressing the multi-strandedness of Bicolano views on death, and their ambiguous, contextual and contested nature. In these three chapters, I have attempted to retain that impression, while exploring the extent to which ideas about death are coherent, centring around themes of imitation, identification and pity, separation and sharing, and the movement between the worlds of the living and the dead. I argued that while pity between the living and the dead must be forgotten, pity may flow to the **Ama** and be called forth from him by those engaged in the attempt to heal their kin, among whom he is in some ways included. In the next section, I will concentrate more closely on the importance of physical appearance, transformation and the arrangement of the face and body, in the context of secular rituals and performances.

*Ritual enables them to close the power gap*

# PART IV

BEAUTY CONTESTS

# 10

---

# Beauty and the idea of 'America'

*Matibayon mag-arog an mga bakla*
*(The bakla are very good at making things resemble each other.)*

**Beauty, mimicry and transformation**

In the previous section, I considered some of the meanings of the term 'imitation' in Bicol in the context of religious acts such as the Passion Play. In this chapter, I turn instead to imitation in secular performances. The reader will recall from the introduction how often it has been suggested that Filipino lowland culture has been eviscerated by the American colonial experience. Even sympathetic observers have sometimes argued that the 'Filipinos were mentally recolonised in a discourse that not only extolled American culture . . . but that also degraded the Spanish colonial past . . . aborting what could have grown into a distinct Filipino civilization' (Mulder, 1991:6).[1] I shall examine what imitation might mean in those areas where the term has been applied most derogatively to the low-lands, that is in elements of popular culture which have the contemporary West, and especially the image of 'America' as viewed from the rural Philippines, as their primary referent.

If the legacy of Spanish Catholicism continues to dominate popular religiosity, it is the legacy of the American colonial period and its schooling system which has made the most obvious impression on public secular life. The Americans demanded from their colony the evidence of the growth of a 'democratic' civic sensibility of a certain kind, and they were extremely successful in eliciting at least its outward signs. The middle classes of each small town organise themselves into prayer-groups for the devotion of the Sacred Heart, but also into groups of Rotarians and Lions. Seminarians training for holy orders play basketball in their spare time. Small primary schools in the barangays field teams of drummers and majorettes in all the major town celebrations, despite the difficulty parents have in raising the money for the uniforms.

Local entertainments and celebrations have also been touched by a deference to 'American' standards and values thus understood. People in rural Bicol still usually spend the time they have to enjoy themselves collectively rather than privately, in fiesta visiting, in dances organised by the barangay adults' organisation or discos for the barangay youth, and in many of the neighbourly events already described. A partial exception to this is the cinema, which people can visit for a few pesos in the local town centre or even in Naga as a special treat; but trips to the cinema would usually be undertaken with several co-godparents, relatives and children, rather then on one's own.[2]

Especially popular whenever the occasion offers, in addition to these pastimes, are both talent contests (**amateuran**) and beauty-contests, which are held for many different categories of entrant, but especially for women and for the **bakla** or male transvestites. The history of beauty-contests in particular is a long one, going back to the Spanish period in which wealthy families fought to have their daughter win a title as a way of promoting her chances of an exceptional marriage;[3] in fact the contest was one in competitive giving; the winner was determined according to the amount of sponsorship money she attracted from her backers, to be donated to the Church.

Although some events in contemporary Calabanga (such as the 'Mrs Calabanga' title to which I refer below) continue to be organised in this way, a shift in the preferences of audiences and organisers in which the **bakla** community was highly active took place in Bicol in the 1960s, towards contests based on American-style meritocratic principles and known as '**brains and beauty lang**' ('brains and beauty only') contests. The organisation of the contests also consciously follows models such as 'Miss World' and 'Miss Universe', both in the selection of events to be staged, and in the construction of series of heats, held often in very small towns, leading to regional and even national-level finals.[4]

Judges at such contests, invited from among the local worthies such as male and female town councillors, doctors, wives of judges, and former contest winners (as well as visiting anthropologists), are asked to make their decision on the basis of points awarded in various categories such as Voice, Presentation, Diction, Artistic Interpretation, Charm and so on.

The official money-competition has been eliminated from such contests, although of course a contestant with a wealthy and interested sponsor willing to promote and to provide costumes and equipment will always be at a distinct advantage.

The cinemas which Bicolanos eagerly attend have a more indirect relationship with 'American' culture. Approximately a third of the larger movie-houses in Naga City show mainly English-language films which are often from the States, and which are attended by those whose education gives them confidence in English, from Catholic girls' school pupils on up the age range. These cinemas are usually air-conditioned, and the ticket prices are higher. The other big Naga venues, as well as the single smaller cinema which usually stands at the centre of little towns like Calabanga, cater to what is slightly impolitely known as the **bakya** ('wooden clog') crowd; that is, the less sophisticated audience not comfortable with English. The movies which are shown here emanate from Manila, from the extremely active national industry which makes and distributes films with local stars in the language of the capital, Tagalog. Most Bicolanos are quite capable of watching their movies in a second language, even if not in the most prestigious one.

Tagalog movies are locally classified into three kinds: **mapangisi** ('something to laugh at'), **laban** ('fighting') and **drama**, i.e. sentimental melodramas, sometimes related to nineteenth- and twentieth-century Filipino popular theatre styles. The **laban** movies (which are often imported from Taiwan) are popular with men, and are mostly martial-arts films involving rebellion, injustice and explosive outbursts of violent fighting. Although these are interesting from several points of view, it is with the other two (home-produced) categories that I am more concerned here. The comedies are often pastiches of Western genres, starring favourite comic actors. *'Starzan'* for instance, which I saw with friends from San Ignacio in 1989, presents a sort of Filipino poor-man's Tarzan who, accompanied by his ever-bungling companion, wins the hand of the lovely mestiza Jane. **Drama** stories centre on love (romantic and familial), the exploitation of the poor and powerless by the wealthy and corrupt, and the triumph of virtue over humiliation. A typical protagonist is the innocent country-girl gone to work as **katabang** to an urban family who abuse her, and in such stories the settings portray a hyperbolically luxurious (if somewhat kitsch) world of brocaded furniture, circular bath tubs and push-button phones, where the spoiled sons of the rich toy with imported foodstuffs at elaborately set tables.[5] Plots however often include elements taken directly from Filipino folk-belief, including witchcraft, possession and matters relating to kinship. In these films, the audience experiences the world of the wealthy 'American' outside at one remove, mediated as it were through a portrayal of the life of the national elite who have access to it.

Each of the key roles in a **drama** – good girl, good guy, bad guy and bad girl (or **contravida**) is played by a nationally famous filmstar with a following among the audience. Actresses such as Sharon Cuneta or Snooky Serna who usually play the heroine are especially important to women as models of beauty and a fashion look described as 'just simple' (**simple lang**); this is in fact highly artificial by Anglo-American standards, but contrasts in its gentle attractiveness with the deliberate sexual provocation of the **contravida**. While one model of beauty may be taken from the luminous images of the mestizo **santos** and **santas** (and one might dress one's little girl to take part in a procession with this in mind), another is taken from the world of the movies; since many of the most admired filmstars are themselves considered 'mestizo/a' in appearance, the two ideals often overlap. In an older age-group, the actress Nora Aunor, herself born to a modest Bicolano family, reminds people of the possibility of being lifted into a different life through beauty and talent, although to most this remains at the level of a fairy-tale.

It is also possible to listen to several Tagalog radio stations and buy Tagalog as well as Bicol newspapers, but people in the barangays rarely buy newspapers and usually prefer the local Bicol-language radio, which features numerous **drama**s of its own, in soap-opera form. These stories are rather similar in tone to the film plots, although of course the visual element is missing.

Although the idea of becoming the next Nora Aunor may be far beyond most people's thoughts, people in Bicol are extremely interested both in the art of giving a successful performance and in the art of making oneself (or others) beautiful. Since, even beauty-contests apart, it is very important to present oneself well in public, the two often go together, and everyone hopes to be found **magayon** (beautiful) or **guapo/pogi** (handsome) or at least to be approved of as being 'respectably dressed' and not to have his outfit mocked as **baduy** (vulgar or clashing). It is these preoccupations which frame not only the most obvious performances, but also many events in ordinary daily life.

### Beauty in the barangay

In an article published in the *Women's Home Companion* during my first stay in Bicol, a journalist voiced a fairly common complaint about the perverse effect on the poor of the 'distorted sense of beauty' fostered by

America; 'parents' with daughters who enter beauty contests, laments the author, 'forsake a harvest's earnings to splurge on the gay neighbourhood beautician . . . and on a banquet for guests' (Hatol, 1988:12).

Although I never knew anyone spend a whole harvest's profit on the beautician, it is true that, for Bicolanos in the barangay, their own and their children's appearance is extremely important, and sending family members well dressed into the world is a source not only of family pride, but also of care for that person and the desire to protect them from 'shame'.[6] What the journalist didn't note, however, was that like the many jokes of those 'who have nothing' which I described in the introduction, the barangay attitude to 'beauty' is also an ironic but genuinely funny comedy, a play on the gap between heartfelt consumer aspiration and the limits of possible achievement.

On any occasion at which dressing-up is required, a fiesta or a barangay dance, for instance, relatives and neighbours will arrange to share some resources, women passing round the powder-puff or piece of scented soap between households. Friends then greet the arrival of each of their workmates, now wearing carefully pressed clothes, and shoes instead of muddy flip-flops, with a cry of teasing but genuinely celebratory admiration, and appreciative clicking noises:

**Abaa-na ini, an gayon-gayon mo na ini! Ay, nakahigh-heels na si Manay, ay! Nakabeauty na !**

(That's too much, you're so beautiful! Ay, Elder Sister's put her high heels on! She's really put her beauty on now!)

Thus the chorus which greeted Nana Trinidad, a married lady then in her late fifties whose pleasant face and strong form showed evidence of decades of work in the ricefields. Everyone else was treated to similar congratulations, for the point is not to embarrass any particular person, but to enjoy a collective transformation of oneself and one's peers, while at the same time gently poking fun at it.

This kind of humour surfaces all the time in relation to the question of 'beauty'; thus while Nana Trinidad and her workmates were actually engaged a few weeks earlier in planting a muddy field full of rice, they heard the amplified Tagalog and American pop-music of the young people's disco drifting across the fields, as the sound-system was tested in preparation for that evening's event. The women in the fields began to joke about the dance, wiggling their hips and holding out their muddy planting-clothes as if they were dancing-clothes, but with their feet firmly stuck in the paddy. This way of dancing as a joke or parody is something women do all the time amongst themselves, miming cheek-to-cheek romantic clinches in a way they would never put into practice with their male partners, with whom public dancing is often accomplished, but usually rather stiffly.

The air of something on the edge of parody attaches to performances which are much more seriously given. At a wedding I attended in the summer of 1989, for instance, formal toasts had been extensively exchanged between the in-laws, and people had settled into groups of men and of women and had continued passing the beer around and pouring toasts. Women always say that they cannot sing 'until they are drunk' and therefore it always happens that someone will eventually be declared so, and will be prevailed upon to 'put aside their shame' (**hale an supog**) and to sing. In contrast to the formal dialectic of the toasts between affines, this singing will always be a 'solo' affair, and the performer is thus somewhat exposed, since except for the local adepts, semi-professionals who have won many competitions, solo singing is always (understandably) felt to constitute somewhat of a risk.

On this afternoon, it was my neighbour Nana Ilar who was declared 'drunk' first. She therefore got up and began to sing one of her favourite party pieces, the melancholy American song which ends:

... but I miss you most of all, my darling,
When Autumn leaves start to fall.

Although she can sing all the most moving scenes of the **Pasion** with great calm, fortitude and accomplishment, and despite the fact that crying in public is not usual when one has not declared oneself 'drunk', Ilar usually ends these 'solo' sessions in tears, as do the other women. What seems to be at issue is not so much the literal (and generally modest) amount of alcohol that anyone has consumed, but the shift into a different register of emotional expression.

Ilar performs her song with some aplomb, and its style is very much to the local taste, its sweetness and melancholy allowing for a general sharing of feelings of 'sentiment' in a context where people are together with those they are close to, and where all kinds of thoughts or memories may add to the atmosphere of vague regret.

Although the specific references of the lyric are not very clear to people (I was often asked to explain the 'Autumn leaves', for instance), I would suggest however that it does make a difference that Ilar should choose to sing in English, something she *only* does when 'drunk'. Since this is not a language she speaks (but is a language she was taught at primary school),

her ability to memorise the lyric is both a more-than-averagely-impressive
display of skill, and therefore an above-average risk. Bicolano audiences
do not like their performers to slip up too much, and when people are not
consciously joking, there is always a seriousness about the intention to get
things right, and a serious sense of élan and achievement about doing so.
Being 'drunk' helps one to take this risk, lessening one's 'shame' at the
thought of falling short.

Moreover, it seems possible that one element in the 'sentimental' and
nostalgic atmosphere of the singing is built precisely out of the origins of
that risk; the loss that the author signified by 'Autumn leaves' makes no
immediate sense in the tropics, but the idea of loss itself does; in singing a
song part of whose meaning escapes one, one evokes, among other losses,
the sadness at not having completely understood, at being excluded in relation to a cultural register which, if one masters it, can open the doors of
possibility and change one's life.

## Overcoming shame and becoming beautiful

The problems of 'removing shame' in a performance come into play even
more forcefully in the more formal setting of the **amateuran**, or singing-
contest. These events, which might take place somewhere within reach of
San Ignacio about once a month, and more often near fiesta, attract
contestants from a wide area. They arrive carefully dressed and carrying
their 'minus-one' tapes, on which the original vocals can be turned down,
so that the performer can sing with the backing track. This is important
for two reasons: firstly, it means they will have learnt the song (I have
watched several people do this) by literally mimicking the performance of
the singer on the tape over and over again; secondly, it is the explanation
for the frequent minor disaster of Bicolano **amateuran** in which the ropey
sound equipment is not equal to the task of eliminating the vocal track,
and the contestant sings a duet with the artist on tape. This is not popular
with audiences, and even less so (thought sometimes defended by competi-
tors) the attempt sometimes made to cover a weak voice by opting for 'lip-
sync' – miming to the sound of the original artist rather than singing
themselves. The **amateuran** are enjoyable, but they are also taken very seriously, and blunders in taste, voice or dress deplored by the spectators.
Young men favour an '**amerikana**' (two-piece suit) while young women
usually essay the '**simple lang**' look of the virtuous film-heroine, and a
degree of decorum is expected.

The key figure at the **amateuran** is the master of ceremonies or **emsee**;
there may be two male **emsee**s or a man and a woman, but never a woman

alone. An **emsee** is a curious mixture of folk character and figure from media entertainment. The person chosen for the job is always someone Bicolanos describe as **masuba** (jokey). Being **masuba** often implies an ability to get away with sexual joking without causing offence; for an **emsee** it means an ability to play with the potential shame and embarrassment of the situation of performing. As Apolinar Mendosa, the barangay captain of Hinulid and one of the two male **Emsees** there put it in part of his patter to the audience:

**'Dapat sa emsee daing supog, ano?'**

('An MC should never feel shame, should he . . . ?')

A reminder perhaps that the other situation in which Bicolanos habitually use **emsees** is at traditional weddings, when they have to set the pace of games in which guests are asked to give as much money as possible to the newlyweds. Since in most contexts in Bicol society shame (**supog**) is positively valued, and to be classed as 'shameless' is heavy criticism, the **emsee** clearly falls into a category of licensed transgressors. Demanding, giving or refusing money is perhaps the quintessential situation in which feelings of **supog** come into play within the barangay, and the **emsee** has to dispense with shame in order to increase the pressure to give, but also to mediate tensions and rivalries, as well as possible feelings of obligation and inadequacy, between the guests, so that neither donors nor recipients finally feel shamed by the amount given at the wedding. A wedding **emsee** is also **masuba**, and it would be quite possible for the same person to perform both kinds of **emsee** role.

Some contest **emsees** adopt a stylised comic manner, laughing hysterically or asking repeated stock questions. This was true of the **emsee** at another local **amateuran**, a local young married man known to be good at the role. As each contestant appeared, he would give a gasp and cry out to the audience (who were highly amused):

**Garo artista! Iba na an pagkaguapo kaini . . . garo mas guapo sakuya, pero kun nakaparigos ako, dai ako napadaog . . .**

('He looks like a star! The handsomeness of this one is really something else . . . could be he's more handsome than me, but if I had had a chance to wash, he wouldn't have got the better of me . . .')

This continued with each contestant, as he pointed to their shoes or suits, demanded to know whether they had fiancees and announced their availability to the young people of the barangay, and so on. Female contestants sometimes, but not always, got off more lightly than the males.

The teasing by the **emsee** does not stop with the introduction of each contestant, since he or she would also comment after each entrant had sung their piece, and often – whatever the standard of the singing – in terms of fulsome praise which came painfully close to sounding like mockery.

People I asked about the **emsee** would often casually remark that he was supposed to **hale an supog** – to remove the contestants' shame, by joking with them and putting them at ease. In the light of this comment, it was always striking how much **supog** the **emsee** seemed to be inflicting on the singers. In fact, I never saw a contestant attempting to match the **emsee**'s banter with their own; instead they would stand meek and still, politely answering the **emsee**'s questions with near-inaudible but formal sentences:

**Emsee:** '. . . my goodness, this one looks like **si Richard Gomez** [a Tagalog film-star] . . . Tell me, where did you get your **amerikana**?'
Contestant: 'Sir, my brother lent it to me.'

The rural teenagers thus embarrassingly compared to major Tagalog filmstars suffered it all with the same self-deprecating downcast eyes and partial smile.

The contrast is all the stronger, then, when the contestant begins to sing. They do not seem to sing as themselves. Rather, they become, as well as their (sometimes considerable) individual talents allow them, a singer, a star, the **artista** to which the **emsee** has just incongruously compared them. Gestures from Western pop performers and the Tagalog singers they influence are choreographed into the performance; careful expressions of emotional excruciation very different from the normal Filipino facial repertoire, and set-piece, conscious singers' movements, spreading the hand with a crescendo or raising and lowering the microphone.

It is no reflection on the skill of the performers (the best of whom may turn professional) to point out that the dramatic shift between normal body-language and forms of expressing emotion and those which obtain during the performances lend the whole occasion a slightly stiff and contrived air. Each performance is a personal transformation, and a shift in language – literally so, because Bicol songs are not used at **amateuran**, where the repertoire is always in English and Tagalog. Favourite songs performed during the summer of 1989 in Calabanga contests included (for women) a current hit called 'Eternal Flame', and for men, besides several sentimental Tagalog hits, the ubiquitous 'My Way', the anthem of middle-class male Filipino drinking sessions. One child performer with a precociously loud voice had been coached in a song in English called 'While

We're Still Young.' The song had fairly explicit references to an adulterous affair which sounded odd to me coming from an eight-year-old, but the Filipino audiences found that the title made it appropriate enough. Two choices of song caused more of a stir: a pretty fourteen-year-old who won the contest by singing the Beatles' hit 'Yesterday' (fairly new to San Ignacio) in an enormously powerful voice, and a diffident young man who sang a famous Tagalog song from the 1950s star Victor Wood, '**Bakit Di Kita Malimot?**' (Tag. 'Why Can't I Forget You?').

This last caused a division of opinion among local audiences. This song, with a mournful, vaguely Latin-American, orchestral accompaniment, builds up to a chorus in which Victor Wood was famous for ending each line on a choking sob:

Why can't I forget you?
Why can't I leave you behind? . . .
Why did you make me love you
If you only wanted to cause me pain? (my trans.)

. . . and so on, each aspect of the original being faithfully reproduced by the performer in Calabanga, sprung like the others out of his acute bash-fulness. While some of the audience enjoyed this revival of an old favourite, a number objected that it was unfashionable. One rival contest-ant disapproved of the high marks the singer had got for his technical abil-ities and took me aside afterwards (for I was one judge at this contest) to advise me that the choice of song was **baduy** (vulgar and unfitting). 'He should have sung something classier, like Shirley Bassey', he reproved me.

Groups of teenagers anywhere in the world practising their favourite songs would of course expose by the small details they had not yet mas-tered, the artificiality of the entire language of pop. Yet there is a difference between American and Bicolano teenagers engaging in these performances. Perhaps it is because the qualities which pop fetishises (sexual love as the source of a person's most truthful experiences and the idea of youthful rebellion, to name but two) are so much less dominant in the lives of families in Bicol barangays than in the life of Western individ-uals. The Bicolano performance – like a performance on the **gamelan** given by talented music-students in England – is also an attempt to perform the cultural context of the piece, and some parts of that context remain a long way off.

### Becoming beautiful

I have said that beauty contests are a common event in rural Bicol life, and I should stress that they take place at all sorts of different levels, and involve many different kinds of people as contestants. The town fiesta proceedings of Calabanga in 1989, for instance, offered the possibility of winning more than a dozen titles, some reserved for unmarried girls (the 'Miss' titles, as they are known) and some for married ladies. All the winners then paraded on floats in the fiesta-day procession. The runners-up each had their own title ('Mrs Health and Hygiene'; 'Miss Temperance', and so on) but the prime title for the matrons was 'Mrs Calabanga'.

I had watched the run-up to this contest with some interest, since Anita, a mother (and spirit-medium) from the neighbouring barangay, was competing for the title. Since this competition is still won by sponsorship, she had also been using her considerable (sometimes oppressive) persuasive abilities and numerous contacts to fill as many of her little donation envelopes as possible. She had hired a yellow sequinned tight-fitting dress and made ready to hire a float and balloons, and to entertain her supporters at a party.

In the event, Anita came third, having raised P.11,000; she and the first two winners were allowed to keep a proportion of the money raised. The first place was taken by a woman who had married a Chinese businessman, and who raised the enormous sum of P.63,000. The new 'Mrs Calabanga' was somewhat younger than Anita (who was then in her fifties) and quite pretty by local standards. Probably anticipating her win, she had dressed in a long, frilly white dress rather like a wedding-gown and accompanied herself on her triumphal walk with three pairs of little children, each in a different style of Filipino or Western formal dress. The watching crowd let out the customary admiring comments of **'Magayon!'** ('Beautiful!') as she went past, and also admired the second and third prize winners in the same way. She was, of course, putting on a tremendous display of status and of the financial power of her backers in the Chinese community, and her self-presentation seemed to comment on the dual kinds of 'beauty' to which the contestants here were staking a claim: on the one hand, personal prettiness (especially 'mestiza' looks) and on the other, those aspects of 'beauty' which can be bought – grand clothes, complete make-up, the evidence of who is behind you, and the affirmative acclamation of the crowd.

'Beauty' in this sense is a protective layer, a covering of status which shelters those who have it. And although the central contests of the Bicol region both for women (the 'Miss Penafrancia') and for **bakla** (the 'Miss Gay Naga City/ Miss Gay Penafrancia') are now run without the money-competition which makes this so apparent, I will argue that this meaning of 'beauty' continues to be part of what makes the contests compelling for performers and audience alike. Both major contests are held at the time of the regional fiesta for the Virgin of Peñafrancia[7] in Naga City, and I will describe the Miss Gay Naga City Contest 1988, at which I was a judge.[8]

It is not the purpose of the present chapter to attempt a comprehensive account of **bakla** identity in Bicol, nor to speak primarily to issues in 'gender theory', but it is of course important to understand something about the lives **bakla** people live, and the peculiar mixture of tolerance and potential lack of respect or even contempt with which they are treated. Like everyone else in Bicol, many **bakla** have parents who are poor farmers or farm labourers. Inside the barangay, **bakla** are in some ways very much accepted. The identity '**bakla**' is offered to little boys who seem happier doing girls' chores and wearing their clothes, and the child gradually either accommodates or angrily rejects it. Such children are sometimes teased, but they are neither ignored nor persecuted. Many mothers calmly admit that one of their children is **bakla**, and most people agree on the identifications; 'That's just how he is', they will say, or 'that's just what's natural to him'.[9] They are not especially interested in the unequivocal definition of how someone came to be that way and usually offer several explanations or none at all.[10] There is a kind of non-authoritarian attitude in Bicol social life generally, which accommodates the **bakla**, so that they are rarely the targets of hatred or prejudiced violence as is sometimes the case for gay or transvestite men and women in the West; however at the same time **bakla** are not always treated as persons of equal dignity compared to other adults.

Their own self-definitions are complex, and often shift according to context. All **bakla** would say they are men 'with women's hearts' who therefore love men, and love to dress in women's clothing and perform female roles. Everyone I met rejected as bizarre and distasteful the dominant Anglo-American interpretation of being 'gay' – that is, being a 'gay' man who desires another similar 'gay' man – and claimed that **bakla** never go out together and love only 'real men' (i.e. non-**bakla**). **Bakla** may however use the imported English word 'gay' to describe themselves,[11] or sometimes, in a curious adoption of another English term, they say they are a 'third sex', neither men nor women. This, at least, is part of the discourse of being **bakla** as people chose to present it to me; the personal realities may be more complex.

The 'real men' with whom the **bakla** fall in love are credited with an invulnerable male sexual identity, which is not thought to be threatened in any way by their relations with **bakla** (although it would be if they themselves chose simultaneously to play the **bakla** social role to other men, in which case they would become **silahis**, i.e. those with ambivalent sexuality).[12] Married men with families who have loved **bakla** are sometimes quite happy to talk about this, ranking it as a sexual exploit similar to having had many female mistresses.

In many ways, the **bakla** adopt the sexual and domestic woman's role in relation to 'real men', perhaps devoting themselves to a live-in boyfriend, and worrying that (as often happens) they will be abandoned because, unlike actual women, they cannot have the children which cement a marital union. This 'feminine' position is however fraught with contradictions. **Bakla** often look for younger boyfriends, to whom they can offer the inducements of financial support in college or in a business, while nonetheless casting themselves as idealised, dependent housewives. 'Real men' moreover tend to cast them as sexual aggressors, almost sexual predators, and in practice if not in theory there remains a certain ambiguity about the nature of sexual relations between the lovers.

These relationships are often sources of unhappiness, and it is not uncommon for **bakla** to be taken advantage of by their boyfriends. Partly for this reason, many adopt a different attitude, more cynical about 'real men' and the chances of a lasting union, and out for a good time. In fact, all **bakla** also define themselves as a group as people whose vulnerability is balanced by their intense powers of attraction and seduction, and claim to be consummately skilled in 'persuading' the boys they fancy (**kursonada**). And while they often say their lives are constrained by the impossibility of becoming 'real women', **bakla** I knew would also express considerable doubt about the desirability of, say, actually having a sex-change operation. As people sometimes put it, as a real woman one has certain limitations of personal freedom and physical strength, and while it would be good to acquire a woman's capacity for pleasure, it would not be desirable to lose a man's. It was even possible at times to see the **bakla** position as one in which one had 'the best of both worlds'.

What I wish to focus on here, however, is the articulation of the **bakla** and the non-**bakla** communities, which takes place mainly through the preferred **bakla** occupations, as seamstresses, hairdressers and beauticians in the many parlours which spring up not only in the big city, but in every tiny town. The 'subculture' of **bakla** life revolves around these parlours, and most although not all **bakla** graduate to them from the barangays, though like all good children they may go home to help with the harvest.

Women and **bakla** in fact divide the beauty and dressmaking businesses between them, and public opinion holds that while women may be more trustworthy, **bakla** are more artful in altering appearances. They therefore occupy a very particular position as mediators of beauty and glamour. As all Bicolanos say: '**Matibayon mag-arog an mga bakla**' ('The **bakla** are very clever at imitating things'), implying a sense of being good not just at mimicry, but at making things look like other things. In the rural barangays as well as the towns, the **bakla** are the experts in transformation; they transform others into beauties in their professional lives, and transform themselves into beauties in their private – or at least their performative – lives.

The **bakla** in fact often seem to assimilate their identity to a language of visibility and hyper-visibility, frequently talking about their charismatic power to seduce as '*exposing ourselves*'. A common **bakla** greeting is to say 'How is your beauty?' instead of 'How are you?' and to substitute in ordinary conversation the phrases 'my beauty' for 'myself' and 'your beauty' for 'yourself'. Non-**bakla** people frequently repeat **bakla** jokes and turns of phrase amongst themselves; little children in the barangays, for instance, are taught another **bakla** greeting to amuse their elders; one person claps the raised hand of a small child and exclaims, '**Apper!** because you are a **bakla!**' After a while, the child learns to raise his hand himself ready for the clap. Exactly what the greeting means is slightly ambiguous; most claim that the **bakla** slang ('**swardspeak**') word '**apper**' is an inversion of the Tagalog '**pare**' – literally 'co-godfather', but used widely to address friends and equals – but some think that '**apper**' is derived from the English word 'appear'. In any case, the point of the game is clear; the adults are teasing the children by claiming to 'reveal' that they are in fact **bakla**; the trick is more amusing to everyone because it is played on very little children who cannot yet speak or understand properly, and who are too young to repudiate the label. At the same time, since this game is so widely used, it is possible to look at it in another way; the **bakla**, supreme experts in imitation, are themselves constantly and universally imitated by other people.

Most **bakla** make their livings in less sophisticated surroundings than they would like. In Calabanga, the parlour was a small, open-fronted shop near the main market next to a grain dealer's. It had a mirror, but no basin, and was run first by Mona and then (after a little disagreement with the landlady) by Linda. Linda's mother, a farmer's wife in her seventies, would drop into the shop each afternoon after shopping for food, and was always treated with politeness and affection by the **bakla** who used the shop as a meeting-place and base for their boyfriend-hunting forays. The customers were mostly women, but with a sprinkling of men.

When Linda's mother was not there, the shop was notable for the continuous card-playing which went on hidden under the table, for the surplus of manicurists which meant that customers had to be shared out, not always without squabbles, and especially for the continuous performance of 'being **bakla**' which Linda and her friends gave for each other. The following description, is taken from notes for a hot afternoon in July.

Linda is on form, keeping up a hysterical conversation while cutting the hair of a young woman into a fashionable bob. Apparently, Linda is paying no attention whatsoever to the haircut, casting occasional sidelong glances at the progress of the work as if it were something somebody else was doing. She pauses, on the other hand, for long periods to strike a pose in front of the mirror and exclaim to the room: '**Magayon!**' (I'm beautiful!) or '**Gi'til!**' (Vanity!). Her client, though, can see that the haircut is going well. A woman friend comes in with a new boyfriend and Linda screams a greeting:

'My Jesus, amiga, you made such a clever choice! . . . He's so good-looking! . . . I'm falling in love . . . do you mind? Do you want a haircut? Let Tess do it – I'm going to do your boyfriend's nails myself.' Linda places a hand over her heart; 'What a choice', she repeats, 'not like Tess, she'll take any man as long as he's big', and then correcting herself with another shriek. 'O **keme**! Don't be angry now, will you?'

Of course, Linda's conversation is an act, but it is an act which all the **bakla** know about; the idea that they are vain, trivial, charming, infuriating, flirtatious and hysterical; an idea represented in talking **keme** – the gay slang (**swardspeak**) for nonsense, mischief and naughtiness. This process of continuously performing an identity was something Linda personally took to extremes, but all the **bakla** I knew could switch in and out of it according to whom they were dealing with.

The leader of the region's **bakla** community is Mr Tata Flores, who runs a successful dressmaking business (and sponsors a basketball team as well as numerous beauty-contestants) in the more luxurious surroundings of Naga City. Tata belongs to one of Bicol's leading families; he grew up speaking English and has worked abroad, and it is he and his friends (male and female) who over the past twenty-five years have turned the 'Miss Gay' contest from a private event held at home into a high-status show which has become a highlight of the year, and which has done much to achieve his ambition of increasing the respect in which the gay community is held in Bicol.[13]

Over the years, Tata has earned for his show a reputation for 'high taste', artistry and technical sophistication which has allowed many of Naga's most respectable progressive citizens to support it. The status of the contest is now such that in 1988 it was officially opened by the talented young mayor of Naga City, who made a speech (in Bicol and English) articulating the wishes of both sides when he claimed that the enormous popularity of the contest '. . . *is a sign that gays are being rendered due recognition and respect in their chosen field and personality . . . the "third sex" is already accepted . . .*' This announcement, with its gloriously economical evocation of the quintessentially American ideology of self-improvement and self-fashioning, placed the show under an umbrella of safe and admirable qualities, a point driven home when the mayor went on to stress the contest's contribution to the civic and business life of the city. The total confidence of the statement was, however, a little political sleight-of-hand, as some elite people are still not entirely sure of their ground with the contest.

But it is equally only because of the responsive chord which the shows themselves have struck with the public of all ages and classes – who throng Naga's main piazza to watch – that these claims were able to carry conviction. By the time of the 1987 show just before my fieldwork, for instance, its fascination was such that a huge and heterogeneous audience sat through a tropical downpour in the unprotected square rather than miss seeing part of the contest. My argument, therefore, is that the Miss Gay contest and its preliminary heats in small towns like Calabanga (equally well attended) are now essentially a popular festival, and that the appeal of the show for a huge non-**bakla** audience both demands and suggests explanations.

I have said that **bakla** are known for their artistry in creating beauty. The crucial and extraordinary thing about the Miss Gay contest is that they create themselves as beauties. As **bakla** see it, the social respect they have won comes from their skill in achieving a dazzling self-transformation. A trader, Oning, explained this:

People say that if you put the Miss Bicolandia show against the Miss Gay the Miss Gay contest is altogether more beautiful than those of real women, and they say that the gays look more truly womanly in their movements when they are . . . modelling on the stage . . .

And I did indeed hear people remark over and over again on the beauty of the **bakla**; it was a subject which fascinated most people who had seen the show; 'The real women are defeated by them; they really look beautiful', was a typical remark. People would speculate on how they achieved their effects, or relate stories about men who fell in love with beautiful **bakla** and courted them as if they were women. What is significant is that, although there was an element of disapproval of the **bakla** and their 'artful' ways, there was equally a genuine excitement and admiration evident at the transformations that they wrought. People may deprecate the **bakla** – but they also enjoy the effects they create.

The audience's recognition that they are like women – or even better – is terribly important to the **bakla**. But when I asked them about the experience of performing in the contest, they always replied in slightly different terms. The experience was always one of happiness, they said, '*When I am up on the stage . . . my feelings are really truly happy.*' But the reason for this happiness was not just that you felt like a woman, but that you felt like a star (**sikat**, 'superstar').

'*If you win*', said Pablo, '*it's as if you are famous (sikat) just for the evening . . . you feel as if you . . . will be recognised . . . if you have been Miss Gay*'. 'Do you feel that you're a woman?' I asked. '*I'm a woman then! And then, I'm really very happy . . . because . . . enough to say . . . its like I'm becoming a superstar.*'[14]

Or as Oning says, '*If you win, it means that you are deserving. That night you're the best. You're the most beautiful, the cleverest . . . That is once in your life that you will have something to say for yourself . . .*' This triumph, however, is achieved only by the exercise of all the **bakla**'s artistry and by the long and exacting practice of walk, smile, pose and English diction in the weeks before the contest. The **bakla** practise with friends and learn from each other's performances. As Oning says, 'You have to research how to be in a beauty contest.' The greatest shame that a **bakla** contestant can imagine is that 'People would find fault with you and say you hadn't studied it.' Not only would one be ridiculed in front of one's fellow-contestants, but in front of the audience whose appreciation of the serious achievement before them is so keenly sought, and the judges with their pencils hovering over the boxes for Poise, Appearance, Originality and Charm. The beauty of the **bakla** is artistry and its successes are hard earned.

## The Miss Gay Naga City Contest, 1988

The following account is taken largely from my fieldnotes for the Miss Gay contest of September 1988.

The preparations have dominated Tata's house for weeks. All Tata's seamstresses[15] are employed making the contestants' orders. Several at once are bent over a shimmering violet and white evening-gown with white and silver flowers embroidered down the front; it has a boned bodice and a tube skirt which break into layers of frills at the knees, thus giving the **bakla** figure plenty of shape. The seamstresses are also fielding **bakla** contestants turning up to register their applications from all over the province; these beauties, as yet dressed only in their everyday street-wear of jeans and feminine top, preen themselves in front of Tata's long mirror. The swimsuit heats are to be held later that week, at Naga City's municipal pool, and Tata has made the swimsuits for the contestants to model, as exact replicas of those in the Miss Bicolandia contest.

On the evening of the finals, the make-up artist Danny is rushing about between faces; I am put into one of Tata's formal creations in cream frills and covered in Revlon in order to pass muster as a judge. I notice that Danny and I have exactly the same make-up, but he can make my fringe stick up higher in the favoured style, as I have more hair. When I join the other judges (three female dignitaries including the vice-mayor, one male councillor, and two female beauty-queens), the stage is brilliantly lit with expensive sound equipment in place, and the plaza is absolutely packed. The **bakla** who are not competing are mostly in women's clothes, and busy with arrangements; Danny has become 'Daniella'; Tata claims he is too old and fat to wear a dress anymore – but perhaps he is just a little too dignified these days.

In fact, the acts are highly accomplished, the dancing fantastic, the audiences' admiration genuine. The **bakla** have chosen stage names –

Figure 10  Jennifer de Assis's angelic smile

Barbra Ledesma from Ligao, Ging-Ging Padilla from Pili, Alice Robles Narvades from Naga – which recall Tagalog filmstars, and old Spanish elites. Most of them are simply dazzling. Jennifer de Assis appears looking fragile in a white, empire-line evening dress trimmed with silver; feeling the admiration of the audience, she lifts up her arms, spreading the cloth like wings, and gives an angelic smile. Claudine Louise Ferrari, with severe waxed chignon and a gown hand-painted with pastel-coloured flowers (she has a rich sponsor in Manila, a boyfriend perhaps), provokes admiring comment even from Tata, who declares her turnout 'quality'. The close-up photos, taken by Naga's photographers and sold in local shops for weeks after the event, reveal a little more the large hands or too-broad shoulders. But for the moment on stage, the **bakla** are beautiful and elated, and the audience is elated with them and caught up in their triumphant beauty.

As the contestants begin to enter to show their daytime outfits, I notice a group of fantastically dressed **bakla** sitting at a table to my right; one has flowing auburn hair and a peacock-coloured satin dress; another is (in a country of short people) almost six feet tall and wears a streaked blonde chignon and a black and pink satin dress with a thigh-high split. These amazing creatures are last year's title-holders, and members of the Naga-Manila beautician elite in their daytime jobs. They sit glamorously sulking at the thought of handing over their crowns in an hour or so's time.

Meanwhile, the other judges and I are working hard to keep track of the multiple boxes on our mark-sheets. The former female beauty-queens take a knowing professional attitude to the event, and most of the women seem at ease with the two sides of the contest, the one very serious and the other a tremendous tease or **keme**, but some of the men are flummoxed by their own reactions to the contestants' allure (a fact of which the **bakla** are well aware), and have to take refuge in a technical approach to marking. Everyone, however, is enjoying themselves.

After the talent section, which featured a lip-sync to Judy Garland's 'New York, New York', and a scene lifted from a Tagalog melodrama in which a famous star portrays a mad beggarwoman, came the questions and answers. The questions, in declamatory English, had been carefully set by Tata to be 'beautiful, not vulgar'. Nevertheless, those on politics and ethics received only vague replies. Other questions, a little less beautiful, seemed easier to answer:

Q: What part of a man's body most attracts you and why?
A: The part of a man's body that most attracts me is . . . whatever part that you think it is.

Q: If you found out that your boyfriend is also gay like you, what is your reaction?
A: I would feel deteriorated [sic], but then we could get together, after all there are plenty of men and we could look for new ones together.

Q: If you were the first gay saint, what is the first miracle that you would do?
A: Well, if it was up to me, I would arrange it so that all the **bakla** would be made into real women!

At three o'clock in the morning, Barbra Ledesma is made Miss Gay Penafrancia and receives her crown from last year's sulking beauties, who are in tears. The audience begins to drift away, but the atmosphere is still one of lightness and festivity. Miss Gay Naga City has her picture taken with her old mother. Someone remarks to Danny the beautician: '*What a waste of your beauty, Danny, that there is no dance.*'

## Difficult transformations

I have argued in this chapter that the Miss Gay Naga City beauty-contest has become a popular festival because at one level it is a triumphant realisation of mastery in a performance genre in which *all* Bicolanos (**bakla** or not) have a common interest. The combined lure of international consumer culture, filtered through the national culture which is centred on Manila, and the legacy of American colonialism which established many new genres of secular performance as the evidence of progress and good citizenship, is one to which people respond powerfully in the Philippines and with good reason. People from all classes, moreover, have the experience of taking part in some such performance, whether in school parades, majorettes practice, the **amateuran** or (in middle-class homes) sitting in the back yard with some friends, some beer and the karaoke set, singing 'My Way'.

I do not want to imply that when people take part in such activities they are necessarily thinking consciously about the problems of 'post-colonialism'; mostly, of course, they are thinking about getting the song right, and enjoying themselves in ways which have in many senses become domesticated as part of the Filipino scene, and which therefore appear banal. Nonetheless, the songs belong to a repertoire of elite education, and to codes of behaviour associated with the American colonial and post-colonial presence in the Philippines. While the elite and middle classes feel themselves to varying extents already in possession of these codes, people in barangays like San Ignacio are excluded from them to a much greater degree especially because of their restricted access to Tagalog and English higher education. Yet in relation to both classes, the **bakla** have been able to establish for themselves a position as purveyors of advanced taste. As Oning says:

People like to see something unusual. It is not an ordinary thing to see and so it has a more beautiful appearance . . . my group [of friends] here are elite people, they have very high taste . . . People are happy to see something so rare . . .

This position rests partly on the very ambivalence of the reputation of the **bakla** as both 'artistic' and 'artificial'. They are conceded a place as the most talented exponents of the widely prized skills of transformation through imitation or replication. At the same time, **bakla** continuously run the risk of being considered pretentious, vulgar or fake ('**ma-arte**'). They enact in even more exaggerated form the Bicolano performer's dilemma, walking the tightrope between the elan of successful performance and the exposure of failure, and part of the popularity of the contest may stem from the fact that these spectacular risks are taken vicariously for the audience, and are taken moreover by a group of people whom one can alternately applaud (thus sharing in their success) and denigrate (thus for poorer people distancing the whole issue in a way reminiscent of the defusing action of Bicol jokes on the subject of money).

The risks which Bicolano performers take, however, seem to apply as much to the moment of 'removing one's shame' and daring to embark on the performance, as to the possibility of completing it imperfectly. This makes sense, if it is recalled that shame (**supog**) is in other contexts an emotion which results when two personages who are widely separated, especially by status differences, are brought into sudden intimacy, and that the 'shame' is felt most by the subordinate party. All performances in elite genres can therefore be thought of as a kind of daring attempt on intimacy with the model imitated, which may raise the status of the performer, or may result in them being considered pretentious. The **bakla** are constantly at risk of being labelled 'shameless' by some non-**bakla** people who consider them financially unreliable and sexually promiscuous, but it is this same ability to 'remove their shame' which enables them to fling themselves into almost-impossible acts of self-transformation. In this sense, one can view Bicolano performances (not despite but because of their 'Westernised' themes) as taking place within a context of typically Southeast Asian ways of dealing with relations to power. Not unlike Atkinson's Wana shamans (Atkinson, 1989), Bicolano beauty-contestants and singers at **amateuran** become the temporary bodily 'lodging places for potency' which are felt to orginate from somewhere 'outside' one's own culture (Errington, 1990:46). The **bakla** epitomise these recapturings of power, not literally through possession, but through a wrapping of the body in symbols of protective status, and a transformation of the persona by proximity to the power it imitates, which are in many ways akin to it.[16]

While Atkinson and Errington tend to typologise whole cultures according to whether they locate potency 'inside' or 'outside' their own boundaries however, in the Bicol context one can see that relations to power, and confidence about how far one might already 'embody' it without having to summon it from the 'outside' world are partially inflected by class. Nonetheless, the **bakla** performances speak to both rich and poor, educated and uneducated, with equal if not identical powers of fascination.

I have deliberately avoided centring the argument of this chapter on the question of 'gender', because I would not wish to say that 'gender' is what the Miss Gay contest is 'really' all about. Despite the significant importation of Euro-American gendered and sexualised notions of identity into the Philippines, I would argue that there are good reasons to think that especially among poorer rural people, these are in no simple sense dominant, nor have they become foundational to people's understandings of their own identity.[17] I would suggest that in the rural barangays, people do not in fact think solely in terms of an inner, more authentic and sexually founded (post-Freudian) self in the way that is claimed to be central to Westerners' constructions of their own individuality. This, however, is not to say that they do not ascribe any importance to physiologically based notions of gender identity. Thus, while it would be true to say that non-**bakla** audiences are interested in the fact that **bakla** have penises but behave like and sometimes look like 'real women'[18] (and can therefore be mocked as not-real women and not-real men), I am not convinced that this observation occupies the same space in the Philippines as a central metaphor for authenticity and inauthenticity as it might in England or America.

The contrast between the 'real', the 'natural' and the 'artificial' indeed at times appears to be drawn at different places in the Philippines from what a European or American might expect, with the artificial being more highly valued. Sally-Ann Ness has noted that in Cebu, 'natural' dancing-styles connote, not what is not cultivated and acquired, but what is not exaggerated (Ness, 1992: 114) and similar observations could be made of the Bicol **simple lang** dress-style. When, in a heat for the Miss Gay contest, one contestant's costume came adrift, revealing first his chest and then his genital area, performers and audience were united in condemning the display as **bastos** (rude, obscene), but it was not the dropping of the mask of gender which scandalised people, so much as the display of body-parts which would be inappropriate for anyone of either gender; as the old lady in front of me remarked indignantly: 'Your breasts are showing and your penis is showing, you child of a trollop!'[19] And it is worth considering that this play on transvestites as the most talented exponents of a valued refined style (*alus*) and simultaneously the most likely to succumb to vulgarity (*kasar*) is also characteristic of various performance genres in Java and elsewhere (Peacock, 1987).

The issue of the 'real' and 'pretend' identities of the **bakla** performers is therefore not necessarily reducible to questions of sexual identity. Nevertheless, Garcia (1996) has recently provided a warning from within the gay and academic communities against underestimating the extent to which the lives of Filipino **bakla** are dominated by the painful attempt to become 'female'. Garcia argues, rightly in my view (and see also Blanc-Szanton, 1990), that the arrival of the Spanish probably shifted the definition of male transvestites away from the categories such as **asog** which were centred on occupation (as spirit-mediums who were 'somewhat like women') and towards a category which prioritised sexual practices and orientations. He claims that one consequence of this has been the stigmatisation of **bakla** as sexual 'inverts', as opposed to their previous empowerment as persons of combined gender.[20] While remaining attentive to these issues, I would suggest that (whatever may be the case in the metropolis) it appears that in Bicol **bakla** self-descriptions are at least not univocal in their insistence on the centrality of becoming 'real women', and indeed it sometimes seems as though this aspiration is presented more for public than for private consumption, as against the idea of 'having the best of both worlds'.

If, historically, **asog** and women occupied important positions as mediators in relation to the spirits, it seems that present-day **bakla** (who are no longer mediums though they may be spirits) have been forced onto a different arena of feminised mediation (which of course they also share with female beauty-contestants). What they are mediating is an American-derived notion of glamour which suggests the power and elite cultural codes of the Philippines' colonisers; the fact that this mediation is often routed through an approximation of the Western models of ideal *femininity* may indeed increase the impact of dichotomous notions of gender on the participants, and may also reflect the curious relationship between women and consumption in the West (Benson, 1996). Becoming beautiful in the Philippines has historically been seen as a protective process, emphasising a person's humanity and right to respect, and conferring (via amulets and tattoos) a layering of power, logics which still apply to the use of **anting** and the practice of embalming the dead. By becoming beautiful in the manner of Miss World, one acquires the armouring of a different cultural repertoire but with unpredictable results;

even the dangers faced by mediums in intimacy with the **tawo** are mitigated by the personal relationship between a healer and her **saro**, but in
imitating the feminine icons of the West, one is endlessly at risk of being
directed into the capitalist task of the production of the self, in which no
'other person', human or supernatural, is involved, and no 'help' is available from an outside source. In that sense, the mediations attempted by
present-day **bakla** could finally be seen as even more difficult and burdensome that those of their audience.

# 11

## Conclusion: oppression, pity and transformation

### The meaning of asking for pity

When our first child died . . . he was buried in a hole in the cemetery . . . the ground there's so wet, when they bury them like that, the bodies come up, so they weigh them down with a stone. It makes you pity them.

I was the one who was sent to the priest, because my husband doesn't know how to borrow money (**disponir**) . . . Ay, I said, I'll have a talk to the priest, I'll get a tomb even if I go into debt . . . 'I'll be your wage-worker, sir', I said to the priest, 'I'll do your washing, if you'll let me, as long as my child has a tomb, because pity the poor thing.' They agree, because what can they do? They know you have nothing . . . So all the three children are buried in the same tomb, and we paid the priest ₱.250.

*(Mrs Irene Mojares)*

This story, told to me one afternoon by one of my co-godmothers, stays in my memory as an evocation in miniature of many others, only a few of which it has been possible to include in this book. The stories have a genuine pathos, but they are not told pathetically, nor in the tone of 'senti-mentality' (**sentimiento**) which Bicolanos often enjoy in their music and fiction. They are stories about pain and lack of power,[1] told by people who are energetic, resourceful, frequently given to ironic joking about their situation, and capable of a complex range of different kinds of verbal per-suasion which may serve to ameliorate the problems they face. The people 'who have nothing' must spend a great deal of time in trying to '**disponir**', that is, not only in borrowing money, but also more broadly in convincing other people with more resources and more power to make available some of what they have, to recognise the existence and the humanity of people poorer and less powerful than themselves.

In the preceding chapters, I have traced some of these interactions as barangay people in Bicol represent them. The different aspects of life and cultural practice discussed in this book are not intended to suggest absolute congruence with each other, and I have wished to emphasise that the construction of a seamless and tightly joineried cultural product is an activity of little interest to most people I knew. Nevertheless, I have argued, it is not misleading to describe a consistency between these contexts at the level of a repertoire of representations of encounters with others, especially powerful others, and their possible, ideal, or feared outcomes. Here, I want to present a somewhat more abstract account of the meaning of 'asking for pity', in order to situate these notions of power more explicitly within an interpretation of lowland history, and to draw out what is unusual about them within the context of Southeast Asian literature and the anthropology of 'identity'.

The Bicolano view of society (both as practice and as ideal) seems to fall between two types more familiar to ethnographic rhetoric. It is neither a view of society as a self-justifying and self-legitimating hierarchy, in which every kind of person occupies her or his rightful place, nor is it a radically egalitarian view, in which hierarchical and rank principles are resisted and inverted. In Bicolano power relationships, I have argued, both more 'egalitarian' and more 'hierarchical' aspects are apparent; the point is, however, that they exist in contrast with each other, but also as variations on each other. In particular, barangay people are greatly concerned with *transformation* from states of greater hierarchy, distance and asymmetry between persons to states of greater balance, intimacy and harmony. This trajectory, or at least the attempt to trace it, can be seen in different forms in each of the contexts described in this book; the difference lies in the degree to which it can be relied on to succeed. Arranged marriage, for example, is ideally expected to follow a path from power inequality and even hostility between the two spouses to harmony and balance between affines, and eventually to intimacy, sharing and undifferentiation. The healer–**saro** relationship, on the other hand, remains poised between 'oppression' and the supportive closeness of 'siblings' or 'companions'.

This preoccupation with social process means that Bicolanos tend to see all relationships as dynamic engagements. There are people 'who have nothing' and those who have wealth, beauty and power, but there is always potential for negotiation and persuasion, through · ·hich the painful gap between the two may be lessened, and the power-deficit of the poor, not eliminated but ameliorated.

This greater closeness between the less and the more powerful, however, does not follow automatically. There are usually at least two paths which any given relationship could take; a suitor may fail to win over his 'reluctant' woman or a **saro** may turn from benefactor into predator. Negotiation is therefore not completed once and then set aside, but becomes a central theme of Bicolano life in the barangay, as its work is repeated over and over again. Partly for this reason, 'those who have nothing' tend to stress the ambivalence of power relationships above all: the way in which patronage and exploitation are two sides of the same coin, an acute awareness of which marks the healer's life with melancholy.

At the same time, Bicolanos do not regard the possession of superior wealth and power as the sign of any internal 'essence', physical or spiritual, by which persons are inherently entitled to their status. Power-holders and the powerless are not different 'kinds' of human being in Bicol; the elite are not thought of as distinguished by the exclusive possession of aristocratic blood or qualified for a happy existence in this life because of the spiritual and moral feats they have performed in some previous incarnation. Fate, luck, human and supernatural patronage, hard work, the mysterious will of God, and the pragmatic mechanisms by which the rich always become richer and the poor become poorer are what tip the scales so unevenly, in Bicolano eyes. Powerful and wealthy persons, therefore, demand recognition and appeasement, and may inspire loyalty and gratitude as well as fear and resentment, but they are not icons of a transcendent order beyond themselves which attracts worship, in the sense that royalty or rank may attract worship, in and of itself. Conversely, nothing about a poor man's essential make-up would exclude him from becoming a rich and powerful member of the elite, given the unlikely circumstances which showered him with wealth.

This is not to say, however, that the possession of power is thought of as a purely material matter; on the contrary, as I have already mentioned, many wealthy and powerful men are thought to have gained access to supernatural assistance, and perhaps to be the holders of **anting** which bring them riches and sexual favours. Bicolanos are in fact always trying to establish and negotiate relationships with various figures of power and, as I have argued, are constantly working out the relative legitimacy of dealings with diverse kinds of spirits, and with Christian saints. Despite the colonial history of the Philippines, moreover, the sources of supernatural power which people find relevant remain resolutely plural, and the boundaries between them are still fluid.

What follows from this is that, although there is no unified and explicit *theory* of personhood and the cultivation of power in Bicol, the dynamics of personal interaction are envisaged in ways which are not totally unlike those in areas such as Java where such theories (linked especially to the formal practice of asceticism) are central to culture and politics (Anderson, 1990; Keeler, 1987: 41–8). In Bicol, despite the relaxed tenor of daily life, encounters with other people are often represented as the mutual, though not always conscious or intentional, testing of power and influence. Social life leads to the discovery of who can 'manage' whom, who will be overwhelmed by whom, or will succumb to another's powers of seduction. The greater the initial social distance between the parties concerned, the more imperatively these idioms come into play, and the more urgent the question becomes as to whether these asymmetries will eventually lead to a greater balance between the two.

Whenever two persons come into contact with each other, at least one of them is considered liable to be transformed by the encounter. The more powerful of the two will be protected from alteration (except in so far as he acquires a follower); the less powerful party will not be able to exert enough influence on him for that. The more powerful person, however, will inevitably change the less powerful, whether that change is for the better or for the worse. Contact with supernaturals can, as we saw, produce an increment of power through proximity, as was the case for devotees who intimately share the experiences of the **Ama**, or it can produce a further depletion of the less powerful person, who may be attacked and predated by the superior power. Repeated contacts of the first kind will gradually wrap the more vulnerable person in layers of protective power; repeated encounters of the second kind will gradually strip these layers away and leave the person exposed. Therefore, any Bicolano considering engaging in a dangerous encounter (especially with a supernatural) will need to assess beforehand what protective resources she has accumulated, or the outcome is likely to be risky if not disastrous.

The notion that persons are potentially changed in every interaction with others, and that they are both at risk of depletion and in search of augmentation in dealings with the more powerful, can be expressed through the theoretical language of exchange. In fact, as I argued in chapters four and nine in particular, the ethnography of the Philippine lowlands has been approached by way of variants on the idea of exchange and 'gift theory' both by the structural functionalists such as Hollnsteiner (1973), and by analysts such as Ileto (1979) and Rafael (1988) who are alert to the existential implications of lowland exchange. The Bicolano 'exchanges' I have described, however, fit somewhat uneasily into most anthropological readings of Mauss (1990). This is partly because many applications of exchange theory tend to present it at the level of system – as a sequence of exchanges whose ordering and consequences are predictably governed by the rules of reciprocity – whereas I would argue that the Bicol material obliges one to focus on the level of tension and uncertainty within systems of exchange, on the ambiguity from an actor's perspective of any particular interaction and its sequel. From the inside, the 'rules of reciprocity' look much less clear-cut.

Another curiosity of Bicolano power relationships seen as exchange, however, occurs at the level of persons and things. A mainstream reading of Mauss would present him as saying that persons are typically linked in exchange by the passing between them of objects (gifts) which contain an aspect of the giver which has a compelling power over the receiver, the 'spirit of the gift' (Mauss, 1990:10). In Bicol, however, it often seems that these mediatory objects have diminished in number, or entirely disappeared. Of course, objects-as-gifts do figure importantly in all sorts of contexts; but when Bicolanos talk about power relationships, what they appear to stress is the direct contact of one person with another, in which the persons concerned become as it were their own mediatory objects. Those who are exposed to overwhelmingly powerful forces risk leaving a part of themselves behind if those forces are predatory, and stand a chance of taking away more of themselves than ever existed before, if they are benevolent. It is because of this peculiarity that I have tried to reflect with some care the ways in which such relationships are not necessarily described by Bicolanos in the language of 'exchange', but through the language of an 'emotional economy' which represents the experiences of such encounters through terms meaning 'shame', 'oppression', 'enslavement', blending and 'becoming used to', and especially love and 'pity'.

It is clear that Bicol is by no means the only place in the Philippines where 'pity' is an important and elaborated concept. On the contrary, it has been very frequently cited, although in the context of quite disparate and sometimes contradictory explanatory frameworks. For the Buid of upland Mindoro, for instance, begging for help, food and compassion are deprecated as acts clearly implicated in unequal relations reminiscent of those of ghosts and lowlanders (Gibson, 1986: 128–9, 163, 188). By complete contrast, the Visayan fishermen discussed by Polo cast all their requests to the spirits of the sea as 'calls' or 'summons' for 'something I need from you' and appeal to them to 'show us your mercy as we call on you' (Polo, 1988: 50 and 39; 1985, 62). Not only this, but the same fishermen also use an appeal to 'mercy' or 'pity' to their fellow-fishermen and nominal equals, whenever one of them is placed in a temporary state of disadvantage and requires food, work or a loan. Expressions such as 'How pitiful I am today. I will have to borrow something from you' or other phrases derived from the Samareno terms **kaluoy**, **intawon**, or **kairo** are, according to Polo, the most common and emphasised ways of making such requests (Polo, 1985: 56).

A similar phenomenon is described by Blanc-Szanton (1972) for the fishermen of Panay, also in the Visayas, in her book *A right to survive*. Blanc-Szanton's book takes as its title the articulation of an ethic which she found to determine the working of fishing and fish-retailing in the village of Igbo in 1967–68, and which leads her to a perceptive rethinking of earlier work on Filipino economic behaviour. One of the earliest ethnographers to document the economic priorities actually articulated by her informants, Blanc-Szanton found that Igbo fishermen claim:

Everyone has a right to survive and provide for his family – a right which transcends all other economic and legal considerations.                          *(1972:129)*

Blanc-Szanton describes various processes of 'sharing' (both in the sense of the division of a commodity, and in the sense of allowing participation in an activity) by which the rights of the very poor to food are respected, while fish-vendors who have been unable to secure access to good catches are nevertheless able to claim the right to 'go along with' another vendor's deal, entitling him to an equal share in the profit (or loss) despite an unequal contribution to the capital (Blanc-Szanton, 1972: 123). Obviously the imperatives of distribution among near-equals are similar to those described by Polo, although either Blanc-Szanton did not report the existence of references to 'pity', or else the people of Igbo use a more insistently egalitarian language to describe what others phrase as the workings of 'compassion'.

For the rice-farmers and agricultural workers of San Ricardo, Central Luzon, Kerkvliet has offered an important analysis of related ethnography within the context of an application and critique of the work of James Scott on 'everyday resistance' in Malaysia (Kerkvliet, 1990: Scott, 1985). Noting the frequent use of the Tagalog term **awa** (pity), Kerkvliet links it, in a way which accords with the observations of other authors and with my own experience, to the appeal to the term **kapwa** (Tagalog and Bicol) meaning 'your fellow human-beings', especially in reference to the rights of the poor to recognition from others (Kerkvliet, 1990: 249; compare also Enriquez, 1991: 105). Kerkvliet offers the significant observation, the implications of which I shall return to below, that by contrast with what Scott claims for the Malay peasant 'moral economy', the rice-workers of San Ricardo phrase their resistance to the oppressive implications of the capitalist re-organisation of agriculture not merely as a 'right to survive' but as a right to be treated with dignity (Kerkvliet, 1990: 176–7) and orientate this claim, not with reference to a traditional past of correct social relations, but to an (implicit) inalienable human claim to be treated as having equal value, despite not having equal power (Kerkvliet, 1990: 269). As if to underline how widespread such idioms are, similar findings are reported by Collier (1997) for hacienda workers in Mindanao, in the Muslim Southern Philippines.

The tendency of writers to date has been to explain such idioms in terms of the history of the particular region under study. Kerkvliet, for example, offers two derivations for the San Ricardo talk of **awa**. Basing his argument on the preception that the Luzon idioms are more radically egalitarian in their implications than those of Scott's Malay villagers' 'moral economy', he first argues that they were forged in the period of the proto-communist Huk rebellions of the 1950s. At a greater distance, he suggests, all such idioms are perhaps determined by Christian meanings, since the terms **awa**, **kapwa** and their correlates are certainly embedded in the religious texts of the Philippine languages (Kerkvliet, 1990:272–3).

While both these factors must be important, I would argue that they cannot account for the widespread occurrence of related ways of talking about power in parts of the Philippines with contrasting histories and relationships to Christianity, including both 'animist' and Muslim regions. I would suggest that what is at issue here is the emergence of a more coherent comparative approach to the cultural construction of power in the lowland Philippines (and perhaps parts of the highlands), which can take account of both the local variations and the broad consistencies of its repertoires, linking those aspects which are undoubtedly 'hierarchical' to those which, like the Igbo 'right to survive', look robustly 'egalitarian'.

It would be as impossible as it is unnecessary to disengage many lowland Filipino terms from the history of Christianity. There is no doubt that the conversion of the lowland Philippines altered the world radically and, as I argued in chapter nine, it is surely right to suppose that it also changed the possibilities of social representation in highly significant ways. As Rafael (1988:167–209) has argued, conversion under the Spanish profoundly challenged and provoked re-organisation in Filipino ideas about social circulation, hierarchy and the sources of power. The interpolation of such idioms with Christianity need not however be taken as a sufficient explanation for their existence. Indeed, it seems that in some ways contemporary Bicolanos have either reversed or resisted some of the changes which Rafael claims accompanied Christianity; for although barangay people have placed the **Ama** and the other saints in the position of their most dependable patron and helper – a position which may not have existed in the same way before the conversion – they have also in many ways defied the logic of the economy of salvation, remaining relatively indifferent to the ideas of heaven and hell, sin and repentance, and the moral superiority of the next world over this one. Even Christianity does not appear to have instituted, for ordinary Bicolano people, an unambiguous and permanent hierarchy of heaven over earth.

### Debt-societies, unpredictable status and capitalism

If an ambiguity about the defining effect of Christianity has dogged the Filipino literature, I have traced in the preceding chapters some aspects of a similar argument which asked how far the apparent oddities of lowland 'culture' (or the apparent lack of it) were to be explained economically, a question which was logically linked to the debate about whether or not the lowlands were 'modernising'. As I mentioned in the introduction, this problem often produced a split between different accounts of the Philippines as either societies of 'patron–clientage' or as societies of 'class'.

Kerkvliet, addressing this issue head on, has produced a careful account of a wide range of factors which would allow a judgement about the pertinence of 'class', defined in several ways, to the community of San Ricardo. He concludes that '. . . people are acutely aware of considerable inequalities and of where everyone is positioned. They emphasise both status, meaning basically standard of living, and class, which refers to roles in production' (1990:14). Whether within the rubrics of 'status' or 'class' however, a 'central dynamic of everyday politics . . . is people trying to make claims on each other and on a range of resources according to their relationships to those superordinate or subordinate to themselves and in terms of their interests and values . . .' (Kerkvliet, 1990: 14) The social situation, in other words, is in constant negotiation between the poorer and the better-off, and while San Ricardo is probably a more politically self-conscious and radical location than San Ignacio (and also differs in its exact history of landord–tenant relations), the tension and fluidity which this description evokes are not unfamiliar from Bicol.

A similar sense of complexity in social relations is evoked by Michael Pinches, who also uses the terminology of class to discuss the politics of a squatter barangay in Manila, whose population originates mainly from Palompom in Leyte (Pinches, 1992). Pinches has two especially interesting emphases for the purposes of the present discussion; firstly, he stresses that social inequality in the Philippines is often expressed by the poor as being defined as much by the humiliating lack of respect afforded them by the rich, as by material hardships, even when these are very severe (Pinches, 1992:71–2 and 1991). Secondly, he stresses that strategies for the escape from such degradation follow two different and contradictory paths, one of which emphasises the solidarity and fraternity of the poor, while the other and often more individualised strategy involves a (frequently disappointing) 'quest for respectability' (Pinches, 1992:77). Again, although in different terminology, Pinches reports the co-existence of two sets of values, one more hierarchical and the other more egalitarian, stating that 'individual status assertions have always existed in a state of tension with the ethos of commonality, mutual help and shared class circumstance, and the *esteem* attributed to those who demonstrated these values' (1992:80; my italics) between which families are forced, often painfully, to negotiate.

Pinches' main argument here is that previous accounts of 'everyday resistance' in the Philippines have tended 'to ignore the contradictory character of resistance' (1992:83). While this argument seems of considerable value, the reader will probably have anticipated my objection. I am not entirely convinced that Philippine evidence leads us to attribute such contradictions only to the particular effects of modern capitalism, as Pinches appears to argue in accord with several others writers (and see also Runcimann 1966: 227–47). In fact, I would be more inclined to stress the resemblances between Pinches' material and the idioms of power I have described for Bicol and other rural lowland contexts. Each of these, it will be recalled, also alluded to 'hierarchical' and 'egalitarian' values which could seem to be contradictory, but which can be reconciled when one thinks of lowland social imagination as stressing the process by which one state is transformed (or partly transformed) into the other. Of course, capitalist economic penetration is everywhere in the Philippines in some senses, but a purely economically derived and short-term explanation for these idioms as 'class' looks less likely when one considers the rural as well as the metropolitan squatter context.

This leads me to suppose that there is at least an 'elective affinity' between such contradictions as Pinches describes, and distinctively ambivalent attitudes to hierarchy and inequality which belong to the much more distant past.

We are perhaps accustomed to think of the co-existence of social inequality with the potential, sometimes more apparent than real, for social mobility as above all a condition of capitalism, especially in those contexts where the effects of the global market everywhere force themselves on our attention. But the combination of social ranking with the ultimate vulnerability of such ranking to movements between all social ranks, within one or more lifetimes, was also the defining characteristic of the 'debt-bondage' ordering of society in the pre-colonial and early colonial Philippines. It will be recalled from the introduction and chapter two that whether in the Visayan or the Tagalog variants of social organisation outlined by W.H. Scott (1985a; 1985b; 1994b) the population of the sixteenth- and seventeenth-century Philippines was said to be divided into three orders, of whom **datus** and freemen (**timawa/maharlika**) formed the minority, supported by the productive majority, the **oripun** (Visayan) or **alipin** (Tagalog), who were all bonded to various degrees.

As mentioned in chapter two, there is some evidence that Filipino elites at the time of Spanish colonisation were beginning to make serious attempts to establish themselves as a permanent and exclusive rank defined by blood. These attempts, however, were interrupted by the Europeans before they could be consolidated, and lowland society in the seventeenth century was therefore still centrally defined by 'a social mobility that ultimately embrace[d] all three classes' (Scott, 1983: 141). Debt-bonded persons could as regularly enter the ranks of the 'freemen' as vice versa (Scott, 1983: 138, 141, 147) but even in the rank-conscious Visayas, **oripun** 'might actually win **datu** status through repute in battle' (Scott, 1983:140). And in all circumstances, here as in the rest of Southeast Asia up to the nineteenth century, 'debt . . . [was] . . . the most fundamental source of Southeast Asian slavery' (Reid, 1983: 159). Moreover, as Rafael reminds us, in such political systems the power of even the most apparently 'aristocratic' of **datus** depends ultimately only on his popularity, his ability to gather followers, to distribute more favours and gifts than he needed to be given and thus 'to elicit signs of deference from others in the community' (Rafael, 1988: 141).

Rafael's reading of social exchange in such conditions is premised on the necessity of having something to return within exchanges with authority, albeit only the signs of one's own deference.[2] While inclusion within the cycles of debt is what guarantees one's social existence, protection and well-being (for, as Reid has remarked in a different context, there was no category of 'free' labour to escape to beyond relations of obligation),[3] it is also what threatens one's extinction. Those who owed everything to their creditors – that is, all their labour – or who were attached as the heavily bonded slaves of persons who themselves were heavily bonded (the **alipin** of **alipin** (Rafael, 1988:145)) were memorably described in the Tagalog areas as **bulislis**, "exposed", like the private parts when one's dress is hitched up – a term which might have reflected a relationship between master and slave' (Scott, 1983:150). Thus, as both Scott and Rafael have made clear, debt-bondage was not an abnormal fact of human relations of society in this period; it *was* the genre in which all social relations (benevolent or oppressive) were constructed (see also Reid, 1983:163). One might expect therefore that it would leave a legacy of complex and ambivalent representations of hierarchy.

Within this system, I would argue, the ambitions of the **datu**s to become a fixed hereditary aristocracy were always in tension with the considerable fluidity of existing social relations; thus the **datu**s of both the Tagalog and the Visayan areas were able at the death of any of their dependents to impose burdensome fines on his heirs, creating a strong tendency for the descendents of the dead man to sink further into debt and obligation. Of course, the elite could choose to impose these fines or waive them, according to their need for labour at a specific time (Scott, 1983:141–2). Dependent persons were, however, often able to take advantage of economic conditions, and transfer themselves, or be transferred, advantageously, and persons still categorised as slaves could in fact hold considerable wealth and acquire many dependents of their own.

The period of the Spanish colonisation of the Philippines was of course (despite the much earlier establishment of the spice trade and Asian commerce) also the period in which Southeast Asia became more directly and heavily implicated in European mercantilism and its money economy. Both Reid (1983: 157) and Scott (1983:138) judge that, at the time of the earliest available descriptions, Filipino debt-bondage had already been affected in significant ways by these developments.[4] Nevertheless, it seems reasonably clear that within the indigenous logic of the Tagalog and Visayan systems, persons were already being exchanged and were exchanging themselves in ways which created explicit equivalences between the value of the debt they owed, or their degree of indentured labour, and articles of exchange value including specific sums of money.

Scott (1983:141) notes the inclusion of slaves together with ceramics, gold, etc. in the elaborate trade in heirloom valuables in the Visayas, and while he suggests that these were usually the most abjectly bonded, especially war-captives and domestic purchases, we saw in chapter two that the implication of accounts such as Alcina's is that in transactions accompanying elite marriage, intimate household slaves were also exchanged, and were given a value which could be quoted in gold taels. Needy persons in all areas of the Philippines would mortgage themselves to others, for specified sums correlated with the number of days of labour they owed per week (Scott, 1983: 142, 144, 146) and the transfer of indenture was also conducted with reference to these sums. People who for one reason or another were more favourably situated could often chose to commute some or all of their labour-dues into payments of valued goods, or of gold articles or money, as well as to pay off the capital for which they had been bonded; thus the sum required to redeem the most onerous duties of a Tagalog **alipin** was recorded as ₱.30 worth of gold, or ₱.60 for freeman status (Scott 1983: 149).

Thus although debt-bondage was not (unlike European slavery) centrally defined by the idea of the 'sale' of one person by another (Reid, 1983: 1–2) understood as the treatment of one person as equivalent to the inanimate property of another,[5] we know that Filipinos were accustomed to think of a convertability between their labour obligations and tribute in other forms which could be substituted for it, a substitution which most people attempted to make, either in part or in total, and which was largely coextensive with a rise in social status. The most 'exposed' persons in Filipino society were those with nothing at all – not even a recognised deference – to render within the cycles of reciprocity; but this was a condition arrived at by a social decline in which *what* one rendered had become decreasingly a matter of choice, and in which, deprived of substitutes, one had eventually been forced to render one's unprotected self.

The enormous and traumatic changes wrought in the Filipino political economy by Spanish colonialism are universally recognised by historians, and clearly involved major re-orientations of the understanding of property with the introduction of alienability of land (Scott, 1994a), and the changing of the definition of 'slavery', as well as a re-orientation of the obligations of ordinary rural Filipinos who were forced to render corvee labour and tribute to the state (see introduction), a burden so heavy as to have reduced the population and the productivity of the Philippines compared to their pre-colonial level. These radical changes defined the way in which the local elites were able to construct a new kind of political power, installing themselves as brokers between the (intendedly non-reciprocal) demands of the Spanish state, and the multiplicitous and multidirectional obligations of Filipino local life (Rafael, 1988:166).

It has equally been agreed, however, that because of the delegation of the collection of tribute and other state demands to the pre-existing indigenous elite, there were surprising continuities in some aspects of the construction of hierarchy throughout the entire Spanish period and beyond (Reid, 1983; Phelan, 1959; Lynch, 1984b). In particular, as Owen has pointed out in a paper specifically addressing the politics of the elite in nineteenth-century Bicol, the status of the **principalia** was defined by exemption from certain state taxes, and the official or unofficial ability to escape such demands on oneself by substituting the work of subordinates, and the ability to coopt state labour-dues for private ends. Owen indeed describes the politics of colonial Bicol as working in two directions; one, 'upwards' through the bureaucratic strategies of the Spanish state, and the other, and more fundamental, political task (Owen, 1992:16) concerning relations 'horizontally' between local elites (now defined through land-ownership and the holding of office) and 'downwards' with dependents. 'These relationships . . . [which would] also carry over into horizontal kinship and marriage alliances . . . remain poorly documented, since the Spanish authorities never cared much about them . . . we can only surmise that in broad terms nineteenth-century **timawas** stood to the **principalia** as pre-Hispanic 'slaves' to their **datu**s or twentieth-century tenants to their landlords' (Owen, 1992:15). Owen further illustrates the centrality of both the continued existence of power experienced as different relative positions in the 'vertical' construction of labour obligations, the extension of debts and the issue of the ability to command 'respect' from one's superiors, including colonial superiors (1992:17).[6]

Given this evidence, it would probably be wrong to explain away my co-godmother Irene's thoughts about the experience of 'asking for pity', as simply a reflection of the immediate economic conditions in which she has to live, after the 'Green Revolution' and at the margins of global capitalism. The near-equivalence which Irene Mojares made between several apparently diverse aspects of her statement '*I'll go into debt if I have to . . . I'll be your wage-worker, sir, if you let me*[7] . . . [They pity you because] . . . *they know you have nothing*' suggests to me that the ways in which the partial intrusion of social relations associated with capitalist standards of production are experienced at present records also a certain continuity (despite the radical disruption of 'vertical relations') with ways of viewing 'oppression' in the lowlands historically.

The statements which less powerful people might have made in the sixteenth century (or even in the nineteenth century) are largely irrecoverable, and cannot be directly compared to those of the people I knew. The exact notions of agency and exchange implicated in historical debt-bondage may always remain somewhat mysterious. One can say, however, that several of those ideas usually regarded as characteristic only of the alienation of labour in modern capitalism – the notion of a fluid 'meritocratic' society in which contradictory valuations are accorded to hierarchical and egalitarian notions, and the possibility of complete 'exposure' in which one can only offer one's labour and nothing more to hierarchical superiors – have their own history in the Philippines in the context of a completely different political economy.

If so, one might consider again the meaning of the Bicolano spirit-mediums' 'sacrifice', the sense in which she has to expose herself to the constant risk of predation from the **tawo** in order to obtain the gift of healing. As I argued in chapter three, this image certainly both draws on the notion of Christian sacrifice as a form of redemption, and at the same time seems to recollect the effort involved in maintaining 'debt' as a socialised category, as something which it is possible to represent as 'help' and not only as 'oppression'. But I would argue that the origins of that socialised understanding of debt as both a benevolent and a potentially predatory relationship extend back into history. The 'sacrifice' of the healer evokes a position of exposure within the context of rural economic relations irrevocably altered by class, but the risk the healer takes, throwing her body and her labour into the breach and exposing them to the will of the **tawo**, could perhaps only be thought of as potentially efficacious in a context where historically even the most vulnerable of persons could hope that some value would be accorded to those moments when he had only himself – and nothing else – to offer in the cycles of exchange. I would argue, therefore, that the inflection of Bicolano representations of exchange by the changes wrought by a particular form of capitalising economy is itself conditioned by assumptions about the production of power which derive from the history of lowland social relations.

At whatever point in history the Filipino poor came to represent the possibility that their own labour – their own existence – would be worthy of recognition, that they could be, in Kerkvliet's phrase, persons of equal value although not of equal power (1990:250), it is clear that this is a fundamental aspect of their present representations, which are nonetheless not 'egalitarian' in any sense generally used in anthropology.

This suggests one further reflection on the ethnography of San Ignacio. The people with whom I lived had suffered a considerable loss in those forms of wealth which Annette Weiner (1976, 1985, 1992) has labelled 'inalienable possessions', that is, objects which are not risked or are only temporarily (as it were, flirtatiously) risked in exchange, and which come to objectify a group's cosmological authentication. Bicolanos, like the Visayans described by Alcina, once held such wealth in the form of traditional Southeast Asian valuables (ceramics, textiles, gold, slaves) some of which would be used in trade and exchange, while others clearly were intended to circulate through marriage etc. only to return to their original 'houses'. The form of such household wealth (although this is another unwritten aspect of lowland history) would have changed extensively over the Spanish period. Unlike the people of Islamic Sulu, who continue to generate 'traditional' valuables through modern migrant work (Johnson, 1997), Bicolano villagers no longer hold historically valued forms of wealth, with the possible exception of women's family gold jewelry.[8] In fact, most people in San Ignacio emphasised the recent and accelerated loss of all forms of transmissable wealth, including much old 'Spanish' gold jewelry, and land, which their grandparents and great-grandparents, ignorant of its real market-value, are said to have sold to buy commercial goods, or to have lost through mortgaging under pressure of debts. Although commercial items (such as tableware as wedding-gifts) have to some extent replaced the older items, the change is clearly seen as linked to people's loss of wealth. The one partial exception to this pattern is perhaps the possession of family saints, which being both circulated and yet retained in a line of inheritance, seem to display many of the properties of the inalienable object.[9] If, in a state they define as impoverishment, Bicolanos have lost many of their 'inalienable possessions', there is perhaps little option but to place into 'sacrificial' value-creating circulations the one inalienable object which remains when one has been denuded of all possible substitutions – oneself.

**The disappearance of the lowlands as a cultural object**
Among the many differences which could be described between the trauma of Spanish colonisation and the trauma of American colonisation is one which has not always been clearly observed; in contrast to the Spanish, who knew that they had come across a heathen culture (with encouraging residual traces of monotheism) which it was their mission to Christianise, the Americans were often unsure that the colony they had acquired was a proper culture at all.[10] Large though the omissions of Spanish documents might be, they did at least pay the compliment of serious attention to any rivals of the Christian God, and thus described in some detail lowland Filipino mediumship, hunting rituals, funerals and marriages and so on. The early American documentation, as well as

popular and travel memoirs of the period, newspapers etc., is notable for the almost complete absence of any reference to such activities as healing. Indeed, they might as well not have existed in the colonial imagination, except when, as happened more often than America's enlightened colonialists would have liked, so-called 'unorthodox' or 'syncretic' activities became associated with 'millenarian' political uprisings against America, in a continuation of the independence movements which had begun against Spain (Ileto, 1979: 75 and passim; McCoy, 1982).

From the American viewpoint, the doctrine of the separation of church and state which was to distinguish the new regime from Spanish 'friar rule' might make it proper that the state take cognisance of religious matters only when they were transmuted into civil unrest. There is also a pervasive anti-Catholic and anti-Hispanic tone in the writings even of relatively unprejudiced and liberal authors like James Le Roy, which associated 'progress' in the new colony firmly with the spread of Protestantism and/or of secularism, and which considers the 'Hispanised' Filipino elite, with their nationalistic interest in the revival of scholarship on the country's 'ancient religions', with dismissive hostility (Le Roy, 1968 (1905):28–9 and 66–95).[11]

Nonetheless, this near-silence on the subject of lowland 'culture' is in extreme contrast to American accounts of the highlands, where 'custom', 'religion' and 'ritual' are some of the primary categories through which local life is evoked. It was not merely that cultural pluralism too formed part of America's notion of itself, it was also that American activities among the Cordillera 'tribes', for example, were explicitly lived out as a nobler reprise of the white American conquest of the Wild West (Jenista, 1987; Rafael 1995b). A variation on this theme is provided by the reminiscences of Mabel Cook Cole, wife of an American anthropologist sent to make collections for the Field Museum of Chicago. Mrs Cole had, she tells us, 'always wished I had been an Indian and could lead a life unhampered by the rules of modern society' (1929:3). On a trip to contact the head-hunting Tinguian, she was able to live out her dream vicariously, albeit the Coles' manner of travelling with loads of tinned roast beef, lowland servants, a rubber bed, a gramophone and an instrument for measuring the heads of 'natives', did not leave them exactly 'unhampered' (Cannell, 1996b).

The title of the book, *Savage Gentlemen*, encompasses some of the contradictions of the narrative, for the main satisfaction which the Tinguian afford the Coles is to be excitingly primitive while displaying a wholly gentlemanly sense of *comme il faut*. Bulakano, the Tinguian leader, introduces the Coles gradually to the world of native custom. 'They have', comments Mabel Cole, 'a very definite way of doing everything. To see them squatting on . . . the floor eating . . . everything with their fingers . . . one would never have suspected them of having strict rules of etiquette, and yet there were times when we felt our own manners very much amiss' (1929:21). This custom is easily recognisable to the American couple as being built on 'tradition' and the ancestral, and the Coles forge good relations with their hosts by their cooperative effort in telling and writing down 'the story of the ancestors . . . whose customs must be followed always' (1929:36).[12]

By contrast, in the plains, Mabel Cole is as enervated as she was invigorated in the mountains, chafes at her role as teacher and longs for the 'wild country' (1929:148). While the Cordillerans are untamed aristocrats, the lowlanders feature prominently in many memoirs as servants (see Rafael, 1995a). In the lowlands, as other lady-writers of the period tell us, one may be very kindly received, but 'Civilisation and the civilised life are a bit slow . . . and the wild tribes and Moros are certainly more picturesque than the Europeanized overclad natives of Manila' (Moses, 1908:147). One is pleasantly surprised by the sophistication of the Manila Christmas (Moses, 1908:195) or one is bored and depressed by the Filipino provincial dances and theatre (Campbell Dauncey, 1906: 57 and 78),[13] but one's emotions are never deeply engaged, and no one thrills to the pleasures of alterity as they do in the uplands. One may even be led to remark, petulantly, that 'There is nothing in these Filipinos, you see' (Campbell Dauncey, 1906:78).

These statements are all the more striking when one considers that healing and spirit-mediumship performances in many respects very similar to those performed by the 'hereditary right' (Cole, 1929:44) of the Tinguian mediums were taking place in the provincial towns where these ladies lived, and also in Manila, as well as in the more inaccessible rural settlements to which many of the American schoolteachers were dispatched. Even the major Catholic processions and festivals, which must have been at least as visually impressive then as now, barely rate a serious mention. It is only when the **insurrectos** or other 'bandits' threaten again that there is a sharpening of focus, and then the language used to describe lowland practices is not one of aristocratic authenticity and the pristine 'savage', but one of inauthenticity, peasant 'superstition' and anomaly. 'Filipino swindler poses as the true saviour', sneered one headline of 1904 (*Manila Times*, 29 April 1904), coopting a Protestant disgust for idolatry in the service of a reproof which recognised – perhaps half with relief –

that there was finally 'something' to the elusive lowlanders. But this 'something', never recognised as an authentic 'culture', is visible only in connection with the threat of political subversion which itself condemns it.

This background, and the manner in which American social science and anthropological fieldtrips were integrated into the series of enquiries by which America took stock of her colony, without doubt explains in large part the legacy of the peculiarly negative definition of lowland culture with which I began this book. It is a characteristic not only of American but of other colonial literatures in Southeast Asia in the nineteenth and twentieth centuries, which pursue certain closely related themes in the representation of colonial relationships. The theme of the 'noble' mountain tribes, for example, is clearly present also in British writing, and there are many similarities between the aspirations expressed by the cowboys of the Cordillera and those of the Brookes, British 'White Rajahs of Sarawak' (Payne, 1986; Brooke, 1992), on whom in fact the American 'white apos' partly modelled themselves (Jenista, 1987: 242). For a confluence of reasons which can only be briefly adumbrated here, such groups imaged for their conquerors the qualities of sturdy independence, political autonomy, self-sufficiency, military traditions and frank trustworthiness. The man of the mountains is above all, to white colonials, the man of honour who will be your worthy enemy or your loyal friend and ally. This image was particularly congenial to the rather bluff, often military, adventurers and dreamers of autonomy who established outposts in the 'wild countries' of the region, and who tended to rule them for a while as fiefs before they became more tightly integrated into the colonial state. The mountain 'tribes' were constructed as noble adversaries, and thus their submission created by reflection the purity of heart of the colonial venture itself and of its harbingers. The plains, by contrast, to the rulers as to their womenfolk, were often seen as the location of sly deceitfulness, boredom, and the evidences of a spoiled culture.

Often, but not always; for the other objects of colonial admiration in Southeast Asia were the many kingdoms of the lowlands and their courts, centres of mystery, refinement and ceremonial. The Brookes divided their attention between the warrior Iban (who of course like the Tinguian were head-hunters) and the sophisticated courts of the Malay rulers, although preferring the former. As John Pemberton has recently shown, Javanese royal ceremonial (**upacara**) became reified under the Dutch into a concept of unchanging 'ritual' through which both Javanese-colonial politics and the claims to power of Java's post-revolutionary rulers have been constructed (Pemberton, 1994:15–16, 189–94). While the Sultanates of the

Southern Philippines could be viewed within this kind of framework (Cook Cole, 1929), the towns and villages of the lowland Christian areas offered no more eastern potentates than noble savages to the colonial gaze. The fact that the tone of American accounts of the lowlands modulates between cheerful condescension and disappointment, suspicion and frustration[14] can therefore be attributed to the vague anxiety and ennui consequent on having obtained a colony much of whose population seemed to have only a highly bastardised form of culture. Like the concept of 'ritual' in Java, the concept of 'culture' in the lowland Philippines has been deeply politically implicated (Cannell, 1996a), the only difference being that it is perhaps more unusual for nation-states than for social classes (Lewis, 1966; Valentine, 1968) for this objectification to unfold historically through the claim that one does not have a proper 'culture' at all.

### Continuity and change in the anthropology of identity

If the culture of the lowland Philippines became a slippery, even a dissolving object to its second colonisers, Bicol and places like it have until recently also been little visible in anthropology. The influential work of Wolters (1982), Anderson (1972) and others has established a powerful approach to Southeast Asia which focusses on divergent political developments of fundamentally connected ideas about power, and especially on the contrast between local states (usually found in the lowlands) and so-called 'egalitarian' or 'tribal' groups situated at the margins of these states. Geertz's famous work (1980) on the Balinese 'Negara' has come to stand for one end of this contrast, while a number of powerful ethnographies of 'marginal' communities defining themselves against the state (Michelle Z. Rosaldo, 1980; Renato Rosaldo, 1980; Gibson, 1986; Atkinson, 1989; Steedly, 1993; Tsing, 1993) stand at the other. This is sophisticated and illuminating work, whose authors are well aware of the limitations as well as the advantages of such a contrast, and of the part which the propaganda of the Southeast Asian states themselves has played in elaborating and maintaining such a distinction (Tambiah, 1985; Vickers, 1989).

It may be, however, that the very fruitfulness of this approach has produced too exclusive a concentration on societies which fit into the more extreme ends of the dichotomy. The anthropological discussion (though from very different motivations) has in fact tended to focus on – and thereby to replicate the idea of – the same categories of society which attracted the American colonials; state or aristocratic systems on the one hand, and anti-state, 'tribal' or 'marginal' communities on the other.[15]

The common ground is perhaps to be explained by the fact that, for anthropologists as well as for lady-discoverers, the guarantee of the 'identity' and therefore the 'authenticity' of any culture has usually been understood as its imperviousness to outside influences, and its ability to build and retain a 'tradition' which remains unchanged over time. It is in discovering such a 'tradition' that one feels one has discovered something of value about someone else, and therefore about oneself. In the context of Southeast Asian states, such 'traditions' are easily located, since these states themselves value and rhetorically stress unchangingness over time as a source of power; for Errington, for example, '"The past" means: potency' in aristocratic Luwu (Errington, 1990:231), especially the potency of the ancestors of the elite. In such a society, one turns backwards to one's origins for authentication, and inwards away from the claims of rivals and the foreign outside.

While Cook Cole associated the possession of 'tradition' closely with Tinguian ancestral authority and aristocratic values, however, anthropologists have seen a wider range of possibilities. Certainly, 'marginal' communities may emphasise their resistance to neighbouring powers or an encompassing state by constructing 'an alternative hierarchy' centred on their own ancestral 'tradition' (Bloch, 1979:167). They may however also choose to develop social mechanisms which restrict the development of internal hierarchy altogether, through an emphasis on sharing and non-exclusivity which often extends either to a rejection of the idea that supernatural authority derives from lineal ancestors (and therefore unequally favours their descendants) and/or through a rejection of processes which limit entry into roles such as shamanship through which supernaturals (perhaps non-lineal local ancestors or other spirits) may be contacted and their power accessed.

This broadly Durkheimian way of thinking has often been used to outstanding effect. Atkinson's account of the 'egalitarian' Wana, for example, shows how the status of such groups is often historically determined. Wana groups appear to have been developing towards a more hierarchical form of organisation, in which the performance of the key *mabolo* ritual was coordinated by the chiefs, with the shamans acting as their officiants. Islamic slave-raids, however, prompted a turn towards a rather non-exclusive form of shamanic practice and a retreat to the hills (Atkinson, 1989:210–12; 318–19) from where the Wana mourn a certain loss of power from their world.

These examples, taken from North American ethnographies, nonetheless closely parallel a discussion of identity and history which has been important in British anthropology, especially through the contributions of

Bloch's (1971, 1986, 1992a, 1992b, 1994) well-known analyses of the relationship between social hierarchy, descent-based kinship and the ways in which ritual works to reproduce and naturalise inequalities, based on extensive writings on the Merina of Madagascar. The Merina are distinguished by their resolute attachment to Merina ancestors as the source of power in this world, by the value they place on the unchanging, and by the strong boundaries they maintain in the attempt to prevent non-Merina people gaining access to this power (Bloch, 1994; 133–45). Where communities are less like the Merina in their attitudes to change, Bloch argues, there are three possibilities. Firstly, they may be labouring under a temporary loss of control over their own lives (perhaps because of conquest or displacement) which is accompanied by loss of confidence in their links with supernaturals. In that case, people will attempt to rebuild their subordination to ancestors or other deities, and regain their line to power. This effort will be made even though, in Bloch's view, like all ritual which he regards as essentially a process of mystification in which contradiction is falsely resolved, it will replicate another form of inequality within the community and the individual (Bloch, 1979; 1986). Secondly, people may be in the midst of a revolution, in which the 'hijacking' of supernatural power to which they do not normally have access plays a part; Merina slaves, for instance, will attempt to incarnate Merina ancestors who are normally banned to them (Bloch, 1994).

The third kind of society most often evoked in Bloch's work is essentially the opposite in its construction of hierarchy and of a continuous identity; that is, it is a society or a moment (sometimes referred to as 'mythological' in a sense derived from Lévi-Strauss's late formulation of the opposition between ritual and myth) in which the ideological elimination of contradiction and irresolvability in life, with the realm of 'unchanging' certainty it supports, is forfeited in favour of an acceptance of competing meanings and a relinquishing of the foundations of hierarchy and domination (Bloch, 1992a:105). Such moments are usually located in societies which have deliberately turned their back on the state, or which have been rejected by it, or are at an immense distance from it, and which are conceived as egalitarian in inclination.

The work of anthropologists such as Stewart (1997) and Astuti (1995) explores this opposition between identity which is a matter of 'being' (as in 'being Merina' – an essence which is inherited) and identity which is a matter of doing; for both these authors, identity can alternatively be constructed not so much by claims about the past, as by action in the present. Stewart's gypsies and Astuti's Vezo, both groups who are in central ways oriented against the state (past or present), are who they are because of certain continuous and distinctive ways of acting (selling horses rather than working the land in one case; specific ways of fishing, following taboos, etc. in the other), and to change these ways of acting is, potentially, to change one's whole identity, at least for the living. As we have seen, however, just as Bicolanos are not like the aristocrats of Luwu or the subjects of the Balinese Negara, so they are also unlike these strongly 'anti-hierarchical' societies. Nor do Bicolanos draw on a notion of what they do to construct a declaration of who they are. In fact, as I stressed in the introduction, Bicolanos are very little given to formal statements about 'who they are' at all, while the making of what we might wish, from an outsider's point of view, to call Bicolano 'identity' is largely conducted through the making and remaking of potentially transformative relationships with others. In particular, it is conducted through the making of asymmetric relationships with human and supernatural superiors, who moreover remain resolutely plural. There are always several sources of power in the Bicolano imagination; they are never absolutely resolved into a coherent hierarchy or collapsed into a single 'syncretic' form. In this, the Bicolano saints and spirits are very unlike the Merina ancestors, who continue to monopolise spiritual legitimacy despite the conversion of Madagascar to Christianity.

On a return visit to Bicol in the summer of 1992, I found the barangay in a state of some religious perplexity. It had been transferred, due to a shift in parish boundaries, to the care of a different priest who had strong opinions on the education of his parishioners, the value of Bible study and the necessity of eradicating superstitious misunderstandings of Catholic ritual. San Ignacio was divided between those who liked this more interventionist approach (some of whom had previously been attracted to the Bible classes offered by Protestant evangelical missionaries) and those who did not. While some were walking across the dark fields one evening a week to 'share' in sessions of Christian moral uplift, therefore, others were avoiding the church.

I was told on my arrival that I had missed the major moment of contention, which had taken place in Lent. As Holy Week approached at the shrine of the **Ama**, the priest had suggested it would be more fitting to have the image removed from his 'house' and placed in the parish church on Holy Wednesday, and that Good Friday be celebrated with a Mass there, omitting or radically foreshortening the usual procession. Resistance to this relocation came of course from the family who own the **Ama** but also from many of his devotees, who began to dream of him speaking to them in appeal: '*Why do you want to bury me already* [i.e. on Wednesday] *when I am not yet dead?*' he reproached them. The **Ama** was not moved to the church – at least, not that year.[16]

The lowland Philippines at the time of colonial contact, unlike the Merina, and unlike the so-called 'Indic kingdoms' of Java, Bali and parts of Sulawesi, never had an indigenous state with an elaborate ideology of kingship. There are however indications that its **datu** class, in the pursuit of a more rigid system of hierarchy which I outlined in relation to marriage in chapter two, may also have been attempting to construct something like a class ancestral cult out of the general Filipino reverences for their families' forbears. Certainly the Jesuit Pedro Chirino thought so, commenting (in the course of a spectacular fulmination against idolatry),

> . . . their paganism . . . consists in adoring and deifying their ancestors, particularly those in the male line, who have been outstanding in courage or in cruelty or in licentiousness and lewdness. Anyone who could get away with it would generally attribute divinity to his aged father upon the latter's death. And the old men themselves would often die acting out this vainglorious lie . . . they would choose for their grave some celebrated site . . . so that [after death he] might be recognized as a god by voyagers and they might adore him and put themselves under his protection.
> *(Chirino, 1969 (1604):297)*

If Chirino is correct, it is likely that such cults had an uneven geographical distribution, and one might suppose that they developed further or were subsequently less disrupted in those parts of the Visayas where, for instance, family ancestors are still claimed by healers as spirit-guides (Magos, 1992). Clearly, however, they did not become a dominant mode of religion in the lowlands; aristocratic ancestors were not elevated to a clearly defined and dominant status, but remained somewhat vaguely distinguished from the many non-ancestral forms of spirits, as, I have argued, they are today.[17]

It is difficult if not impossible to know much about what might have happened in the intervening centuries, although we have seen that some attenuated role remains for family **anitos**, and that in some other respects they appear to have been replaced as family patrons by Catholic saints.[18] My point here is that Filipino history (like Wana history) is by no means entirely unmarked by the attempt to 'fix' the ancestral and relations of authority; and we saw in the chapters on marriage that ordinary Filipinos have inherited some of the rituals of the elite as *one* (but only one) of the registers through which they attempt to construct their own value, although events have now made that attempt somewhat precarious.[19] Some aspects of the range of practices involved in Bicolano spirit-mediumship,

too, such as the methods of the healers who work 'in their own voices' and
the **paraanitos** healer Tiang Delia, can, as we saw, be understood as
attempts to hold onto practices associated with a time in the past when
previous generations knew how to create greater degrees of control. There
are elements of Bicolano life which do concern a nostalgia for the superior
knowledge of ancestors, and for efficacious and known ways of doing
things.

The other register in which we saw people like the **parabahon** Mamay
Etring act and speak, however, is one which envisages the continuous
process of transformation through time; a principle of change so total that
it even encompasses the supernaturals (under God).[20] Even the 'dead
Christ' is a Christ who grows, and grows old. Just as the hierarchical structure of Bicolano life is set against a vision of the constant (if distant)
potential of even the most powerless persons to initiate some change, some
movement through the hierarchy, some mitigation of the inequalities of
power, so the recollected 'traditions' of marriage and mediumship are
themselves only semi-permanent, not sempiternal; as the Age of the Child
replaces the Age of the Father they too for better or worse may be gradually carried away through time.[21]

I argued in chapters one and two that the claim of women in San
Ignacio to value in marriage is constructed as the outcome of – although
largely not by explicit reference to – one long history of shifting constructions of value, which are themselves always thought of in at least two
different ways (the value of reluctance overcome versus the value of freely
and mutually blending wills). It is perhaps this double history, this hesitation between ways of regarding social relations, persons, objects and time
as fluid, and viewing them as fixed and arranged in an unequivocal hierarchy, which is the background to the 'double-sidedness' we have seen in
several contexts in ordinary Bicolano life in the present. But in Bicol
history, the moments in which particular social relationships seem certain
are always qualified and, in the end, it is only the process by which relationships are made and promise transformation which endures.

**Knowing the words**

The Spanish traveller Guerra, passing through Southern Bicol in 1856,
stopped to watch the production of a **commedia** (a folk drama with
Hispanic origins). His comments on the performance were not favourable:

The performers had chosen a play from Persian history. The language was Spanish
and the dresses were, to say the least, eccentric . . . The actors walked on, chattering

their parts, which not one of them understood, and moving their arms up and down . . . their countenances were entirely devoid of expression and they spoke like automatons.                                                    *(Jagor, 1965 (1875): 79)*[22]

The performers of this Spanish play were probably not from the elite and therefore probably not among those few Filipinos who were ever truly fluent in Spanish; however even in the later nineteenth century when these plays were translated into Bicol, European commentators still found the

acting remarkable for its woodenness, claiming with Feodor Jagor that they 'found it difficult to understand how [the Bicolanos] were persuaded to spend so much time and money upon a matter they seemed so thoroughly indifferent to'.

*(Jagor, 1965 (1875): 79)*

One theme of this book has been the problem of the claimed lack of cultural distinctiveness of the lowland Philippines, a claim which reaches its height in the recoil which many European and American vistors expressed from the 'imitativeness' (read: lack of authenticity) of the islands. What did this imitativeness signify? My argument has been that lowland society is constituted neither as an achieved society of ancestral tradition, nor as an 'egalitarian' society of persons who make themselves through distinctive activity. It is instead, surely, as both Ileto's and Rafael's discussions of society seen through debt and exchange prompt us to accept, still today a society where process is relational; where persons are represented as formed, through interactions with others and the biassed but finally mutable displacements of power which are involved in those interactions.[23] In that case, as I argued in chapter ten, 'imitation' is another form of relation which contains within itself for Bicolanos the possibility of transformation.

One aspect of the fact that Bicolanos insist so little on the possession of a 'culture' in the sense of a set of unchanging laws and customs is that much which is probably continuous in local practice goes unarticulated and unannounced. I described in chapter three how the **palihion** or death-customs are widely practised while seeming to have become largely 'unspeakable', and the nature of the **aswang** even more so. So many of the automatic reactions of Bicol life – like pulling the hair on the crown of the head to prevent soul-loss when someone faints – are lived but are not consciously claimed or even admitted to exist. Living in a Bicol barangay was like living in a landscape haunted by seemingly ancient gestures, gestures whose significance was clearly in excess of the words by which people ever referred to them, as though bodies and emotions relinquish their habitual practices much more slowly than words or even thoughts.

In this place where meaning often seems to be so elusive, I was haunted by something else rarely considered as a social fact: the expression on people's faces, and especially the faces in performance some of which I described in chapter ten. It was not only the spectacularly presented faces of the beauty-contests which haunted me, however, but equally (for they seemed to have something to do with each other) the faces of my friends engaged in 'reading' the **Pasion**-text, the 'pairs' of readers catching each other's eye to coordinate a complex point in the ornamentation, expressions transformed by the act of shared concentration, by the use of a skill and a genre so well mastered as to allow the pleasure of improvisation. It is this which demands an explanation and a response.

In many societies which value 'tradition' and the unchanging, and which emphasise above all the existence of a single or dominant supernatural authority, it may be convincingly argued that ritual presents a monolithic reading of 'the truth' to its participants ('real life comes from the Merina ancestors', for example), and it is in fact the property of ritual as such to impose this 'truth' upon its participants, and to separate them from their own ordinary knowledge of the contradictions of life and death (Bloch, 1986: 157–95). However, where (as in Bicol) there are many overlapping variations on rituals directed at a collection of supernaturals whose exact powers and relationships to each other are subject to speculation (and have been over several centuries without apparently reaching a final resolution), the problems of reading the meaning of participation in ritual must necessarily differ. While religious understanding in Bicol is by no means unstructured – everyone believes in the Catholic God; everyone understands the general character of the invisible people – much of its detail is thought of as only known provisionally. Indeed, given that the spirits and even the saints themselves are not immune to change, it would be difficult for things to be otherwise. In particular, the practices of different healers relativise religious orthodoxy, since they are so different from each other, and hold a range of different positions on the correct dealings of spirits with Christian deities and the elusive, semi-ancestral **anitos**.

In addition, Bicolano rituals are complicated by the historical overlay of different forms connected to different periods of colonial rule, and the changing demands and proscriptions of those rulers. If Filipino lowland history is the history of people who had always to learn to relate to the demands of external powers, then contemporary Bicolano practice is in some ways a palimpsest, the layering on top of each other of all those constructed relations. In this situation, what is difficult is not to resist the overwhelmingly unitary meaning of a single ritual message, for every ritual contact with supernatural power in Bicol is relativised by every other contact with a different kind of power, and their mutual standing is always somewhat uncertain. What is difficult is to reconcile the demands of these powers in a context in which no such solution is felt to be permanent. If this is 'alienation', it requires considerably more concentrated effort of Bicolanos than (it would seem) of the Merina or other descent-focussed people, and that effort in itself makes a difference to what ritual means.

This effort, moreover, is not just intense, but creative. Each layer of Filipino history, and each kind of superior power to whom Bicolanos may wish to relate, typically requires the learning and performance of a range of 'texts' (written, musical or otherwise), many of them literally in lan-gauges other than Bicol. Creativity works in two ways in Bicol ritual; firstly, there is the innovative effort and play which derives from the uncer-tainty of ritual process, and which marks Bicol healing seances in particu-lar. Secondly, there is the creativity which, like the improvisational creativity of a jazz player, follows from the successful mastery of one such cultural text, creating a moment in which ordinary Bicolanos too feel that they 'know the words', and are therefore able to express themselves within them. It is the pleasure of succeeding in that effort which one sees in the faces of the **Pasion** readers and, more fragilely, of the beauty queens.

Within the familiar Durkheimian framework of anthropology, then, one might say that paradoxically what is most enduring in Bicol history is something which has nothing to do with fixity and resistance to change as such, but which is a model of process. Bicol ritual itself could be seen as reproducing not an ideology which opposes transcendent fixity to the impermanence of human life, but a model of power which is never fixed or still because it is inherent in and accessible only through relations of exchange between persons. Moreover, although these relations are essen-tially those between unequals, the people 'who have nothing' about whom this book is written are clear in their emphasis on the lack of closure in such relations – hierarchy may or may not remain, but even the most pow-erless persons may – in fact must – place the kernel of humanity which commands recognition and constitutes value within the relations of debt and pity, and hope gradually to be able to wrap it round in protective layers of alliance, patronage and wealth.

Perhaps it is not so surprising then if Bicolanos do not fetishise rituals as the guarantors of continuity in the same way that societies interested in 'tradition' may do, but seem to expect them too to change. The model of asymmetrical relations that I have outlined is cast by Bicolanos – above all when they are nostalgic for times of greater prosperity and control – as a conversation, and it is the idea of modes of persuasive speech which they regret rather than any particular ritual as such. While rituals often do attempt to 'fix' for a while techniques which present people in an advantageous conversational position – healers confident of the powers of summoning, for example, or future affines elaborating the rhetorical play between 'begging for pity' and 'talking face to face and opposite each other', it is not totally unexpected if these relationships change, if one needs to begin a new conversation elsewhere, or modify the approach of the old one, even losing ground and ending up in a less advantageous position. But the idea of the efficacy of conversation remains.

This leads me to the two final points I wish to make. Firstly, Bicol is a place which sits oddly in anthropological discussions because its 'identity' seems guaranteed neither by its own claims to the possession of unchanging authenticity, nor by its involvement in political and cultural 'resistance', nor by its deliberate withdrawal to the position of 'marginality'. Bicolano people do not have a triumphalist view of their own culture, nor do they in everyday life reach complete resolutions to the problems of power and power relations. This should suggest to us, perhaps, that ambiguity, irony and irresolution are also kinds of social fact, not to be explained away simply as a way-station en route to a higher degree of cultural certainty, any more than they are to be portrayed as the 'post-modernist' fragmentation of some former cultural coherence. It is in these areas of irresolution and complex meaning that much that is important in Bicol life takes place; the point of Bicolano conversations is not just the conclusion they might reach, but the course of the conversation itself. Secondly, ideas and idioms of feeling about power and pity, love and oppression, balance and accommodation, are as much a part of ordinary marital relationships, and dealings between parents and children, as they are part of the wedding rituals which may recall the aristocratic Houses of distant history.[24] If the system of arranged marriage and the rituals which accompany it should waste away still further, therefore, the double-sidedness of Bicolano idioms of power means there is no reason to suppose that whole way of speaking kinship through the idioms of persuasion, reluctance and pity would go with it; people may simply speak more of marriages which are made by the meeting of wills, and less of those which are not. Potency, finally, for the people 'who have nothing' is not 'the past'; it is the structure of intimate life, and the painful conundrums of unequal relations for people of equal value are written in the way a young woman turns away from her new husband in the middle of the night, or reaches out to touch him.

# Appendix: Rotation of land

Esteban Mendez: rotation of the land belonging to his father

Diagram 3a  Division of holding in Placido's generation

Domingo Mendez = ? (name 'forgotten' by great-grandchildren)

Placido    Cipriano    Aquilino    Gloria

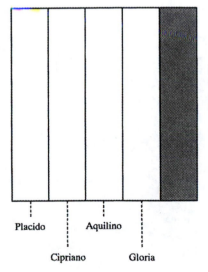

Placido        Aquilino

Cipriano        Gloria

Section to pay notary's
expenses, subsequently
available for rotation
between the four siblings

Diagram 3b  Placido's descendants in 1989

( ) = deceased

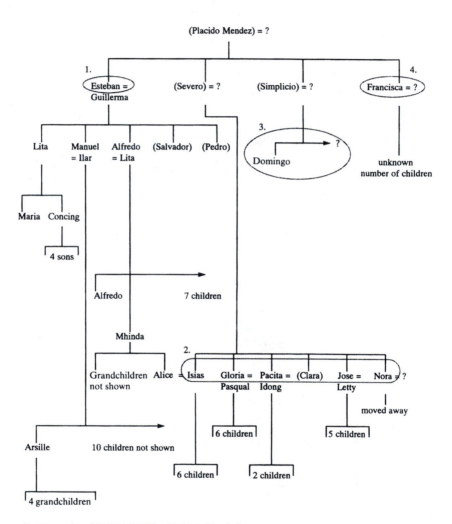

Rotation order of PARALIBOT land indicated by circles

Diagram 4  Bardog family (**paralibot** saint)

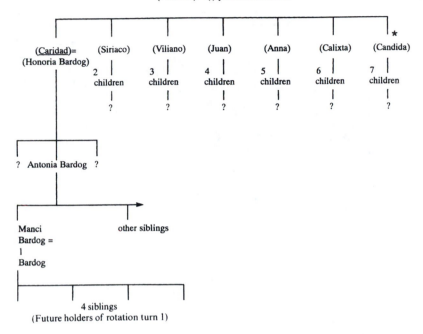

(? Celesto) = (/) purchasers of saint

? Antonia Bardog ?

Manci
Bardog =
1
Bardog

4 siblings
(Future holders of rotation turn 1)

Rotation marked by numerical order. N.B. Data highly incomplete because respondents had 'forgotten' kinship details.

*NB Siblings not in age order

Note: Caridad was the original donee of the saint

Diagram 5  Circulation of Sophia de Jose, Santa Cruz

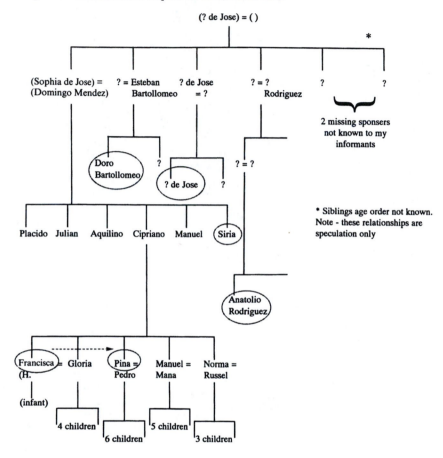

Rotation marked by circles: correct order unknown, as it had been 'forgotten' by kin.

# Notes

**Introduction: mountains and plains**

1 The majority of the most substantial accounts (ethnographic or historical) of the lowlands have focussed on either Tagalog-speaking parts of Luzon, or the Visayan region, and not on Bicol. Among the published exceptions (and not including here the body of technical work on development), some of the most important contemporary work has been done by historians Norman Owen (1982, 1984, 1989a and b, 1990, 1992), Francisco Mallari (especially 1987), John N. Schumacher, S.J. (1981) and Dañilo M. Gerona (1988b, 1990) as well as by social scientist Frank Lynch, SJ (c.1956, 1959, 1963, 1972, 1973a 1973b, 1974, 1975, 1984a), economist and anthropologist Jeanne Frances I. Illo (particularly *Irrigation in the Philippines: impact on women and their households*, 1988; and 'Who heads the household: women and households in the Philippines', 1992, although much of her work on Quezon Province, such as Illo 1990 and 1995, is also illuminating for Bicol) and the linguist and dictionary-writer Malcolm Mintz (1985, 1991, 1992, 1996). Useful compilations and commentaries on Bicol literature, and local historical surveys have been published by Maria Lilia F. Realubit (1976, 1983), Jaime T. Malanyaon (1990, 1991), Luis Camera Dery (1991), James O'Brien, S.J. (1968) and the earlier work by Mariano G. del Prado (1938) and work by Domingo E. Abella (1954) on Bicol church history. Important late-Spanish and American period sources on Bicol include Marius John (1940), the travelogues of Feodor Jagor (1965; first published 1875) and Juan Alvarez de Guerra (1887), the parochial survey of the province by the Franciscan Felix de Huerta (1865), Archbishop Francisco Gainza's republication of Marcos de Lisboa's 1754 Bicol dictionary (1866) and Jose Castaño's account (presumably for a nationalist elite audience) of Bicol's 'ancient religion' (1895). Early Spanish accounts of Bicol (or rather, of the provinces of Albay, Sorsogon and Ambos Camarines) are scattered and often slight, but some references of interest for the area which later became Camarines Sur may be found in Blair and Robertson's immense compilation of documents, *The Philippine Islands, 1493–1898*, vol. 5, 93–100 (Miguel de Loarca's description of Bicol and dispute with the Jesuit Salazar), vol. 7, 41–4 (on early Bicol fervour for conversion), vol. 16, 74–89 (Morga's *Successos de las*

*islas Filipinas* of 1609), vol. 17, 209–11 (on the early works in Bicol of de Lisboa and other missionaries), vol. 18: 1, 17 (on the Moro raids) and 93–111 (anonymous account of Bicol in 1618), vol. 23: 228 (Fray Juan de Medina on the Augustinians in Bicol), vol. 28: 300–58 (on the Augustinian recollects), vol. 34: 387–91 (anonymous Relation of the Philippine islands c. 1587), vol. 35: 284–7 (seventeenth-century Franciscan missions in Bicol) and 312–14 (grammatical works in Bicol by Augustinians and Franciscans), vol. 52: 29–90 (Siniblado de Mas's account of mortuary and birth rituals written in 1842, claiming continuities with the pre-conquest period). References to early Spanish works with special relevance for Filipino religion generally are given in chapters three to seven, but it is worth noting the value for Bicol of Pedro Chirino's 1604 account, *Relacion de las islas Filipinas/The Philippines in 1600*. Schumacher's useful compilation of extracts from documents, *Readings in Philippine church history* (1987) quotes a number of other major sources on the conversion period which include references to Bicol, such as Francisco Colin, Francisco de Sta Ines, Diego Aduarte, Marcelo de Ribadeneira, Gaspar de San Augustin and others (Schumacher, 1987: especially 49–51; 70–6; 83–5).

2 Jose Rizal, the 'Father of Filipino Nationalism', executed by the Spanish on unsubstantiated charges in 1896, and author in 1887 of the Filipino classic *Noli mi Tangere* ('The Lost Eden') (Rizal, 1961). Benedict Anderson discusses his work as part of the new nationalistic imagination (Anderson, 1983: 33–5; 130–1).

3 'Culture' is not a term with much purchase in rural Bicol; although there is a certain awareness of the value of 'heritage' in national (and nationalist) politics, it appears to be less significant than in other areas of the islands (compare Ness, 1992: 184–5). The term people usually use is **ugali mi**, 'our ways'. A discussion of this issue is given in the conclusion.

4 While Spanish government in the Philippines was famously indirect and the peninsular Spanish population in the islands extremely thin, the archipelago became more significant to Spain after its empire was fractured by the Latin American revolutions in the mid-nineteenth century (Steinberg 1982:25; Mayuga and Cross, 1984:37–8).

5 Spanish economic exactions appear to have stunted both productivity and population growth in the islands, compared to the immediate pre-colonial period (Reid, 1988:16).

6 Spanish policy in Bicol and other Philippine provinces (by contrast with Mexico and the former Inca Empire) was to missionise from the first in native Filipino languages. Both Augustinians and Franciscans compiled catechisms, grammars, vocabularies and many religious texts and hymns in Bicol (although children were taught the Spanish alphabet with hornbooks, not the indigenous writing method).

7 The closing of Subic Bay and Clark Bases was scheduled only in 1991, and was agreed by a majority of one.

8 On the painful circumstances of many Filipino migrant workers see Wynne, 1979; Anderson, 1993; Paganoni, 1984, and (on the meanings of the Flor Contemplacion case) Rafael (1997:277–9).

9 Over the period in which this project has moved from fieldwork to thesis, and

then (slowly) to book form, the beginnings of a renaissance in work on the Philippines has been taking place, and no slight is intended to the many outstanding colleagues and scholars both inside and outside the Philippines whose work has contributed to my thinking in ways which are too numerous to list, but which will be obvious to them.

10 The Philippine CCP used Maoist-inspired terminology which classed Filipino society as 'semi-feudal' and 'semi-Imperialist' – labels which implied that little good could be expected of the Filipino masses without a significant change in consciousness led by the party (see Tornquist, 1991; Rocamora, 1991 and Coumans, 1993 and 1996).

11 To borrow Benedict Anderson's phrase (see *Language and power, exploring political cultures in Indonesia,* Ithaca, NY: Cornell University Press, 1990).

12 In C. Holt (ed.), *Culture and politics in Indonesia,* Ithaca, NY: Cornell University Press.

13 I refer the reader to Anderson's impeccably clear and discriminating essay for all the necessary qualifications as to the precise nature of the causality, continuity and regionality here under discussion.

14 The question of how far different Southeast Asian cultures share the same idea of 'potency' or differ from each other in important respects is an interesting one.

15 I would like to acknowledge here the importance which Vince Rafael's extraordinarily imaginative and stimulating work has had for me since I first read *Contracting Colonialism* in the final months of my fieldwork in 1989. Although the main areas of my fieldwork and the themes of pity, oppression and transformation were by that time already making themselves irresistibly felt in all the conversations I had with people around me, Vince's work set them in a new context which has continued to be a source of inspiration and interest to me since that date.

16 The Bicol word **boot** (feelings, intentions) is the nearest correlate to Tagalog **loob**, but Bicolanos do not consistently use idioms of the **boot** to describe the 'self'. Bicolanos may also refer to the **kalag** (dead soul), the **espiritu** (living soul), to '**buhay ko/mo**' ('my/your life') in describing themselves, as well as simply using personal pronouns in conjuction with verbs explaining interpersonal processes (**daog ako**; I was defeated, etc.) See chapter three.

17 The relationship between my argument and the observations of other authors on 'pity' and its Tagalog correlates (Ileto, 1979:230; Rafael, 1988:145) is given in the conclusion.

18 The introduction describes Calabanga and Naga as they were in my first period of fieldwork. The boom years of the 'Tiger economies' had begun to affect the Philippines by the mid-1990s, with a rash of rapid construction of condominiums and businesses, and by late 1997 Calabanga town centre had relocated its market slightly away from the central piazza, and the construction of several new civic buildings in concrete and other modern materials had contributed to its elevation to second-class municipal status, a reflection of the aims of its mayor and town council. Some national-level funding had also been accessed for the improvement of roads and other facilities. These changes were to a lesser extent also observable in the barangays, where there had been

new building by some of the better-off residents, while others remained in extremely modest or impoverished conditions. While San Ignacio had never been a homogeneous community, it seemed that differentials in consumption were to some extent being increased. How and whether these patterns would be sustained post-slump remains to be seen. The improvement to the barangay road in 1997 and the increase in traffic seemed to suggest that San Ignacio would gradually become more like the barangays of the town proper.

19 The market has since been moved to a new site to prevent these disturbances.

20 San Ignacio had a population of just over 1,500, Calabanga a population of 54,261 and Naga a population of 115,329 in 1990 (Philippines National Statistics Office).

21 On the effects of multiply-layered agricultural mortgaging, see Satoru Nishimura, 'Agricultural development in Western Visaya: pawning land, overseas workers and *porsiyentuhan*', Paper presented to the International Philippine Studies Conference, Honolulu, Hawaii, April 1996. Nishimura also notes the common practice of informally mortgaging out farming rights rather than land ownership rights (1996:11). Cathy McIlwaine has also noted the profound effect of mortgaging of rights in farming in Cebu (personal communication).

22 This information was collected together with Jeanne Illo, whom I would like to thank.

23 Since Calabanga has historically been a frontier zone on the fringes of the wooded areas, it seems possible that this 'smallholder' identification reflects the last vestiges of the pre-twentieth-century movements of population towards 'free' unoccupied cultivable lands in times of demographic pressure (Owen, 1984:26–9). Certainly Calabanga grew considerably in size in the nineteenth century and also in the 1920s – the former growth possibly reflecting the end of the threat of Moro pirate slave-raiding which had continued to make this area periodically unsafe throughout the Spanish period (Mallari, 1987; 1990). From the location of their relatives, and some other indicators, I have the impression that some people in San Ignacio may originally have come to the area from Partido.

24 Lynch said much the same thing in a different theoretical language in his study of Canaman (1959).

25 **Pamaghat** is also given to new mothers.

26 There were ₱.30 to £1 sterling in 1988.

27 Middle- and upper-class Bicolanos face a different set of dilemmas; they may participate more fully in consumer capitalism, but when they leave home to work or travel abroad they may sometimes be treated (especially by immigration officials) as second-class citizens of the global culture.

28 The normal terms of polite address for known persons older than the speaker in Bicol are **Manoy** (older brother) and **Manay** (older sister), or **Nana** (aunt) and **Mamay** (uncle), or **Lola** (grandmother) and **Lolo** (grandfather), depending on relative age.

29 I discuss dressing-up in detail in chapter ten.

30 'Ay, garo nananamitan mo iyan giraray!'

31 In one family's house, the radio was covered with a cloth from the shrine of the

**Amang Hinulid** (prized as a help during labour), the two objects being I suppose of similar value and beauty.

32 On the incommensurability of humans and spirits as a theme in Malagasy spirit mediumship, see Michael Lambek's *Human spirits* (1981).

### 1: Marriage stories: speaking of reluctance and control

1 The idea that parents promise their children in repayment of an obligation is paralleled in religious vows (**promesas**), where a child may be committed by its parent to some future religious act – even an act they will not perform until they are themselves adult. Parents may also promise their sons to the priesthood – a promise which the children feel as fairly binding.

2 **Padi** (co-godfather) and **madi** (co-godmother) are frequently used terms of address in Bicol. When a child is baptised, his mother and all his godmothers all will call each other **madi**, and his father and all his godfathers will all call each other **padi**. The terms imply equality, mutual hospitality and support, and such relationships vary between the ceremonious and the intimate. The old healer is using the term pre-emptively (and therefore coercively) in talking to Severina's father.

3 The connection between sharing sex and sharing food is strongly made in these contexts, so that cooking for a new husband signifies a willingness to accept him sexually.

4 **Bukid** – uplands, forests, 'the sticks' (see introduction). **Taga-barangay** or **barangay na barangay** I have approximated as 'peasant'. I would like to thank Marilyn Flores for her many irreverent contributions to my research.

5 Readers who so wish should be able to look back to find concrete examples in the narratives of chapter one of many of the points articulated as principles of a system in chapter two.

6 Fieldwork correspondence between Bicol and Sylhet, Bangladesh, with Katy Gardner originally brought home to me the strength of the contrast between the way Bicolanos and people in more didactic cultures fended off the silly questions of the anthropologist; while I was often told that Filipinos have no culture, Katy was being told, 'We do things this way because it is the will of Allah.'

7 See chapter eight for a description of one such riddling game, played in Lent. Although the Bicol 'folklore' movement is not very strong, there is a certain amount of revivalism. One Bicol language radio programme, broadcast on Sunday evenings and popular in the barangay, mixes old-fashioned Bicol songs with a kind of improvised verse-form debate (**balagtasan**) between two contestants, for which expert perfomers are sought in remote corners of the region. It is my impression that (mostly male) local political speech-making still draws indirectly on these rhetorical styles, although this is beyond the scope of the present discussion.

8 The stories quoted in this chapter were told by women between the ages of twenty-five and seventy-plus; since exact birthdates were not known by all my informants, their approximate ages in 1988–89 are indicated after their names, to provide some idea of relative age, e.g. '(20–30 yrs)'. Unfortunately the accounts I have from teenagers were on the whole less detailed, an omission I

hope to remedy in further research; perhaps because I was known to have a partner, I spent more time with married women than with the younger, unmarried kids. People to whom I fell into the category of 'older sister' were also often shyer about talking to me about their love-lives.

9  The formalities of Bicol weddings are explained in chapter two, but the stories which follow may be better understood with reference to the following outline. The groom's parents should make a visit to the bride's house with a formal proposal (**presentar**) and often another visit to set the details of the wedding (**sungkohan**). The groom, who bears all the wedding-costs, must then build a palm-leaf canopy at the bride's house (**tuytoy**) and the wedding feast is held there. Until the post-war period, and sometimes into the 1960s, the groom was expected to do brideservice (**magbantay**) for several months or a year before the wedding; this is now extremely rare.

10  That is, her father's uncle, who 'begged for her' (asked to adopt her) as a baby. Adoption between relatives (especially between siblings and those who are 'like siblings') is common in Bicol, both where the baby's biological parents are in financial difficulties, and where the adoptive parents are unable to have children of their own. An account of adoption in Cebu is given in Yu and Liu, 1980.

11  **Turubigan**, a hopscotch-like game, the grid for which is marked with trickles of water on the dry ground.

12  The phrase **magribay tasa** (exchange of cups) applies specifically to a double wedding in which a brother and sister from one family marry a sister and a brother from another family; the phrase can comfortably be extended to apply to cousins (who are always said to be 'like siblings'), and arguably to other combinations, for instance a brother and sister from one family marrying an uncle and niece from another family.

To anticipate the interpretation offered in the next two chapters: the interest which this kind of exchange evokes seems to be based on its ambiguous placement between the symmetry which emphasises the equality of the two families, and the asymmetry or directionality of the exchange (each side being seen from another perspective as taking a sister from the other). This latter way of viewing the exchange, which stresses the asymmetrical (and implicitly hierarchical) side of marriage, creates the atmosphere of high-spirited emulation in which one side 'presenting' for the girl spurs the other side on to 'present' also for their intended bride, and not to be 'overtaken' as Nana Adora says.

13  This unusual use of a respect title in a proposal rather than the egalitarian **padi/madi** reflects Emiliano's parents' position as employees of their future in-laws.

14  'Maimonon siya na marhay.' The same word is used to describe husbands' 'jealousy' especially male restrictions on women's social movement. There seems to be an implied idea that Adora's stepfather was 'selfishly' preventing the proper circulation of a woman (not even his own daughter) and the establishment of relationships of affinity and wider relatedness. Interestingly Pertierra (1983:335–7) suggests that Visayan and Bicolano (but not Ilocano) women are seen as threats to men's attempts to control a 'transcendent' social reciprocity, because both the local valuation of female beauty and the tradition of female migrant labour prompt male fears of wayward female circulation.

15 See chapter four for a discussion of Auring as a spirit-medium and her relationship to her spirit-companion, Clara.

16 i.e. the **Amang Hinulid**, the local miraculous saint mentioned in the introduction, and see chapters seven to nine.

17 When I returned to Bicol in 1992, I interviewed many of the husbands of the women quoted here. A full description of their side of the story will unfortunately have to await another publication, for reasons of space. However, it is worth noting that these stories of male allure seem to fall within the Southeast Asian tradition which sees sexual allure as one form of 'potency' in Anderson's sense, sometimes associated with the possession of amulets.

18 Jean-Paul Dumont's *Visayan vignettes: ethnographic traces of a Philippine island* describes how the people of Siquijor contrast **gugma** (real and familial love) with **amor** (romance) and **love** (using the English term, to evoke modern, American-style sexual relationships) (Dumont, 1992:193–204). The Bicolano contrast between 'real' and 'learnt' love using Bicol-language terms does not seem to reflect quite the same preoccupations (although Bicolano people are also interested in the nature of modern romance) and is not simply a consequence of Americanisation.

19 The normal terms used by Bicolanos are **palad** (palm) and **suwerte** (luck).

20 Edita later met another young man and had started a family when I returned to Bicol in 1992.

21 I have used both English words in this text to translate Bicol **herak**, which can be closer to one meaning or the other according to context. This is not an accident, since it reflects the way in which perspectives on power relationships are always shifting in Bicol, either over time or according to the viewpoint of the participant. In instances where the multiple meanings of the word seem especially important, the reader is alerted by the inclusion of the Bicol term.

22 I am not here suggesting that women 'stage' either reluctance or spirit-possession in order to obtain practical concessions from their husbands (contrast Lewis, 1971:77, and see an important critique of his argument in Boddy, 1989:139–42), but that the structural compulsion of women to obey itself has in this culture the logical implication that women are owed something in return, which becomes the foundation of one form of value for women.

23 Note however that this is not like the systems classically attributed to 'honour' societies in the Mediterranean and elsewhere (see, e.g., Brandes, 1981; Pitt-Rivers, 1977; Abu-Lughod, 1986). Firstly, the gender system is at times bifurcated but not actually dualistic, and secondly, the issue of resistance and persuasion is not premissed on the idea that the man should try to seduce the woman while the woman guards her sexual purity; virginity is not an issue of central interest in the rural lowland Philippines (Blanc-Szanton, 1990:351–2).

## 2: Kinship and the ritualisation of marriage

1 Levels of early written evidence for the state societies of Indonesia and elsewhere are of course much greater than for the Philippines of the same period, which appears not to have had record-keeping courts before the arrival of the Spanish.

2 See Gibson (1986: 61–71) for a trenchant account of these earlier controversies

in relation to the Buid of Mindoro. There are of course illuminating exceptions: Dumont, 1992: 143–86 on kinship and class in Siquijor; Eviota (1992) on
the political economy of gender; Garcia (1996) on sexual orientation; Blanc-
Szanton's (1990) pioneering article; McCoy (1994) on families and the state.

3 Errington's work has been both highly influential and (as is often the case with
very illuminating comparative ideas) somewhat controversial. Errington herself
points to the way in which the categories of 'Exchange' and 'Centrism' are not
absolute distinctions, for she sees them as variations on each other (1989: 269).
This is not the appropriate point at which to offer an extended discussion of the
strengths and weaknesses of her ethnography of Luwu; however, I should note
that I use it in this chapter as one instance of the anthropological formulation
of how aristocratic and monarchical *ideologies* of this type might function in
their modern form, rather than as an account of the political interpolation
between Luwu aristocrats and the Indonesian state, or even of how women
experience such a system. Although Errington is drawing on Anderson's (1990)
seminal essay, many of her assumptions about monarchical power are widely
echoed in other writers on 'Indic kingship', e.g. Geertz (1980) and Tambiah
(1985).

4 Explanations for why women hold power less often are given in terms of other
idioms e.g. for the Wana as described by Atkinson and the Meratus described
by Tsing, in terms of women's general tendency to journey less far than men
in search of prowess and power (Atkinson and Errington, 1990:124; 228)
Obviously, this does not amount to an 'equal' position for women – but this is
not what the authors are arguing.

5 The label 'level societies' covers people with extremely different ideas of what it
is to be 'level': contrast Buid, Wana, Ilongot – a point which the argument as
formulated perhaps does not sufficiently cover.

6 Within Southeast Asia, Lévi-Strauss himself had focussed on the 'East
Indonesian' ('Exchange') area.

7 People say in this and other contexts (e.g. the discussion of infidelity) that
**'Daog an kasal sa sundo'** ('Real union defeats a wedding').

8 On the economically cooperative nature of marriage in Bicol see Illo (1992:193
and 1988:52–3; 60, 68).

9 Just as it seemed they looked for and created a sexualisation of previously non-
sexually determined identities, see Garcia (1996) and Blanc-Szanton (1990:
358).

10 See Illo (1995) on how misleading it is to translate the Tagaglog **maybahay** as
'housewife'.

11 The weaving of cloth continued some time after the collapse of the international **abaca** trade (see Owen, 1984), and is still carried out in some very few
towns for local sales. Of course, the raising of pigs and chickens, the growing of
vegetables, etc. is still the business of women and glossed as 'for the house'.

12 i.e. the immediate neighbourhood, or compound.

13 Interestingly, these phrases appear to be drawn from Franciscan eschatology,
reflecting the influence of the Franciscan order in Bicol. The same eschatology
is elaborately developed in parts of the Andes (Platt, c.1987 and Phelan, 1970),
and it is possible that in Bicol too it has deliberately millenarian overtones.

14 I would expect the shift away from arranged marriages to be less marked in areas where the retention of farming property has been more stable; certainly, in areas of Rinconada and Albay, bridewealth and brideservice were still being negotiated at high levels into the 1960s.

15 I suspect that what makes sense of these complex shifts in occupation is that women moved into various 'male' activities *on however small a scale*, to help support their families, while men (defined as prouder) only moved into those 'female' activities where there was, at least for a time, a reasonable sum to be earned (real returns on agricultural labour rose for a short while in the 1970s, and then fell).

16 The massive entry of young women into poorly paid wage employment, for instance the garment industry which Chant and McIlwane (1995) chronicle for the Visayas, has not been paralleled on the same scale in Bicol, which is classed as one of the poorest regions of the Philippines. This is partly because Bicol was seemingly deliberately by-passed for infrastructural development during the Marcos years, when it had a reputatation as a pro-Aquino area.

17 Jocano (1989:188) notes the derivation of this term from **dugang**, to add on.

18 Or it could be viewed as playing on the idea of being permitted to keep a 'sibling' for oneself; in the context of Lévi-Strauss's famous characterisation of marriage as mediating the tension between the desire to give and the desire to keep for oneself (Lévi-Strauss, 1969:42–3), one might almost say this was a Bicol vision of having the best of both worlds. On Filipino interest in the relationship between incest and twins, see Hart (1966: 66).

19 People say that one should not marry one's fourth cousin or any closer relative, a prohibition which must partly reflect the rulings of the Catholic church. However, as Jean-Paul Dumont has illuminatingly explained for a similar situation (1992:151–55) in situations of multiple intermarriage, degrees of relatedness may often be determinable only by memory and interpretation.

20 There are in fact more than two surnames in the barangay; people with these surnames tend to mention this more often! However, most people with other surnames can be treated as either being, having been, or being about to become a member of the 'two' by marriage or cognatic links; otherwise, people content themselves by saying 'most of us here are Guiro/Gavez; we are all one stomach'.

21 *Hulit sa mga bagong kinasal, o qui Adan* ('Homily for newlyweds, or Adam's homily', my trans.), n.d., Naga City: Cecilio Press. Page numbers in the remainder of this section refer to this.

22 For an account of even more elaborate Bicol marriage celebrations in the 1960s see O'Brien, *The historical and cultural heritage of the Bicol people* (1966:337–8). For a detailed acount of similar Visayan marriages at the same period see Quisumbing, *Marriage customs in rural Cebu* (1965).

23 Unorthodox, 'pro-sex' Adam and Eve stories which celebrate marriage rather then deplore the origin of sin are found all over the Philippines. Compare the Bicol 'Adam's **hulit**' for instance to an Ilongo-language version from Panay: *Mga laggay sa bag-ong nacasal agud sila manginbulahon* ('La Panayana', 1927). Such texts seem to be linked to popular versions of older creation myths focussed on a man–woman pair who classically emerge from a bamboo-stalk,

and some versions of such myths are still in contemporary currency (Magos, 1986: appendix; Mercado, 1975:168–71). Chirino (1604 (1969): 297) cites a version of this myth common in the 1600s.

24 In the youth of the speaker's generation, Bicol-language plays were still mounted in the barangay quite frequently. See Fernandez (1996) on the history of Filipino popular dramas.

25 Lit. 'approach' – the special meal of chicken, rice and wine, classically coconut palm wine. For other accounts of rhetorical jousting and courtship offerings, see Jocano (1969a:70–2), Quisumbing (1965: 21–3). For the **balak** (competitions between lovers in spontaneous poetry, obviously linked to the more recent practice of asking for and obtaining an answering song in serenades) see Alcina (1668, Part I, Book 3: 34–5).

26 **Atang**; lit., a food offering cast on the waves for spirits. Compare Castaño (1895:27).

27 **ambag** payments are ideally supposed to be equal to or twice as much as the gift that was given to one's own family by the family now marrying a son. The phrasing of this rule as always containing an alternative (equal or double) is possibly linked to the general ambivalence between equality and hierarchy between transacting parties which I note at several points in the context of exchange between affines.

28 Unless they are looking after the old couple in the house. This duty tends to be taken on, either by the youngest child and his/her spouse, or by the oldest child and his/her spouse, depending on family circumstances and negotiations. The couple who tends the old people in their last years has the right to continue to live in the main house after their death.

29 Alcina spent thirty-five years in the Visayas especially Samar.

30 I do not mean to suggest here an anomalous notion of 'property'. The Spanish both introduced for the first time a notion of land as private property (Scott, 1994a) and altered its definition in many ways, including by the banning of Philippine slavery.

31 It is tempting to draw comparisons here with the taking of life in head-hunting societies, although this view is rejected by the Rosaldos for the Ilongot (see e.g. Michelle Z. Rosaldo, 1980: 174).

32 Obviously, similar to the **pusaka** of many other Southeast Asian societies. See e.g. Kotilainen (1992).

33 The payment of a dowry gift by both sides for the establishment of the couple, however, remained at this point distinct from brideprice.

34 Ref. Alcina, Part I, Book 4: 180. This was also true for Bicol. Gerona (1988b:34–5) describes an eighteenth-century courtship ritual involving an armed assault on the house of the bride, which drew up its ladders as if repelling a raiding party, as was done throughout the lowlands (Polo, 1988: 9, 14) and marriage payments which included spears. The pattern of movement is in fact very similar to that employed by the Ilongot when making pacts to end an episode of fighting, and the Ilongot explicitly equate these truces with courtship (R. Rosaldo, 1980: 65). On the interpolated symbolism of conquest and marriage see Bloch's (1992a:73) treatment of Phylactou's (1989) account of Ladhaki marriage.

35 Compare *Political systems of highland Burma* (E. Leach (1970)).

36 An epic song cited by Alcina (1668: Part I, Book 4: 260–9) (the *Candu* or *Caranduman* of Datong Somanga) tells of a datu who courts a high-ranking princess. Eroticism is expressed through the request for and the withholding of the lover's gift of betel-nut, and through the posing of and performance of 'impossible' tasks. It is the princess, not her father, who finally accepts and even pursues her suitor in this story after an extended display of reluctance. My reading would be that high politics could sometimes be played out through erotics by both men and women. For lower-ranking people, presumably, the political constraints on choice of spouse were not so powerful.

37 With the exception of work such as Pemberton's which aims to integrate the analysis of the contemporary Indonesian state with an understanding of the ideology of kinship (in this case, of marriage in Java; Pemberton, 1994: 169–80 and 197–235).

38 Although not their slaves.

39 See Errington (1989:270) saying in Luwu, 'He speaks and there is no response, he speaks and there is no contradiction.'

40 Loarca the counter-reformation priest gives as the explanation for this the fact that the commoners 'had no property' to dispose of, and therefore were not in need of the rituals of bridewealth – reasoning which would earn him honourable mention in many a marxist anthropological account. It is hard to know whether he was right (Loarca, 1582: 155–61).

41 See Magos (1978:25–37) for an account of similar practices apparently still current in Antique, Panay.

42 A preliminary exploration of this question is given in Cannell, 1996b 'Opportunities for improvement; American education and "home economics" in the Philippines'. unpublished paper presented to the Association of Asian Studies Conference, Honolulu, Hawaii.

43 Not all the aspects by which the Bicolano house is tied into a wider cosmology have been erased, however, as the chapters on spirit-mediumship should indicate.

44 Although Ilongot kinship is not obviously constructed in the language of the virilocal house.

45 Compare Suzanne A. Brenner's 'Why women rule the roost; rethinking Javanese ideologies of gender and self-control' in (eds.) A. Ong and M. Peletz (1995: 19–50).

### 3: Introduction: healing and the 'people who have nothing'

1 Tuesdays and Fridays are the days when healers work throughout Bicol and also elsewhere in the lowlands (see e.g. Magos, 1986:122). These are days when the spirits are strong; – and so the healers' spirit-companions are strong. One healer in Libmanan explained to me in a metaphor drawn from 'counter-insurgency' that 'if you want to mount an ambush [on the spirits causing illness] you have to make sure the enemy is at home'. Friday is of course also significant as the day of Christ's death, which adds to its arcane associations. Spirits are also more powerful at certain times of day, including noon and six o'clock.

2 I estimate that I met and talked to at least twenty-five healers in Calabanga,

Libmanan and Naga, and heard in detail about five or six others who were already dead at the time of my fieldwork, but who were remembered by their patients and relatives whom I knew well. I knew only two healers in Naga, because I was concentrating on Calabanga and Libmanan, but there were undoubtedly many more.

3 By driving the sorcery-object deep into the body and round the circulatory system.

4 But not vice versa; menstruation, like childbirth, is more a time of vulnerability to external influences than of pollution, and women in these states are protected, not avoided.

5 It can be 'removed' by wetting your fingers with saliva and touching the child's stomach with them; if this is not done, **usog** can be fatal, and one must willingly and immediately do this if asked, without taking offence. Some people are known to have a tendency to inflict **usog**, and mothers with new babies may try to avoid them.

6 This point is also made in Part three, on the living and the dead.

7 I am not presenting this section as an exhaustive examination of Bicolano spirit-mediumship in all its aspects, but mainly as it bears on the exploration of these idioms. I have therefore not referred at length to the very extensive literature on spirit-mediumship, shamanism and possession in Southeast Asia and elsewhere. Some key references would include the classic literature on Siberian shamanism, including the debate over the shamanism–possession distinction (Shirokogoroff, 1935; Eliade, 1951; Douglas, 1970; de Heusch, 1962. Lewis (1986: 78–94) reviews this literature helpfully, and astutely points out that the ethnography does not support an absolute distinction between the two phenomena. Karim (1981) shows how inappropriate such a split is for the Ma'Betisek in Malaysia. It is certainly helpful to view the Bicol material as covering a spectrum from possession healing to more shamanistic healing, as I do in the following chapter (though I would hesitate to apply any of Lewis's conclusions on the functions of female possession to Bicol). The Amazonian literature often discusses hallucinogens in shamanism (Chagnon, 1971), but one strand of the Southeast Asian literature has been concerned with possession as a psychological symptom, even as evidence of culture-specific neuroses or personality disorders (Spiro, 1967; 1982). For the Philippines, Bulatao (1977) looks at trance states as a clinical psychologist, while Magos (1986) discusses Panay healing as an ideology and practice functional for Igkado society. In recent approaches, Karim (1990) and Nasuruddin (1990) look at possession within Malay understandings of emotion, while Obeyesekere (1981) finds a new way to combine anthropological and pyschoanalytic symbolic analysis.

8 Being 'accompanied' logically seems to imply that both the person and the **tawo** are in two places at once; if I ever suggested this to a healer, they would concur, but without much conviction, it seemed to me. The important aspects are that the person's **espiritu** is potentially lost in the world of the **tawo**, and that an unfortunate 'exchange' (**ribay**) has taken place; the exact logistics of that exchange remain unclear at least to me. There is a name for soul-loss (**anayo**) which is not caused by the **tawo** but by looking into water, dust, etc., but this seems to be falling into disuse as a category.

9 The word **ribay** or swop is also used to describe this method, which seems to be a very old one, as is **atang**, to release an offering onto rivers or the sea for the spirits.

## 4: Spirit mediums and spirit-companions

1 **Katabang** (literally co-helper) means a domestic help, almost always an unmarried girl and sometimes a poorer relation of the employing family.

2 Demetrio (1968:16) notes that the Visayan **baylan** or shaman goes missing from her home during her initiatory encounters with the spirits, and that these contacts carry the risk of madness, or of failure to return from the spirit world (effectively, death).

3 I know of no detailed examination of the relationship between healers and their spirit-companions in the lowland Philippines. The most famous early Spanish accounts emphasise the 'demonic' possession of female mediums, (usually called **bailan** or **babaylanes**). See Chirino (1604:296–305), Loarca (1582:170–2), Alcina (1668: Part I, Book 4:211–58), de Morga (in Blair and Robertson, 1903–9, 16:132) and San Augustin (quoted in Schumacher, 1987: 256–7). The connections between Visayan **balabylanes** and peasant uprisings are given in Cullemar (1986), Hart (1966) and McCoy (1982), and for the Tagalog region by Ileto (1979). Magos (1992) describes contemporary Visayan '**ma-aram**' shamans in Panay. More general surveys of lowland healing, shamanism and possession, usually under the label of 'anitism' (worship of **anitos**) can also be found in Hislop (1971), Jocano (1969b), Mercado (1975), Demetrio (1968), Natividad (1979) and Schumacher (1984). The turn of the century saw an awakening of interest among elite nationalist circles in compilations on popular religion, see Blumentritt's *Diccionario mitologico* (1895), de los Reyes' *La religion antigua de los Filipinos* (1909), and (on Bicol) Castano's *Breve noticia . . .* (1895) as well as the specimen of a healer's book of prayers/spells collected by Retana (1894).

4 (Si poon ko, nagpoon kong . . . pagkainaki ko, talagang ini bagang garo api-apihon ako sa mga kairiba-iba ko.)

5 Lightning is associated with a wide but somewhat puzzling range of beliefs in Bicol; it is attracted to bright shiny objects (mirrors, gold teeth) which must be hidden from it; it can be 'cut' with knives which may be placed sticking out of the corners of the house; in mysterious and amorphous ways, it is also associated with the spirits.

6 *Pace* Hagey (1980:ii–iii) who claims that healing is simply becoming an entrepreneurial activity as other sources of subsistence are undermined.

7 She was confident about discussing for instance the way to perform the food offerings for the rice paddy and **atang** on the sea, and belief in the viscera-sucking witches or **aswang**. In this relative security with the status of arcane knowledge, she was closer to the Libmanan healer, Tiang Delia, whom I discuss in the second chapter of this section.

8 On the attribution of ethnic groups to spirits, see Natividad (1979:93) on **agta** spirits. On the cultural importance of **agta** and **remontados** in Bicol, see Castano (1895:11–18).

9 Compare Keeler on Javanese spirit-mediums: 'To maintain their prestige,

[mediums]. . .of any sort must never expressly demand payment for their services. To do so would prove their cupidity and selfishness, traits that would necessarily vitiate all claims to potency' (1987:116).

10 And granddaughter and niece of well-known healers – again she does not stress this when she talks about her vocation.

11 **Sanib**, one of the words used in Bicol for a state of possession, literally means 'to wear one thing over another' (Mintz and Britanico, 1985:469). See the second chapter of this section for a discussion of variations between healers in the way possession is envisaged.

12 **simple lang** – a phrase which is repeatedly used to describe people's favourite filmstars of the Tagalog melodramas, such as Sharon Cuneta, who, although artfully dressed and made up, avoid the 'vamp' style associated with the **contra-vida**, and usually play the 'good' woman.

13 **Ning pag ako pirming aarogon kayan garo makulugon pirmi an boot mo pirmi kang poproblemahon garo diyan ka sana man mapuli sainda. Nagsasabi ngani daa kun gusto mo ngaya kuonon daa ako. May beses natatakot man**. The halting quality of the statement is there in Bicol, and I think certainly underlines the rather painful, mysterious and reflective nature of the thought, since Auring usually speaks with fluency and panache.

14 Donn Hart (1966:68) records that, in Leyte, people say they are taken by the spirits as lover, playmates and slaves to live in the invisible world for seven years. No such time limit is specified in Bicol.

15 'Gusay', the word Auring used, equals either a variant on **gutay**, 'to pay off a debt in small instalments' (Mintz and Britanico, 1985:298) or **gusi**, the local word for share-cropping and splitting the harvest (see description of share-cropping with saints, in chapter nine).

16 **bastang garo dai ako niya pag-apihon, habo niya**.

17 For a number of other examples of both male and female healers stories, see Cannell (1991: 75–219).

18 See Atkinson (1989:255–78) on the former, and Ileto (1979) and McCoy (1982) on the latter. Impressionistically, I would say that men tend to prefer this kind of healing, and various other more spectacular forms – association with **maligno**, use of **anting**, firewalking, counter-sorcery etc. – to everyday mediumship. This implies complex historical questions which I would like to pursue elsewhere about gendered shifts in healing over time. It appears that the balance of numbers has shifted in favour of women healers over the past fifty years, and there are some indications that this is associated with a generalised perception that there has been a devaluation of male forms of persuasion, oratory and command, and an increased resort to feminised forms, in several different arenas of Bicol life. There are no hard and fast gender divisions in Bicol healing, however.

19 Compare Boddy (1989: 264) on healing as a counter-hegemonic space; however, Bicol healing does not seem to have quite this quality of neat inversions. Perhaps closer to the Bicol view of healing is Steedly's (1993: 136–7) notion of the 'obtuse' whose purpose is to avoid reduction to any single meaning, or Lambek's (1981) discussion of the way in which healing is 'about' healing itself.

20 Local interpretations often reflected ideas of cultural change and cultural loss;

social scientists at the Ateneo de Naga discussed with me their impression that Bicolano healing had become corrupted in the post-war period by models of demonic possession based on American movies (Jesus de Volante, personal communication). While it is very possible that healers may include more possession techniques at present than they did in the 1950s, the history of possession in Bicol is actually a long and complex one, as noted in this chapter.

21 As was well known to Lynch (1984a:64–84), Hollnsteiner (1973), and others in post-war lowland ethnography; see for instance Enriquez (1986) on 'Kapwa: a core concept in Filipino social psychology'.

22 Ness is a trained choreographer, and provides acute and perceptive descriptions of Filipino gesture.

23 See chapter four for the apparent sexual implications of possession for Auring and their relationship to her account of her marriage. On spirits as lovers and seducers, see Hart (1966:68).

24 In bereavement the person's own soul is weakened, and they are liable to 'follow' the dead (see below, chapter seven). Bereaved healers are thus vulnerable to being 'taken' in possession; at Auring's mother-in-law's funeral when Clara 'entered' Auring (also then pregnant) to pay her last respects, people commented that it was an 'unchancy' thing.

25 Many healers' stories circle round these themes, e.g. Zeny, Helen and Agustin. Another man I know (marrying a woman he loved) was interrupted by a male **saro** which effectively prevented him consummating his marriage for several months.

26 One reason people often cite for giving up children, is that several of their young children die in succession, with the implication that they are perhaps being predated by the **saro** in return for his gifts.

27 See below, chapter six.

28 On the idea of exchange – or alternatively of money – as evil, see also Parry in Parry and Bloch (1989); the exploration of this theme in the context of the history of Christianity is of course familiar from earlier writers, most obviously Weber (1992) and Tawney (1926).

29 Compare Kerkvliet (1990:165; 173).

30 Such disputes do not only apply to land and cultivation rights, as other assets are treated in analogous ways. A local passenger-motorcycle driver, for instance, used his 'driving rights' (he did not own the bike) as security to raise a loan, with repayment arranged on the 'share-cropping' system, as a proportion of his income. A disagreement arose when it was claimed that he had raised two such loans at once against the same security.

31 Johnson (1995a; 1995b).

32 Another way to see this would be that the healer refuses any sum which puts in doubt the fact that she – or rather her **saro** – is the benefactor and the patient the recipient.

33 Unmilled rice, still in the husk.

## 5: Spirit mediums and seance forms: changing relations to the spirit world

1 Further examples of this variety which space precludes including here can be found in Cannell (1991: 74–219).

2 Atkinson's (1989) account of Wana shamanism is outstanding for its account

of how shamanism is significant at many different levels, including the aesthetic, and must be regarded as equally 'art and politics'.

3 It is impossible to avoid a sexual connotation for this phrase in English. While not absent from the Bicol **maglaog sa hawak**, this did not seem to be uppermost in most people's minds either when saying the words or when watching a medium lying on the ground while the **saro** 'enters' either through the head or through the feet. The Bicol association with a guest entering a house, which Bicolanos sometimes mention explicitly, would not be obvious in English.

4 Spoons tapped on chiming glass or on plates seem to be the modern Bicolano equivalent of the gongs and bells with which spirits all over Southeast Asia are summoned. On the use of gongs and bells in highland Mindoro, see Gibson (1986:75) and in contemporary Panay see Jocano (1969a:72) and Magos (1986:66); on Southeast Asian gongs see Reid (1988:210–13).

5 Poor Mamay Lino was literally 'singing' in a low monotone.

6 As is often the case, there were family connections, Nana Nening being Mamay Lino's cousin on his father's side. She lives in a nearby barangay.

7 **Kamangyan** (grey powder, from storax gum used, according to some, to call the **anitos**) and **incenso** (yellow crystals, for the **duende**).

8 Of the sort called **salapi**, that is, 50 centavos.

9 The second of these two names is obviously based on Pontius Pilate, who of course is known from the Passion story; the first might mean something like 'Grandfather Fed-up', but this is not entirely clear to me. As becomes clear below, these two **tawo** are named intermediaries who are asked to fetch the culprit.

10 **Dai mo na mapaparawili sa saindang nagpaparawili saimo.** This conveys a sense of Lino gazing enchanted at his spirit-seducers, unable to break free.

11 Pieces of Church paraphernalia and gestures associated with priests are often used in healing to protect the weakened and open person against invasion by the wrong sort of spirits. This 'policing' role is, like much else in Bicol healing, never made explicit. See Endicott (1970:133–9) on boundaries in Malay magic.

12 The reader may remember Helen and the interfering spirit who obliged her to marry Agustin, from chapter one.

13 Bicol **sampot**. On the similarity between possession and the covering of a medium with a cloth, see Graham on the Iban (1987:59); on cloth/clothes as a means of transforming identity as a medium is possessed by a powerful spirit, see Graham (1987:89) on the Iban transvestite medium, and Morris (1994:53–74) on Northern Thai spirit mediumship. Among the many works on the symbolic and transformative power of cloth, and on links between cloth and status in Southeast Asia, see Ruth Barnes (1993:29–44).

14 The blurring of the personality of healer and spirit-companion is common even in contexts in which it is theoretically strongly denied, as among Malay **main petri** practitioners (Laderman, 1991: 32, 50, 58).

15 Snakes feature in Bicol stories as wealth-giving but risky patrons. When born as a supernatural 'twin' of a child, snake twins cause trouble because they do not want to be parted from their siblings. See Rudolph (1988); references to snake-twins as a sign that a child may become a healer are often found in the popular press: see M.Z.R. (1989) and Mandreza (1989).

16 By reading the pulse, matching finger-lengths on the hands, and other signs.

17 I do not know whether Nening ever uses this kind of practice, although the healer Tiang Delia, and others, certainly do.

18 Duels with swords or knives crop up in plays and folk religious performances (such as the **Santacruzan**) as well as in healing in Bicol. A duel could be seen as the overtly aggressive counterpart of balanced, emulative conversation or verbal jousting, matching one side against another (as cock-fight aficionados also do with their birds). On sword-play in Cebuano folk dance, see Ness (1992:145–6); on sword-fights in Filipino **komedya**, see Fernandez (1996:63, 66, 69).

19 According to Luis's family, Pitong had approached the raging spirit, who had refused to talk to all other healers, and said quietly: '*Don't do that my friend, we're friends now, good friends . . .*' The spirit immediately calmed down, and Pitong was able to grasp and blow on his head, so that he left and Luis returned to his senses.

20 The spirit had first demanded that Luis's wife pour very hot water on his head, much to her alarm. This gesture seems both parodic baptism, and reference to healers' practice of blowing on the crown of the head to send away spirits and call back souls.

21 Keeler (1987:108–40) describes Central Javanese disdain for mediums as opposed to non-possessed healers, which suggests that Islam as well as Christianity may have had the effect of heightening ambivalence towards possession in Southeast Asia, although it is clear in Keeler's argument that the Javanese viewpoint is equally defined by complex local discourses on the value of self-control and ascetic exercises.

22 As in many parts of the Catholic world, there is a division between the more old-fashioned and less interventionist parish priests, and those who – partly in response to the threat from fundamentalist Protestants seeking converts – are seeking to change popular worship to focus on conscience, Bible study, the 'sharing' of spritual experience, and so on. In 1992, people were split in their response to these changes, although in an area where the value of reading religious texts is so strongly felt, the appeal of Bible study is powerful.

23 See Jocano (1969a:104–5) for an account from Panay, similar to the Bicol version. For a contrasting interpretation see Natividad (1979:87), who suggests that the spirits may have more power than humans in the world because they were its autochthons.

24 **Sakop**, the word used to describe an area under the influence, rule or protection, human or supernatural (as in the **sakop** of the local patron saint).

25 Filipino priests, especially native Bicolanos, are often familiar with the **tawo** from their own upbringing.

26 An earlier version of this argument appeared in Cannell (1995a).

27 A full discussion of the Bicol idea of madness is beyond my scope here, but it has considerable overlap with completely uncontrolled possession, and is similarly described as temporarily or permanently 'losing your person-hood/consciousness (**pagkatawo**)'. It need not be literally identified with possession by the spirits, however. Sadly, Zenobia's daughter had also suffered periods of fear of madness.

28 Healers in Bicol do not often have **libritos**, but they do have **orasion**, and use a number of them in their daily practice, especially **pangontra** (protective charms). I would like to thank Mrs Sideria Azanes for teaching me one such **pangontra**. Drawn around the sign of a cross are a series of letters standing (in a slightly mysterious way) for the formula: *Sa marumpot na Espiritu/sara Be Bolo me/ Yoto divan dome /me dios me Bolo/mia Beduara Amen/Jesus.* A striking example of a nineteenth-century Pangasinan **librito** confiscated from a 'bandit' by a member of the Dominican order (R.P.FR. Casimiro Lafuente) is reproduced in Retana (1894) as *Un libro de aniterias.* On the possession of **orasion** as an indicator of 'shamanic' power see McCoy (1982:162) and Demetrio (1990:281).

29 Journeys over mountains often feature in dreams of the spirit-world, and mountains, caves and rivers form the Philippines' magical topography, and are associated with spirits, the ancestors and the dead. The fact that magical power is sought in caves may be linked to the pre-Hispanic practice of jar burials in caves (Scott, 1984:24–5; Alcina, 1668:Part I, Book 3: 258–63; Dery, 1991:252). The traveller Feodor Jagor, who spent time in the Philippines between 1859 and 1873, notes the high value placed on jars in the Libmanan area of Bicol (Jagor, 1965:124–6) and describes ancient Visayan burial sites with jars (Jagor, 1965:186–90). Demetrio (1990:104) mentions a culture-hero who brought back the first jars from the land of the dead. On caves, mountains and pools as the sites of some of most famous syncretic/nativistic Filipino cults, see Elesterio (1989:11 and photographs 1 and 2). Western Visayan cave/water complexes have been relatively well discussed (see for instance Eugenio, 1987:319) but little is written about Bicol sacred caves and mountains (although there are many), probably because in general Bicolanos do not present them as a coherent cosmology.

30 Possibly, swallowing your book of spells at the moment of death was thought to protect the healer against the predations of the spirits and defend against their pull towards the invisible world. It also seems to point to a low rate of inherited **libritos**!

31 He lists categories of **anitos/diwata**s ('the souls of the deceased') who inhabit the ricefields, mountains and seas, **kalag** (souls of the dead), **umulagad** (guardian spirits) and numerous named **divata**s or 'phantasms' corresponding to present-day **engkanto**s, (de los Reyes, 1909:39, 122, 125–5) and comments on the confusion of some of these with 'devils' by the 'romanists' (de los Reyes, 1909: 126), for he was both patriot and schismatic (Scott, 1985d:266). This author also stresses the division of spirits into protective and predatory roles.

### 6: Coda: the birthday-parties of the spirits

1 Possibly there is an association with Rizal's heroine (Rizal (1958)1887).

2 Space prevents me from giving more details here of Tiang Delia's extremely interesting healing practice, but a fuller account is given in Cannell (1991:187–215).

3 I would like here to record my appreciation for Tiang Delia's help and that of her family, neighbours and the **anitos**.

4 i.e. a Philippine-made 'American' brand.

5 Although I was never told this in Bicol, several authors record that in the

Visayas it is even said that **anitos** or **diwatas** or **tawo** although supernaturals, have a life-cycle and can die (Demetrio, 1968:137; Hart, 1966:68). Given the overlap between saints and **anitos**, this observation may be suggestive in relation to the life-cycle of the **Ama** (see chapters seven to nine).

### 7: The living and the dead

1  **Aswang**: viscera-sucking or sniffing witches feeding on the moribund and the newly dead.

2  I wondered at first whether this evasiveness was due to prohibitions on speaking about death-practices. However, I am assured by friends who grew up in Bicol in the 1950s that **palihion** were something their grandparents explicitly *insisted* they should learn.

3  For an interesting photograph of the embalmed corpse of 'an obscure beautician called Archie' see James Fenton's account of 'The Snap Revolution'. (Fenton, 1986:74).

4  **Aswang** beliefs involve a great many details which I do not include here for reasons of space. Pertierra (1983:319–37) gives a comparative account of 'viscera-suckers' in different regions of the Philippines, and other references are given in Gerona (1988b:33); Jocano (1969b:ch.13); Demetrio (1990:187–9, 318); Rafael (1988:190–1). Important early sources include Castano (1895:22–5, 41), de los Reyes (1909:113, 127), de Plasencia (1589:192–3), Loarca (1582:131). Lynch (1949:401–27 and 1963) gives a comprehensive description of the Bicolano **aswang** and the **korokoro** omen bird, transmission of **aswang** status, ways of curing it, etc. My own data are not in contradiction to Lynch's on any point, although my informants provided much less detail (however, Lynch collated material from throughout the Bicol region).

5  For contrasting European beliefs on the link between bodily decomposition and unwelcome visits from the dead, and the role of embalming in preventing both, see Barber (1988:174–94).

6  The Bicol phrase used is **pigpaparong niya sinda**. Sniffing is often an echo of eating in Bicol.

7  People in San Ignacio stressed the idea of flying **aswang** since one man, still alive in 1989, was said to have been one, although it was maintained that he had ceased to be active. He had flown by smearing an ointment on his arms by moonlight on the seashore, and uttering the words **'lampas nguog!'** (over the coconut palms!).

8  Bicol **Naghigda na**, lit. 'lain down already'. The phrase is used euphemistically.

9  Mirrors are also turned to the wall by some people during a thunderstorm, to stop the lightning coming through them into the house, and there are some indications that they are seen as something through which spirits and souls can pass.

10  It is usual for rubbish to be allowed to accumulate during the wake. A neighbour will stay behind while the others attend the funeral, sweep out the house and burn the rubbish, before the guests arrive back to eat. (See also Magos, 1978:216.) Connectedly, **kalag** are said to be 'afraid of a broom', and brooms can be propped protectively over sleeping babies.

11  **Inay** means mother, Noel's parents' term of address for Teresita – but this is an

example of kin terms becoming habitual so that people even in the wrong generation use them.

12 In other contexts, these games usually centre on religious arcana or lofty moral sentiments.

13 Her dead husband's youngest sister.

14 To lose consciousness (**pagkatawo**) would be to be at risk of 'following' the dead person.

15 There are still areas of Camarines Sur where a simple church blessing (with water and incense, but no communion) is used instead of the expensive Requiem Mass. Occasionally someone in a remote hamlet has to be buried without access to the priest, in which case prayers will be said (e.g. by catechists).

16 Some people attributed it to the Chinese influence, the Chinese being thought of by Bicolanos as a notably wealthy ethnic group, as well as being identified with respect for ancestors.

17 To stop the dogs getting at it; embalmers tell gruesome stories about the tipping of blood into rivers, etc.

18 **Pambalon**. This is from the word **balon** which means food or provisions to take with you on a journey. Feeding the dead is important in Bicol, although I am not sure how far the analogy between food and the Mass can be pushed here.

19 Compare the account of preparing a body without embalming to make it beautiful and prevent odours of decomposition in rural Panay in Magos (1978:213) and a similar account in Jocano, (1969a:113–14). Gerona (1988b:33) comments that the sacrifice of a slave to protect a high-ranking person from predation in the afterlife (presumably by acting as a substitute) was common in Bicol in the seventeenth century. Spanish sources on the burial and treatment of the corpse, describing body decoration and embalming, include Alcina (1668:Part I, Book 3: 242–60); Loarca (1582: 136); Chirino (1604:326–8). Scott (1984:24–8) comments on the archaeological evidence in the Philippines, while Reid (1988:75–90) describes the use of body decoration as a status marker throughout Southeast Asia.

20 For an account of religious texts on death used by the Spanish in the Philippines, see Rafael (1988:167–209). For a general (if controversial) attempt to put together a history of European ideas of death, see Aries (1977).

21 An association of ideas was suggested in one anecdote I was told after being assured that embalming prevents a return from the dead; my informant commented that a young Filipina film star who had recently died had been found, when embalmed, to have '**aswanged**' entrails. (She had apparently died of anorexia nervosa.)

22 Niels Mulder, in a paper based on mainly middle-class people in Manila, has a similar finding. He argues that Filipinos are relatively uninterested in the ideas of sin, confession, punishment in hell and expiation in purgatory stressed in other Catholicisms, and that 'all Filipinos go to heaven' (Mulder, 1987). In this he echoes Isabelo de los Reyes, who stated baldly, 'no es Filipina el idea del infierno' (de los Reyes, 1909:45) and claimed that Filipinos also had only a rather general idea of Paradise (1909:41–6) – that is, that it was not very nearly tied into an understanding of sin. Contrary views can be found, though mostly

among interested parties: early missionaries claimed that seventeenth-century Bicolanos were among the most fervent in performing penance and attending confession and Mass; Schumacher (1987:61–2; 83) quotes Ribadeneira on this point.

23 Occasionally I would be told more precisely imagined ideas of heaven (always introduced rather doubtingly by 'they say . . .' or 'the old people said'). People recalled hearing that in heaven one could only talk with one's co-godparents; therefore it is a good idea to have plenty of these. One could see, but not talk to, one's spouse. There may be a connection with the idea that co-godparenthood is ideally a relationship of equality in the Philippines; there may also be a connection with the fact that co-godparenthood (and, in a sense, first marriage) are relationships created by the power of the Church (compare Bloch and Guggenheim 1981).

24 Some people say it is the third day after the death; perhaps the confusion results from the fact that the period between death and burial has now been greatly extended.

25 **sambitan**, to name someone, with a sense of calling them. The word is related to the calling of the name of the deceased at funerals, **manambitan**.

26 Compare Catedra's account of the All Souls' Day visits of the dead among transhumant farmers in the Asturias region of northern Spain (Catedra, 1992:336–7). The culture of Catedra's **vacqueiros** forms an interesting comparison to this material, since they are similar in their relative lack of stress on orthodox Catholic notions of heaven, hell and purgatory (Catedra, 1992:289), but different in the way they understand the nature of the journey of the dead, and relations between the dead and the living.

27 For the debate on the meaning of prescribed 'flatness of affect' in the face of death, see Geertz (1960:72–6) and Wikan, on 'managing turbulent hearts' in Bali (Wikan,1990).

28 Many marginalised communities with a knowledge of both their own and the majority/outside culture move ambivalently between the two, or attempt to talk to outsiders only in their own terms (Pina-Cabral, 1986:vii–viii; 31; 112). Michelle Z. Rosaldo describes how evangelised Ilongot denied their recent involvement in head-hunting, but when she played her friends a tape of their head-hunting songs, it aroused intense emotions, anger and grief (1980:53–60).

**8: The funeral of the 'dead Christ'**
1 Interesting perspectives on saints as mediators in European Catholicism can be found in Geary (1988), Brown (1981), Christian (1972) and Pina-Cabral (1986). Other examples of Filipino saints who arrive by water are San Vicente de Ferrer in Negros (Locsin-Nava, 1987:86–7) and the Sto Niño of Cebu, who also first appeared as a formless lump of wood (Ness, 1992: 76).

2 The actual origins of the statue are hard to decipher and locally disputed. It is unusually finely made, and some people say it came by ship from Spain (which might mean Mexico) but carved saints can also be commissioned in the workshops of Quiapo, Manila. It has been in Calabanga for at least sixty years, arguably 180 years (three generations) and possibly longer.

3 A local patriot is said to have once tried to replace the saint's **mestizo** head with

a Filipino one: the carpentry instruments bounced off the **Ama**, but the patriot became extremely ill. Local people conclude that the **Ama** prefers his mixed European-Filipino identity.

4 There is an ambiguity in the literature over whether Tranquillino Hernandez, former barangay captain of Polangui and author of the dedicatory letter which opens the Bicol **Pasion**, or Archbishop Gainza himself, is the actual translator of the Bicol version. Javellana's scholarly edition of the Tagalog Passion (Javellana 1988:235), for instance, lists Gainza as translator, and 1867 as the first year of publication). In my view, however, the preface to the Bicol **Pasion** appears to imply that Gainza was commissioner and perhaps collaborator, but that Hernandez was the prime translator, and I have therefore referenced accordingly. For a further discussion of some aspects of the evidence, see Cannell (1997). On the complex textual genealogy of the Tagalog Passion, see Tiongson (1976); Javellana (1983; 1984; 1988; 1990); Santiago (1988); Lumbera (1986). On Archbishop Gainza's efforts to create a renaissance in Bicol-language religious texts, see Abella (1954:171–82).

5 My feeling, however, is that many complete or partial Bicol-language versions of the Passion story may have existed before 1866, in private possession and perhaps in some forms of public circulation too, alongside other performances in Tagalog but perhaps with a Bicol musical idiom which had already diverged from Tagalog Passion-chant (since the two musical forms are now quite different from one another). The evidence here, both textual and musical, is hard to interpret and no full study has yet been completed on the Passion in Bicol.

6 And, some suggest, pocket rather too much of the donations intended for the completion of the shrine.

7 Perhaps because she recognised it as a supernatural gift, similar to the **anting** of the **tawo**.

8 Frank Lynch describes the Bicol Easter and Christmas cycles as of near-equal importance (c. 1956:87–92), and it is true that folk performances telling the Christmas story (the search for an inn; the **Pastores** or visit of the shepherds) persisted in Calabanga until the mid-1960s. They are now mostly performed by cultural revival groups, especially schoolteachers. However, Father Lynch may also have been seeing through the eyes of orthodox Church liturgy to some extent.

9 It also occurs during the **Traslacion** of the Virgin of Peñafrancia, the patron saint of the Bicol region.

10 Participation in this procession, which includes mandolin-players and singers, is also a form of religious devotion.

**9: Kinship, reciprocity and devotions to the saints**

1 On Spanish **promesas** ('instrumental prayers'), one of the oldest among five types of popular prayer in the Nansa Valley, see Christian (1972:114–25).

2 Such as a statue as Balongay, another **Hinulid**, which I was shown. It is often hinted that even less famous saints have grown while in their family's possession.

3 See chapter two.

4 Either at their parents' death, or (anticipatorily) at marriage.

5 Because Bicol has a wet-season and a dry-season crop each year. Sometimes siblings try to ensure that everyone has a fair share of the higher yielding wet-season harvests.

6 I make no attempt here to discuss the way these principles are translated into practice. In the situation of land shortage which prevails in Calabanga, short-term land-use arrangements are extraordinarily complex. However equality between siblings and fair sharing with parents and landlords remain central to disputes over land.

7 Examples of the way **paralibot** land arrangements arise, and of cases of inherited devotions to saints, are given in Cannell, 1991: 451–60. For a diagramatic example of the inheritance and **paralibot** circulation of land and saints, see p. 257.

8 For instance, the **invension** of the Calabanga San Antonio.

9 It will be recalled that the distribution of food at the shrine formed part of the Good Friday vigil of the **Ama**.

10 The transferability of devotions within families is also noted by Zialcita (1986) for Bulacan, Pampanga and Laguna.

11 This is an approximate quotation from the **Pasion** text (Hernandez, 1984, (1866):146)

12 Among the **hulit** most often picked out were those beginning 'O Christians who are sinners . . . think of becoming better . . . you have only one soul; what if it should not live . . .' and 'O child disobedient to your parents, your father and mother, this is the example to imitate, the humble deeds of Jesus . . .' (Hernandez, 1984 (1866): 185–6 and 41–42 my trans.). I do not want to suggest that the instructions to repent were not understood by people in Calabanga. However, the text of the **hulit** is decidedly more focussed on sin and eschatology than their glosses and discussions of it ever were.

13 In fact I heard this appeal to pious sentiment made only once, in Lent, when people are much more self-conscious than at other times about the need for appropriate Christian sentiments. This woman was also making a strong claim about her relationship with her children in the face of rather stressful and unideal circumstances, and also in the face of some local criticisms of her own respectability.

14 Especially Marina Warner (1976).

15 Leonor's promise in this case was to visit the **Ama**'s shrine seven Fridays in a row. She made several such promises while her children were small.

16 One family I knew began a series of readings of the **Pasion** in 1989 to fulfil a vow conditional on their daughter living to be seven years old. Another man decided to cancel his promise, made for the birth of a son, when the child died. The priest rebuked him, but said that if he maintained the devotion he might have another son, as in fact happened.

17 Zialcita (1986) makes the same observation with respect to devotions involving blood-shedding. He notes that the emphasis on bodily healing in these practices runs counter to most of the history of Catholic teaching, which has associated physical disciplines with the subduing of the body (Zialcita, 1986:61).

18  Both Christian (1972:181–87) and Catedra (1992:336–8) address closely related problems in the ethnography of northern Spain.

19  On the struggle for control of mediation within Christianity, see Leach's seminal essay, 'Melchisedech and the emperor' (Leach, 1972).

20  This appears to be true of most if not all Southeast Asian double-burial contexts. On the ritual treatment of decomposition, the fear of the odour of the corpse and the reclamation of the cleaned bones as ancestral objects see for instance Metcalfe (1982:esp. 83–4, 133, 177) on Borneo, Siegel (1986: 268–273) on Java, Freeman (1970: 6 and photograph 8a) on the Iban.

21  Moving saints are of course found in European Catholic miracles, (on moving Spanish crucifixes, see Christian, 1992), but to my knowledge the saint with an entire life-cycle is a specifically Filipino phenomenon.

## 10:  Beauty and the idea of 'America'

1  The argument of many nationalistically minded Filipinos is that American influence was both more baleful and more pervasive than Spanish, especially since it came disguised as beneficence (Salazar, 1991). I would not argue with the sometimes baleful influence of American rule either colonially or post-independence, but I would argue with the entirely negative definition of all lowland culture which incorporates 'American' elements as an insecure and dependent 'colonial mentality' (Mulder, 1991:7).

2  Although a young man might invite a girl he was courting to the cinema or to have a snack in the town, – generally in the daytime, not the evening.

3  Imelda Marcos famously began her career and met Marcos through becoming winner of a beauty-contest in Leyte (Pedrosa, 1987:69). Barcenas (1989:14) describes Bicol contests in their present form as dating back to the end of the Spanish period, although it is possible that they developed in part out of the many religious processions which involve Mary as the Queen of Heaven, Queen Isabella or Queen Helena in the **Santacruzan** (story of the finding of the True Cross). (Santos, 1982: 35–6; Fernandez, 1996:11,100). On money contests, see Lynch (c.1956:102)

4  Barcenas (1989: 14) claims that national-level competitions 'started long ago . . . just when America began to rule our country . . .'

5  There is unfortunately no space at present to describe in any detail the films which I watched with friends in Bicol, although they bear on issues discussed in this book in various ways, especially on the representation of kinship.

6  Beauty contests apart, the importance and financial burden of clothes presses down on people in all sorts of circumstances, especially for example, for primary-school graduation ceremonies.

7  The contests are therefore integrated into the region's major religious festival, which includes a famous fluvial procession of the Peñafrancia Virgin. I will not discuss the women's contests here, since it is the **bakla** contest which is most famous and most anticipated by a wide popular audience.

8  Such is the fascination with beauty contests and transvestitism in Bicol that in 1989 a local college in Naga staged a transvestite contest which was specifically not for **bakla** men. Tata was rather pleased, and took the imitation as a sincere form of flattery, though several of the **bakla** speculated that the contestants might not be so 'macho' as they made out.

9 Fathers may find the identity of their sons more difficult to accept, but many families take it with rather little fuss. **Bakla** relatives feature among people's recollections of their parents' and grandparents' generations.

10 These explanations seemed to me quite eclectic; people sometimes mentioned an aspect of heredity, but without much conviction, and sometimes **bakla** themselves suggested (as is sometimes said in the West) that being dressed in girls' clothes or given girls' tasks as children had changed them, although parents tend to see such behaviour as chosen by the child.

11 The people I knew in Naga City, who had much longer education and more exposure to American materials than those in the barangays, sometimes read newspapers and circulars which came directly or indirectly from gay communities in the States. Nonetheless, they also were surprised to know that 'gays' love other 'gays' in America, and considered this either a dubious way to behave, or a misdescription. On the other hand, when Tata's sister once got out the video of *Kiss of the Spider Woman* for the shop-workers, thinking they would identify with the 'Latin-American' style of homosexuality there portrayed, the **bakla** found the film of no relevance to them at all.

12 Compare the interesting and detailed work of Mark Johnson on the **bantut** of the southern Philippines (Johnson, 1994 and 1997), whose identities are much more unambiguously focussed on penetrator/penetrated roles in sexual intercourse. I may be understating this factor in Bicol, but it is also clear from Johnson's work that the particularities of local Islam shape the ways in which sex is used as a metaphor for threat and defence.

13 After my departure in 1992, Tata was successful in getting elected as a city councillor (**kagawad**) for Naga City, during which time he was fondly known as the 'ka-gay-wad'.

14 Irvine (1982) notes in an appendix that Thai transvestites in the Chiang Mai area also hold beauty contests: 'In another form of acting, individual **kathooi** can find momentary celebration', writes Irvine. 'This is when they participate in their own fashion and beauty contests which take place within the village monastery as part of the local fair. Dressed and made up like women, and moving, often convincingly, like them, they can enjoy momentary attention and often general admiration for their convincing performance' (1982:477). I find it intriguing that Irvine's description and my own seem to echo each other in references to the celebratory aspect which I here call 'the happiness of the **bakla**', and which is linked to the opposing possibility of public shame and private distress (Irvine, 1982:467).

15 Some of Tata's seamstresses are themselves **bakla**, and others are women. I would like to take this opportunity to thank Tata, Tina and his staff and friends for their time, hospitality and help while I was in Bicol, and for allowing me to be one of the judges at their superb event.

16 Rural popular performers in Thailand may claim to be literally possessed by the spirits of famous Western figures such as Michael Jackson (Coeli Barry, personal communication).

17 Blanc-Szanton (1990) takes a similar view on Iloilo. If there is no reason to typecast pre-colonial gender-relations as ideally complementary (Eviota, 1992: 33–37), there is also no reason to accept that contemporary gender is totally determined by colonial and Western imperatives, and my own reading of the

Bicol situation as well as others suggests that it is not (see e.g. Illo 1995). Moreover, it seems likely that local concepts of internality and externality of the person do not necessarily correspond to the (post-Freudian) model of the internal, sexually founded and authentic 'self' versus the external self, at least until more work has been done on the significance attached to sexuality in specific locations. For a very interesting reading of those aspects of gender relations which *were* highly determined by American-period colonial relationships, however, see Rafael (1995a).

18  The ways in which dominant Western ideologies of the person create a fascination with cross-dressing as a contrast between apparent and 'real/physical/natural' gender is of course the subject of Judith Butler's influential writings on transvestitism as 'masquerade' (Butler, 1990:46–54; 1993:121–42).

19  Compare Siegel (1986:114, 116) for audiences shocked into 'imitative' crudeness by breaches of propriety on the Surakarta stage.

20  On the notion of combined genders in shamanism, and the relative lack of stress on issues of sexuality, compare Graham's account of the Iban; Iban transvestite shamans could either be impotent and celibate, or become the 'wives' of men (Graham, 1987 esp. 147–51).

## 11: Conclusion: oppression, pity and transformation

1  This story was told to me on an afternoon when my co-godmother Irene had just come out of hospital, following an emergency caesarian after which she had been unable to pay for painkillers or antibiotics.

2  Albeit Rafael seems to be suggesting (in reference to Siegel, 1986 and Derrida, 1985) that these cycles of exchange of signs are themselves a kind of phantasm; the compulsive recreation of a hierarchical distance which they both wish to eliminate and cannot do without. I am grateful to Danilyn Rutherford for illuminating discussions on this point.

3  Reid is here discussing the maritime mercantile states of early modern Southeast Asia, where debt-slaves who received manumission would often re-indenture themselves to a different master/creditor (Reid, 1983: 168). This despite the fact that such cities surely represented the most innovative social environments of the period.

4  Reid in particular classes the Philippines societies as 'transitional' (Reid, 1983:163) between 'closed' systems of slavery, linked in part with the retention of labour for rice-agriculture which emphasised the ritual differentiation and non-transferability of slave status and 'open' systems typical of the maritime cities such as Malacca and Aceh, where the recruitment of population was a priority and where the status of slaves was gradually transformed into that of ordinary (bonded) citizens. (Reid, 1983: 166–67)

5  Scott rightly points out that sixteenth- and seventeenth-century Europeans did not reject 'slavery' on these grounds, which have prevailed since the eighteenth century abolitionist movement, but on the basis of a distinction between the rightness of subjection of non-Christians and Christians (or members of the Spanish Empire, regarded as equivalent).

6  This is I think the most useful way to read Lynch's account of Canaman, a town almost adjoining Calabanga, as composed essentially of two social

groups ('big people and little people') in the 1950s (Lynch, 1959). I would not follow Lynch's argument about the harmonious functionality of the two social classes.

7 It will be recalled that the Bicol sermon for married couples quoted in chapter two exhorts the groom not to treat his bride as his 'wage-worker'.

8 I am grateful to Smita Lahiri for interesting discussions on the possible significance of gold wealth and pawnshops in the Christian Philippines.

9 They also quite often belong specifically to women. It is interesting that Rineke Coumans observed in Marinduque the existence of 'double' sets of family saints, the more luxurious belonging to the elite, while the smaller, odder and apparently older images belonged to the poorer families (Coumans, personal communication).

10 Two separate but related discussions of American reactions to the lowlands c. 1900 are given in Cannell 1996a and 1996b.

11 See Le Roy (1968:74) for a dismissal of the Filipino **ilustrado** Isabelo de los Reyes as a notoriety-seeking charlatan, and all links between insurrection and 'native' religion as 'imposture'. De los Reyes' major collection on historical religion is *La Religion Antigua de los Filipinos* (1909) (Imprente de el Rinacimento, Madrid) and an appreciation of his significance in anti-imperialist politics is given in Scott (1985:285–300).

12 The Coles seem to have managed better than their friend William Jones, who was killed by the Ilongot in the final weeks of his visit to them (Michelle Z. Rosaldo, 1980:2).

13 Mrs Campbell Dauncey is one of the few English rather than American female memoirists of the period, and source of some acerbically superior remarks on the follies of the American manner of running a colony. She is also, however, one of the few authors to mention any kind of Catholic procession or celebration, despite the obvious impressiveness of such spectacles (see Cannell 1998).

14 For a cross-section of samples of the tone of American colonial discourse in the Philippines, see the authors of the *Discrepant histories* collection edited by Vicente Rafael (1995c) especially Ileto's piece on anti-cholera measures, Warwick Anderson's piece on laboratory medicine and Michael Salman's piece on Philippine penology.

15 Every generalisation of this kind brings to mind its own exceptions, and I do not intend here to appear to ignore the existence of notable ethnographies on Southeast Asian peasants. Discussions of peasant identity tend to centre either on problems of economic change and transformation from a Marxian (Kahn, 1980) or Foucauldian (Ong, 1987) perspective, though Kahn (1993) later integrates a forceful critique of the discourse of the Sumatran 'peasant' under colonialism. Other studies view peasant religion and culture from the viewpoint of the 'big tradition/little tradition' critique (which itself replicates the centre–periphery dichotomy) or to critique it by presenting local religion as logically coherent, as in Tambiah's groundbreaking (1970) study of Thai village Buddhism.

16 At the time of going to press, the **Ama**'s funeral was still being conducted from his own shrine on Good Friday. The innovatory priest had transferred to another parish.

17 It is difficult if not impossible to know what might have happened in the intervening centuries.

18 On the overlapping of Catholic saint and pre-Catholic **anitos/diwata** and other
ancestral/deity images, see Ness (1992: 74), Natividad (1979:102), Hislop (1971:
145–50), Lynch (1984c:114–15), Jocano (1965, 1967), Fernando and Zialcita
(1991:116, 154).

19 In this sense, there seems to be some correspondence with an early, and more
crudely Durkheimian point made by Bloch on situations where ritual forms
appear loose and innovative (*Man*, 1979, 14 (1): 165–7) rather than rigid and
tied to transcendental certainty. Bloch claims that the 'unstable' (167) rather
than stereotypical character of such rituals is due to an unsuccessful attempt to
assert one (ritualised) hierarchy against another; when populations feel more
securely in control, they will assert their ritualised identity more strongly (and
authority will have re-established itself within the community). As discussed
below, I believe this only partially describes the variability of ritual in Bicol.

20 See Hislop (1971: 68) for a reference to Visayan **anitos** who are even said to die.

21 Maurice Bloch has drawn on an earlier version of these arguments (Cannell,
1991) in his article 'Internal and external memory: different ways of being in
history' (Bloch, 1992b), and I have found Bloch's contrast between Bicolano
attitudes to time and those of Yemeni and other peoples very helpful in thinking about these issues. While Bloch is right to stress that 'identity' in Bicol is
processual, however, he somewhat oversimplifies the contrast with past-ori-
ented societies when he says, for example, that 'For [Bicolanos] the distant past
is a week, and fading memory is gradually replaced by newer constituting
events' (Bloch, 1992b:9).

22 Realubit (1983:217–18) also quotes this passage in Jagor in her history of Bicol
literature and drama. Note that the date of 1875 refers to the first Spanish
edition of Jagor's work, which was preceded by a German edition first published in 1873.

23 The view given by my ethnography is of course as I have emphasised primarily
the view of one group of people – poorer villagers; one could expect that
wealthier people would place more emphasis on the preservation of inherited
objects and of genealogies, and on themselves as patrons. See Coumans (1996)
for a study which compares the attitudes of elite and barangay in Marinduque
in the context of a Liberation theology movement.

24 Ileto notes that within the language of millenarian peasant uprisings in the
Philippines, 'Begging and the acceptance of . . . protective care [can] create, not
a subordinate–superordinate relationship, but a horizontal one akin to love'
(Ileto, 1979:230). My point, however, is that *at all times* and *in all contexts* in
the Philippines lowlands, the language of 'love' and the language of 'power' are
in fact mutually constructing.

# Bibliography

Abella, Domingo B., 1954. *Bikol Annals: a collection of vignettes of Philippine history,* vol. I. *Manila.* Privately published.

Abu-Lughod, Lila, 1986. *Veiled sentiments: honor and poetry in a Bedouin society.* Berkeley: University of California Press.

Aduarte, Fray Diego, 1905 (originally 1640). *History of the Dominican Province of the Holy Rosary, by Fray Diego Aduarte, O.P.,* in Blair and Robertson, *The Philippine Islands* (55 volumes), vol. 30; 19–321.

Alcina, Francisco de, S.J., (1688). *The Munoz text of Alcina's history of the Bisayan islands (1688).* Part I, vols. 3 and 4. Preliminary translation by Paul S. Leitz, Loyola University. Philippine Studies Program, Department of Anthropology, University of Chicago, 1970.

Anderson, Benedict R. O'G., 1983. *Imagined communities: reflections on the origins and spread of nationalism.* London and New York: Verso.

   1990 (originally published 1972). 'The idea of power in Javanese culture' in B.R.O'G. Anderson, *Language and power: exploring political cultures in Indonesia.* Ithaca: Cornell University Press.

Anderson, Bridget, 1993. *Britain's secret slaves: an investigation into the plight of overseas domestic workers in the United Kingdom.* London: Anti-Slavery International.

Anderson, Warwick, 1995. '"Where every prospect pleases and only man is vile": laboratory medicine as colonial discourse', in Vicente L. Rafael (ed. ) 1995d, 83–112.

Anonymous, 1903 (originally published 1649). *Entrada de la seraphica religion de nuestro P.S. Francisco en las islas Philipinas* (translated as 'Entrance of the seraphic order of our father St Francis into the Philippine islands'), vol. 7: 280–313, in E.H. Blair and J.A. Robertson (eds.), 1903–9. *The Philippine islands, 1493–1898.* 55 volumes. Cleveland: A.H. Clark.

Aries, Philippe, 1977. *The hour of our death.* Harmondsworth: Penguin Books.

Astuti, Rita, 1995. *People of the sea.* Cambridge: Cambridge University Press.

Atkinson, Jane Monnig, 1989. *The art and politics of Wana shamanism.* Berkeley: University of California Press.

   1990. 'How gender makes a difference in Wana society', in Jane Monnig

Atkinson and Shelly Errington (eds.), *Power and difference: gender in island Southeast Asia*. Stanford: Stanford University Press; 59–94.

Atkinson, Jane Monning and S. Errington (eds.), 1990. *Power and difference: gender in island Southeast Asia*. Stanford: Stanford University Press.

Barber, Paul, 1988. *Vampires, burial and death: folklore and reality*. New York and London: Yale University Press.

Barcenas, Diosdado C., 1989. 'The beauties of yesteryears'. *Women's Journal* 17: 14–17 (April 22). Manila: Philippine Journalists, Inc.

Barker, Nicholas H., 1994. 'Flesh and blood: animistic elements of the Passion of Christ in the Philippines'. Paper presented to the European Conference of Philippine Studies at the School of Oriental and African Studies, London, April 1994.

Barnes, Ruth, 1922. 'Women as headhunters: the making and meaning of textiles in a Southeast Asian context', in R. Barnes and J.B. Eicher (eds.), *Dress and gender: making and meaning*. Providence and Oxford: Berg.

Barnes, Ruth and Joanne B. Eicher, 1992. *Dress and gender: making and meaning*. Providence and Oxford: Berg.

Benson, Susan, 1996. 'Body health and eating disorders', in K. Woodward and L. Jaynes (eds.), *Media, culture and identity*. London: Open University Press.

Beyer, H. Otley, 1979. 'The Philippines before Magellan', in Mauro Garcia (ed.), *Readings in Philippine history*. Manila: Filipiniana Book Guild.

Blair, E.H. and J.A. Robertson (eds.), 1903–9. *The Philippine islands, 1493–1898*. 55 volumes. Cleveland: A.H. Clark.

Blanc-Szanton, Maria Cristina, 1972. *A right to survive: subsistence marketing in a lowland Philippine town*. The Pennsylvania State University, reprinted under authority of Presidential Decree no. 285, as amended by Presidential Decree no. 400, by the Institute of Philippine Culture, Ateneo de Manila University, PO Box 154, Manila 2801, Philippines.

    1990. 'Collision of cultures: historical reformulations of gender in the lowland Visayas, Philippines', in J.M. Atkinson and S. Errington (eds.), *Power and difference: gender in island Southeast Asia*. Stamford: Stamford University Press.

Bloch, Maurice, 1971. *Placing the dead: tombs, ancestral houses and kinship organization among the Merina of Madagascar*. London and New York: Seminar Press.

    1979. 'Knowing the world or hiding it?' Correspondence with M.F.C. Bourdillon in *Man* (N.S.) 14(1): 165–7.

    1986. *From blessing to violence. History and ideology in the circumcision ritual of the Merina of Madagascar*. Cambridge: Cambridge University Press.

    1989a. 'Marriage among equals', in *Ritual, history and power: selected papers in anthropology*. London: Athlone Press.

    1989b. *Ritual, history and power: selected papers in anthropology*. London: Athlone Press.

    1992a. *Prey into hunter: the politics of religious experience*. Cambridge: Cambridge University Press.

    1992b. 'Internal and external memory: different ways of being in history'. *Suomen antropologi I* 17:3–15.

1994. 'The slaves, the king and Mary in the slums of Antananarivo', in N. Thomas and C. Humphrey (eds.), *Shamanism, history and the state.* Ann Arbor: Michigan University Press.

Bloch, M. and S. Guggenheim, 1981. 'Compadrazgo, baptism and the symbolism of a second birth'. *Man* (N.S.) 16: 376–86.

Bloch, Maurice and Jonathan Parry (eds.), 1982. *Death and the regeneration of life.* Cambridge: Cambridge University Press.

Blumentritt, Ferdinand, 1895. '*Diccionario mitologico de Filipinas*', in W.E. Retana (ed.), *Archivo del bibliofilo Filipino* (1895–1905), vol. II. Madrid: Imprenta de la viuda de M. Minuesa de los Rios.

Boddy, Janice, 1989. *Wombs and alien spirits: women, men and the Zar cult in northern Sudan.* London: University of Wisconsin Press.

Boon, James, 1990. 'Balinese twins times two: gender, birth-order and "household" in Indonesia/Indo-Europe', in J.M. Atkinson and S. Errington (eds.), *Power and difference: gender in island Southeast Asia.* Stanford: Stanford University Press.

Borra, Teresita, 1984. 'An economic analysis of the Philippine Manpower Export Industry', in Fr. Anthony Paganoni (comp.), *Migration from the Philippines.* Quezon City: Scalabrinians.

Bourdieu, Pierre, 1977. *Outline of a theory of practice,* translated by Richard Nice. London and New York: Routledge and Kegan Paul.

Brandes, Stanley, 1981. 'Like wounded stags: male sexual ideology in an Andalusian town', in S.B. Ortner and H. Whitehead (eds.), *Sexual meanings: the cultural construction of gender and sexuality.* Cambridge: Cambridge University Press.

Brenner, Suzanne A., 1995. 'Why woman rule the roost: rethinking Javanese ideologies of gender and self control', in A. Ong and M. Peletz (eds.), *Bewitching women, pious men: gender and body politics in Southeast Asia.* Berkeley: University of California Press.

Brooke, Margaret, Ranee of Sarawak, 1992 (originally published 1913). *My life in Sarawak.* Singapore and Oxford: Oxford University Press.

Brown, Peter, 1981. *The cult of the saints: its rise and function in Latin Christianity.* London: SCM Press Ltd.

Bulatao, Jaime, 1977. 'Keynote speech: altered state of consciousness in Philippine religion', in L.N. Mercado (ed.), *Filipino religious psychology.* Manila: Pambansang Samahan sa Sikolohiyang Pilipino and the Divine Word University.

1984. 'Bulatao special group studies', cited in Frank Lynch, 'Social acceptance reconsidered', in *Philippine society and the individual; selected essays of Frank Lynch, 1949–76.* ed. Aram A. Yengoyan and Perla Q. Makil, 23–9. Ann Arbor: Centre for South and Southeast Asian Studies, University of Michigan.

Butler, Judith, 1990. *Gender trouble: feminism and the subversion of identity.* New York: Routledge.

1993. *Bodies that matter: on the discursive limits of 'sex'.* London: Routledge.

Camaligan Committee, 1953. *History and cultural life in Camaligan.* Bureau of Education Schoolteachers' Committee Reports.

Campbell Dauncey, Mrs, 1906. *An Englishwoman in the Philippines.* London: John Murray.

Cannell, Fenella, 1991. 'Catholicism, spirit mediums and the ideal of beauty in a Bicolano community, Philippines'. PhD thesis, University of London.

1995a. 'The imitation of Christ in Bicol, Philippines'. *Journal of the Royal Anthropological Institute (N.S.)* 1: 377–94.

1995b. 'The power of appearances: beauty, mimicry and transformation in Bicol', in Vicente L. Rafael (ed.), 1995d, 223–58.

1996a. 'The Age of the Father and the Age of the Child: ritual and "ritualization" in Bicol, Philippines'. Paper delivered at the International Philippine Studies Conference, Honolulu, Hawaii, April 1996.

1996b. 'Opportunities for improvement: home economics in the Philippines'. Paper delivered at the Association of Asian Studies Conference, Honolulu, Hawaii, April 1996.

1997. 'Reading as gift and writing as theft in the Philippine lowlands'. Paper presented to the first of two workshops entitled '"Words and things"; the anthropology of Christianity' held at the Departments of Anthropology, Manchester and London School of Economics: meeting one, Manchester, May 16th, 1997.

1998. 'Immaterial culture; idolatry and colonialism in the lowland Philippines'. Paper presented at the Workshop series 'The long-term consequences of colonialism', Department of Anthropology, University College London, March 1998.

Carsten, Janet, 1987. 'Women, kinship and community in a Malay fishing village in Pulau, Langkawi, Kedah, Malaysia'. PhD thesis, University of London.

1991. 'Children in-between: fostering and the process of kinship in Pulau Lankawi, Malaysia'. *Man* (N.S.) 26: 425–48.

1995. 'Houses in Langkawi: stable structures or mobile homes?' in J. Carsten and S. Hugh-Jones (eds.), *About the house. Lévi-Strauss and beyond.* Cambridge: Cambridge University Press.

Castano, Fray Jose, 1895. *Breve noticia acerca del origen, religion, creecias y superstitiones de los antiquos indios del Bicol: Escrito expresamente para el ARCHIVO,* in W.E. Retana (comp.), *Archivo del bibliofilo Filipino,* vol. I: 323–80 Madrid: Imprenta de la Viuda de M. Minuesa de los Rios.

Catedra, Maria, 1992. *The world, other worlds: sickness, suicide, death and the afterlife among the Vaquieros de Alzada of Spain* (translated from Spanish by William Christian Jr). Princeton: Princeton University Press.

Census, 1990. *Census of Population and Housing Report no. 3–24E (Camarines Sur); Social and demographic characteristics.* Report of the Philippines National Statistics Office, Manila.

Chagnon, Napoleon, with Philip le Quesne and James A. Cook, 1971. 'Yanomamo hallucinogens: anthropological, botanical and chemical findings'. *Current Anthropology* 12: 72–82.

Chant, Sylvia and Cathy McIlwaine, 1995. *Women of a lesser cost: female labour, foreign exchange and Philippine development.* London: Pluto Press.

Chirino, Pedro, S.J., 1969 (original 1604). *Relacion de las islas Filipinas/The Philippines in 1600* (translated by Ramon Echevarria). Manila: Historical Conservation Society.

Christian, William A., Jr, 1972. *Person and God in a Spanish valley.* Princeton: Princeton University Press.

1992. *Moving crucifixes in modern Spain.* Princeton: Princeton University Press.

Collier, Christopher (Kit), 1997. 'Revolution as a process of articulation: the case of Davao'. Paper presented to the European Conference of Philippine Studies, I.R.S.E.A., Aix-en-Provence, France, April 1997.

Conklin, Harold C., 1964. 'Ethnogenealogical method', in *Explorations in Cultural Anthropology,* ed. W.H. Goodenough. New York: McGraw-Hill.

Constantino, Renato, 1969. *The making of a Filipino. A story of Filipino colonial politics.* Quezon City: Malaya Books.

1976. 'Identity and consciousness: the Philippine experience', *Journal of Contemporary Asia* 6 (1) 5–28 and 6 (2) 129–47.

1978a. *Neocolonial identity and counter consciousness: essays on cultural decolonization.* London: Merlin Press.

1978b. *The Philippines: the continuing past.* Quezon City: Foundation for Nationalist Studies.

Cook Cole, Mabel, 1929. *Savage gentlemen.* New York: D. Van Norstrand Company Ltd.

Coumans, Catherine (Rineke), 1991. 'Aspects of structurally organized versus everyday forms of rural resistance in the Philippines'. Paper presented at the European Conference of Philippine Studies, C.A.S.A., University of Amsterdam, 1991.

1993. 'Building basic Christian communities: religion, symbolism and ideology in a national movement to change local level power relations in the Philippines'. PhD thesis, McMaster University, Canada.

1996. '"Re-Christianization" in Marinduque'. Paper delivered at the International Philippine Studies Conference, East-West Centre, University of Hawaii at Manoa, Honolulu, Hawaii, April 1996.

Cullamar, Evelyn Tan, 1986. *Babaylanism in Negros, 1896–1907.* Quexon City: New Day Publishers.

Dahlberg, Andrea, 1987. 'Transcendence of bodily suffering: an anthropological study of English Catholics at Lourdes'. PhD thesis, University of London.

Davis, William G., 1968. 'Economic relations and social relationships in a Philippine marketplace: capital accumulation in a peasant economy', in R. van Niel (ed.), *Asian studies at Hawaii* 2: 1–28. Honolulu: Asian Studies Program, University of Hawaii.

1973. *Social relations in a Philippine market: self interest and subjectivity.* Berkeley and London: University of California Press.

De Heusch, Luc, 1962. 'Cultes de possession et religons initiatiques de salut en Afrique', in *Annales du Centre d'Etudes des Religions,* vol. 2. Brussels: Institut de Sociologie de l'Université Libre de Bruxelles.

De Huerta, M.S.P.C. Fransisco Fray Felix, c.1865. *Estado Geographico, Topografico, Estadistico, Historico-Religioso, de la Santa Y Apostolica Provincia de S. Gregorio Magno.* Binondo: Imprenta de M. Sanchez.

De los Reyes, Isabelo, 1900. *La religion del 'Katipunan' osea la antigua de los filipinos tal como ahora la resucita la Asociacion de los hijos del pueblo ('Katipunan'), la promovedora de la revolucion filipina con la segunda parte inedita, hasta ahora, en la que se dar concer la organizacion del Katipunan, y se desarrolla la anterior doctrina religiosa con afirmaciones mas concretas y modernas, por Isabelo de los Reyes Y Florentino.* Publicado por la delegacion filipina en Europa. Madrid: Tipolit. de J. Corvales.

1909. *La Religion Antigua de los Filipinas.* Kiapo (Quiapo) Manila: Imprente de El Rinascimiento.

Demetrio, Fr Francisco R., S.J., 1968. 'The Engkanto belief; an essay in interpretation'. *Philippine Sociological Review,* 16: 136–43.

1978. 'Indigenous religions and Christianity in the modernization process of the Philippines', in *Agham-Tao; Papers of the First National Convention of UGAT, U.P. at Los Banos, 14–16 April, 1978,* vol. I, no. 1, 1978: 89–111.

1990. *Myths and symbols Philippines.* Manila: National Bookstore.

Demetrio, F.R., G. Cordero-Fernando and Fernando N. Zialcita, 1991. *The soul book.* Manila: GCF Books.

Derrida, Jacques, 1985. 'Des tours de Babel', in Joseph F. Graham (ed.) *Difference in translation,* 167–85. Ithaca, NY: Cornell University Press.

Dery, Luis Camara, 1991. *From Ibalon to Sorsogon: a historical survey of Sorsogon province to 1905.* Quezon City: New Day.

Douglas, Mary, 1970. *Natural symbols: explorations in cosmology.* London: Barrie, and Rockliff: The Crescent Press.

Dumont, Jean-Paul, 1992. *Visayan vignettes: ethnographic traces of a Philippine island.* Chicago: University of Chicago Press.

1994. 'Matrons, maids, and mistresses: Philippine domestic encounters'. *Philippine Quarterly of Culture and Society* 22: 174–91.

Durkheim, Emile, 1984. *The division of labour* (translated by Halls). London: MacMillan.

Echauz, Roustiano, 1978. *Apuntas historias de la isla de Negroes/Sketches of the island of Negroes* (translated by D.V. Hart). Athens, Ohio: Centre for International Studies, Ohio University.

Elesterio, Fernando G., 1989. *Three essays on Philippine religious culture.* Manila: De La Salle University Press.

Eliade, Mircea, 1951. *Le chamanisme et les techniques archaïques de l'exstase.* Paris: Librarie Payot.

1964. *Shamanism; archaic techniques of ecstacy.* Princeton: Princeton University Press.

1989. *Shamanism: archaic techniques of ecstacy.* London: Arkana (Penguin Group).

Embree, J.F., 1950. 'Thailand: a loosely structured social system'. *American Anthropologist* 52: 181–93.

Endicott, K.M., 1970. *An analysis of Malay magic.* London: Oxford University Press.

Enriquez, Virgilio G., 1986. '**Kapwa**; a core concept in Filipino social psychology', ed. Virgilio G. Enriquez (ed.), *Philippine world view.* Singapore: Institute of Southeast Asian Studies.

also published as Enriquez, 1991, in *SA 21; selected readings, Department of Sociology-Anthropology.* Quezon City, Ateneo de Manila Office of Research and Publications, 98–105.

Errington, Shelly, 1989. *Meaning and power in a Southeast Asian realm.* Princeton: Princeton University Press.

1990. 'Recasting sex, gender and power: a theoretical and regional overview', in J.M. Atkinson and S. Errington (eds.), *Power and difference: gender in island Southeast Asia.*

Eugenio, Damiana L., 1987. 'Philippine legendary'. *Danyag, Journal of Studies in the Social Sciences, Humanities, Education, and the Basic and Applied Sciences* (University of the Philippines in the Visayas) 3: 287–319.

Eviota, Elizabeth Uy, 1992. *The political economy of gender: women and the sexual division of labor in the Philippines.* London and New Jersey: Zed Books.

Fee, Mary H., 1910. *A woman's impressions of the Philippines.* Chicago: A.C. Mc Ching and Co.

Fenton, James, 1986. *The snap revolution: James Fenton in the Philippines (Granta 18).* Cambridge: Granta Publications Ltd.

Fernandez, Doreen G., 1996. *Palabas: essays on Philippine theatre history.* Quezon City: Ateneo de Manila University Press.

Freeman, Derek, 1970. *Report on the Iban.* London: Athlone Press.

Garcia, Neil, 1996. *Bakla: Philippine gay culture, the last thirty years.* Quezon City: University of the Philippines.

Geary, Patrick, 1988. 'Sacred commodities: the circulation of medieval relics', in Arjun Appadurai (ed.), *The social life of things: commodities in cultural perspective.* Cambridge: Cambridge University Press.

Geddes, W.R., 1968. *Nine Dayak nights.* Oxford: Oxford University Press.

Geertz, Clifford, 1960. *The religion of Java.* Chicago and London: Chicago University Press.

1964. *The religion of Java:* Free Press of Glencoe: Collier-Macmillan.

1980. *Negara: the theatre state in 19th century Bali.* Princeton: Princeton University Press.

Gerona, Danilo Madrid, 1988a. 'The early evangelisation of the Bikol region'. *Kinaadman (Wisdom): The Journal of the Southern Philippines* 10: 91–104.

1988b. *From epic to history: a brief introduction to Bicol history.* City of Naga: Ateneo de Naga University Press.

1990. 'The Franciscan evangelisation and the Bikolano response 1578–1700'. *Kinaadman (Wisdom): The Journal of the Southern Philippines* 12: 97–113.

Gibson, Thomas, 1986. *Sacrifice and sharing in the Philippine highlands. Religion and society among the Buid of Mindoro.* London: Athlone Press.

Goodno, James B., 1991. *The Philippines. Land of broken promises.* London and New Jersey: Zed Books.

Graham, Penelope, 1987. *Iban shamanism: an analysis of the ethnographic literature.* Occasional paper of the Department of Anthropology, Research School of Pacific Studies, Canberra, Australian National University.

Guerra, Juan Alvarez de, 1887. *Viajes por Filipinas: de Manila a Albay.* Madrid: Imprenta de Fortanet.

Guerrero, Milagros C., 1996. 'Sources on women's role in Philippine history, 1590–1898. Texts and countertexts'. Paper presented to the International Conference on Philippine Studies, East-West Centre, University of Hawaii at Manoa, April 1996, Honolulu, Hawaii.

Hagey, Rebecca Susan, 1980. 'Healing entrepreneurship in the Philippines'. PhD thesis, Ann Arbor, University of Michigan.

Hart, Donn V., 1966. 'The Filipino villager and his spirits'. *Solidarity* 1 (4): 65–71.

1977. *Compadrinazgo: Ritual kinship in the Philippines.* Dekalb: Northern Illinois University Press.

Hatol, Mag Cruz, 1988. 'A national preoccupation with beauty'. *Women's Home Companion* 16: 12 (July 13). Manila: Philippine Journalists Inc.

Hegel, G.W.F., 1975. *Early theological writings* (translated by T.M. Knox). Philadelphia: University of Pennsylvania Press.

Hernandez, Tranquilino, 1984 (originally published 1866). *Casaysayan can mahal na Passion ni Jesucristo Cagurangnanta: na sucat ipaglaad nin puso nin siisay man na magbasa. ("Pasion Bicol").* Translation commissioned by Archbishop Francisco Gainza, Archbishop of Nueva Carceres. Manila: U.S.T. Press.

Hislop, Stephen K., 1971. 'Anitism, a survey of religious beliefs native to the Philippines'. *Asian Studies* 9: 144–56.

Hollnsteiner, Mary R., 1973. 'Reciprocity in the lowland Philippines', in F. Lynch and A. de Guzman II (eds.), *Four readings in Philippine values* (third revised and enlarged edition). IPC papers No. 2. Quezon City: Ateneo de Manila University Press.

Hoskins, Janet, 1990. 'Doubling deities, descent and personhood: an exploration of Kodi gender categories', in Jane Monnig Atkinson and Shelly Errington (eds.), *Power and difference: gender in island Southeast Asia*, 273–306.

Ileto, Reynaldo Clemena, 1979. *Pasyon and revolution. Popular movements in the Philippines, 1840–1910.* Quezon City: Ateneo de Manila University Press.

   1995. 'Cholera and the origins of the American sanitary order in the Philippines', in Vicente L. Rafael (ed.), 1995d, 51–82.

Illo, Jeanne Frances I., 1985. 'Wives at work: patterns of labor force participation in two rice-farming villages in the Philippines', in *Women in rice farming; proceedings of a conference on women in rice farming systems.* International Rice Research Institute (I.R.R.I.). Aldershot, Hants, and Vermont, USA: Gower Publishing Company Ltd.

   1988. *Irrigation in the Philippines: impact on women and their households.* Bangkok: The Population Council, Regional Office for South and East Asia.

   1990. *Fishers, traders, farmers, wives: the life stories of ten women in a fishing village.* Quezon City: Ateneo de Manila University Press.

   1992. 'Who heads the household? Women in households in the Philippines', in K. Saradamoni (ed.), *Finding the household: conceptual and methodological issues.* Women and the Household in Asia, vol. V. New Delhi: Sage.

   1995. 'Redefining the *maybahay* or housewife: reflections on the nature of women's work in the Philippines', in W.J. Karim (ed.), *'Male' and 'female' in developing Southeast Asia.* Oxford: Berg.

Illo, Jeanne Frances I. and Ricardo R. San Andres, 1978. *Beyond share tenancy: a socioeconomic study of the effects of agrarian programs in Bicol river basin, Camarines Sur, 1974 and 1977: Final report submitted to the Bicol River Basin Development Program by the Social Survey Research Unit (Naga City).* Institute of the Philippine Culture, 30 September 1978. Quezon City: Ateneo de Manila University.

Irvine, Walter Raymond Beattie, 1982. 'The Thai-Yuan "madman" and the "modernising, developing, Thai nation" as bounded entities under threat; a study in the replication of a single image'. PhD thesis, University of London.

Jagor, Feodor, 1965 (1875). *Travels in the Philippines (Reisen in der Philippinnen)*. Manila: Filipiniana Book Guild. First Spanish edition published as Jagor, F., 1875. *Viajes por Filipinas, traducios del aleman por S. Vidal Y Soler*. Madrid: Imprenta, Estereotipo y Glavanoplastia de Aribau y C.a (Sucesores de Rivadeneyra), Impresores de Camara de S.M.

Javellana, Rene, B.S.J., 1983. 'Pasyon genealogy and annotated bibliography'. *Philippine Studies* 31: 451–67.

—— 1984. 'The sources of Aquino de Belen's Pasyon'. *Philippine Studies* 32: 305–21.

—— 1988. *Casaysayan nang Pasiong mahal ni Jesuscristong Panginoon natin na sucat ipagalab nang puso nang sinomang babasa (with an introduction, annotations and translation of the 1882 edition)*. Quezon City: Ateneo de Manila University Press.

—— 1990. 'Gaspar Aquino de Belen's poetic universe: a key to his metaphorical theology'. *Philippine Studies* 38: 28–44.

Jenista, Frank Lawrence, 1987. *The white apos: American governors on the Cordillera central*. Quezon City: New Day.

Jensen, Erik, 1974. *The Iban and their religion*. Oxford: Clarendon Press.

Jocano, F. Landa, 1965. 'Conversion and the patterning of Christian experience in Malitbog, Central Panay, Philippines'. *Philippine Sociological Review* 13: 96–119.

—— 1967. 'Filipino Catholicism: a case study in religious change'. *Asian Studies* 5: 42–64.

—— 1969a. *Growing up in a Philippine Barrio*. New York: Holt, Rinehart and Winston.

—— 1969b. (1966). *The traditional world of Malitbog*. Community Development Research Council. Quezon City: University of the Philippines Press.

—— 1982. *The Ilocanos: an ethnography of family and community life in the Ilocos region*. Quezon City: University of Philippines, Diliman.

—— 1989. 'Kinship and technological change: a study from Western Visayas, Philippines', in Y. Kikuchi (ed.), *Philippine kinship and society*. Quezon City: New Day Publishers.

John, Marius, 1940. *Philippine saga*. New York: House of Field.

Johnson, Mark, 1994. 'Cross-gendered men and homosexuality in the Southern Philippines: ethnicity, political violence and the protocols of engendered sexuality among the Muslim Taussug and Sama'. Paper delivered at the European Conference of Philippine Studies, School of Oriental and African Studies, London, April 1994.

—— 1995a. 'Remembrances and debts: encompassing the alien'. Unpublished paper.

—— 1995b. 'Remembrances, identity, cultural transformation and transgender men in the Southern Philippines'. *International Journal of Comparative Race and Ethnic Studies* 2 (1): 116–32.

—— 1995c. *Beauty and power: identity, cultural transformation and transgendering in the Southern Philippines*. PhD thesis, University of London.

—— 1997. *Beauty and power: transgendering and cultural transformation in the Southern Philippines*. Oxford: Berg.

Kahn, Joel S., 1980. *Minangkabau social formations: Indonesian peasants and the world economy*. Cambridge: Cambridge University Press.

1993. *Constituting the Minangkabau: peasants, culture and modernity in colonial Indonesia.* Providence and Oxford: Berg.

Karim, Wazir Jahan, 1981. *Ma'Batisek concepts of living things.* London: Athlone Press.

Karim, Wazir Jahan (ed.), 1990. *Emotions of culture. A Malay perspective.* Oxford: Oxford University Press.

Karnow, Stanley, 1990. *In our own image: America's empire in the Philippines.* London: Century.

Kayne, Sargent, 1907. *Anting-anting stories and other strange tales of the Filipinas.* Boston: Sherman, French and Company.

Keeler, Ward, 1987. *Javanese shadow-play, Javanese selves.* Princeton: Princeton University Press.

Kerkvliet, Benedict, 1990. *Everyday politics in the Philippines: class and status relations in a Central Luzon village.* Berkeley: University of California Press.

Kikuchi, Yasushi, 1991. *Uncrystallized Philippine society: a social anthropological analysis.* Quezon City: New Day Publishers.

Kotilainen, Eija-Maija, 1992. *'When the bones are left'. A study of material culture of central Sulawesi.* Helsinki: Transactions of the Finnish Anthropological Society no. 31.

Kuipers, Joel C., 1990. *Power in performance: the creation of textual authority in Weyewa ritual speech.* Philadelphia: University of Pennsylvania Press.

Laderman, Carol, 1991. *Taming the winds of desire. Psychology, medicine, and aesthetics in Malay shamanship performance.* Berkeley: University of California Press.

Lambek, Michael, 1981. *Human spirits: a cultural account of trance in Mayotte.* Cambridge: Cambridge University Press.

Lan, David, 1985. *Guns and rain. Guerillas and spirit mediums in Zimbabwe.* London: James Curry.

Le Roy, James, 1968 (1905). *Philippine life in town and country.* Published as *The Philippines circa 1900, Book one.* Manila: Filipiniana Book Guild.

Leach, Edmund, 1970 (originally published 1954). *Political systems of highland Burma: a study of Kachin social structure.* London: Athlone Press.

1972. 'Melchisedech and the emperor: icons of subversion and orthodoxy', in E. Leach and D.A. Aycock (eds.), *Structuralist interpretation of biblical myth.* Cambridge: Cambridge University Press.

Leach, Edmund and D. Alan Aycock (eds.), 1983. *Structuralist interpretation of biblical myth.* Cambridge: Cambridge University Press.

Lévi-Strauss, Claude, 1969 (originally published 1949). *The elementary structures of kinship.* Boston: Beacon Press.

1983a. *The way of the masks* (translated by S. Modelski). London: Jonathan Cape.

1983b. 'Histoire et ethnologie'. *Annales* 38: 1217–31.

1984. *Paroles données.* Paris: Plon.

1987. *Anthropology and myth: Lectures 1951–82.* Oxford: Blackwell.

1991. 'Maison', in P. Bonte and M. Izard (eds.), *Dictionnaire de l'ethnologie et de l'anthropologie.* Paris: Presses Universitaires de France.

Lewis, I. M., 1971. *Ecstatic religion: an anthropological study of spirit possession and shamanism.* Harmondsworth: Penguin Books.

1986. *Religion in context: cults and charisma.* Cambridge: Cambridge University Press.

Lewis, Oscar, 1966. *The children of Sanchez.* Harmondsworth: Penguin Books.

Lisboa, Fr Marcos de, 1865. *Vocabulario de la lengua Bicol: compuesto per el M.R.P. Fr. Marcos de Lisboa (Reimpreso de espensas del Exmo. Imo. y Rmo. Dr. Fr. Francisco Gainza. Arzobispado etc.).* Manila: Establecimiento Tipografidad de Colegio de Santo Tomas.

Loarca, Miguel de, 1582–87. 'Relacion de las islas Filipinas', in E.H. Blair and J.A. Robertson (eds.), 1903–9. *The Philippine islands, 1493–1898.* 55 vols., vol. 5: 34–187. Cleveland: A.H. Clark.

Locsin-Nava, Cecilia, 1987. 'Recurrent motifs in Negrenese waterlore'. *Danyag; Journal of Studies in the Social Sciences, Humanities, Education, and the Basic and Applied Sciences.* University of the Philippines in the Visayas. 2: 68–79.

Lumbera, Bienvenido, 1986. *Tagalog poetry 1570–1898: tradition and influence on its development.* Quezon City: Ateneo de Manila University Press.

Lynch, Frank, S.J., 1949. 'An mga Asuang: A Bicol belief', in *Philippine Social Sciences and Humanities Review* 14 (December 1949): 401–28 (also published in Yengoyan and Makil (eds.), 1984).

c. 1956. 'Folk Catholicism in the Philippines'. Unpublished typescript. Library of Institute of Philippine Culture, Ateneo de Manila University, Quezon City, Philippines.

1959. *Social class in a Bikol town.* Frank Lynch assisted by Augusto V. Plopinion and Wilfredo F. Arce. Research series no. 1. Philippine Studies Program, Department of Anthropology, University of Chicago.

1963. *Bikol area sources collection (Religious beliefs and behaviour series).* Bikol Areas Survey, vol. I. Naga: Ateneo de Naga.

1973a. (third revised and enlarged edition). 'Social acceptance reconsidered', in F. Lynch and A. de Guzman II (eds.), *Four readings on Philippine values.* IPC papers no. 2. Quezon City: Ateneo de Manila Press.

1973b. *What rice farmers of Camarines Sur say they want from Philippine government.* SSRU Research Report Series no. 1. Naga City: Social Survey Research Unit, Ateneo de Naga.

1974. *Rice farm harvest and practice in Camarines Sur: Do compact farms, Masagana gg and the Samahang Ngayon make a difference?* SSRU Research Report Series no. 2. Naga City: Social Survey Research Unit, Ateneo de Naga.

1984a. 'Social acceptance reconsidered', in Aram A. Yengoyan and Perla S. Makil (eds), 23–39. Also published as Lynch, 1991. 'Social acceptance reconsidered'. *SA 21: selected readings.* Department of Sociology – Anthropology. Quezon City: Ateneo de Manila University Press.

1984b. 'Big people and little people; social class in the rural Philippines', Aram A. Yengoyan and Perla S. Makil (eds.) 92–9.

1984c. 'An mga aswang: a Bicol belief', in Aram A. Yengoyan and Perla S. Makil (eds.), 75–197.

1984d. 'Folk Catholicism in the Philippines', in A. Yengoyan and Perla S. Makil (eds.) 197–227.

1984e. '"Town fiesta": an anthropologist's view', in Aram A. Yengoyan and Perla S. Makil (eds.) 209–27.

Lynch, Frank, S.J., (ed.), 1972. *View from the paddy: empirical studies of Philippine rice farming and tenancy.* Quezon City: Institute of Philippine Culture. Also published in *Philippine Sociological Review* 20 (1972): 1–2.

Lynch, Frank, S.J. and Alfonso de Guzman II (eds.), 1973 (third revised and enlarged edition). *Four readings on Philippine values.* IPC papers no. 2. Quezon City: Ateneo de Manila Press.

Lynch, Frank, S.J. and Jeanne Frances I. Illo (eds.), 1975. *Patterns of income distribution and household spending in Bicol River Baisin.* SSRU Research Report Series no. 13. Naga City: Social Survey Research Unit, Ateneo de Naga.

McDonald, Mark, 1982. 'Urbanization and class in Iloilo'. *Philippine Studies* 30: 15–31.

Macdonald, Charles, 1991. 'Comparative mythology; from island Southeast Asia to the New World?' Draft paper presented to the European Conference of Philippine Studies. C.A.S.A. University Amsterdam, April 24–26, 1991.

Macdonald, Charles et al. (eds.), 1987. *De la hutte au palais: sociétés 'à maison' en Asie du Sud-Est insulaire.* Paris: C.N.R.S.

Maceda, Jose, Leonor Orosa Gogiungco, and Lucrecia R. Kasilag, 1980. 'Philippine music' entry in *New Grove dictionary of music and musicians*, ed. Stanley Sadie, 631–53. London: Macmillan.

Madigan, Francis, S.J., 1972. *Birth and death in Cagayan de Oro: population dynamics in a medium-sized Philippine city.* Quezon City: Ateneo de Manila University Press.

Magboo, Nemesio, 1922. *Ligaya sa langit at mundo: catua-tuang pamgangnac ng mahal na Virgen sa maralitang cueva o portel ng Belen.* Manila: J. Martinez.

Magos, Alicia B., 1978. 'The Ma-aram in a Kinaraya society'. MA thesis, University of the Philippines Diliman, Quezon City.

1986. 'The ideological basis and social context of Ma-Aram practice in a Kinaray-a society'. PhD thesis, University of the Philippines Diliman, Quezon City.

1992. *The enduring Ma-Aram tradition: an ethnography of a Kinaray-a village in Antique.* Quezon City: New Day.

Malanyaon, Jaime T., 1990. *Tambobong nin mga piniling tataramon sa Bikol (Bikol–English thesaurus).* Naga City: AMS Press.

1991. *Istorya kan Kabikolan* (Kabikolan: a history). Naga City: AMS Press.

Mallari, Francisco, S.J., 1983. 'The remontados of Isarog', *Kinaadman (Wisdom): The Journal of the Southern Philippines* 5: 103–17.

1987. 'Defenses of Bicol towns in the 19th century'. *Philippine Studies* 35: 191–210.

1990. 'Camarines towns under siege'. *Philippine Studies* 38: 453–76.

Manalong, Priscilla S., 1982. 'Philippine values, norms and technological innovation'. *Philippine Social Science and Humanities Review* vol. XLVI.

Mandreza, Kit, 1989. 'The snake twin'. *Women's Journal* 17: 44–6. (July 1). Manila: Philippine Journalists Inc.

Manila Bureau of Printing, 1915. *The Philippine islands: their industrial and commercial possibilities; the country and the people*. Official catalog of the Philippine Exhibit at the Panama-Pacific International Exposition of 1915.

Marasigan, Vicente, S.J., 1982. 'Tatlong persona solo dios'. *Philippine Studies* 30: 552–63.

1985. *A Banahaw guru: symbolic deeds of Agapito Illustrismo*. Quezon City: Ateneo de Manila University Press.

Martinez, M.R.P. Fr. Domingo, 1905. *Catecismo de la Doctrina Cristiana en Idioma Bicol*. Manila: Colegio de Sto. Tomas.

Mas, Siniblado de (originally published 1842). *Internal political condition of the Philippines*, vol. 52: 29–90, in E.H. Blair and J.A. Robertson (eds.), *The Philippine islands, 1493–1898*. 1903–9. 55 volumes. Cleveland: A.H. Clark.

Mataragnon, Rita H., 1984. 'God of the rich, God of the poor'. *Philippine Studies* 32: 5–27.

1985. 'Modernization and religion: must they move in opposite directions?' *Philippine Studies* 33: 164–75.

Mauss, Marcel, 1966. *The gift: forms and functions of exchange in archaic societies* (tran. I. Cunnison). London: Cohen and West.

1990. *The gift; the form and reason for exchange in archaic societies* (translated by W.D. Halls, with a foreword by Mary Douglas). London: Routledge. (Originally published as *Essai sur le don*, 1950, by Presses Universitaires de France in *Sociologie et Anthropologie*.)

Mayuga, Sylvia, and H.B. Cross, 1984. 'Historical quilt', in S. Mayuga et al., *Insight Guide, Philippines*. London: APA Productions (Harrap).

McCoy, Alfred W., 1982. 'Baylan: animist religion and Philippine peasant ideology'. *Philippine Quarterly of Culture and Society* 10: 141–94.

1994. 'An anarchy of families: the historiography of state and family in the Philippines', in A.W. McCoy (ed.), *An anarchy of families: state and family in the Philippines*. Quezon City: Ateneo de Manila University Press.

McKinnon, Susan, 1991. *From a shattered sun. Hierarchy, gender and alliance in the Tanimbar islands*. Madison: University of Wisconsin Press.

Mercado, Leonardo N., 1975. *Elements of Filipino philosophy*. Tacloban City: Divine Word University Press.

Metcalfe, Peter, 1982. *A Borneo journey into death: Berewan eschatology from its rituals*. Philadelphia: University of Pennsylvania Press.

Mintz, Malcolm, 1991. 'Anger and verse: two vocabulary subsets in Bikol'. *Vical 2: Western Austronesian and contact languages, papers from the 5th international conference on Austronesian linguistics*. Auckland: Linguistics Society of New Zealand.

1992. 'Insights into pre-Hispanic Bikol society'. Paper presented at the International Philippine Studies Conference, Australian National University, Canberra, Australia, July 1992.

1996. 'Prehispanic terms for war and conflict'. Paper presented at the International Philippine Studies Conference, East-West Centre, University of Hawaii at Manao, Honolulu, Hawaii, April 1996.

Mintz, Malcolm and Jose Rosario Britanico, 1985. *Bikol–English dictionary/Diksionariong Bikol–Ingles*. Quezon City: New Day.

Morais, Robert J., 1981. *Social relations in a Philippine town.* Special Report no. 19. Illinois: Center for Southeast Asian Studies, Northern Illinois University.

Morris, Rosalind C., 1994. 'The empress's new clothes: dressing and redressing modernity in Northern Thai spirit mediumship', in L. Milgram and P. van Esterik (eds.), *The transformative power of cloth in Southeast Asia.* Montreal and Toronto: Canadian Council for Southeast Asian Studies, Museum for Textiles.

Moses, Edith, 1908. *Unofficial letters of an official's wife.* New York: D. Appleton and Company.

Mulder, Niels, 1987. 'All Filipinos go to heaven.' Mimeograph copy of a working paper, Beilefeld.

1990a. *Appreciating lowland Christian Filipino culture.* Bielefeld: Southeast Asia Programme Working Paper no. 141.

1990b. 'Philippine textbooks and the national self-image'. *Philippine Studies* 38: 84–102.

1991. 'The cultural process of lowland Christian Filipino society'. Paper presented at the European Conference on Philippine Studies, C.A.S.A. University Amsterdam, April 1991.

1992. *Inside Southeast Asia: Thai, Javanese and Filipino interpretations of everyday life.* Bangkok: Editions Duang Kamol.

Murray, Francis J., Jr, 1973. 'Lowland social organisation II: Ambilineal kin groups in a Central Luzon barrio'. *Philippine Sociological Review* 21: 159–68.

M.Z.R., 1989. 'His twin brother was a horse'. *Women's Journal* 17: 50 (August 12). Manila: Philippine Journalists Inc.

Nasuruddin, Mohamed Ghouse, 1990. 'Dancing to ecstasy on the hobby horse' in W.J. Karim (ed.), *Emotions of culture. A Malay perspective.* Singapore: Oxford University Press.

Natividad, Mateo C., 1979. 'An ethnology of inganktos: Filipino folk Catholicism'. Master's thesis, Northern Illinois University.

Ness, Sally-Ann, 1992. *Body, movement and culture: kinesthetic and visual symbolism in a Philippine community.* Philadelphia: University of Pennsylvania Press.

Nishimura, Satoru, 1996. 'Agricultural development in Western Visaya: pawning land, overseas workers and *Porsiyentuhan*'. Paper presented at the International Conference of Philippine Studies, East-West Centre, University of Hawaii at Manoa, Honolulu, Hawaii, April 1996.

O'Brian, James, S.J. (ed.), 1968 (first edition 1966). *The historical and cultural heritage of the Bikol people: a textbook for the use of the Ateneo de Naga.* Naga City: Cyclostyled.

Obeyesekere, Gananath, 1981. *Medusa's hair: an essay on personal symbols and religious experience.* Chicago: University of Chicago Press.

Ocampo, Ambeth R., 1990. *Rizal without the overcoat.* Pasig, Metro Manila: Anvil Publishing.

Ong, Aihwa, 1987. *Spirits of resistance and capitalist discipline: factory women in Malaysia.* Albany: State University of New York Press.

Owen, Norman G., 1982. 'Abaca in Kabikolan: prosperity without progress', in A.W. McCoy and Ed C. de Jesus (eds.), *Philippine social history: global trade and local transformations.* Quezon City: Ateneo de Manila University Press.

1984. *Prosperity without progress: Manila hemp and material life in the colonial Philippines.* Quezon City: Ateneo de Manila University Press.

1989a. 'Subsistence in the slump: agricultural adjustment in the provincial Philippines', in I. Brown (ed.), *The economies of Africa and Asia in the interwar depression.* London: Routledge.

1989b. 'Age statement and misstatement in the nineteenth-century Philippines: some preliminary findings', in *Annales de Démographie Historique, 1988, Société de Démographie Historique,* 328–48. E.H.E.S.S., Paris, 1989.

1990. 'Problems in Partido: 1741–1810'. *Philippine Studies* 38: 421–53.

1992. 'The power of the principalia: local politics in early 19th century Kabikolan'. Paper presented at the Fourth International Philippine Studies Conference, Canberra, 1–3 July.

Paganoni, Fr Anthony (comp.), 1984. *Migration from the Philippines.* Quezon City: Scalabrinians.

'La Panayana', 1927. *Mga Laggay sa bag-ong nacascal agud sila maginbulahon.* Iloilo: Imprenta Lib. Y Encuadernacia, Mundurriao.

Parry, Jonathan, 1979. *Caste and kinship in Kangra.* London: Routledge and Keegan Paul.

1986. 'The gift, the Indian gift and the "Indian gift"'. *Man* (N.S.) 21: 453–73.

1994. *Death in Banaras.* Lewis Henry Morgan Lectures 1988. New York and Cambridge: Cambridge University Press.

Parry, Jonathan and Maurice Bloch, 1989. *Money and the morality of exchange.* Cambridge: Cambridge University Press.

Payne, Robert, 1986. *The white rajahs of Sarawak.* Singapore and Oxford: Oxford University Press.

Peacock, James, 1987. *Rites of modernization: symbols and social aspects of Indonesian proletarian drama.* Chicago: University of Chicago Press.

Pedrosa, Carmen Navarro, 1987. *Imelda Marcos. The rise and fall of one of the world's most powerful women.* London: Weidenfeld and Nicolson.

Pemberton, John, 1994. *On the subject of 'Java'.* Ithaca: Cornell University Press.

Pertierra, Raul, 1983. 'Viscera suckers and female sociality: the Philippine asuang'. *Philippine Studies* 38: 319–37.

Phelan, John Leddy, 1959. *The hispanicization of the Philippines: Spanish aims and Southeast Asian responses 1565–1700.* Madison: University of Wisconsin Press.

1970. *The millenial kingdom of the Franciscans in the New World.* Berkeley: University of California Press.

Philippine National Statistics Office, 1990. *1990 Census of population and housing report No. 3: social, economic and demographic characteristics.* Report of the Philippines National Statistics Office, Camarines Sur. Manila: Philippines National Statistics Office.

Phylactou, Maria, 1989. 'Household organisation and marriage in Ladakh'. PhD thesis, University of London.

Pina-Cabral, Joao de, 1986. *Sons of Adam, daughters of Eve: the peasant worldview of the Alto Minho.* Oxford: Clarendon Press.

Pinches, Michael, 1991. 'The working-class experience of shame, inequality and people power in Tatalon, Manila', in B.J. Kerkvliet and Resil B. Mojares (eds.), *From Marcos to Aquino: local perspectives in political transition in the Philippines.* Quezon City: Ateneo de Manila University Press.

1992. 'Proletarian ritual: class degradation and the dialectic of resistance in Manila'. *Pilipinas* 19: 69–92 (Fall 1992).

Pitt-Rivers, Julian, 1961. *People of the Sierra.* Chicago: University of Chicago Press.

1977. *The fate of Shechem, or the politics of sex: essays in the anthropology of the Mediterranean.* Cambridge: Cambridge University Press.

Plasencia, Juan de, (originally published c. 1589). 'The customs of the Tagalogs', vol. 7: 136–96, in E.H. Blair and J.A. Robertson (eds.), *The Philippine islands, 1493–1898.* 1903–9. 55 volumes. Cleveland: A.H. Clark.

Platt, Tristan, c.1987. 'The sound of light in Northern Potosi'. Unpublished paper, delivered to the London School of Economics Research Seminar in Anthropology, 1987.

1996. *Guerreros de Cristo: cofradias misa solar y guerra regenerativa en una doctrina Macha.* Traduccion de Luis H. Antezana. La Paz, Bolivia: Azur, Plural.

Polo, Jaime Biron, 1985. 'Of metaphors and men: the Binalayan fishcorral ritual as a contract in a social spectrum'. *Philippine Sociological Review* 33: 54–63.

1988. *Rethinking Philippine popular symbols: moments of domination and resistance in the province of Leyte.* Quezon City: The Research Forum.

del Prado, Mariano G., 1938. *Ibalon: ethnography of the Bikol region* (translated by Maria Lilia F. Realubit). Legazpi: AMS Press.

Quisumbing, Lourdes R., 1965. *Marriage customs in rural Cebu.* Cebu City, Philippines: The University of San Carlos (Divine Word University).

Rafael, Vicente L., 1988. *Contracting colonialism; translation and Christian conversion in Tagalog society under early Spanish rule.* Manila: Ateneo de Manila University Press.

1995a. 'Colonial domesticity: white woman and the United States rule in the Philippines'. *American Literature* 67(4): 639–66 (December).

1995b. 'Mimetic subjects; engendering race at the edge of empire'. *Differences: A Journal of Feminist Cultural Studies* 7(2): 127–49.

1995c. 'Nationalism, imagery and the Filipino intelligentsia in the nineteenth century', in Vicente L. Rafael (ed.), 1995d, 133–58.

1995d. *Discrepant Histories; translocal essays on Filipino cultures.* Philadelphia: Temple University Press and Manila: Anvil Publishing.

1997. '"Your grief is our gossip": overseas Filipinos and other spectral presences'. *Public Culture* 9: 267–91.

Realubit, Maria Lilia F., 1976. *The Bikol dramatic tradition.* Quezon City: University of the Philippines. City of Naga: A.M.S. Press.

1983. *Bikols of the Philippines.* City of Naga: A.M.S. Press.

1990. 'Contemporary Bikol writing'. *Philippine Studies* 38: 500–29.

Reid, Anthony, 1988. *Southeast Asia in the age of commerce, 1450–1680,* vol. I: *The lands below the winds.* New Haven and London: Yale University Press.

Reid, Anthony, (ed.), 1983. *Slavery, bondage and dependency in Southeast Asia.* With the assistance of Jennifer Brewster. St Lucia and New York: University of Queensland.

Retana, Wenceslao E., 1894. *Un libro de aniterias: supersticiones de los Indios Filipinos.* Madrid: Imprenta de la Viuda de M. Minuesa de los Rios.

1895–1905. *Archivo del bibliofilo Filipino; recopilacion de documentos historicos, cientificos, literarias, y politicos, y estudios bibliograficos por W.E. Retana.* 5 vols. Madrid: Imprenta de la Viuda de M. Minuesa de los Rios.

Reyes, Emmanuel A, 1989. *Notes on Philippine Cinema* Manila. De La Salle University Press.

Reyes, Romana P. de los and Sylvia Ma. G Jopillo, 1988. *Partnership in irrigation; farmers and government in agency-managed systems.* Quezon City, I.P.C.: Ateneo de Manila University.

Rizal, Jose, 1958 (2nd edn 1961) (originally published 1887). *Noli mi tangere.* (translated as *The lost Eden* by Leon Ma. Guerrero). Hong Kong and London: Q.C.R. Martinez.

Rocamora, Joel, 1991. 'The NDF program: 1973–1990 – A textual analysis'. Draft paper presented at the European Conference on Philippine Studies, C.A.S.A., University of Amsterdam, March 1991.

Rosaldo, Michelle Z., 1980. *Knowledge and passion. Ilongot notions of self and social life.* Cambridge: Cambridge University Press.

Rosaldo, Renato, 1980. *Ilongot headhunting 1883–1974: a study in society and history.* Stanford: Stanford University Press.

Rudolph, Ebermut, 1988. 'The snake-twins of the Philippines: observations of the alter-ego complex'. *Philippine Studies* 16: 45–77.

Runcimann, W.G., 1966. *Relative deprivation and social justice: a study of attitudes to inequality in 20th century England.* London: Routledge and Keegan Paul.

Rutherford, Danilyn Fox, 1997. 'Raiding the land of the foreigners: power, history and difference in Biak, Irian Jaya, Indonesia'. PhD thesis, Cornell University.

Rutten, Rosanne, 1982. *Women workers of hacienda Milagros: wage labour and household subsistence on a Philippine sugarcane plantation.* Amsterdam: Anthropologisch-Sociologisch Centrum, Universiteit van Amsterdam.

1990. *Artisans and entrepreneurs in the rural Philippines: making a living and gaining wealth in two commercialised crafts.* Amsterdam: VU University Press.

1991. 'The rise of provincial entrepreneurs in Philippine crafts'. Paper presented to the European conference on Philippine Studies, C.A.S.A., Amsterdam, 1991.

Salaman, Michael, 1995. '"Nothing without labor": penology, discipline and independence in the Philippines under United States rule', in Vicente L. Rafael (ed.), 1995d, 113–32.

Salazar, Manuel B., 1971. *Tronco del mundo: an aguiagui kan kinaban bago magabot si Jesucristo sa ipag-awit.* Naga City: Cecilio.

Salazar, Zeus A., 1991. 'Philippine studies and Pilipinolohiya: two heuristic views in the study of matters Filipino'. Paper presented at the European Conference on Philippine Studies, C.A.S.A., University of Amsterdam, April, 1991.

de San Antonio, Fray San Fransisco, 1977 (originally published 1738). *Cronicas de las Provincia de San Gregoria Magno/The Philippine Chronicles of Fray San Antonio.* Book I (translation from Spanish by D. Pedro Picornell). Manila: Historical Conservation Society.

Santiago, Luciano P.R., 1988. 'Doctor Don Mariano Benerve Pilapil (1759–1818): passion and transformation'. *Philippine Quarterly of Culture and Society* 16: 19–43.

Santos, Luz Mendoza, 1982. *Mary in the Philippines: a votive offering*. Manila: L.M. Santos.

Schumacher, John N., S.J. (ed.), 1981. *Revolutionary clergy: the Filipino clergy and the nationalist movement, 1850–1903*. Quezon City: Ateneo de Manila University Press.

1984. 'Syncretism in Philippine Catholicism: its historical causes'. *Philippine Studies* 32: 251–72.

1987 (second edition). *Readings in Philippine church history*. Loyola School of Theology. Quezon City: Ateneo de Manila University Press.

1991. 'Religious aspects of the revolution in Bicol'. *Philippine Studies* 39: 230–41

Scott, James, 1985. *Weapons of the weak. Everyday forms of peasant resistance*. New Haven and London: Yale University Press.

Scott, William Henry, 1983. 'Oripun and Alipin in the Philippines', in A. Reid (ed.), *Slavery, bondage and dependency in Southeast Asia*, 138–55. University of Queensland: St Lucia and New York.

1984. *Prehispanic source materials for the study of Philippine history*. Quezon City, Philippines: New Day Publishers.

1985a. 'Filipino class structure in the 16th century' in W.H. Scott, *Cracks in the parchment curtain and other essays in Philippine history*, 96–126. Quezon City: New Day.

1985b. 'Class structure in the unhispanised Philippines', in W.H. Scott, *Cracks in the parchment curtain and other essays in Philippine history*, 127–48. Quezon City: New Day.

1985c. 'A minority reaction to American imperialism: Isabelo de los Reyes' in W.H. Scott, *Cracks in the parchment curtain and other essays in Philippine history*, 285–300. Quezon City: New Day.

1985d. 'Isabelo de los Reyes, *Provinciano* and nationalist', in W.H. Scott, *Cracks in the parchment curtain and other essays in Philippine history*, 226–84. Quezon City: New Day.

1994a. 'Prehispanic Filipino concepts of land rights'. *Philippine Quarterly of Culture and Society* 22: 165–73.

1994b. *Barangay: sixteenth century Philippine culture and society*. Quezon City: Ateneo de Manila University Press.

Shimizu, Hiromu, 1991. 'Filipino children in family and society: growing up in a many-people environment', in *SA 21, Selected readings*. Department of Sociology – Anthropology. Quezon City: Ateneo de Manila University Press.

Shirokogoroff, S.M., 1935. *The psychomental complex of the Tungas*. London: Kegan Paul.

Siegel, James T., 1986. *Solo in the new order: language and hierarchy in an Indonesian city*. Princeton: Princeton University Press.

Spiro, Melford E., 1967. *Burmese supernaturalism: a study in the explanation and reduction of suffering*. Englewood Cliffs: Prentice-Hall.

1982 (originally printed 1970). *Buddhism and society; a great tradition and its Burmese vicissitudes*. Berkeley and Los Angeles: University of California Press.

Steedly, Mary Margaret, 1993. *Hanging without a rope: narrative experience in colonial and postcolonial Karoland*. Princeton: Princeton University Press.

Steinberg, David Joel, 1982. *The Philippines: a singular and a plural place.* Boulder, Colorado: Westview Press.

Stewart, Michael, 1997. *The time of the gypsies.* London. Westview Press.

Tagle, Ramon A., Jr., 1994. 'Population control: enduring values, changed horizons', in Rene B. Javellana S.J. (ed.), *Morality, religion and the Filipino: essays on honor of Bitalana R. Gorospe, S.J.* Quezon City: Ateneo de Manila University Press.

Tambiah, Stanley J., 1970. *Buddhism and the spirit cults in North-east Thailand.* Cambridge: Cambridge University Press.

 1985. 'The galactic polity in Southeast Asia', in *Culture, thought and social action.* Cambridge, Mass.: Harvard University Press. Also published in *World conqueror and world renouncer* (1976), 102–31.

Tan, Michael L., 1987. *Usug, Kulam, Pasma; traditional concepts of health and illness in the Philippines.* Research reports no. 3. With Lorna P. Makil and Mary Grenough, M.M., Editorial consultants. Quezon City: AKAP (Alay Kapwa Kilusang Pangkalusugan).

Taussig, Michael, 1980. *The devil and commodity fetishism in South America.* Chapell Hill: University of North Carolina Press.

Tawney, R.H., 1926. *Religion and the rise of capitalism, a study.* With a prefatory note by Charles Gore. London, Murray.

Thomas, Nicholas and Caroline Humphrey (eds.), 1994. *Shamanism, history and the state.* Ann Arbor: University of Michigan.

Tiongson, Nicanor G., 1976. 'Pasyon: the best-known Filipino book'. *Archipelago* 4(3): 30–8.

Tornquist, Olle, 1991. 'Communists and democracy in the Philippines'. Paper presented at the European Conference on Philippine Studies, Amsterdam, March 1991.

Tremillios, Ricardo D., 1992. 'The Lenten practice of Pasyon as Southeast Asian theatre: a structural analysis of protocol and performance'. Paper presented at the International Philippine Studies Conference, Australian National University, Canberra, July 1992.

Tsing, Anna Lowenhaupt, 1990. 'Gender and performance in Meratus dispute settlement', in Atkinson and Errington (eds.), 1990: 95–126.

 1993. *In the realm of the diamond queen: marginality in an out-of-the-way place.* Princeton: Princeton University Press.

Valentine, Charles A., 1968. *Culture and poverty: critique and counter-proposals.* Chicago: Chicago University Press.

Vengco, Sabino A., 1984. 'Another look at inculturation'. *Philippine Studies* 32: 181–97.

Vickers, Adrian 1989. *Bali: a paradise created.* New York: Periplus Books.

Warner, Marina, 1976. *Alone of all her sex: the myth and the cult of the Virgin Mary.* New York: Knopf.

Waterson, Roxanna, 1990. *The living house; an anthropology of architecture in Southeast Asia.* Kuala Lumpur: Oxford University Press.

 1995. 'Houses and hierarchies in island Southeast Asia', in Janet Carsten and Stephen Hugh-Jones (eds.) *About the house,* Cambridge: Cambridge University Press.

Watson, Rubie, 1985. *Inequality among brothers. Class and kinship in South China.* Cambridge: Cambridge University Press.

Weber, Max, 1992 (previous edition of this translation 1930), translated [from the German] by Talcott Parsons. *The Protestant ethic and the spirit of capitalism, introduction by Anthony Giddens.* London: Routledge (translation of: 'Die protestantische Ethik und der "Geist" des Kapitalismus').

Weiner, Annette B., 1976. *Women of value, men of renown: new perspectives in Trobriand exchange.* Austin: University of Texas Press.

1985. 'Inalienable wealth'. *American Ethnologist* 12: 52–65.

1992. *Inalienable possessions: the paradox of keeping-while-giving.* Berkeley, Los Angeles, Oxford: University of California Press.

Wikan, Unni, 1990. *Managing turbulent hearts: a Balinese formula for living.* Chicago and London: University of Chicago Press.

Wolters, O.W., 1982. *History, culture and religion in Southeast Asian perspectives.* Singapore: Institute of Southeast Asian Studies.

Worcester, Dean, C., 1913. 'The non-Christian peoples of the Philippine islands'. *The National Geographic Magazine* 24 (11).

Wynne, Alison, 1979. *No time for crying: stories of Philippine women who care for their country and its people.* Kowloon: Resource Centre for Philippine Concerns.

Yengoyan, Aram A. and Perla S. Makil, 1984. *Philippine society and the individual; selected essays of Frank Lynch, 1949–76.* Michigan Papers on South and Southeast Asia no. 24. Ann Arbor: University of Michigan Center for South and Southeast Asian Studies.

Yu, Elena and William T. Liu, 1980. *Fertility and kinship in the Philippines.* Notre Dame and London: University of Notre Dame Press.

Zialcita, Fernando, N., 1986. 'Popular Interpretations of the Passion of Christ'. *Philippine Sociological Review* 34: 56–62.

# Index

*Cambridge Studies in Social and Cultural Anthropology*

*available in paperback